SLAVERY:

LETTERS AND SPEECHES,

BY

HORACE MANN,

THE FIRST SECRETARY OF THE MASSACHUSETTS BOARD OF EDUCATION.

BOSTON:

PUBLISHED BY B. B. MUSSEY & CO.

1853.

TO

THE YOUNG MEN

OF

MASSACHUSETTS

THIS VOLUME IS AFFECTIONATELY

Dedicated

BY

THE AUTHOR.

This work comes from one in whose mind present Memories are taking the place of early Hopes. It is specially addressed to those in whose minds future Memories will soon take the place of present Hopes. Hence a fitting occasion presents itself for the statement of a few principles, by whose unerring guidance the exulting Hopes of Youth may always be transformed into the happy Memories of Age.

The Youth of all climes and times have a common attribute. The desire of happiness is a universal desire. God fixes this element in the core of life. Far back in our moral organization, before human conduct can come in to control or modify, this longing for happiness, this hope of future welfare, is radicated in the soul; so that it seems to have been the first attribute which was taken for the constitution of our nature, and around which the other attributes were gathered, rather to have been added to the rest as a secondary or incident. The desire of some form of happiness being secured, as a motive power, it seems to have been left very much to the option of each individual to select his own objects of enjoyment, whether noble or ignoble, and to devise his own means for obtaining them, whether righteous or unrighteous.

The emulous and aspiring youth of a Free People will always find much of their private, and most of their public welfare, indissolubly connected with the institutions and laws of their country. In these, therefore, their interest is both public and personal; — it pertains to the citizen as well as to the man. All great moral questions, though touching them but lightly at first, will come closer and closer home, as long as they live; — growing into greater importance for their posthumous memory than for their living fame, and affecting the fortunes of their posterity even more than their own.

Though all Young Men are substantially alike in their desire of well being, yet, in regard to the guiding principles by which the objects of hope are pursued, in order to obtain happiness, three marked distinctions, or classes, exist among them.

1. There are those who adopt with implicit and unquestioning faith the views of their parents, or of the circle, or caste, into which they were thrown by the accident of birth. They never venture to explore or wander outside of the ideas and opinions among which they were born and bred. For them, an hereditary boundary encloses thought, belief, hope. Whether the opinions amid which they live are insular in their narrowness, or continental in their breadth; whether they belong to the earth, came up from the dark regions below, or descended from the realms of purity above, they are taken into the receptive soul, as unfledged birds take whatever food is offered them, from friend or foe, with closed eye and opened mouth. Even if practically right, therefore, they are never rationally right, for they have never discerned between good and ill; and all their convictions, whether true or untrue, rest upon the foundation of bigotry alone.

2. The second class look eagerly beyond family or caste. They anxiously inquire what views, what dogmas, are in the ascendant

among men, — what party predominates or outvotes, what avowals or professions will most readily open avenues to wealth, propitiate power, win patronage, insure advancement. Finding where the preponderance of forces lies, they attach themselves to the stronger. No matter whether the tide ebbs or flows, they drift with the current. If popular views change, they change, "like a wave driven with the wind and tossed;" like a chameleon, changing its color with every contact.

Some of this class, more sagacious, though not less false to principle, than the rest, ascend an eminence, whence they can survey the direction of forces, mark the future point and period of their union, and then they strike at once for the spot whither those forces are converging They, not less than their fellows, warp eternal principles to suit the vice of the hour, only it is an hour somewhat future, instead of the present one.

3. But there is a third class of Young Men who are true to the sacred instincts of virtue, and devoutly reverent of duty. They seek, not for the time-hallowed, but for the truth-hallowed. They have learnt that, in the divine classification, there are but two great objects in the universe, — God and Mankind. These are the only existences recognized in those two supreme laws, which, by divine prerogative, hold all other laws in their embrace. Hence the two resulting and all-comprehending duties, — love to God and love to Man. The convictions and sentiments which belong to the Brotherhood of the one, stand upon the same basis of authority as those which belong to the Fatherhood of the other. Hence all other entities and possibilities, — opulence, power, fame, genius, things present, or things to come, — are, and forever must be, secondary and subordinate to these primary and everlasting laws. No names so lofty, no multitude so large, that they can abolish these truths, or abstract one jot or tittle from their binding force, in this life, or in any life. They are coëternal with their Author; unchangeable as He, and moral life and moral death wait upon their award.

When the Young Man of this class looks within himself, he finds the constitution of his own moral nature to be such, that annihilation with truth is better than the most favored existence with error. And when he looks without himself, he sees there is a God enthroned above, mightier than every "god of this world," and that there is a divine law higher than any laws of fallible men. Hence he knows that Right and Truth will assuredly triumph, and that all who oppose them will be scattered as the whirlwind scatters the chaff. The patriarchs sold Joseph into Egypt; yet God was with him, and raised him to honor, and at last put the lives of his treacherous brethren into his hands.

Whatever may be the peculiar madness of the hour, in whatever direction the gauds of wealth may beckon, or the prizes of ambition call, let the Young Man remember, *that* only can be honorable which is just, that only can be safe which is right. Hence, though the perfumed breezes of flattery may entice him on one side, and a storm of maledictions beat fiercely against him on the other, let him consecrate himself to Justice and Truth, and be inspired with the faith that, though the earth should quake or the heavens fall, an omniscient eye will over-watch, and an omniscient arm will protect him.

Among the wiles of the sorceress that beguile the young to their ruin there is no more seductive, yet fallacious temptation, than the value which seems to belong to the passing hour, and to the pleasures it may bring. How infinitely small a part of existence is the present day, or year! How insignificant its point compared with the ages to come! What are its huzzas, its ostentation, and its pride, when placed in the balance against the eternity of rewards that crown allegiance to duty? O, how insane and fatuous to barter the undecaying honors of the future for the transitory joys of the present! In the future, lies the wealth of every man; the present is only an opportunity to make its title secure. The temporizer must snatch from hour to hour at some new expedient, which, if he fails to seize, he sinks to perdition. The virtuous man binds himself to a principle, and soars securely through all worlds.

Nothing stands upon a more adamantine basis of truth than the principles which decide between Human Freedom and Human Slavery. These eternal principles happen now, in a peculiar degree, to be implicated in the shifting and uncertain current of politics; and political storms may seem for a time to overwhelm them. But the cloud which obscures the sun does not annihilate it; and these principles are sure to emerge and shine unclouded in their native splendor forever. Every act, whether of individuals or of governments, whether committed in past days or in our day, which compromises the sacred principles of Human Freedom, or postpones its interests to other interests, is set down, in the calendar of fate, for ultimate and universal execration. This is just as certain as it is that the great crimes of the race committed in past ages, — the persecutions of the early Christians, the tortures of the Inquisition, or the atrocities of the African Slave trade, — are now condemned by the awful verdict of history and the ever-sounding reprobation of mankind. In the spread of Christianity, in the advance of civilization, in the moral development of the people, a tribunal is now preparing, which will pronounce sentence of condemnation against the abetters of slavery, to be promulgated as from Sinai, and preserved in the archives of eternity. The Progress of the Age bears us on, not only to a forward, but to an upward point; and what we now say against the apostates to duty and the traitors of mankind, in past ages, however much they may have been honored, caressed, and rewarded in their day, will soon be said of every one amongst ourselves who leads or joins the band of conspirators against the Rights of Man.

Every Young Man, however obscure or powerless he may seem, can do something for the cause of freedom. Whatever disadvantages the youth may labor under, they have one all-compensating advantage. A longer period of life is before them, and deeds which can only be accomplished through years of labor, they can achieve. But our success depends infinitely less upon our strength than upon our motive. When we supply the virtuous will, God supplies the power; so that the result corresponds, not to our weakness, but to his omnipotence. We are thus made able

> ———— "to join
> Our partial movements with the master wheel
> Of the great world, *and serve that sacred end,*
> *Which He, the unerring Reason, keeps in view.*"

Those Young Men of Massachusetts, then, of the noble lineage of the Pilgrims, who have been nursed amid the influences of sanctuary and school, in whose bosoms is the sacred depository of future and boundless hopes, but who are now counselled to abandon their integrity, who are brought into peril of being corrupted by the lures of wealth, or fascinated by the dazzling of worldly honors, or swept away by the pressure of the multitude that do evil, I adjure to stand fast and immovable on those sacred and eternal principles of Human Liberty which came down to us *through* the fires of oppression and the agony and blood of martyrs, but came *from* God;— principles that can never suffer the decays of time, which kings nor senates of kings can ever abolish, and which, however much the passions of men may seek to taint or defile them, are ever beautiful and fair, as the names of all their disciples shall hereafter be. I call upon Young Men to throw themselves forward in imagination into middle life, or old age, and there behold how these mighty questions will look in the retrospect of time, when the brilliant robes which now gild the tempter are gone, and only the ghastly fiend remains; when the passion that prompted the crime is dead, and only the remorse survives. Think not of luxury, or wealth, or ignoble ease, but only of an heroic conflict, careless of the present strength of the foe. Take no bribe from the hand of power, in whatever disguise of beauty it may come, but spurn it and its author alike. Let your future manhood realize the generous aspirations of your youth; and, amid the seductions of the present hour, prize only the jubilant memories you can lay up for old age. It may grieve you to break friendships, but truth and duty are your nearest friends. It may be painful to live amongst those who upbraid and condemn you; but be a coward when virtue is in peril, and your own accusing conscience you must live with forever. Study those exemplars of excellence who came purified and resplendent out of fiery trials. It is said of Francis the First, that when he read the valorous exploits of Gaston de Foix, he wept tears of emulation. Rejoice, then, though marshalled in the fore front of battle when the Rights of Humanity are in danger, and you shall rejoice again and forever in their triumph. Read and ponder what was so nobly said by one of the heathen of the old world, and be ashamed, yea, weep for your country and your kind, if the Christianity of America has fallen below the paganism of Rome. Seneca says, —

"Virtue covets danger; and whatever may be her aim, she never stops to consider how much she may suffer, since her sufferings are a part of her glory. Military men glory in their scars. With exultation they point us to their blood flowing in an honorable cause. Though they who return *unharmed* from the field of battle may have done as many and as noble deeds, yet it is the *wounded* soldier who receives double honors. God provides for those whom he would make most honorable, by furnishing them with opportunities for achieving valiant and noble deeds. Hence he strews difficulties along their path. It is in the storm you see who is worthy to be a pilot; and in battle, who is the soldier. . . . . How can I know with what constancy and endurance one will bear up against reproach and obloquy and popular odium, if he has grown old amidst the applauses of the world, if he has never encountered misfortune, and has been followed by the indiscriminating favor of men? . . . . Be not affrighted, I beseech you, at the dangers which were intended by the immortal gods only as stimulants to exertion. The season of calamity is virtue's opportunity. *They*, rather, are to be esteemed wretched, who lie torpid in luxurious ease, whom a sluggish calm detains on the great voyage, like vessels that lie weltering on a sea without a gale. Whom God approves and loves, he exercises, and tries them again and again, and thus inures them to hardship; but those whom he designs to enervate, he spares and indulges and saves them from impending ills. . . . . The *bravest* of the army are they whom the commander selects for the most perilous service. The general details his choicest men to send on secret expeditions by night, or to explore an unknown way, or to dislodge a garrison from their entrenchments. No man chosen for such an enterprise is ever heard to say, '*My commander has wronged and dishonored me,*' but rather, '*He has known well whom to choose.*' Such, too, is the language of those who are required to suffer what would make the timid and the ignoble weep. We stand honored in the divine regards when the great experiment, *how much human nature can endure for a virtuous cause*, is tried in ourselves. . . . . As teachers deal with their scholars, so God deals with good men. He demands most of those in whom he has most confidence." *

West Newton, October, 1851.

CONTENTS.

1

LETTER

Accepting the Nomination for the Thirtieth Congress, made by the Whig Convention of District No. 8, March, 1848.

Gentlemen;

Your communication of the 16th inst., being directed to Newton, (instead of West Newton, where I reside,) did not reach me until this morning. I thank you cordially for the kind expressions of personal regard with which you have been pleased to accompany it. You inform me that at a convention of delegates assembled in Dedham, on Wednesday, the 15th inst., I was nominated as a candidate to fill the vacancy in Congress occasioned by the death of the great and good man whose irreparable loss we, his constituents, with a nation for our fellow-mourners, deplore.

At first thought, the idea of being the immediate successor of John Quincy Adams in the councils of the nation might well cause any man to shrink back from the inevitable contrast. But it is obvious, on a moment's reflection, that the difference is so trivial between all the men whom he has left, compared with the disparity between them and him, as to render it of little consequence, in this respect, who shall succeed him; and the people in the Eighth District, in their descent from Mr. Adams to any successor, must break and bear the shock of the fall, as best they can.

I most heartily concur with you in that estimate of the services, and veneration for the character, of our late representative, which your resolutions so eloquently express. To be fired by his example, to imi-rate his diligence and fidelity in the discharge of every trust, to emulate his moral intrepidity, which always preferred to stand alone by the right, rather than to join the retinue and receive the plaudits of millions, as a champion of the wrong, — this would be, in the beautiful language of the Roman historian, " to ascend to glory by the path of virtue."

One of the resolutions adopted by your convention declares the three following things : —

1. That the successor of Mr. Adams, on the floor of Congress, should be a man " whose principles shall be in consonance with those of his predecessor."

2. That his fidelity to the great principles of human freedom shall be unwavering. And, —

3. That his " voice and vote shall on all occasions be exercised in extending and securing liberty to the human race."

Permit me to reäffirm these sentiments with my whole heart. Should the responsibilities of that successorship ever be devolved upon me, I shall endeavor so to fulfil them, that these dead words should become a living soul. I should deem it not only an object of duty, but of the highest ambition, to contend for the noble principles you have here expressed, as Mr. Adams contended for them ; though, unhappily, it would be only as a David in Saul's armor. Bear with me for a moment while I enlarge upon these sentiments.

1. " *In consonance with his principles.*" — I believe it was the sovereign rule of Mr. Adams's life to act in obedience to his convictions of duty. Truth was his guide. His conscience was non-elastic. He did not strain at a gnat before company, on account of its size, and then, privately, swallow a camel. His patriotism was coëxtensive with his country ; it could not be crushed and squeezed in between party lines. Though liable to err, — and what human being is not ? — yet his principles were believed by him to be in accordance

with the great moral laws of the universe. They were thought out from duty and religion, and not carved out of expediency. When invested with patronage, he never dismissed a man from office because he was a political opponent, and never appointed one to office merely because he was a political friend. Hence he drew from Mr. Holmes, of South Carolina, this noble eulogium, — a eulogium, considering the part of the country from which it came, as honorable to its author as to its object, — that "he crushed no heart beneath the rude grasp of proscription; he left no heritage of widows' cries or orphans' tears." Could all the honors which Mr. Adams ever won from offices held under the first five Presidents of the United States, and from a public service, which, commencing more than fifty years ago, continued to the day of his death, be concentrated in one effulgent blaze, they would be less far-shining and inextinguishable than the honor of sacrificing his election for a second presidential term, because he would not, in order to obtain it, prostitute the patronage and power which the constitution had placed in his hands. I regard this as the sublimest spectacle in his long and varied career. He stood within reach of an object of ambition doubtless dearer to him than life. He could have laid his hands upon it. The "still, small voice" said, No! Without a murmur, he saw it taken and borne away in triumph by another. Compared with this, the block of many a martyr has been an easy resting-place.

2. "*Unwavering fidelity to the great principles of human freedom.*" — The Declaration of American Independence, in 1776, was the first complete assertion of human rights, on an extensive scale, ever made by mankind. Less than three quarters of a century have elapsed, and already the greatest portion of the civilized world has felt the influence of that Declaration. France, for years, has had a constitutional monarchy;

perhaps, to-day, her government is republican. Holland and Belgium are comparatively free. Almost all the states of the Germanic Confederation have a written constitution, and a legislature with a popular branch. Prussia has lately commenced a representative system. The iron rule of Austria is relaxed under the fervent heat which liberty reflects from surrounding nations. Naples and Sicily have just burst the bonds of tyranny. In Rome and the States of the Church, where, under the influence of religious and political despotism, the heart of Freedom was supposed to be petrified into insoluble hardness, that heart is now beginning to pulsate with a new life, and to throb with sympathy for humanity. Great Britain and Denmark have emancipated their slaves in the West Indies. Measures are now in progress to ameliorate the condition of Russian serfs. Even half-barbarous, Mahometan Tunis has yielded to the tide of free principles. To what bar of judgment will our own posterity bring us, what doom of infamy will history pronounce upon us, if the United States shall hereafter be found the only portion of Christendom where the principles of our own Declaration of Independence are violated in the persons of millions of our people ?

3. " *The exercise, on all occasions, of voice and vote, in extending and securing liberty to the human race.*" — There is a crisis in our affairs. A territory, in extent far exceeding that of the thirteen original states, when they repelled the power of Great Britain, has lately been added, or is, doubtless, about to be added, to our national domain. The expanse of this territory is so vast, that it may be divided into a dozen sections, and these sections may be erected into separate states, each one of which shall be so large that Massachusetts would seem but an inconsiderable court-yard, if placed in front of it. Parts of this territory are fertile and salubrious. It is capable of supporting millions and

millions of human beings, of the same generation. The numbers of the successive generations, which in the providence of God are to inhabit it, will be as the leaves of the forest, or the sands on the sea-shore. Each one of these is to be a living soul, with its joys and sorrows, its hopes and fears, its susceptibilities of exaltation or of abasement. Each one will be capable of being formed into the image of God, or of being deformed into the image of all that is anti-godlike.

These countless millions are to be our kindred; many of them, perhaps, our own descendants ; at any rate, our brethren of the human family; for has not God "made of one blood all nations of men to dwell upon all the face of the earth"? In rights, in character, in happiness ; in freedom or in vassalage ; in the glorious immunities and prerogatives of knowledge, or in the debasement and superstitions of ignorance; in their upward-looking aspiration and love of moral excellence, or in their downward-looking, prone-rushing, and brutish appetites and passions, what shall these millions of our fellow-creatures be? I put it as a practical question, What shall these millions of our fellow-creatures be? — for it is more than probable that this very generation, — nay, that the actors in public affairs, before the sands of the present year shall have run out, — will prescribe and foreördain their doom. That doom will be what our present conduct predestines.

If we enact laws and establish institutions, under whose benign influences that vast tract of territory shall at length teem with myriads of human beings, each one a free-born man; each one enjoying the inalienable right of "life, liberty, and the pursuit of happiness;" each one free for the cultivation of his capacities, and free in the choice and in the rewards of his labor; — if we do this, although the grand results may not manifest themselves for a thousand years, yet when the fulness of time shall come, the equity and the honor of framing these laws and institutions will belong to us, as much as though the glorious consummation could be realized to-morrow. On the other hand, if we so shape the mould in which their fortunes are to be cast, that, for them or for any portion of them, there shall be servitude instead of liberty, ignorance instead of education, debasement instead of dignity, the indulgence of bestial appetites instead of the sanctities and securities of domestic life, — then, until the mountains shall crumble away by age, until the arches of the skies shall fall in rottenness, these mountains and these arches will never cease to echo back the execrations upon our memory of all the great and good men of the world. And this retribution, I believe, will come suddenly, as well as last forever.

In one of the South-western States a vast subterranean cave has been discovered, deep down in whose chambers there is a pool of water, on which no beam of sunlight ever shines. A sightless fish is said to inhabit this rayless pool. In this animal, indeed, the rudiments of a visual organ are supposed to be dimly discernible; but of an orb to refract the rays of light, or of a retina to receive them, there is no trace. Naturalists suppose that the progenitors of these animals, in ages long gone by, possessed the power of vision; but that, being buried in these depths by some convulsion of nature, long disuse at first impaired, at length extinguished, and has at last obliterated the visual organ itself. The animal has sunk in the scale of being, until its senses are accommodated to the blackness of darkness in which it dwells. Were this account wholly fabulous, it has the strongest verisimilitude, and doubtless describes what would actually occur under the circumstances supposed.

Thus will it be with faculties above the surface of the earth, as well as below it. Thus will it be with human beings, as well as with the lower orders of creation. Thus will it be with our own brethren or children, should we shut up from them the book of knowledge, or seal their senses so that they could not read it. Thus will it be with all our God-given faculties, just so far as they are debarred from legitimate exercise upon their appropriate objects. The love of knowledge will die out, when it ceases to be stimulated by the means of knowledge. Self-respect will die out, under the ever-present sense of inferiority. The sentiments of truth and duty will die out, when cunning and falsehood can obtain more gratifications than frankness and honesty. The noblest impulses of the human soul, the most sacred affections of the human heart, will die out, when every sphere is closed against their exercise. When such a dreadful work is doing, or threatens to be done, can any one stand listlessly by, see it perpetrated, and then expect to excuse himself, under the false, impious pretext of Cain, "Am I my brother's keeper?"

Fully, then, do I agree with you and the delegates of the convention you represent, in saying that the successor of Mr. Adams should be one "whose voice and vote shall, on all occasions, be exercised in extending and securing liberty to the human race." Of course I do not understand you to imply any violation of the constitution of the United States, which every representative swears to support.

Permit me to say a word personal to myself. For eleven years, I have been estranged from all political excitements. During this whole period, I have attended no political meeting of any kind whatever. I have contented myself with the right of private judgment and the right of voting, though it has usually so happened that my official duties have demanded my absence from home at the time of the fall elections. I have deemed this abstinence from *actively* mingling in political contests both a matter of duty towards opposing political parties, and a proper means of subserving the best interests of the cause in which I had embarked. I hoped too, by so doing, to assist in rearing men even better than those now belonging to any party.

The nature of my duties also, and all my intercourse and associations, have attracted me towards whatever is worthy and beneficent in all parties, rather than towards what is peculiar to any one. Not believing in political pledges, I should have had the honor to decline giving any to you, had you not had the first and greater honor of asking none from me. After what I have said above in favor of liberty for all mankind, it would be a strange contradiction did I consent to be myself a slave of party. The hands which you raised in behalf of yourselves and your constituents, when you voted for the noble sentiments contained in the resolution I have quoted, could never degrade themselves by forging a fetter for the free mind of another, or fastening one upon it ; and the hand with which I have penned my hearty response to those sentiments can never stretch itself out to take a fetter on. Should your nomination, therefore, be accepted and be successful, it must be with the explicit understanding between us that I shall always be open to receive the advice of my constituents, shall always welcome their counsel, always be most grateful for their suggestions, but that, in the last resort, my own sense of duty must be the only arbiter. Should differences arise, the law opens an honorable escape for both parties, — declination on my part, substitution on yours.

I must add, in closing, that so far as personal preferences are concerned, I infinitely prefer remaining in my present position, with all its labor and its thanklessness, to any office in the gift of the people. I had hoped and intended, either in a public or private capacity, to spend my life in advancing the great cause of the people's education. Two considerations alone could tempt me to abandon this purpose. The first is important. The enactment of laws which shall cover waste territory, to be applied to the myriads of human beings who are hereafter to occupy that territory, is a work which seems to precede and outrank even education itself. Whether a wide expanse of country shall be filled with beings to whom education is permitted, or with those to whom it is denied, — with those whom humanity and the law make it a duty to teach, or with those whom inhumanity and the law make it a *legal* duty not to teach, seems preliminary to all questions respecting the best systems and methods for rendering education effective.

The other consideration is comparatively unimportant; though, for the time being, it has embarrassed me greatly. I now learn that expectations were excited at your convention, that if a nomination were tendered me, it would not be declined. Had I anticipated the favorable regards of the convention, or foreseen that such expectations would be raised, I should not have hearkened to the proposition for a moment; and I may be permitted to add, that when I saw my name announced in the papers, my first act was to prepare a letter of declination. It was only when I went to deliver the letter that I learnt what had been done, and that, in the opinion of persons whose judgment I am bound to respect, I had been so far committed by my too partial friends, as that no option remained.

Yielding to these considerations, I submit myself to the decision of my fellow-citizens.

With sentiments of high personal regard,

I am, gentlemen,

Your friend and servant,

HORACE MANN.

Hon. THOMAS FRENCH, President; SAMUEL C. MANN, JOHN K. CORBETT, EDWARD CREHORE, Esqs., Secretaries.

WEST NEWTON, March 21, 1848.

SPEECH

DELIVERED IN THE HOUSE OF REPRESENTATIVES OF THE UNITED STATES, JUNE 30, 1848, ON THE RIGHT OF CONGRESS TO LEGISLATE FOR THE TERRITORIES OF THE UNITED STATES, AND ITS DUTY TO EXCLUDE SLAVERY THEREFROM.

MR. CHAIRMAN ;

I have listened with interest, both yesterday and to-day, to speeches on what is called the "Presidential Question." I propose to discuss a question of far greater magnitude, — the question of the age, — one whose consequences will not end with the ensuing four years, but will reach forward to the setting of the sun of time.

Sir, our position is this: The United States finds itself the owner of a vast region of country at the west, now almost vacant of inhabitants. Parts of this region are salubrious and fertile. We have reason to suppose, that, in addition to the treasures of wealth which industry may gather from its surface, there are mineral treasures beneath it, — riches garnered up of old in subterranean chambers, and only awaiting the application of intelligence and skill to be converted into the means of human improvement and happiness. These regions, it is true, lie remote from our place of residence. Their shores are washed by another sea, and it is no figure of speech to say that another sky bends over them. So remote are they, that their hours are not as our hours, nor their day as our day ; and yet, such are the wonderful improvements in art, in modern times, as to make it no rash anticipation, that, before this century shall have closed, the inhabitants on the Atlantic shores will be able to visit their brethren on the Pacific in ten days; and that intelligence will be transmitted and returned between the eastern and the western oceans in ten minutes. That country, therefore, will be rapidly filled, and we shall be brought into intimate relations with it, and, notwithstanding its distance, into proximity to it.

Now, in the providence of God, it has fallen to our lot to legislate for this unoccupied, or but partially occupied, expanse. Its great future hangs upon our decision. Not only degrees of latitude and longitude, but vast tracts of time, — ages and centuries, — seem at our disposal. As are the institutions which we form and establish there, so will be the men whom these institutions, in their turn, will form. Nature works by fixed laws; but we can bring this or that combination of circumstances under the operation of her laws, and thus determine results. Here springs up our responsibility. One class of institutions will gather there one class of men, who will develop one set of characteristics; another class of institutions will gather there another class of men, who will develop other characteristics. Hence their futurity is to depend upon our present action. Hence the acts we are to perform seem to partake of the nature of creation, rather than of legislation. Standing upon the elevation which we now occupy, and looking over into that empty world, "yet void," if not "without form," but soon to be filled with multitudinous life, and reflecting upon our power to give form and character to that life, and almost to foreördain what it shall be, I feel as though it would be no irreverence to compare our condition to that of the Creator before he fashioned the "lord" of this lower world; for we, like Him, can ingraft one set of attributes, or another set of attributes, upon a whole race of men. In approaching this subject, therefore, I feel a sense of responsibility corresponding to the infinite, — I speak literally, — the *infinite* interests which it embraces.

As far as the time allowed me will permit, I propose to discuss two questions. The first is, "*Whether Congress can lawfully legislate on the subject of slavery in the territories.*"

On this question a new and most extraordinary doctrine has lately been broached. A new reading of the constitution has been discovered. It is averred that the 3d section of the 4th article, giving Congress power "to dispose of, and make all needful rules and regulations respecting the territory or other property belonging to the United States," only gives power to legislate for the land *as land*. It is admitted that Congress may legislate for the land *as land*, — geologically or botanically considered, — perhaps for the beasts that roam upon its surface, or the fishes that swim in its waters; but it is denied that Congress possesses any power to determine the laws and the institutions of those who shall inhabit that "land."

But compare this with any other object of purchase or possession. When Texas was admitted into the Union, it transferred its "navy" to the United States; in other words, the United States bought, and of course owned, the navy of Texas. What power had Congress over this navy, after the purchase? According to the new doctrine, it could pass laws for the hull, the masts, and the sails of the Texan ships, but would have no power to navigate them by officers and men. It might govern the ships as so much wood, iron, and cordage, but would have no authority over commanders or crews.

But we are challenged to show any clause in the constitution which confers an *express* power to legislate over the territories we possess. I challenge our opponents to show any clause which confers express power to acquire those territories themselves. If, then, the power to acquire exists, it exists by implication and inference ; and if the power *to acquire* be an implied one, the power *to govern what is acquired* must be implied also. For, for what purpose does any man acquire property but to govern and control it ? What does a buyer pay for, if it be not the right to " dispose of " ? Such is the doctrine of the Supreme Court of the United States : " The right to govern," says Chief Justice Marshall, " may be the inevitable consequence of the right to acquire." *Amer. Ins. Co.* vs. *Canter*, 1 *Peters*, 542. See also *McCullough* vs. *Maryland*, 4 *Wheat.* 422. *The Cherokee Nation* vs. *Georgia*, 5 *Peters*, 44. *United States* vs. *Gratiot*, 14 *Peters*, 537.

But I refer to the express words of the constitution, as ample and effective in conferring all the power that is claimed. " Congress may dispose of, and make all needful rules and regulations," &c. If Congress may " dispose of " this land, then it may sell it. Inseparable from the right to sell is the right to define the terms of sale. The seller may affix such conditions and limitations as he pleases to the thing sold. If this be not so, then the buyer may dictate his terms to the seller. Answer these simple questions : Supposing the United States to own land in fee simple, then, is the government under guardianship, or disabled by minority ? Is it *non compos mentis ?* If no such disability applies to it, then it may sell. It may sell the fee simple, or it may carve out a lesser estate, and sell that. It may incorporate such terms and conditions as it pleases into its deed or patent of sale. It may make an outright quitclaim, or it may reserve the minerals for its own use, or the navigable streams for public highways, as it did in regard to the territory north-west of the river Ohio. It may insert the conditions and limitations in each deed or patent ; or, where the grantees are numerous, it may make general "rules and regulations," which are understood to be a part of each contract, and are therefore binding upon each purchaser. No man is compelled to buy; but if any one does buy, he buys subject to the "rules and regulations" expressed in the grant; and neither he, nor his grantees, nor his or their heirs after them, can complain. I want, therefore, no better foundation for legislating over the territories than the fact of ownership in the United States. Grant this, and all is granted. If I own a farm, or a shop, I may, as owner, prescribe the conditions of its transfer to another. If he does not like my conditions, then let him abandon the negotiation; if he accedes to the conditions, then let him abide by them, and hold his peace.

Sir, in the state to which I belong, we hold temperance to be a great blessing, as well as a great virtue; and intemperance to be a great curse, as well as a great sin. I know of incorporated companies there, who have purchased large tracts of land for manufacturing purposes. They well know how essential is the sobriety of workmen to the profitableness of their work; they know, too, how wasteful and destructive is inebriety. In disposing of their land, therefore, to the men whom they would gather about them and employ, they incorporate the provision, as a fundamental article in the deed of grant, that ardent spirits shall never be sold upon the premises; and thus they shut up, at once, one of the most densely-thronged gateways of hell. Have they not a right to do so, from the mere fact of ownership? Would any judge or lawyer doubt the validity of such a condition; or would any sensible man ever doubt its wisdom or humanity? Pecuniarily and morally, this comes under the head of "needful rules and regulations." If tipplers do not like them, let them stagger away, and seek their residence elsewhere.

But the United States is not merely a land owner; it is a sovereignty. As such, it exercises all constitutional jurisdiction over all its territories. Whence, but from this right of sovereignty, does the government obtain its power of saying that no man shall purchase land of the natives, or aborigines; and that, if you wish to buy land in the territories, you shall come to the government for it? Is there any express power in the constitution authorizing Congress to say to all the citizens of the United States, "If you wish to buy ungranted land in the territories, you must come to us, for no one else can sell, or shall sell"? This right, sustained by all our legislation and adjudications, covers the whole ground. *Lessee of Johnson et al.* vs. *McIntosh*, 8 *Wheaton*, 543; 5 *Cond. Rep.* 515.

But, leaving the constitution, it is denied that there are precedents. The honorable gentlemen from Virginia [Mr. Bayly] has not only contested the power of Congress to legislate on the subject of slavery in the territories, but he has denied the existence of precedents to sustain this power. Sir, it would have been an assertion far less bold, to deny the existence of precedents for the election of a President of the United States; for the instances of the latter have been far less frequent than of the former. Congress has legislated on the subject of slavery in the territories all the way up from the adoption of the constitution to the present time; and this legislation has been sustained by the judiciary of both the general and state governments, and carried into execution by the executive power of both. See *Menard* vs. *Aspasia*, 5 *Peters*, 505; *Phebe et al.* vs. *Jay*, *Breese's Rep.* 210; *Hogg* vs. *The Zanesville Canal Co.*, 5 *Ohio Rep.* 410; *Martin's Louisiana Rep. N. S.* 699; *Spooner* vs. *McConnell*, 1 *McLean's Rep.* 341; *Harvey* vs. *Deeker*, *Walker's Mississippi Rep.* 36; *Rachael* vs. *Walker*, 4 *Missouri Rep.* 350.

So far as the uniform practice of sixty years can settle a doubtful, or confirm an admitted right, this power of legislating over the territories has been taken from the region of doubt, and established upon the basis of acknowledged authority. In legislating for all that is now Ohio, Indiana, Illinois, Wisconsin, Michigan, Iowa, Missouri, Arkansas, Mississippi, Louisiana, and Florida, we have legislated on the subject of slavery in the territories. Sixty years of legislation on one side, and not a denial of the right on the other.

But the gentleman from Virginia [Mr. Bayly] says, that the action of Congress in regard to the territories has been rather that of constitution-making than of law-making. Suppose this to be true; does not the greater include the less? If Congress could make a constitution for all the territories, — an organic, fundamental law, — a law of laws, — could it not, had it so pleased, make the law itself? A constitution prescribes to the legislature what it shall do, and what it shall not do; it commands, prohibits, and binds men by oaths to support itself. It says, "Hitherto SHALT thou come, and no farther." And if Congress can do this, can it not make the local law itself? Can aught be more preposterous? As if we could *command* others to do what we have no right to do ourselves, and prohibit others from doing what lies beyond our own jurisdiction! Surely, to decree on what subjects a community shall legislate, and on what they shall not legislate, is the exercise of the highest power.

But Congress has not stopped with the exercise of the constitution-making power. In various forms, and at all times, it has legislated for the territories, in the strictest sense of the word *legislation*. It has legislated again and again, and ten times again, on this very subject of slavery. See the act of 1794, prohibiting the slave trade from "any port *or place*" in the United States. Could any citizen of the United States, under this act, have gone into one of our territories and there have fitted out vessels for the slave trade? Surely he could, if Congress had no right to legislate over territories only as so much land and water.

By statute 1798, chapter 28, § 7, slaves were forbidden to be brought into the Mississippi Territory from without the United States, and all slaves so brought in *were made free.*

So the act of 1800, chapter 51, in further prohibition of the slave trade, applied to all citizens of the United States, whether living in territories or in organized states. Did not this legislation cover the territories?

By statute 1804, chapter 38, § 10, three classes of slaves were forbidden to be introduced into the Orleans Territory.

Statute 1807, chapter 22, prohibiting the importation of slaves after January 1, 1808, prohibited their importation into the territories in express terms.

Statute 1818, chapter 91, statute 1819, chapter 101, and statute 1820, chapter 113, prohibiting the slave trade, and making it piracy, expressly included all the territories of the United States.

Statute 1819, chapter 21, authorized the President to provide for the safe-keeping of slaves imported from Africa, and for their removal to their home in that land. Under this law, the President might have established a depot for slaves within the limits of our territories, on the gulf, or on the Mississippi.

By statute 1820, chapter 22, § 8, Congress established what has been called the Missouri compromise line, thereby expressly legislating on the subject of slavery. So of Texas. See *Jo. Res. March* 1, 1851.

By statute 1819, chapter 93, statute 1821, chapter 39, § 2, and statute 1822, chapter 13, § 9, Congress legislated on the subject of slavery in the Territory of Florida.

Does it not seem almost incredible that a defender and champion of slavery should deny the power of Congress to legislate on the subject of slavery in the territories? If Congress has no such power, by what right can a master recapture a fugitive slave escaping into a territory? The constitution says, "No person held to service, or labor, in one *state*, escaping into another," — that is, another *state*, — "shall be discharged from such service, or labor," &c. The act of 1793, chapter 7, § 3, provides that when a person held to labor," &c., "shall escape into any other of the said states, *or territory*," he may be taken. By what other law than this can a runaway slave be retaken *in a territory?* If Congress has no power to legislate on the subject of slavery in any territory, then, surely, it cannot legislate for the capture of a fugitive slave in a territory. The argument cuts both ways. The knife wounds him who would use it to wound his fellow.

Further than this. If slavery is claimed to be one of the common subjects of legislation, then any legislation by Congress for the territories, on any of the common subjects of legislation, is a precedent, going to prove its right to legislate on slavery itself. If Congress may legislate on one subject belonging to a class, then it may legislate on any other subject belonging to the same class. Now, Congress has legislated for the territories on almost the whole circle of subjects belonging to common legislation. It has legislated on the elective franchise, on the pecuniary qualifications and residence of candidates for office, on the militia, on oaths, on the *per diem* and mileage of members, &c., &c. By statute 1811, chapter 21, § 3, authorizing the Territory of Orleans to form a constitution, it was provided that all legislative proceedings and judicial records should be kept and promulgated in the English language. Cannot Congress make provision for the rights of the people, as well as for the language in which the laws and records defining those rights shall be expressed? Any language is sweet to the ears of man which gives him the right of trial by jury, of habeas corpus, of religious freedom, and of life, limb, and liberty; but accursed is that language, and fit only for the realms below, which deprives an immortal being of the rights of intelligence and of freedom; of the right to himself, and the dearer rights of family.

But all this is by no means the strongest part of the evidence with which our statutes and judicial decisions abound, showing the power of Congress to legislate over territories. From the beginning, Congress has not only legislated over the territories, but it has appointed and controlled the agents of legislation.

The general structure of the legislature in several of the earlier territorial governments was this: It consisted of a governor and of two houses, — an upper and a lower. Without an exception, where a governor has been appointed, Congress has always reserved his appointment to itself, or to the President. The governor so appointed has always had a veto power over the two houses; and Congress has always reserved to itself, or to the President, a veto power, not only over him, but over him and both the houses besides. Congress has often interfered also with the appointment of the upper house, leaving only the lower house to be chosen exclusively by the people of the territory; and it has determined even for the lower house the qualifications both of electors and of elected. Further still: the power of removing the governor, at pleasure, has always been reserved to Congress, or to the President.

Look at this: Congress determines for the territory the qualifications of electors and elected, — at least in the first instance. No law of the territorial legislature is valid until approved by the governor. Though approved by the governor, it may be annulled by Congress, or by the President; and the governor is appointed, and may be removed at pleasure, by Congress or by the President.

To be more specific, I give the following outline of some of the territorial governments:—

Ohio Territory, statute 1789, *chapter* 8.—A governor for four years, nominated by the President, approved by the Senate, with power to appoint all subordinate civil and military officers.

A secretary for four years, appointed in the same way.

Three judges, to hold office during good behavior. Governor and judges the sole legislature, until the district shall contain five thousand free male inhabitants. Then,—

A House of Assembly, chosen by qualified electors, for two years.

A legislative council of five, to hold office for five years. The House of Assembly to choose ten men, five of whom are to be selected by the President and approved by the Senate. These five to be the "Legislative Council."

A governor, as before, with an unconditional veto, and a right to convene, prorogue, and dissolve the Assembly.

Power given to the President to revoke the commissions of governor and secretary.

Indiana Territory, statute 1800, *chapter* 41.—Similar to that of Ohio. At first, the lower house to consist of not more than nine, nor less than seven.

Mississippi Territory, statute 1800, *chapter* 50.—Similar to that of Indiana.

Michigan Territory, statute 1805, *chapter* 5.—Similar to that of Indiana.

Illinois Territory, statute 1809, *chapter* 13.—Similar to that of Indiana.

Alabama Territory, statute 1817, *chapter* 59. — Similar to that of Indiana.

Winconsin Territory, statute 1836, *chapter* 54. — Governor for three years, appointed as above, and removable by the President, with power to appoint officers and grant pardons. Unconditional veto.

Secretary for four years, removable by the President. In the absence, or during the inability, of the governor, to perform his duties.

Legislative Assembly to consist of a Council and a House of Representatives, to be chosen for two years. Congress to have an unconditional veto, to be exercised on laws approved by the governor.

Louisiana Territory, statute 1803, *chapter* 1. — Sole dictatorial power given to the President of the United States; and the army and navy of the United States placed at his command to govern the territorial inhabitants. — (This was under Mr. Jefferson, a strict constructionist.)

Territory of Orleans, statute 1804, *chapter* 38. — Governor nominated by the President, approved by the Senate, tenure of office three years. Removable by the President. Secretary for four years, to be governor in case, &c.

Legislative Council of thirteen, to be annually appointed by the President.

Governor and Council, of course, a reciprocal negative on each other. Congress an unconditional veto on both.

District of Louisiana, statute 1804, *chapter* 38. — To be governed by the governor and judges of the Territory of Indiana.

Congress an unconditional veto on all their laws.

Missouri Territory, statute 1812, *chapter* 95. — A governor, appointable and removable as above.

Secretary, the same.

A Legislative Council of nine. Eighteen persons

to be nominated by the House of Representatives for the territory; nine of these to be selected and appointed by the President and Senate. A House of Representatives, to be chosen by the people.

Arkansas Territory, statute 1819, *chapter* 49. — A governor and secretary, appointable and removable as above.

All legislative power vested in the governor and in the judges of the superior court.

When a majority of the *freeholders* should elect, then they might adopt the form of government of Missouri.

East and West Florida, statute 1819, *chapter* 93. — *Statute* 1821, *chapter* 29. — *Statute* 1822, *chapter* 13. From March 3, 1819, to March 30, 1822, the government vested solely in the President of the United States, and to be exercised by such officers as he should appoint.

After March 30, 1822, a governor and secretary, appointable and removable as above.

All legislative power vested in the governor, and in thirteen persons, called a legislative council, to be appointed annually by the President.

Yet, sir, notwithstanding all this legislation of Congress for the territories, on the subject of slavery itself; notwithstanding its legislation on a great class of subjects of which slavery is acknowledged to be one; notwithstanding its appointment, in some cases, of the legislative power of the territory, — making its own agent, the governor, removable at pleasure, — giving him a veto, in the first place, and reserving to itself a veto when he has approved; notwithstanding the exercise, in other cases, of full, absolute sovereignty over the inhabitants of the territories, and all their interests; and, notwithstanding such has been the practice of the government for sixty years, under Jefferson, Madison, Monroe, Jackson, and others, it is now denied that

Congress has any right to legislate on the subject of slavery in the territories. Sir, with a class of politicians in this country, it has come to this, that slavery is the only sacred thing in existence. It is self-existent, like a god, and human power cannot prevent it. From year to year, it goes on conquering and to conquer, and human power cannot dethrone it.

Sir, I will present another argument on this subject, and I do not see how any jurist or statesman can invalidate it.

Government is one, but its functions are several. They are legislative, judicial, executive. These functions are coördinate; each supposes the other two. There must be a legislature to enact laws; there must be a judiciary to expound the laws enacted, and point out the individuals against whom they are to be enforced; there must be an executive arm to enforce the decisions of the courts. In every theory of government, where one of these exist, the others exist. Under our constitution they are divided into three parts, and apportioned among three coördinate bodies. Whoever denies one of these must deny them all.

If the government of the United States, therefore, has no right to *legislate* for the territories, it has no right to *adjudicate* for the territories; if it has no right to *adjudicate*, then it has no right to *enforce* the decisions of the judicial tribunals. These rights must stand or fall together. He who takes from this government the law-making power, in regard to territories, strikes also the balances of justice from the hands of the judge, and the mace of authority from those of the executive. There is no escape from this conclusion. The constitution gives no more authority to adjudge suits in the territories, or to execute the decisions of the territorial courts, than it does to legislate. If Congress has no power over territory, only *as land*, then what does this land want of judges and marshals?

Is it not obvious, then, that this new reading of the constitution sets aside the whole legislative, judicial, and executive administration of this government over territories, since the adoption of the constitution? It makes the whole of it invalid. The Presidents, all members of Congress, all judges upon the bench, have been in a dream for the last sixty years, and are now waked up and recalled to their senses by the charm of a newly-discovered reading of the constitution.

Hitherto, sir, I have not directed my remarks to the actual legislation by Congress on the subject of slavery in the North-western Territory, so called. That territory was consecrated to freedom by the ordinance of 1787. It has been said that the *Confederation* had no power to pass such an ordinance. But whether this be so or not, is immaterial, for *Congress* has ratified the ordinance again and again. The first Congress at its first session passed an act whose preamble is as follows: "Whereas, in order that the ordinance of the United States, in Congress assembled, for the government of the territory north-west of the river Ohio, may continue to have full effect," &c. It then proceeds to modify some parts of the ordinance, and to adopt all the rest.*

In the second section of the act of 1800, chaper 41, establishing the Indiana Territory, it is expressly provided that its government shall be "in all respects similar to that provided by the ordinance of 1787."

In the act of 1802, chapter 40, section 5, authorizing Ohio to form a constitution and state government, this ordinance of 1787 is three times referred to as a valid and existing engagement, and it has always been held to be so by the courts of Ohio.

So in the act of 1816, chapter 57, section 4, author-

* Mr. Madison thought the original ordinance to be clearly invalid. See Federalist, No. 38. It is just as clear that he thought the constitution gave validity to it. See Federalist, No. 43.

izing the erection of Indiana into a state, the ordinance is again recognized, and is made a part of the fundamental law of the state.

So in the act of 1818, chapter 67, section 4, authorizing Illinois to become a state.

So in the act of 1805, chapter 5, section 2, establishing the Territory of Michigan.

So of Wisconsin. See. act of 1847, chapter 53, in connection with the constitution of Wisconsin.

But all this is tedious and superfluous. I have gone into this detail, because I understand the gentleman from Virginia [Mr. BAYLY] to have denied this adoption and these recognitions of the ordinance. I hazard nothing in saying that the ordinance of 1787 has been expressly referred to as valid, or expressly or impliedly reënacted, a dozen times, by the Congress of the United States; and, in the state courts of Ohio, Illinois, Louisiana, Mississippi, and Missouri, it has been adjudged to be constitutional. How, then, is it possible for any mind, amenable to legal rules for the decision of legal questions, to say that Congress cannot legislate, or has not legislated, (except once or twice inadvertently,) on the subject of slavery in the territories?

On this part of the argument, I have only a concluding remark to submit. The position I am contesting affirms generally that Congress cannot legislate upon the subject of slavery in the territories. The *inexpediency* of so legislating is further advocated on the ground that it is repugnant to democratical principles to debar the inhabitants of the territories from governing themselves. Must the free men of the territories, it is asked, have laws made for them by others? No! It is anti-democratic, monarchical, intolerable. All men have the right of self-government; and this principle holds true with regard to the inhabitants of territories, as well as the inhabitants of states.

Now, if these declarations were a sincere and honest affirmation of human rights, I should respect them and honor their authors. Did this doctrine grow out of a jealousy for the rights of man, a fear of usurpation, an assertion of the principle of self-government, I should sympathize with it, while I denied its legality. But, sir, it is the most painful aspect of this whole case, that the very object and purpose of claiming these ample and sovereign rights for the inhabitants of the territories is, that they may deny *all* rights to a portion of their fellow-beings within them. Enlarge, aggrandize, the rights of the territorial settlers! And why? Because, by so doing, you enable them to abolish all rights for a whole class of human beings. This claim, then, is not made for the purpose of making freemen more free, but for making slaves more enslaved. The reason for denying to Congress the power to legislate for the territories, is the fear that Congress will prevent slavery in them. The reason for claiming the supreme right of legislation for the territorial inhabitants, is the hope that they will establish slavery within their borders. Must not that democracy be false which begets slavery as its natural offspring?

If it has now been demonstrated that Congress has uniformly legislated, and can legislate, on the subject of slavery in the territories, I proceed to consider the next question. *Is it expedient to exclude slavery from them?*

Here, on the threshold, we are confronted with the claim that the gates shall be thrown wide open to the admission of slavery into the broad western world; because, otherwise, the southern or slave states would be debarred from enjoying their share of the common property of the Union.

I meet this claim with a counter-claim. If, on the one hand, the consecration of this soil to freedom will exclude the slaveholders of the south, it is just as true, on the other hand, that the desecration of it to slavery will exclude the freemen of the north. We, at the north, know too well the foundations of worldly prosperity and happiness; we know too well the sources of social and moral welfare, ever voluntarily to blend our fortunes with those of a community where slavery is tolerated. If our demand for free territory, then, excludes them, their demand for slave territory excludes us. Not one in five hundred of the freemen of the north could ever be induced to take his family and domicile himself in a territory where slavery exists. They know that the institution would impoverish their estate, demoralize their children, and harrow their own consciences with an ever-present sense of guilt, until those consciences, by force of habit and induration, should pass into that callous and more deplorable state, where continuous crime could be committed without the feeling of remorse.

Sir, let me read a passage from Dr. Channing, written in 1798, — fifty years ago, — when, at the early age of nineteen, he lived for some time in Richmond, Virginia, as a tutor in a private family. While there, he wrote a letter, of which the following is an extract: —

"There is one object here which always depresses me. It is *slavery*. This alone would prevent me from ever settling in Virginia. Language cannot express my detestation of it. Master and slave! Nature never made such a distinction, or established such a relation. Man, when forced to substitute the will of another for his own, ceases to be a moral agent; his title to the name of man is extinguished; he becomes a mere machine in the hands of his oppressor. No empire is so valuable as the empire of one's self. No right is so inseparable from humanity, and so necessary to the improvement of our species, as the right of exerting the powers which nature has given us in the pursuit of any and of every good which we can obtain without doing injury to others. Should you desire it, I will give you some idea of the situation and character of the negroes in Virginia. It is a subject so degrading to humanity, that I cannot dwell on it with pleasure. I should be obliged to show you every vice, heightened by every meanness, and added to every misery. The influence of slavery on the whites is almost as fatal as on the blacks themselves."

This was written fifty years ago, by a young man from New England, only nineteen years old. I know that, on all subjects of philanthropy and ethics, Dr. Channing was half a century in advance of his age. But the sentiments he expressed on this subject, at the close of the last century, are now the prevalent, deep-seated feelings of northern men, excepting, perhaps, a few cases where these feelings have been corrupted by interest.

I repeat, then, that the north cannot shut out the south from the new territories by a law for excluding slavery, more effectually than the south will shut out the north by the fact of introducing slavery. Even admitting, then, that the *law* is equal for both north and south, I will show that all the *equity* is on the side of the north.

Sir, from the establishment of our independence by the treaty of 1783 to the time of the adoption of the constitution, and for years afterwards, no trace is to be found of an intention to enlarge the bounds of our republic ; and it is well known that the treaty of 1803, for acquiring Louisiana, was acknowledged by Mr. Jefferson, who made it, to be unconstitutional. In 1787, the Magna Charta of perpetual freedom was secured to the North-west Territory. But the article excluding slavery from it had an earlier date than 1787. On the 1st of March, 1784, Congress voted to accept a session from the state of Virginia of her claim to the territory north-west of the Ohio river. The subject of providing a government for this and other territory was referred to a committee consisting of Mr. Jefferson, Mr. Chase of Maryland, and Mr. Howell of Rhode Island. On the 19th of April, 1784, their report was considered. That report contained the following ever-memorable clause: —

"That after the year 1800, of the Christian era, there shall be neither slavery nor involuntary servitude in any of the said states, [they were spoken of as states, because it was always contemplated to erect the territories into states,] otherwise than in punishment of crimes whereof the party shall have been convicted to have been personally guilty."

Sir, we hear much said in our day of the Wilmot proviso against slavery. In former years, great credit has been given to Mr. Nathan Dane, of Massachusetts, for originating the sixth article, (against slavery), in the ordinance of 1787. Sir, it is a misnomer to call this restrictive clause the "Wilmot proviso." It is the *Jefferson proviso*, and Mr. Jefferson should have the honor of it; and would to Heaven that our southern friends, who kneel so devoutly at his shrine, could be animated by that lofty spirit of freedom, that love for the rights of man, which alone can make their acts of devotion sacred.

But what is most material to be observed here is, that the plan of government reported by Mr. Jefferson, and acted upon by the Congress at that time, embraced all the "western territory." It embraced all the "territory ceded, or *to be ceded*, by individual states to the United States." — See *Journals of Congress, April* 23, 1784. If, then, we leave out Kentucky and Tennessee, as being parts of Virginia and North Carolina, all the residue of the territory north *or south* of the Ohio river, within the treaty limits of the United States, was intended, by the "Jefferson proviso," to be rescued from the doom of slavery. For that proviso there were sixteen votes, and only seven against it. Yet so singularly were these seven votes distributed, and so large a majority of the states did it require to pass an act, that it was lost. The whole of the representation from seven states voted for it unanimously. Only two states voted unanimously against it. Had but one of Mr. Jefferson's colleagues voted with him, and had Mr. Spaight, of North Carolina, voted for it, the restrictive clause in the report would have stood. But a minority of seven from the slave-holding states controlled a majority of sixteen from the free states, — ominous even at that early day of a fate that has now relentlessly pursued us for sixty years.

That vote was certainly no more than a fair representation of the feeling of the country against slavery at that time. It was with such a feeling that the "compromises of the constitution," as they are called, were entered into. Nobody dreaded or dreamed of the extension of slavery beyond its then existing limits. Yet, behold its aggressive march! Besides Kentucky and Tennessee, which I omit, for reasons before intimated, seven new slave states have been added to the Union, — Mississippi, Alabama, Missouri, Arkansas, Louisiana, Florida, and Texas, — the last five out of territory not belonging to us at the adoption of the constitution; while only one free state, Iowa, has been added during all this time, out of such newly-acquired territory.*

* Here Mr. HILLIARD, of Alabama, rose to ask if the south, by the Missouri compromise, had not surrendered its right to carry slavery north of the compromise line? His question was not understood. If it had been, it would have been replied, that the existence of slavery at New Orleans, and a few other places in Louisiana, at the time of the treaty with France, by no means established the right to carry it to the Pacific Ocean, if the treaty extended so far. Slavery being against natural right, can only exist by virtue of positive law, backed by force sufficient to protect it. It could not lawfully exist, therefore, in any part of Louisiana, which had not been laid out, organized, and subjected to the civil jurisdiction of the government. Such was not the case with any part of the territory north of the compromise line, and therefore nothing was surrendered. On the other hand, in the formation of the territorial governments of Orleans, Missouri, Arkan-

But there is another fact, which shows that the slaveholders have already had their full share of territory, however wide the boundaries of this country may hereafter become.

I have seen the number of *actual slaveholders* variously estimated; but the highest estimate I have ever seen is *three hundred thousand.* Allowing six persons to a family, this number would represent a white population of eighteen hundred thousand.

Mr. Gayle, of Alabama, interrupted and said: If the gentleman from Massachusetts has been informed that the number of slaveholders is only 300,000, then I will tell him his information is utterly false.

Mr. Mann. Will the gentleman tell me how many there are?

Mr. Gayle. Ten times as many.

Mr. Mann. Ten times as many! Ten times 300,000 is 3,000,000; and allowing six persons to each family, this would give a population of 18,000,000 directly connected with slaveholding; while the whole free population of the south, in 1840, was considerably less than five millions!

Mr. Meade, of Virginia, here interposed and said, that where the father or mother owned slaves, they were considered the joint property of the family. I think, if you include the grown and the young, there are about three millions interested in slave property.

Mr. Mann resumed. My data lead me to believe that the number does not now exceed two millions; but, at the time of the adoption of the constitution, the number directly connected with slaveholding must have been less than one million. Yet this one million have

sas, and Florida, a vast extent of country was surrendered to slavery. And this is independent of the question whether Congress, by the constitution, has any more right to establish slavery *any where* than it has to establish an inquisition, create an order of nobility, or anoint a king.

already managed to acquire the broad States of Missouri, Arkansas, Louisiana, Florida, and Texas, beyond the limits of the treaty of 1783; when, at the time the "compromises of the constitution" were entered into, not one of the parties supposed that we should ever acquire territory beyond those limits. And this has been done for the benefit, (if it be a benefit,) of that one million of slaveholders, against what is now a free population of fifteen millions. And, in addition to this, it is to be considered that the non-slaveholding population of the slave states have as direct and deep an interest as any part of the country, adverse to the extension of slavery. If all our new territory be doomed to slavery, where can the non-slaveholders of the slaveholding states emigrate to? Are they not to be considered? Has one half the population of the slaveholding states rights, which are paramount, not only to the rights of the other half, but to the rights of all the free states besides? for such is the claim. No, sir. I say that, if slavery were no moral or political evil, yet, according to all principles of justice and equity, the slaveholders have already obtained their full share of territory, though all the residue of this continent were to be annexed to the Union, and we were to become, in the insane language of the day, "an ocean-bound republic."

I now proceed to consider the nature and effects of slavery, as a reason why new-born communities should be exempted from it. First, let me treat of its economical or financial, and, secondly, of its moral aspects.

Though slaves are said to be property, they are the preventers, the wasters, the antagonists of property. So far from facilitating the increase of individual or national wealth, slavery retards both. It blasts worldly prosperity. Other things being equal, a free people will thrive and prosper, in a mere worldly sense, more than a people divided into masters and slaves. Were we so constituted as to care for nothing, to aspire to nothing, beyond mere temporal well being, this well being would counsel us to abolish slavery wherever it exists, and to repel its approach wherever it threatens.

Enslave a man, and you destroy his ambition, his enterprise, his capacity. In the constitution of human nature, the desire of bettering one's condition is the mainspring of effort. The first touch of slavery snaps this spring. The slave does not participate in the value of the wealth he creates. All he earns another seizes. A free man labors, not only to improve his own condition, but to better the condition of his children. The mighty impulse of parental affection repays for diligence, and makes exertion sweet. The slave's heart never beats with this high emotion. However industrious and frugal he may be, he has nothing to bequeath to his children, — or nothing save the sad bonds he himself has worn. Fear may make him work, but hope — never. When he moves his tardy limbs, it is because of the suffering that goads him from behind, and not from the bright prospects that beckon him forward in the race.

What would a slave owner at the south think, should he come to Massachusetts, and there see a farmer seize upon his hired man, call in a surgeon, and cut off all the flexor muscles of his arms and legs? I do not ask what he would think of his humanity, but what would he think of his sanity? Yet the planter does more than this when he makes a man a slave. He cuts deeper than the muscles; he destroys the spirit that moves the muscles.

In all ages of the world, among all nations, wherever the earnings of the laborer have been stolen from him, his energies have gone with his earnings. Under the villeinage system of England, the villeins were a low, idle, spiritless race; dead to responsibility; grovelling in their desires; resistant of labor; without enterprise; without foresight. This principle is now exemplified in the landlord and tenant system of Ireland. If a tenant is to be no better off for the improvements he makes on an estate, he will not make the improvements. Look at the seigniories of New York, — the anti-rent districts as they are now called; — every man acquainted with the subject knows that both people and husbandry are half a century behind the condition of contiguous fee-simple proprietorships. All history illustrates the principle, that when property is insecure, it will not be earned. If a despot can seize and confiscate the property of his subject at pleasure, the subject will not acquire property, and thereby give to himself the conspicuousness that invites the plunder. And if this be so when property is merely insecure, what must be the effect when a man has no property whatever in his earnings? Who does not know that a slave, who can rationally hope to purchase his freedom, will do all the work he ever did before, and earn his freedom-money besides? Slavery, therefore, though claiming to be a kind of property, is the bane of property; and the more slaves there are found in the inventory of a nation's wealth, the less in value will the aggregate of that inventory be.

This is *one* of the reasons why slave labor is so much less efficient than free labor. The former can never compete with the latter; and while the greater service is performed with cheerfulness, the smaller is extorted by fear. Just as certain as that the locomotive can outrun the horse, and the lightning outspeed the locomotive, just so certain is it that he who is animated by the hopes and the rewards of freedom will outstrip the disheartened and fear-driven slave.

The intelligent freeman can afford to live well, dress decently, and occupy a comfortable tenement. A scanty subsistence, a squalid garb, a mean and dilapidated hovel, proclaim the degradation of the slave. The slave states gain millions of dollars every year from the privations, the mean food, clothing, and shelter to which the slaves are subjected; and yet they grow rich less rapidly than states where millions of dollars are annually expended for the comforts and conveniences of the laborer. More is lost in production than is gained by privation.

A universal concomitant of slavery is, that it makes white labor disreputable. Being disreputable, it is shunned. The pecuniary loss resulting from this is incalculable. Dry up the myriad headsprings of the Mississippi, and where would be the mighty volume of waters which now bear navies on their bosom, and lift the ocean itself above its level, by their outpouring flood? Abolish those sources of wealth, which consist in the personal industry of every man, and of each member of every man's family, and that wide-spread thrift, and competence, and elegance, which are both the reward and the stimulus of labor, will be abolished with them. Forego the means, and you forfeit the end. You must use the instrument if you would have the product. Nothing but the feeling of independence, the conscious security of working for one's self and one's family, will, in the present state of the world, make labor profitable.

I know it has been recently said in this capital, and by high authority, that, with the exception of menial services, it is not disreputable at the south for a white man to labor. There are two ways, each independent of the other, to disprove this assertion. One of them consists in the testimony of a host of intelligent witnesses acquainted with the condition of things at the south. I might quote page after page from various sources; but, as the assertion comes from a gentleman belonging to South Carolina, [Mr. CALHOUN, of the Senate,] I will meet it with the statement of another gentleman belonging to the same state. I refer to Mr. William Gregg, of Charleston, a gentleman who is extensively acquainted with the social condition of men, both north and south.

In that state, according to the last census, there were about 150,000 free whites *over twelve years of age.* "Of this class," says Mr. Gregg, "fifty thousand are non-producers."* I suppose South Carolina to be as thrifty a slave state as there is, perhaps excepting Georgia; yet here is one third part of the population, old enough to work and able to work, who are idle, and of course vicious, — non-producers, but the worst kind of consumers.

Another answer to the above assertion is, that if white labor were reputable at the south, and white men were industrious, the whole country would be a garden, — a terrestrial paradise, — so far as neatness, abundance, and beauty are concerned. *Where are the* RESULTS *of this respected and honored white labor?* In a country where few expenses are necessary to ward off the rigors of winter; where the richest staples of the world are produced; where cattle and flocks need but little shelter, and sometimes none; if man superadded his industry to the bounties of nature, want would be wholly unknown, competence would give place to opulence, and the highest decorations of art would mingle with the glowing beauties of nature.

But hear Mr. Gregg: —

"My recent visit to the northern states has fully satisfied me that the true secret of our difficulties lies in the want of energy on the part of our capitalists, and ignorance and laziness on the part of those who ought to labor. We need never look for thrift while we permit our immense timber forests, granite quarries, and mines to lie idle, and supply ourselves with hewn granite, pine boards, laths, shingles, &c.,

* Essays on Domestic Industry, or an Inquiry into the Expediency of establishing Cotton Manufactories in South Carolina, 1845.

furnished by the *lazy* dogs of the north. Ah! worse than this; we see our back-country farmers, many of whom are too lazy to mend a broken gate, or repair the fences to protect their crops from the neighboring stock, actually supplied with their axe, hoe, and broom handles, pitchforks, rakes, &c., by the *indolent* mountaineers of New Hampshire and Massachusetts. The time was, when every old woman had her gourd, from which the country gardens were supplied with seed. We now find it more convenient to permit this duty to devolve on our careful friends, the Yankees. Even our boat oars, and handspikes for rolling logs, are furnished, ready-made, to our hand," &c. "Need I add, to further exemplify our excessive indolence, that the Charleston market is supplied with fish and wild game by northern men, who come out here as regularly as the winter comes, for this purpose, and from our own waters and forests often realize, in the course of one winter, a sufficiency to purchase a small farm in New England." — *Essays*, page 8.

Again: —

"It is only necessary to travel over the sterile mountains of Connecticut, Massachusetts, Vermont, and New Hampshire, to learn the true secret of our difficulties," — "to learn the difference between indolence and industry, extravagance and economy. We there see the scenery which would take the place of our unpainted mansions, dilapidated cabins, with mud chimneys, and no windows, broken-down rail fences, fields overgrown with weeds, and thrown away half exhausted, to be taken up by pine thickets; beef cattle unprotected from the inclemency of winter, and so poor as barely to preserve life." — *Essays*, page 7.

And again: —

"Shall we pass unnoticed the thousands of poor, ignorant, degraded white people among us, who, in this land of plenty, live in comparative nakedness and starvation? Many a one is reared in *proud* South Carolina, from birth to manhood, who has never passed a month in which he has not, some part of the time, been stinted for meat. Many a mother is there who will tell you that her children are but scantily supplied with bread, and much more scantily with meat, and if they be clad with comfortable raiment, it is at the expense of these scanty allowances of food. These may be startling statements, but they are nevertheless true; and if not believed in Charleston, the members of our legislature, who have traversed the state in electioneering campaigns, can attest their truth." — *Essays*, page 22.

After such statements as these; after the testimony of hundreds and hundreds of eye-witnesses; after the proofs furnished by the aggregates of products, published in our Patent Office Reports, it is drawing a little too heavily on our credulity to say that the white man at the south is industrious. Industry manifests itself by its results, as the sun manifests itself by shining.

But slavery is hostile to the pecuniary advancement of the community in another way. The slave must be kept in ignorance. He must not be educated, lest with education should come a knowledge of his natural rights, and the means of escape or the power of vengeance. To secure the abolition of his freedom, the growth of his mind must be abolished. His education, therefore, is prohibited by statute under terrible penalties.

Now, a man is weak in his muscles; he is strong only in his faculties. In physical strength how much superior is an ox or a horse to a man; in fleetness, the dromedary or the eagle. It is through mental strength only that man becomes the superior and governor of all animals.

It was not the design of Providence that the work of the world should be performed by muscular strength. God has filled the earth and imbued the elements with energies of greater power than that of all the inhabitants of a thousand planets like ours. Whence come our necessaries and our luxuries? — those comforts and appliances that make the difference between a houseless, wandering tribe of Indians in the far west, and a

New England village. They do not come wholly or principally from the original, unassisted strength of the human arm, but from the employment, through intelligence and skill, of those great natural forces with which the bountiful Creator has filled every part of the material universe. Caloric, gravitation, expansibility, compressibility, electricity, chemical affinities and repulsions, spontaneous velocities,—these are the mighty agents which the intellect of man harnesses to the car of improvement. The application of water, and wind, and steam, to the propulsion of machinery, and to the transportation of men and merchandise from place to place, has added ten thousand fold to the actual products of human industry. How small the wheel which the stoutest laborer can turn, and how soon will he be weary! Compare this with a wheel driving a thousand spindles or looms, which a stream of water can turn, and never tire. A locomotive will take five hundred men, and bear them on their journey hundreds of miles in a day. Look at these same five hundred men, starting from the same point, and attempting the same distance, with all the pedestrian's or the equestrian's toil and tardiness. The cotton mills of Massachusetts will turn out more cloth, in one day, than could have been manufactured by all the inhabitants of the eastern continent during the tenth century. On an element which, in ancient times, was supposed to be exclusively within the control of the gods, and where it was deemed impious for human power to intrude, even there the gigantic forces of nature, which human science and skill have enlisted in their service, confront and overcome the raging of the elements,—breasting tempests and tides, escaping reefs and lee shores, and careering triumphant around the globe. The velocity of winds, the weight of waters, and the rage of steam, are powers, each one of which is infinitely stronger than all the strength of all the nations and races of mankind, were it all gathered into a single arm. And all these energies are given us on one condition, — the condition of intelligence, that is, of education.

Had God intended that the work of the world should be done by human bones and sinews, he would have given us an arm as solid and strong as the shaft of a steam engine; and enabled us to stand, day and night, and turn the crank of a steamship while sailing to Liverpool or Calcutta. Had God designed the human muscles to do the work of the world, then, instead of the ingredients of gunpowder or gun cotton, and the expansive force of heat, he would have given us hands which could take a granite quarry and break its solid acres into suitable and symmetrical blocks, as easily as we now open an orange. Had he intended us for bearing burdens, he would have given us Atlantean shoulders, by which we could carry the vast freights of rail-car and steamship, as a porter carries his pack. He would have given us lungs by which we could blow fleets before us, and wings to sweep over ocean wastes. But, instead of iron arms, and Atlantean shoulders, and the lungs of Boreas, he has given us a mind, a soul, a capacity of acquiring knowledge, and thus of appropriating all these energies of nature to our own use. Instead of a telescopic and microscopic eye, he has given us power to invent the telescope and the microscope. Instead of ten thousand fingers, he has given us genius inventive of the power loom and the printing press. Without a cultivated intellect, man is among the weakest of all the dynamical forces of nature; with a cultivated intellect, he commands them all.

And now, what does the slave maker do? He abolishes this mighty power of the intellect, and uses only the weak, degraded, and half-animated forces of the human limbs. A thousand slaves may stand by a river, and to them it is only an object of fear or of superstition. An educated man surpasses the ancient idea of a river god; he stands by the Penobscot, the Kennebec, the Merrimack, or the Connecticut; he commands each of them to do more work than could be performed by a hundred thousand men, — to saw timber, to make cloth, to grind corn, — and they obey. Ignorant slaves stand upon a coal mine, and to them it is only a worthless part of the inanimate earth. An educated man uses the same mine to print a million of books. Slaves will seek to obtain the same crop from the same field, year after year, though the *pabulum* of that crop is exhausted; the educated man, with his chemist's eye, sees not only the minutest atoms of earth, but the imponderable gases that permeate it, and he is rewarded with an unbroken succession of luxuriant harvests.

Nor are these advantages confined to those departments of nature where her mightiest forces are brought into requisition. In accomplishing whatever requires delicacy and precision, nature is as much more perfect than man as she is more powerful in whatever requires strength. Whether in great or in small operations, all the improvements in the mechanical and the useful arts come as directly from intelligence as a bird comes out of a shell, or the beautiful colors of a flower out of sunshine. The slave worker is forever prying at the short end of Nature's lever, and using the back instead of the edge of her finest instruments.

Sir, the most abundant proof exists, derived from all departments of human industry, that uneducated labor is comparatively unprofitable labor. I have before me the statements of a number of the most intelligent gentlemen of Massachusetts, affirming this fact as the result of an experience extending over many years. In Massachusetts we have no native-born child wholly without school instruction; but the degrees of attainment, of mental development, are various. Half a dozen years ago, the Secretary of the Massachusetts Board of Education obtained statements from large numbers of our master manufacturers, authenticated from the books of their respective establishments, and covering a series of years, the result of which was, that increased wages were found in connection with increased intelligence, just as certainly as increased heat raises the mercury in the thermometer. Foreigners, and those coming from other states, who made their marks when they receipted their bills, earned the least; those who had a moderate or limited education occupied a middle ground on the pay-roll; while the intelligent young women who worked in the mills in winter, and taught schools in summer, crowned the list. The larger capital, in the form of intelligence, yielded the larger interest in the form of wages. This inquiry was not confined to manufactures, but was extended to other departments of business, where the results of labor could be made the subject of exact measurement.

This is universally so. The mechanic sees it, when he compares the work of a stupid with that of an awakened mind. The traveller sees it, when he passes from an educated into an uneducated nation. Sir, I have seen countries in Europe, lying side by side, where, without compass or chart, without bound or landmark, I could run the line of demarcation between the two, by the broad, legible characters which ignorance has written on roads, fields, houses, and the persons of men, women, and children, on one side, and which knowledge has inscribed on the other.

This difference is most striking in the mechanic arts, but it is clearly visible also in husbandry. Not the most fertile soil, not mines of silver and gold, can make a nation rich, without intelligence. Who ever had a more fertile soil than the Egyptians? Who have handled more silver and gold than the Spaniards? The universal cultivation of the mind and heart is the only true source of opulence; — the cultivation of the mind, by which to lay hold on the treasures of nature; the cultivation of the heart, by which to devote those treasures to beneficent uses. Where this cultivation exists, no matter how barren the soil or ungenial the clime, there comfort and competence will abound; for it is the intellectual and moral condition of the cultivator that impoverishes the soil or makes it teem with abundance. He who disobeys the law of God in regard to the culture of the intellectual and spiritual nature, may live in the valley of the Nile, but he can rear only the "lean kine" of Pharaoh; but he who obeys the highest law may dwell in the cold and inhospitable regions of Scotland or of New England, and "well-formed and fat-fleshed kine" shall feed on all his meadows. If Pharaoh will be a taskmaster, and will not let the bondmen go free, the corn in his field shall be the "seven thin ears blasted by the east wind;" but if he will obey the commandments of the Lord, then behold there shall be "seven ears of corn upon one stalk, all rank and good." Sir, the sweat of a slave poisons the soil upon which it falls; his breath is mildew to every green thing; his tear withers the verdure it drops upon.

But slavery makes the general education of the whites impossible. You cannot have general education without Common Schools. Common Schools cannot exist where the population is sparse. Where slaves till the soil, or do the principal part of whatever work is done, the free population must be sparse. Slavery, then, by an inexorable law, denies general education to the whites. The providence of God is just and retributive. Create a serf caste, and debar them from education, and you necessarily debar a great portion of the privileged class from education also. It is impossible, in the present state of things, or in any state of things which can be foreseen, to have free and universal education in a slave state. The difficulty is insurmountable. For a well-organized system of Common Schools, there should be two hundred children, at least, living in such proximity to each other that the oldest of them can come together to a central school. It is not enough to gather from within a circle of half a dozen miles' diameter fifty or sixty children for a single school. This brings all ages and all studies into the same room. A good system requires a separation of school children into four, or at least into three, classes, according to ages and attainments. Without this gradation, a school is bereft of more than half its efficiency. Now, this can never be done in an agricultural community where there are two classes of men — one to do all the work, and the other to seize all the profits. With New England habits of industry, and with that diversified labor which would be sure to spring from intelligence, the State of Virginia, which skirts us here on the south, would support all the population of the New England states, and fill them with abundance.

Mr. Bayly. We have as great a population as New England now.

Mr. Mann. As great a population as New England!!

Mr. Bayly. We send fifteen representatives.

[A voice. And how many of them represent slaves?]

Mr. Mann. Massachusetts alone sends ten representatives.

[A voice. And the rest of New England twenty-one more.]

Mr. Mann. I say, sir, the single State of Virginia could support in abundance the whole population of New England. With such a free population, the school children would be so numerous that public schools might be opened within three or four miles of each other all over its territory, — the light of each of which, blending with its neighboring lights, would illumine the whole land. They would be schools, too, in point of cheapness, within every man's means. The degrading idea of pauper schools would be discarded forever. But what is the condition of Virginia now? One quarter part of all its adult free white population are unable to read or write, and were proclaimed to be so by a late governor, in his annual message, without producing any reform. Their remedy is to choose a governor who will not proclaim such a fact. When has Virginia, in any state or national election, given a majority equal to the number of its voters unable to read or write? A *republican* government supported by the two pillars of Slavery and Ignorance!

In South Carolina there is also a fund for the support of pauper schools; but this had become so useless, and was so disdained by its objects, that a late governor of the state, in his annual message, recommended that it should be withdrawn from them altogether.

Yet in many of the slave states there are beautiful paper systems of Common Schools, — dead laws in the statute books, — and the census tells us how profitless they have been. In 1840, in the fifteen slave states and territories, there were only 201,085 scholars at the primary schools. In the same class of schools in the free states, there were 1,626,028, — eight times as many. New York alone had 502,367, or two and a half times as many. The scholars in the primary schools of Ohio alone, outnumbered all those in the fifteen slave states and territories by more than 17,000. In the slave states, almost one tenth part of the free white population over twenty years of age are unable to read and write. In the free states, less than one in one hundred and fifty; and at least four fifths of these are foreigners, who ought not to be included in the computation. Many of the slave states, too, have munificent school funds. Kentucky has one of more than a million of dollars; Tennessee, of two millions; yet, in 1837, Governor Clarke, of Kentucky, declared, in his message to the legislature, that "one third of the adult population were unable to write their names;" and in the State of Tennessee, according to the last census, there were 58,531 of the same description of persons. Surely it would take more than five of these to make three freemen; for the more a state has of them, the less of intelligent freedom will there be in it. And if the schools in the slave states are compared with the schools in the free states, the deficiency in quality will be found as great as the deficiency in number.

Sir, during the last ten years I have had a most extensive correspondence with the intelligent friends of education in the slave states. They yearn for progress, but they cannot obtain it. They procure laws to be passed, but there is no one to execute them. They set forth the benefits and the blessings of education; but they speak in a vacuum, and no one hears the appeal. If a parent wishes to educate his children, he must send them from home, and thus suffer a sort of bereavement, even while they live; or he must employ a tutor or governess in his family, which few are able to do. The rich may do it, but what becomes of the children of the poor? In cities the obstacles are less; but the number of persons resident in cities is relatively small. All this is the inevitable consequence of slavery; and it is as impossible for free, thorough, universal education to coëxist with slavery as for two bodies to occupy the same space at the same time. Slavery would abolish education, if it should invade a free state; education would abolish slavery, if it *could* invade a slave state.

Destroying common education, slavery destroys the

fruits of common education, — the inventive mind, practical talent, the power of adapting means to ends in the business of life. Whence have come all those mechanical and scientific improvements and inventions which have enriched the world with so many comforts, and adorned it with so many beauties; which to-day give enjoyments and luxuries to a common family in a New England village, that neither Queen Elizabeth of England nor any of her proud court ever dreamed of, but a little more than two centuries ago? Among whom have these improvements originated? All history and experience affirm that they have come, and must come, from people among whom education is most generous and unconfined. Increase the *constituency*, if I may so speak, of developed intellect, and you increase in an equal ratio the chances of inventive, creative genius. From what part of our own country has come the application of steam to the propulsion of boats for commercial purposes, or of wheels for manufacturing purposes? Where have the various and almost infinite improvements been made which have resulted in the present perfection of cotton and woollen machinery? Whence came the invention of the cotton-gin, and the great improvements in railroads? Where was born the mighty genius who invented the first lightning rod, which sends the electric fluid harmless into the earth; or that other genius, not less beneficent, who invented the second lightning rod, which sends the same fluid from city to city on messages of business or of affection? Sir, these are results which you can no more have without common education, without imbuing the public mind with the elements of knowledge, than you can have corn without planting, or harvests without sunshine.

Look into the Patent Office reports, and see in what sections of country mechanical improvements and the application of science to the useful arts have originated.

Out of *five hundred and seventy-two* patents issued in 1847, only *sixty-six* went to the slave states. The patents annually issued, it is true, are a mingled heap of chaff and wheat, but some of it is wheat worthy of Olympus. I think the Patent Office reports show that at least six or eight times as many patents have been taken out for the north as for the south. What improvements will a slave ever make in agricultural implements; in the manufacture of metals; in preparing wool, cotton, silk, fur, or paper; in chemical processes; in the application of steam; in philosophical, nautical, or optical instruments; in civil engineering, architecture, the construction of roads, canals, wharves, bridges, docks, piers, &c.; in hydraulics or pneumatics; in the application of the mechanical powers; in household furniture, or wearing apparel; in printing, binding, engraving, &c., &c.? This question, when put in reference to slaves, appears ridiculous; and yet it is no more absurd, when asked in reference to an ignorant slave, than when asked in reference to an uneducated white man. The fact that the latter is a voter makes no difference, notwithstanding the common opinion, in certain latitudes, that it does. All such improvements come from minds which have had an early awakening, and been put on scientific trains of thought in their childhood and youth, — a thing utterly impossible for the people at large, without Common Schools.

These are causes; now look at effects. In the New England states, the iron manufacture is twenty times as much, according to the population, as it is in Virginia; and yet Virginia has far more of the ore than they. In cotton, we can hardly find a fraction low enough to express the difference. The ship-building in Maine and Massachusetts is thirty-five times as much as in Virginia. The north comes to the south, cuts their timber, carries it home, manufactures it, and then brings it back, wrought into a hundred different forms, to be sold to those who would see it rot before their eyes.

Can any man give a reason why Norfolk should not have grown like New York, other than the difference in the institutions of the people? Jamestown was settled before Plymouth, and had *natural* advantages superior to it. Plymouth now has a population of between seven and eight thousand, is worth two millions of dollars, and taxed itself last year, for schools and schoolhouses, more than seven thousand dollars. I ought rather to say, that it invested more than seven thousand dollars in a kind of stock that yields a hundred per cent. income. How many bats there may be in the ruins of Jamestown, the last census does not inform us.

The books printed at the south I suppose not to be equal to *one fiftieth* part of the number printed at the north. In maps, charts, engravings, and so forth, the elements of comparison exist only on one side.

Out of universal education come genius, skill, and enterprise, and the desire of bettering one's condition. Industry and frugality are their concomitants. Diversified labor secures a home market. Diligence earns much, but the absence of the vices of indolence saves more. Hence comforts abound, while capital accumulates. After the home consumption is supplied, there is a surplus for export. The balance of trade is favorable. All the higher institutions of learning and religion can be liberally supported. These institutions impart an elevated and moral tone to society. Hence efforts for all kinds of social ameliorations. Temperance societies spring up. Societies for preventing crime; for saving from pauperism; for the reform of prisons and the reformation of prisoners; for peace; for sending missionaries to the heathen; for diffusing the gospel, — all these, where a sound education is

5

given, grow up, in the order of Providence, as an oak grows out of an acorn.

In one thing the south has excelled, — in training statesmen. The primary and the ultimate effects of slavery upon this fact are so well set forth in a late sermon by Dr. Bushnell, of Hartford, Connecticut, that I will read a passage from it: —

"And here, since this institution of slavery, entering into the fortunes of our history, complicates in so many ways the disorders we suffer, I must pause a few moments to sketch its characteristics. Slavery, it is not to be denied, is an essentially barbarous institution. It gives us, too, that sign which is the perpetual distinction of barbarism, that it has no law of progress. The highest level it reaches is the level at which it begins. Indeed, we need not scruple to allow that it has yielded us one considerable advantage, in virtue of the fact that it produces its best condition first. For while the northern people were generally delving in labor, for many generations, to create a condition of comfort, slavery set the masters at once on a footing of ease, gave them leisure for elegant intercourse, for unprofessional studies, and seasoned their character thus with that kind of cultivation which distinguishes men of society. A class of statesmen were thus raised up, who were prepared to figure as leaders in scenes of public life, where so much depends on manners and social address. But now the scale is changing. Free labor is rising, at length, into a state of wealth and comfort, to take the lead of American society. Meanwhile, the foster-sons of slavery, — the high families, the statesmen, — gradually receding in character, as they must under this vicious institution, are receding also in power and influence, and have been ever since the revolution. Slavery is a condition against nature; the curse of nature, therefore, is on it, and it bows to its doom by a law as irresistible as gravity. It produces a condition of ease which is not the reward of labor, and a state of degradation which is not the curse of idleness. Therefore, the ease it enjoys cannot but end in a curse, and the degradation it suffers cannot rise into a blessing. It nourishes imperious and violent passions. It makes the masters solitary sheiks on their estates, forbidding thus the possibility of public schools, and preventing also that condensed form of society which is necessary to the vigorous maintenance of churches. Education and religion thus displaced, the dinner table only remains, and on this hangs, in great part, the keeping of the social state. But however highly we may estimate the humanizing power of hospitality, it cannot be regarded as any sufficient spring of character. It is neither a school nor a gospel. And when it comes of self-indulgence, or only seeks relief for the tedium of an idle life, scarcely does it bring with it the blessings of a virtue. The accomplishments it yields are of a mock quality, rather than of a real, having about the same relation to a substantial and finished culture that honor has to character. This kind of currency will pass no longer; for, it is not expense without comfort, or splendor set in disorder, as diamonds in pewter; it is not air in place of elegance, or assurance substituted for ease; neither is it to be master of a fluent speech, or to garnish the same with stale quotations from the classics; much less is it to live in the Don Juan vein, accepting barbarism by poetic inspiration, — the same by which a late noble poet, drawing out of Turks and pirates, became the chosen laureate of slavery, — not any or all of these can make up such a style of man, or of life, as we in this age demand. We have come up now to a point where we look for true intellectual refinement, and a ripe state of personal culture. But how clearly is it seen to be a violation of its own laws, for slavery to produce a genuine scholar, or a man who, in any department of excellence, unless it be in politics, is not a full century behind his time? And if we ask for what is dearer and better still, for a pure Christian morality, the youth of slavery are trained in no such habits as are most congenial to virtue. The point of honor is the only principle many of them know. Violence and dissipation bring down every succeeding generation to a state continually lower; so that now, after a hundred and fifty years are passed, the slaveholding territory may be described as a vast missionary ground, and one so uncomfortable to the faithful ministry of Christ, by reason of its jealous tempers, and the known repugnance it has to many of the first maxims of the gospel, that scarcely a missionary can be found to enter it. Connected with this moral decay, the resources of nature also are exhausted, and her fertile territories changed to a desert, by the uncreating power of a spendthrift institution. And then, having made a waste where God had made a garden, slavery gathers up the relics of bankruptcy, and the baser relics still of virtue and all manly enterprise, and goes forth to renew, on a virgin soil, its dismal and forlorn history. Thus, at length, has been produced what may be called the bowie-knife style of civilization, and the new west of the south is overrun by it, — a spirit of blood which defies all laws of God and man; — honorable, but not honest; prompt to resent an injury, slack to discharge a debt; educated to ease, and readier, of course, when the means of living fail, to find them at the gambling table or the race-ground, than in any work of industry, — probably squandering the means of living there, to relieve the tedium of ease itself."

The free schools of the north lead to the common diffusion of knowledge, and the equalization of society. The private schools of the south divide men into patricians and plebeians; so that, in the latter, a nuisance grows out of education itself. In the public schools of New York there are libraries now amounting to more than a million of volumes. In the schools of Massachusetts the number of volumes is relatively less, but the quality is greatly superior. In each of these states, within half an hour's walk of the poorest farm-house or mechanic's shop, there is a library, free and open to every child, containing works of history, biography, travels, ethics, natural science, &c., &c., which will supply him with the noblest capital of intelligence, wherewith to commence the business of making himself a useful and intelligent citizen. With the exception of New Orleans, (whose free schools were commenced and have been presided over by a Massachusetts man,) and three or four other cities, all the libraries in the public schools of the slave states could be carried in a schoolboy's satchel. The libraries of all the universities and colleges of the south contain 223,416 volumes; those of the north, 593,897 volumes. The libraries of southern theological schools, 22,800; those of northern, 102,080.

Look into Silliman's Journal, or the volumes of the American Academy of Arts and Sciences, and inquire whence the communications came. Where live the historians of the country, Sparks, Prescott, Bancroft; the poets, Whittier, Bryant, Longfellow, Lowell; the jurists, Story, Kent, Wheaton; the classic models of writing, Channing, Everett, Irving; the female writers, Miss Sedgwick, Mrs. Sigourney, and Mrs. Child? All this proceeds from no superiority of natural endowment on the one side, or inferiority on the other. The Southern States are all within what may be called "the latitudes of genius;" for there is a small belt around the globe, comprising but a few degrees of latitude, which has produced all the distinguished men who have ever lived. I say this difference results from no difference in natural endowment. The mental endowments at the south are equal to those in any part of the world. But it comes because, in one quarter, the common atmosphere is vivified with knowledge, electric with ideas, while slavery gathers its Bœotian fogs over the other. What West Point has been to our armies in Mexico, that, and more than that, good schools would be to the intelligence and industrial prosperity of our country.

It may seem a little out of place, but I cannot forbear here adverting to one point, which, as a lover of children and as a parent, touches me more deeply than any other. To whom are intrusted, at the south, the early care and nurture of children? It has been thought by many educators and metaphysicians, that children learn as much before the age of seven years as ever afterwards. Who, at the south, administers this early knowledge, — these ideas, these views, that have such sovereign efficacy in the formation of adult character? Who has the custody of children during this ductile, forming, receptive period of life, — a period when the mind absorbs whatever is brought into contact with it? Sir, the children of the south, more or less, and generally *more*, are tended and nurtured by slaves. Ignorance, superstition, vulgarity, passion, and perhaps impurity, are the breasts at which they nurse. Whatever afflictions God may see fit to bring upon me, whatever other mercies He may withhold, may He give me none but persons of intelligence, of refinement, and of moral excellence, to walk with my children during the imitative years of their existence, and to lead them in the paths of knowledge, and breathe into their hearts the breath of a moral and religious life.

Before considering the moral character of slavery, I wish to advert for a moment to the position which we occupy as one of the nations of the earth, in this advancing period of the world's civilization. Nations, like individuals, have a character. The date of the latter is counted by years; that of the former, by centuries. No man can have any self-respect, who is not solicitous about his posthumous reputation. No man can be a patriot who feels neither joy nor shame at the idea of the honor or the infamy which his age and his country shall leave behind them. Nations, like individuals, have characteristic objects of ambition. Greece coveted the arts; Rome gloried in war; but liberty has been the goddess of our idolatry. Amid the storms of freedom were we cradled; in the struggles of freedom have our joints been knit; on the rich aliment of freedom have we grown to our present stature. With a somewhat too boastful spirit, perhaps, have we challenged the admiration of the world for our devotion to liberty; but an enthusiasm for the rights of man is so holy a passion, that even its excesses are not devoid of the beautiful. We have not only won freedom for ourselves, but we have taught its sacred lessons to others. The shout of "Death to tyrants, and freedom for man!" which pealed through this country seventy years ago, has at length reached across the Atlantic; and whoever has given an attentive ear to the sounds which have come back to us, within the last few months, from the European world, cannot have failed to perceive that they were only the far-travelled echoes of the American Declaration of Independence. But in the divine face of our liberty there has been one foul, demoniac feature. Whenever her votaries would approach her to worship, they have been fain to draw a veil over one part of her visage, to conceal its hideousness. Whence came this deformity on her otherwise fair and celestial countenance? Sad is the story, but it must be told. Her mother was a vampire. As the daughter lay helpless in her arms, the beldam tore open her living flesh, and feasted upon her lifeblood. Hence this unsightly wound, that affrights whoever beholds it. But, sir, I must leave dallying with these ambiguous metaphors. One wants the plain, sinewy, Saxon tongue to tell of deeds that should have shamed devils. Great Britain was the mother. Her American colonies were the daughter. The mother lusted for gold. To get it, she made partnership with robbery and death. Shackles, chains, and weapons for human butchery, were her outfit in trade. She made Africa her hunting-ground. She made its people her prey, and the unwilling colonies her market-place. She broke into the Ethiop's home, as a wolf into a sheepfold at midnight. She set the continent a-flame, that she might seize the affrighted inhabitants as they ran shrieking from their blazing hamlets. The aged and the infant she left for the vultures; but the strong men and the strong women she drove, scourged and bleeding, to the shore. Packed and stowed like merchandise between unventilated decks, so close that the tempest without could not ruffle the pestilential air within, the voyage was begun. Once a day the hatches were opened, to receive food and to disgorge the dead. Thousands and thousands of corpses, which she plunged into the ocean from the decks of her slave ships, she counted only as the tare of commerce. The blue monsters of the deep became familiar with her pathway, and, not more remorseless than she, they shared her plunder. At length the accursed vessel reached the foreign shore. And there, monsters of the land, fiercer and feller than any that roam the watery plains, rewarded the robber by purchasing his spoils.

For more than a century did the madness of this traffic rage. During all those years, the clock of eternity never counted out a minute that did not witness the cruel death, by treachery or violence, of some son or daughter, some father or mother, of Africa. The three millions of slaves that now darken our southern horizon are the progeny of these progenitors, — a doomed race, fated and suffering from sire to son. But the enormities of the mother country did not pass without remonstrance. Many of the colonies expostulated against, and rebuked them. The New England colonies, New Jersey, Pennsylvania, Virginia, presented to the throne the most humble and suppliant petitions, praying for the abolition of the trade. The colonial legislatures passed laws against it. But their petitions were spurned from the throne. Their laws were vetoed by the governors. In informal negotiations attempted with the ministers of the crown, the friends of the slave were made to understand that royalty turned an adder's ear to their prayers. The profoundest feelings of lamentation and abhorrence were kindled in the bosoms of his western subjects by this flagitious conduct of the king. In that dark catalogue of crimes, which led our fathers to forswear allegiance to the British throne, its refusal to prohibit the slave trade to the colonies is made one of the most prominent of those political offences which are said to "define a tyrant." In the original draught of the Declaration of Independence, as prepared by Mr. Jefferson, this crime of King George the Third is set forth in the following words:—

> " He has waged cruel war against human nature itself, violating its most sacred rights of life and liberty in the persons of a distant people who never offended him, captivating and carrying them into slavery in another hemisphere, or to incur a miserable death in their transportation thither. This piratical warfare, the opprobrium of infidel powers, is the warfare of the CHRISTIAN King of Great Britain. Determined to keep a market where MEN should be bought and sold, he has prostituted his negative for suppressing every legislative attempt to prohibit or to restrain this execrable commerce."

Now, if the King of Great Britain prostituted his negative that slavery might not be restricted, what, in after times, shall be said of those who prostitute their affirmative that it may be extended? Yet it is now proposed, in some of the state legislatures, and in this Capitol, to do precisely the same thing, in regard to the Territory of Oregon, which was done by Great Britain to her transatlantic possessions; not merely to legalize slavery there, but to prohibit its inhabitants from prohibiting *it.* Though three thousand miles west of Great Britain, she had certain constitutional rights over us, and could affect our destiny. Though the inhabitants of Oregon are three thousand miles west of us, yet we have certain constitutional rights over them, and can affect their destiny. Great Britain annulled our laws for prohibiting slavery; we propose to annul an existing law of Oregon prohibiting slavery. If the execrations of mankind are yet too feeble and too few to punish Great Britain for her wickedness, what scope, what fulness, what eternity of execration and anathema will be a sufficient retribution upon us, if we volunteer to copy her example? It was in the eighteenth century when the mother country thus made merchandise of human beings, — a time when liberty was a forbidden word in the languages of Europe. It is in the nineteenth century that we propose to reënact, and on an ampler scale, the same execrable villany, — a time when liberty is the rallying cry of all Christendom. So great has been the progress of liberal ideas within the last century, that what was venial at its beginning is unpardonable at its close. To drive coffles of slaves from here to Oregon, in the middle of the nineteenth century, is more infamous than it was to bring cargoes of slaves from Africa here, in the middle of the eighteenth. Yet such is the period that men would select to perpetuate and increase the horrors of this traffic.

Sir, how often, on this floor, have indignant remonstrances been addressed to the north, for agitating the subject of slavery? How often have we at the north been told that we were inciting insurrection, fomenting a servile war, putting the black man's knife to the white man's throat. The air of this hall has been filled, its walls have been, as it were, sculptured, by southern eloquence, with images of devastated towns, of murdered men and ravished women ; and, as a defence against the iniquities of the institution, they have universally put in the plea that the calamity was entailed upon them by the mother country, that it made a part of the world they were born into, and therefore they could not help it. I have always been disposed to allow its full weight to this palliation. But if they now insist upon perpetrating against the whole western world, which happens at present to be under our control, the same wrongs which, in darker days, Great Britain perpetrated against them, they will forfeit every claim to sympathy. Sir, here is a test. Let not southern men, who would now force slavery upon new regions, ever deny that their slavery at home is a chosen, voluntary, beloved crime.

But let us look, sir, at the moral character of slavery. It is proposed not merely to continue this institution where it now exists, but to extend it to the Pacific Ocean, — to spread it over the vast slopes of the Rocky Mountains. Sir, the conduct of governments, like the conduct of individuals, is subject to the laws and the retributions of Providence. If, therefore, there is any ingredient of wrong in this institution, we ought not to adopt it, or to permit it, even though it should pour wealth in golden showers over the whole surface of the land. In speaking of the moral character of slavery, sir, I mean to utter no word for the purpose of wounding the feelings of any man. On the other hand, I mean not to wound the cause of truth by abstaining from the utterance of any word which I ought to speak.

The institution of slavery is against natural right. Jurists, from the time of Justinian; orators, from the time of Cicero; poets, from the time of Homer, declare it to be wrong. The writers on moral or ethical science, — the expounders of the law of nations and of God, — denounce slavery as an invasion of the rights of man. They find no warrant for it in the eternal principles of justice and equity; and in that great division which they set forth between right and wrong, they arrange slavery in the catalogue of crime. All the noblest instincts of human nature rebel against it. Whatever has been taught by sage, or sung by poet, in favor of freedom, is a virtual condemnation of slavery. Whenever we applaud the great champions of liberty, who, by the sacrifice of life in the cause of freedom, have won the homage of the world and an immortality of fame, we record the testimony of our hearts against slavery. Wherever patriotism and philanthropy have glowed brightest; wherever piety and a devout religious sentiment have burned most fervently, there has been the most decided recognition of the universal rights of man.

Sir, let us analyze this subject, and see if slavery be not the most compact, and concentrated, and condensed system of wrong which the depravity of man has ever invented. Slavery is said to have had its origin in war. It is claimed that the captor had a right to take the life of his captive; and that if he spared that life he made it his own, and thus acquired a right to control it. I deny the right of the captor to the life of his captive; and even if this right were conceded, I deny his right to the life of the captive's offspring. But this relation between captor and captive precludes the idea of peace; for no peace can be made where there is no free agency. Peace being precluded, it follows inevitably that the state of war continues. Hence, the state of slavery is a state of war; and though active hostilities may have ceased, they are liable to break out, and may rightfully break out, at any moment. How long must our fellow-citizens, who were enslaved in Algiers, have continued in slavery, before they would have lost the right of escape or of resistance?

The gentleman from Virginia, [Mr. Bocock,] in his speech this morning, put the right of the slaveholder upon a somewhat different ground. He said a man might acquire property in a horse before the existence of civil society, by catching a wild one. And so, he added, one man might acquire property in another man, by subduing him to his will. The superior force gave the right, whether to the horse or to the man. Now, if this be so, and if at any time the superior force should change sides, then it follows inevitably that the relation of the parties might be rightfully changed by a new appeal to force.

The same gentleman claims Bible authority for slavery. He says, "I see slavery there tolerated, I had almost said inculcated. I see such language as this: 'Both thy bondmen and thy bondmaids shall be of the heathen that are round about you; of them shall you buy bondmen and bondmaids; and ye shall take them as an inheritance for your children after you, to inherit them for a possession,'" &c. Does not the gentleman know that, by the same authority, the Israelitish slaves were commanded to despoil their Egyptian masters, and to escape from bondage? Surely the latter is as good an authority as the former. If the gentleman's argument is sound, he is bound to advocate a repeal of the act of 1793. If the gentleman's argument is sound, the free states, instead of surrendering fugitive slaves to their masters, are bound to give those masters a Red Sea reception and embrace; and the escape of the children of Israel into Canaan is a direct precedent for the underground railroad to Canada.

Both the gentleman from Kentucky, [Mr. FRENCH,] yesterday, and the gentleman from Virginia, to-day, spoke repeatedly, and without the slightest discrimination, of "a slave and a horse," "a slave and a mule," &c. What should we think, sir, of a teacher for our children, or even of a tender of our cattle, who did not recognize the difference between men and mules, — between humanity and horse-flesh? What should we think, if, on opening a work, claiming to be a scientific treatise on zoölogy, we should find the author to be ignorant of the difference between biped and quadruped, or between men and birds, or men and fishes? Yet such errors would be trifling compared with those which have been made through all this debate. They would be simple errors in natural history, perhaps harmless; but these are errors, — fatal errors, — in humanity and Christian ethics. No, sir; all the legislation of the slave states proves that they do not treat, and cannot treat, a human being as an animal. I will show that they are ever trying to degrade him into an animal, although they can never succeed.

This conscious idea that the state of slavery is a

state of war, — a state in which superior force keeps inferior force down, — develops and manifests itself perpetually. It exhibits itself in the statute books of the slave states, prohibiting the education of slaves, making it highly penal to teach them so much as the alphabet; dispersing and punishing all meetings where they come together in quest of knowledge. Look into the statute books of the free states, and you will find law after law, encouragement after encouragement, to secure the diffusion of knowledge. Look into the statute books of the slave states, and you find law after law, penalty after penalty, to secure the extinction of knowledge. Who has not read with delight those books which have been written, both in England and in this country, entitled "The Pursuit of Knowledge under Difficulties," giving the biographies of illustrious men, who, by an undaunted and indomitable spirit, had risen from poverty and obscurity to the heights of eminence, and blessed the world with their achievements in literature, in science, and in morals? Yet here, in what we call republican America, are fifteen great states, vying with each other to see which will bring the blackest and most impervious pall of ignorance over three millions of human beings; nay, which can do most to stretch this pall across the continent, from the Atlantic to the Pacific.

Is not knowledge a good? Is it not one of the most precious bounties which the all-bountiful Giver has bestowed upon the human race? Sir John Herschel, possessed of ample wealth, his capacious mind stored with the treasures of knowledge, surrounded by the most learned society in the most cultivated metropolis in the world, says, "If I were to pray for a taste which should stand me in stead, under every variety of circumstances, and be a source of happiness and cheerfulness to me through life, and a shield against its ills, however things might go amiss, and the world frown upon me, it would be a taste for reading." Yet it is now proposed to colonize the broad regions of the west with millions of our fellow-beings, who shall never be able to read a book, or write a word; to whom knowledge shall bring no delight in childhood, no relief in the weary hours of sickness or convalescence, no solace in the decrepitude of age; who shall perceive nothing of the beauties of art, who shall know nothing of the wonders of science, who shall never reach any lofty, intellectual conception of the attributes of their great Creator; — deaf to all the hosannas of praise which nature sings to her Maker; blind in this magnificent temple which God has builded.

Sir, it is one of the noblest attributes of man that he can derive knowledge from his predecessors. We possess the accumulated learning of ages. From ten thousand confluent streams, the river of truth, widened and deepened, has come down to us; and it is among our choicest delights, that if we can add to its volume, as it rolls on, it will bear a richer freight of blessings to our successors. But it is here proposed to annul this beneficent law of nature; to repel this proffered bounty of Heaven. It is proposed to create a race of men, to whom all the lights of experience shall be extinguished; whose hundredth generation shall be as ignorant and as barbarous as its first.

Sir, I hold all voluntary ignorance to be a crime; I hold all enforced ignorance to be a greater crime. Knowledge is essential to all rational enjoyment; it is essential to the full and adequate performance of every duty. Whoever intercepts knowledge, therefore, on its passage to a human soul; whoever strikes down the hand that is outstretched to grasp it, is guilty of one of the most heinous of offences. Add to your virtue knowledge, says the apostle; but here the command is, Be-cloud and be-little by ignorance whatever virtue you may possess.

Sir, let me justify the earnestness of these expressions by describing the transition of feeling through which I have lately passed. I come from a community where knowledge ranks next to virtue in the classification of blessings. On the tenth day of April last, the day before I left home for this place, I attended the dedication of a schoolhouse in Boston which had cost $70,000. The mayor presided, and much of the intelligence and worth of the city was present on the occasion. I see by a paper which I have this day received, that another schoolhouse, in the same city, was dedicated on Monday of the present week. It was there stated by the mayor that the cost of the city schoolhouses which had been completed within the last three months was $200,000. On Tuesday of this week, a new high schoolhouse in the city of Cambridge was dedicated. Mr. Everett, the president of Harvard College, was present, and addressed the assembly in a long, and, I need not add, a most beautiful speech. That schoolhouse, with two others to be dedicated within a week, will have cost $25,000. Last week, in the neighboring city of Charlestown, a new high schoolhouse, of a most splendid and costly character, was dedicated by the mayor and city government, by clergy and laity. But it is not mayors of cities and presidents of colleges alone that engage in the work of consecrating temples of education to the service of the young. Since I have been here, the governor of the commonwealth, Mr. Briggs, went to Newburyport, a distance of forty miles, to attend the dedication of a schoolhouse which cost $25,000. On a late occasion, when the same excellent chief magistrate travelled forty miles to attend the dedication of a schoolhouse in the country, some speaker congratulated the audience because the governor of the commonwealth had come down from the executive chair to honor the occasion. "No," said he, "I have come up to the occasion to be honored by it." Within the last year, $200,000 have been given by individuals to Harvard College. Within a little longer time than this, the other two colleges in the state have received, together, a still larger endowment from individuals or the state.

These measures are part of a great system which we are carrying on for the elevation of the race. Last year, the voters of Massachusetts, in their respective towns, voluntarily taxed themselves about a million of dollars for the support of Common Schools. We have an old law on the statute book, requiring towns to tax themselves for the support of public schools; but the people have long since lost sight of this law in the munificence of their contributions. Massachusetts is now erecting a reform school for vagrant and exposed children, — so many of whom come to us from abroad, — which will cost the state more than a hundred thousand dollars. An unknown individual has given twenty thousand dollars towards it. We educate all our deaf and dumb and blind. An appropriation was made by the last legislature to establish a school for idiots, in imitation of those beautiful institutions in Paris, in Switzerland, and in Berlin, where the most revolting and malicious of this deplorable class are tamed into docility, made lovers of order and neatness, and capable of performing many valuable services. The future teacher of this school is now abroad, preparing himself for his work. A few years ago, Mr. Everett, the present president of Harvard College, then governor of the commonwealth, spoke the deep *convictions* of Massachusetts people, when, in a public address on education, he exhorted the fathers and mothers of Massachusetts in the following words: "Save," said he, "save, spare, scrape, stint, starve, do any thing but steal," to educate your children. And Doctor Howe, the noble-hearted director of the Institution for the Blind, lately uttered the deepest *sentiments* of our citizens, when, in speaking of our duties to the blind, the deaf and dumb, and the idiotic, he said, "The sight of any human being left to brutish ignorance is always demoralizing to the beholders. There floats not upon the stream of life a wreck of humanity so utterly shattered and crippled, but that its signals of distress should challenge attention and command assistance."

Sir, it was all glowing and fervid with sentiments like these, that, a few weeks ago, I entered this House, — sentiments transfused into my soul from without, even if I had no vital spark of nobleness to kindle them within. Imagine, then, my strong revulsion of feeling, when the first set, elaborate speech which I heard, was that of the gentleman from Virginia, proposing to extend ignorance to the uttermost bounds of this republic, — to legalize it, to enforce it, to necessitate it, and make it eternal. Since him, many others have advocated the same abhorrent doctrine. Not satisfied with dooming a whole race of our fellow-beings to mental darkness, impervious and everlasting, — not satisfied with drawing this black curtain of ignorance between man and nature, between the human soul and its God, from the Atlantic to the Rio Grande, across half the continent, — they desire to increase this race ten, twenty millions more, and to unfold and spread out this black curtain across the other half of the continent. When, sir, in the halls of legislation, men advocate measures like this, it is no figure of speech to say that their words are the clankings of multitudinous fetters; each gesture of their arms tears human flesh with ten thousand whips; each exhalation of their breath spreads clouds of moral darkness from horizon to horizon.

Twenty years ago, a sharp sensation ran through the nerves of the civilized world, at the story of a young man named Caspar Hauser, found in the city of Nuremberg, in Bavaria. Though sixteen or seventeen years of age, he could not walk nor talk. He heard without understanding; he saw without perceiving; he moved without definite purpose. It was the soul of an infant in the body of an adult. After he had learned to speak, he related that, from his earliest recollection, he had always been kept in a hole so small, that he could not stretch out his limbs, where he saw no light, heard no sound, nor even witnessed the face of the attendant who brought him his scanty food. For many years conjecture was rife concerning his history, and all Germany was searched to discover his origin. After a long period of fruitless inquiry and speculation, public opinion settled down into the belief that he was the victim of some great unnatural crime; that he was the heir to some throne, and had been sequestered by ambition; or the inheritor of vast wealth, and had been hidden away by cupidity; or the offspring of criminal indulgence, and had been buried alive to avoid exposure and shame. A German, Von Feuerbach, published an account of Caspar, entitled "The Example of a Crime on the Life of the Soul." But why go to Europe to be thrilled with the pathos of a human being shrouded from the light of nature, and cut off from a knowledge of duty and of God? To-day, in this boasted land of light and liberty, there are three million Caspar Hausers; and, as if this were not enough, it is proposed to multiply their number tenfold, and to fill up all the western world with these proofs of human avarice and guilt. It is proposed that we ourselves should create and should publish to the world, not one, but untold millions of "Examples of *a Crime on the Life of the Soul.*" It is proposed that the self-styled freemen, the self-styled Christians, of fifteen great states in this American Union, shall engage in the work of procreating, rearing, and *selling* Caspar Hausers, often from their own loins; and if any further development of soul or of body is allowed to the American victims than was permitted to the Bavarian child, it is only because such development will increase their market value at the barracoons. It is not from any difference of motive, but only the better to insure that motive's indulgence. The slave child must be allowed to use his limbs, or how could he drudge out his life in the service of his master? The slave infant must be taught to walk, or how, *under the shadow of this thrice-glorious Capitol*, could he join a coffle for New Orleans?

I know, sir, that it has been said, within a short time past, that Caspar Hauser was an impostor, and his story a fiction. Would to God that this could ever be said of his fellow-victims in America!.

For another reason slavery is an unspeakable wrong. The slave is debarred from testifying against a white man. The courts will not hear him as a witness. By the principles of the common law, if any man suffers violence at the hands of another, he can prefer his complaint to magistrates, or to the grand juries of the courts, who are bound to give him redress. Hence the law is said to hold up its shield before every man for his protection. It surrounds him in the crowded street and in the solitary place. It guards his treasures with greater vigilance than locks or iron safes; and against meditated aggressions upon himself, his wife, or his children, it fastens his doors every night more securely than triple bolts of brass. But all these sacred protections are denied to the slave. While subjected to the law of force, he is shut out from the law of right. To suffer injury is his, but never to obtain redress. For personal cruelties, for stripes that shiver his flesh, and blows that break his bones, for robbery or for murder, neither he nor his friends can have preventive, remedy, or recompense. The father, who is a slave, may see son or daughter scored, mangled, mutilated, or ravished before his eyes, and he must be dumb as a sheep before its shearers. The wife may be dishonored in the presence of the husband, and, if he remonstrates or rebels, the miscreant who could burn with the lust will burn not less fiercely with a vengeance to be glutted upon his foiler.

Suppose, suddenly, by some disastrous change in the order of nature, an entire kingdom or community were to be enveloped in total darkness, — to have no day, no dawn, but midnight evermore! Into what infinite forms of violence and wrong would the depraved passions of the human heart spring up, when no longer restrained by the light of day, and the dangers of exposure! So far as legal rights against his oppressors are concerned, the slave lives in such a world of darkness. A hundred of his fellows may stand around him and witness the wrongs he suffers, but not one of them can appeal to jury, magistrate, or judge, for punishment or redress. The wickedest white man, in a company of slaves, bears a charmed life. There is not one of the fell passions that rages in his bosom which he cannot indulge with wantonness and to satiety, and the court has no ears to hear the complaint of the victim. How dearly does every honorable man prize character! The law denies the slave a character; for, however traduced, legal vindication is impossible.

And yet, infinitely flagrant as the anomaly is, the slave is amenable to the laws of the land for all offences which he may commit against others, though he is powerless to protect himself by the same law from offences which others may commit against him. He may suffer all wrong, and the courts will not hearken to his testimony; but for the first wrong he does, the same courts inflict their severest punishments upon him. This is the reciprocity of slave law, — to be forever liable to be proved guilty, but never able to prove himself innocent; to be subject to all punishments, but, through his own oath, to no protection. Hear what is said by the highest judicial tribunal of South Carolina: "Although slaves are held to be the absolute property of their owners, yet they have the power of committing crimes." — *2d Nott and McCord's Rep.*, p. 179. A negro is so far amenable to the common law, that he may be one of three to constitute the number necessary to make a riot. — *1st Bay's Rep.*, 358. By the laws of the same state, a negro may be himself stolen, and he has no redress; but if he steals a negro from another, he shall be hung. — *2d Nott and McCord's Rep.*, 179. [*An example of this penalty suffered by a slave.*] This is the way that slave legislatures and slave judicatories construe the command of Christ, "Whatsoever ye would that men should do unto you, do ye also the same unto them." Nay, by the laws of some of the slave states, where master and slave are engaged in a joint act, the slave is indictable, while the master is not.

What rights are more sacred or more dear to us than the conjugal and the parental? No savage nation, however far removed from the frontiers of civilization, has ever yet been discovered, where these rights were unknown or unhonored. The beasts of the forest feel and respect them. It is only in the land of slaves that they are blotted out and annihilated.

Slavery is an unspeakable wrong to the conscience The word "conscience" conveys a complex idea. It includes conscientiousness; that is, the sentiment or instinct of right and wrong; and also intelligence, which is the guide of this sentiment. *Conscience*, then, implies both the desire or impulse to do right, and also a knowledge of what is right. Nature endows us with the sentiment, but the knowledge we must acquire. Hence we speak of an "enlightened conscience," meaning thereby not only the moral sense, but that knowledge of circumstances, relations, tendencies and results, which is necessary in order to guide the moral sense to just conclusions. Each of these elements is equally necessary to enable a man to feel rightly and to act rightly. Mere knowledge, without the moral sense, can take no cognizance of the everlasting distinctions between right and wrong; and so the blind instinct, unguided by knowledge, will be forever at fault in its conclusions. The two were made to coëxist and operate together by Him who made the human soul. But the impious hand of man divorces these twin capacities, wherever it denies knowledge. If one of these coördinate powers in the mental realm be annulled by the legislature, it may be called *law;* but it is repugnant to every law and attribute of God.

But, not satisfied with having invaded the human soul, and annihilated one of its most sacred attributes, in the persons of three millions of our fellow-men; not satisfied with having killed the conscience, as far as it can be killed by human device, and human force, in an entire race; we are now invoked to multiply that race, to extend it over regions yet unscathed by its existence, and there to call into being other millions of men, upon whose souls, and upon the souls of whose posterity, the same unholy spoliation shall be committed forever.

Slavery is an unspeakable wrong to the religious nature of man. The dearest and most precious of all human rights is the right of private judgment in matters of religion. I am interested in nothing else so much as in the attributes of my Creator, and in the relations which he has established between me and himself, for time and for eternity. To investigate for myself these relations, and their momentous consequences; to "search the Scriptures;" to explore the works of God in the outward and visible universe; to ask counsel of the sages and divines of the ages gone by, — these are rights which it would be sacrilege in me to surrender; which it is a worse sacrilege in any human being or human government to usurp. Yet, by denying education to the slave, you destroy not merely the *right*, but the *power*, of personal examination in regard to all that most nearly concerns the soul's interests. Who so base as not to reverence the mighty champions of religious freedom, in days when the dungeon, the rack, and the fagot were the arguments of a government theology? Who does not reverence, I say, Wickliffe, Huss, Luther, and the whole army of martyrs whose blood reddened the axe of English intolerance? Yet it was only for this right of private judgment, for this independence of another man's control in religious concernments, that the godlike champions of religious liberty perilled themselves and perished. Yet it is this very religious despotism over millions of men which it is now proposed, not to destroy, but to create. It is proposed not to break old fetters and cast them away, but to forge new ones and rivet them on. Sir, on the continent of Europe, and in the Tower of London, I have seen the axes, the chains, and other horrid implements of death, by which the great defenders of freedom for the soul were brought to their final doom, — by which political and religious liberty was cloven down; but fairer and lovelier to the view were axe and chain, and all the ghastly implements of death ever invented by religious bigotry or civil despotism to wring and torture freedom out of the soul of man; — fairer and lovelier were they all than the parchment roll of this House on which shall be inscribed a law for profaning one additional foot of American soil with the curse of slavery.

After the above speech was delivered, I was referred to a Tract, written by a Virginian, on the subject of slavery; and, by the politeness of its author, I have since obtained a copy of it. It is entitled, "*Address to the People of West Virginia; showing that Slavery is injurious to the public welfare, and that it may be gradually abolished, without detriment to the rights and interests of Slaveholders.* BY A SLAVEHOLDER OF WEST VIRGINIA. Lexington: R. C. Noel. 1847." This Address was written by the Rev. Henry Ruffner, D. D., president of Lexington College, Lexington, Va. Some of the passages of this Address are so striking; it is throughout so corroborative of one of the arguments contained in the speech; and coming, as it does, from a Virginian, an eye-witness of the effects of slavery, and a holder of slaves, that I have thought it would be useful to append them. The extracts, of course, are not, as here, consecutive.

Nowhere, since time began, have the two systems of slave labor and free labor been subjected to so fair and so decisive a trial of their effects on public prosperity as in these United States. Here the two systems have worked side by side for ages, under such equal circumstances, both political and physical, and with such ample time and opportunity for each to work out its proper effects, that all must admit the experiment to be now complete, and the result decisive. No man of common sense, who has observed this result, can doubt for a moment that the system of free labor promotes the growth and prosperity of states in a much higher degree than the system of slave labor. In the first settlement of a country, when labor is scarce and dear, slavery may give a temporary impulse to improvement; but even this is not the case, except in warm climates, and where free men are scarce and either sickly or lazy; and when we have said this, we have said all that experience in the United States warrants us to say, in favor of the policy of employing slave labor.

It is the common remark of all who have travelled through the United States, that the free states and the slave states exhibit a striking contrast in their appearance. In the older free states are seen all the tokens of prosperity ; — a dense and increasing population ; thriving villages, towns, and cities ; a neat and productive agriculture, growing manufactures, and active commerce.

In the older parts of the slave states, — with a few local exceptions, — are seen, on the contrary, too evident signs of stagnation, or of positive decay ; — a sparse population, a slovenly cultivation spread over vast fields that are wearing out, among others already worn out and desolate ; villages and towns, " few and far between," rarely growing, often decaying, sometimes mere remnants of what they were, sometimes deserted ruins, haunted only by owls ; generally no manufactures, nor even trades, except the indispensable few ; commerce and navigation abandoned, as far as possible, to the people of the free states ; and generally, instead of the stir and bustle of industry, a dull and dreamy stillness, broken, if broke at all, only by the wordy brawl of politics.

New England and the middle states of New York, New Jersey, and Pennsylvania contained, in 1790, 1,968,000 inhabitants, and in 1840, 6,760,000 ; having gained, in this period, 243 per cent.

The four old slave states had, in 1790, a population of 1,473,000, and in 1840, of 3,279,000 ; having gained, in the same period, 122 per cent., just about half as much, in proportion, as the free states. They ought to have gained about twice as much ; for they had at first only seven inhabitants to the square mile, when the free states not only had upwards of twelve, but, on the whole, much inferior advantages of soil and climate. Even cold, barren New England, though more than twice as thickly peopled, grew in population at a faster rate than these old slave states.

About half the territory of these old slave states is new country, and has comparatively few slaves. On this part the increase of population has chiefly taken place. On the old slave-labored lowlands, a singular phenomena has appeared ;

there, within the bounds of these rapidly growing United States, — yes, there, population has been long at a stand; yes, over wide regions, — especially in Virginia, — it has declined, and a new wilderness is gaining upon the cultivated land! What has done this work of desolation? Not war, nor pestilence; not oppression of rulers, civil or ecclesiastical; but *slavery*, a curse more destructive in its effects than any of them. It were hard to find, in old king-ridden, priest-ridden, overtaxed Europe, so large a country, where, within twenty years past, such a growing poverty and desolation have appeared.

It is in the last period of ten years, from 1830 to 1840, that this consuming plague of slavery has shown its worst effects in the old Southern States. Including the increase in their newly-settled and western counties, they gained in population only 7½ per cent.; while cold, barren, thickly peopled New England gained 15, and the old Middle States 26 per cent. East Virginia actually fell off 26,000 in population; and, with the exception of Richmond and one or two other towns, her population continues to decline. Old Virginia was the first to sow this land of ours with slavery; she is also the first to reap the full harvest of destruction. Her lowland neighbors of Maryland and the Carolinas were not far behind at the *seeding;* nor are they far behind at the ingathering of desolation.

Let us take the rich and beautiful State of Kentucky, compared with her free neighbor Ohio. The slaves of Kentucky have composed less than a fourth part of her population. But mark their effect upon the comparative growth of the state. In the year 1800, Kentucky contained 221,000 inhabitants, and Ohio, 45,000. In forty years, the population of Kentucky had risen to 780,000; that of Ohio to 1,519,000. This wonderful difference could not be owing to any natural superiority of the Ohio country. Kentucky is nearly as large, nearly as fertile, and quite equal, in other gifts of nature. She had greatly the advantage, too, in the outset of this forty years' race of population. She started with 5½ inhabitants to the square mile, and came out with 20: Ohio started with one inhabitant to the square mile, and came out with 38. Kentucky had full possession of her territory at the beginning. Much of Ohio was then, and for a long time afterwards, in possession of the Indians. Ohio is by this time considerably more than twice as thickly peopled as Kentucky ; yet she still gains, both by natural increase and by the influx of emigrants ; while Kentucky has for twenty years been receiving much fewer emigrants than Ohio, and multitudes of her citizens have been yearly moving off to newer and yet newer countries.

Compare this natural increase with the census returns, and it appears that, in the ten years from 1830 to 1840, Virginia lost by emigration no fewer than 375,000 of her people, of whom East Virginia lost 304,000, and West Virginia 71,000. At this rate Virginia supplies the west every ten years with a population equal in number to the population of the State of Mississippi in 1840!

Some Virginia politicians, proudly, — yes, *proudly*, fellow-citizens, — call our old commonwealth *The Mother of States!* These *enlightened* patriots might pay her a still higher compliment, by calling her *The Grandmother* of States. For our part, we are grieved and mortified to think of the lean and haggard condition of our venerable mother. Her black children have sucked her so dry, that now, for a long time past, she has not milk enough for her offspring, either black or white.

She has sent, — or we should rather say, she has driven, — from her soil at least one third of all the emigrants who have gone from the old states to the new. More than another third have gone from the other old slave states. Many of these multitudes, who have left the slave states, have shunned the regions of slavery, and settled in the free countries of the west. These were generally industrious and enterprising white men, who found, by sad experience, that a country of slaves was not the country for them. It is a truth, a certain truth, that *slavery drives free laborers, — farmers, mechanics, and all, and some of the best of them too, — out of the country, and fills their places with negroes.*

It is admitted on all hands, that slave labor is better adapted to agriculture than to any other branch of industry ; and that, if not good for agriculture, it is really good for nothing.

Therefore, since in agriculture slave labor is proved to be far less productive than free labor, *slavery is demonstrated to be not only unprofitable, but deeply injurious to the public prosperity.*

We do not mean that slave labor can never earn any thing for him that employs it. The question is between free labor and slave labor. He that chooses to employ a sort of labor that yields only half as much to the hand as another sort would yield, makes a choice that is not only unprofitable, but deeply injurious to his interest.

Agriculture in the slave states may be characterized in general by two epithets, *extensive*, *exhaustive*, — which in all agricultural countries forebode two things, *impoverishment*, *depopulation*. The general system of slaveholding farmers and planters, in all times and places, has been, and now is, and ever will be, to cultivate much land, badly, for present gain, — in short, to kill the goose that lays the golden egg. They cannot do otherwise with laborers who work by compulsion, for the benefit only of their masters, and whose sole interest in the matter is to do as little and to consume as much as possible.

This ruinous system of large farms cultivated by slaves showed its effects in Italy, eighteen hundred years ago, when the Roman empire was at the height of its grandeur.

Pliny, a writer of that age, in his Natural History, (Book 18, c. 1–7,) tells us, that while the small farms of former times were cultivated by freemen, and even great commanders did not disdain to labor with their own hands, agriculture flourished, and provisions were abundant; but that afterwards, when the lands were engrossed by a few great proprietors, and cultivated by fettered and branded slaves, the country was ruined, and corn had to be imported. The same system was spreading ruin over the provinces, and thus the prosperity of the empire was undermined. Pliny denounces, as the worst of all, the system of having large estates in the country cultivated by slaves, or indeed, says he, "*to have any thing done by men who labor without hope of reward*."

So Livy, the great Roman historian, observed, some years before Pliny, (Book 6, c. 12,) that "innumerable multitudes of men formerly inhabited those parts of Italy, where, in his time, none but slaves redeemed the country from desertion;" — that is, a dense population of free laborers had been succeeded by a sparse population of slaves.

Even the common mechanical trades do not flourish in a slave state. Some mechanical operations must, indeed, be performed in every civilized country; but the general rule in the south is, to import from abroad every fabricated thing that can be carried in ships, such as household furniture, boats, boards, laths, carts, ploughs, axes, and axehelves, besides innumerable other things, which free communities are accustomed to make for themselves. What is most wonderful is, that the forests and iron mines of the south supply, in great part, the materials out of which these things are made. The northern freemen come with their ships, carry home the timber and pig iron, work them up, supply their own wants with a part, and then sell the rest at a good profit in the southern markets. Now, although mechanics, by setting up their shops in the south, could save all these freights and profits, yet so it is, that northern mechanics will not settle in the south, and the southern mechanics are undersold by their northern competitors.

Now connect with these wonderful facts another fact, and the mystery is solved. The number of mechanics, in different parts of the south, is in the inverse ratio of the number of slaves; or in other words, where the slaves form the largest proportion of the inhabitants, there the mechanics and manufacturers form the least. In those parts only where the slaves are comparatively few, are many mechanics and artificers to be found; but even in these parts they do not flourish as the same useful class of men flourish in the free states. Even in our Valley of Virginia, remote from the sea, many of our mechanics can hardly stand against northern competition. This can be attributed only to slavery, which paralyzes our energies, disperses our population, and keeps us few and poor, in spite of the bountiful gifts of nature with which a benign Providence has endowed our country.

Of all the states in this Union, not one has on the whole such various and abundant resources for manufacturing as our own Virginia, both East and West. Only think of her vast forests of timber, her mountains of iron, her regions of stone coal, her valleys of limestone and marble, her fountains of salt, her immense sheep-walks for wool, her vicinity to the cotton fields, her innumerable waterfalls, her bays, harbors, and rivers for circulating products on every side; — in short, every material and every convenience necessary for manufacturing industry.

Above all, think of Richmond, nature's chosen site for the greatest manufacturing city in America,—her beds of coal and iron, just at hand, her incomparable water power, her tide-water navigation, conducting sea vessels from the foot of her falls, and above them her fine canal to the mountains, through which lie the shortest routes from the eastern tides to the great rivers of the west and the south-west. Think, also, that this Richmond, in old Virginia, "the mother of states," has enjoyed these unparalleled advantages ever since the United States became a nation;—and then think again, that this same Richmond, the metropolis of all Virginia, has fewer manufactures than a third-rate New England town;—fewer,—not than the new city of Lowell, which is beyond all comparison,—but fewer than the obscure place called Fall River, among the barren hills of Massachusetts;—and then, fellow-citizens, what will you think,—what *must* you think,—of the cause of this strange phenomenon? Or, to enlarge the scope of the question: What must you think has caused Virginians in general to neglect their superlative advantages for manufacturing industry?—to disregard the evident suggestions of nature, pointing out to them this fruitful source of population, wealth, and comfort?

Say not that this state of things is chargeable to the *apathy* of Virginians. That is nothing to the purpose, for it does not go to the bottom of the subject. What causes the apathy? That is the question.

The last census gave also the cost of constructing new buildings in each state, exclusive of the value of the materials. The amount of this is a good test of the increase of wealth in a country. To compare different states in this particular, we must divide the total cost of building by the number of inhabitants, and see what the average will be for each inhabitant. We find that it is in Massachusetts, **$3·60**; in Connecticut, **$3·50**; in New York, **$3·00**; in New Jersey, **$2·70**; in Pennsylvania, **$3·10**; in Maryland, **$2·30**; and in Virginia, **$1·10**.

No state has greater conveniences for ship navigation and ship building than Virginia. Yet on all her fine tide waters she has little shipping; and what she has is composed almost wholly of small bay craft and a few coasting schooners.

We do not blame our southern people for abstaining from

all employments of this kind. What could they do? Set their negroes to building ships? Who ever imagined such an absurdity? But could they not hire white men to do such things? No; for, in the first place, southern white men have no skill in such matters; and, in the second place, northern workmen cannot be hired in the south, without receiving a heavy premium for working in a slave state.

The boast of our West Virginia is the good city of Wheeling. Would that she was six times as large, that she might equal Pittsburg, and that she grew five times as fast, that she might keep up with her!

We glory in Wheeling, because she only, in Virginia, deserves to be called a manufacturing town. For this her citizens deserve to be crowned, — not with laurel, — but with the solid gold of prosperity. But how came it that Wheeling, and next to her, Wellsburg, — of all the towns in Virginia, — should become manufacturing towns? Answer: They breathe the atmosphere of free states, almost touching them on both sides. But again; seeing that Wheeling, as a seat for manufactures, is equal to Pittsburg, and inferior to no town in America, except Richmond; and that, moreover, she has almost no slaves; why is Wheeling so far behind Pittsburg, and comparatively so slow in her growth? Answer: She is in a country in which slavery is established by law.

We shall explain, by examples, how a few slaves in a country may do its citizens more immediate injury than a large number.

When a white family own fifty or one hundred slaves, they can, so long as their land produces well, afford to be indolent and expensive in their habits; for though each yields only a small profit, yet each member of the family has ten or fifteen of these black work-animals to toil for his support. It is not until the fields grow old, and the crops grow short, and the negroes and the overseer take nearly all, that the day of ruin can be no longer postponed. If the family be not *very* indolent and *very* expensive, this inevitable day may not come before the third generation. But the ruin of small slaveholders is often accomplished in a single lifetime.

When a white family own five or ten slaves, they cannot afford to be indolent and expensive in their habits; for one black drudge cannot support one white gentleman or lady.

Yet, because they are slaveholders, this family will feel some aspirations for a life of easy gentility; and because field work and kitchen work are negroes' work, the young gentlemen will dislike to go with the negroes to dirty field work, and the young ladies will dislike to join the black sluts in any sort of household labor. Such unthrifty sentiments are the natural consequence of introducing slaves among the families of a country, especially negro slaves. They infallibly grow and spread, creating among the white families a distaste for all servile labor, and a desire to procure slaves who may take all drudgery off their hands. Thus general industry gives way by degrees to indolent relaxation, false notions of dignity and refinement, and a taste for fashionable luxuries. Then debts slyly accumulate. The result is, that many families are compelled by their embarrassments to sell off and leave the country. Many who are unable to buy slaves leave it also, because they feel degraded, and cannot prosper, where slavery exists. Citizens of the valley! is it not so? Is not this the chief reason why your beautiful country does not prosper like the northern valleys?

We have examined the census of counties for the last thirty or forty years, in Maryland, Virginia, and North Carolina, with the view to discover the law of population in the northern slave states. The following are among the general results: —

When a county had at first comparatively few slaves, the slave population, except near the free borders, gained upon the whites, and most rapidly in the older parts of the country.

The population, as a whole, increased so long as the slaves were fewer than the whites, but more slowly as the numbers approached to equality. In our valley, a smaller proportion of slaves had the effect of a larger one in East Virginia, to retard the increase of population.

When the slaves became as numerous as the whites in the eastern and older parts of the country, population came to a stand; when they outnumbered the whites, it declined. Consequently, the slave population has tended to diffuse itself equally over the country, rising more rapidly as it was further below the white population, and going down when it had risen above them.

The price of cotton has regulated the price of negroes in Virginia; and so it must continue to do; because slave labor is unprofitable here, and nothing keeps up the price of slaves but their value as a marketable commodity in the south. Eastern negroes and western cattle are alike in this, that, if the market abroad go down or be closed, both sorts of animals, the horned and the woolly-headed, become a worthless drug at home. The fact is, that our eastern brethren must send off, on any terms, the increase of their slaves, because their impoverished country cannot sustain even its present stock of negroes. We join not the English and American abolition cry about "slave-breeding" in East Virginia, as if it were a chosen occupation, and therefore a reproachful one. It is no such thing, but a case of dire necessity, and many a heartache does it cost the good people there. But behold in the east the doleful consequences of letting slavery grow up to an oppressive and heart-sickening burden upon a community! Cast it off, West Virginians, whilst yet you have the power; for if you let it descend unbroken to your children, it will have grown to a mountain of misery upon their heads.

Good policy will require the Southern States, ere long, to close their markets against northern negroes. When the southern slave market is closed, or when, by the reduced profits of slave labor in the south, it becomes glutted,—then the stream of Virginia negroes, heretofore pouring down upon the south, will be thrown back upon the state, and, like a river dammed up, must spread itself over the whole territory of the commonwealth. The head spring in East Virginia cannot contain itself; it must find vent; it will shed its black streams through every gap of the Blue Ridge and pour over the Alleghany, till it is checked by abolitionism on the borders. But even abolitionism cannot finally stop it. Abolitionism itself will tolerate slavery, when slaveholders grow sick and tired of it.

In plain terms, fellow-citizens, eastern slaveholders will come with their multitudes of slaves to settle upon the fresh lands of West Virginia. Eastern slaves will be sent by thousands for a market in West Virginia. Every valley will echo with the cry, "Negroes! Negroes for sale! Dog cheap! Dog cheap!" And because they are dog cheap, many of our people will buy them. We have shown how slavery has prepared the people for this; how a little slavery makes way for more, and how the law of slave increase operates to fill up every part of the country to the same level with slaves.

And then, fellow-citizens, when you have suffered your country to be filled with negro slaves instead of white freemen; when its population shall be as motley as Joseph's coat of many colors; as ring-streaked and speckled as father Jacob's flock was in Padan Aram, — what will the white basis of representation avail you, if you obtain it? Whether you obtain it or not, East Virginia will have triumphed; or, rather, *slavery* will have triumphed, and all Virginia will have become a land of darkness and of the shadow of death.

Then, by a forbearance which has no merit, and a supineness which has no excuse, you will have given to your children, for their inheritance, this lovely land blackened with a negro population, — the offscourings of Eastern Virginia, the fag-end of slavery, the loathsome dregs of that cup of abomination which has already sickened to death the eastern half of our commonwealth.

Delay, not, then, we beseech you, to raise a barrier against this Stygian inundation, to stand at the Blue Ridge, and with sovereign energy say to this Black Sea of misery, "Hitherto shalt thou come, and no farther."

SKETCH

Of the Opening Argument in the Case of, the United States *vs.* Daniel Drayton, indicted, (in forty-one several Bills of Indictment,) for stealing and carrying away, in the Schooner Pearl, a Cargo of Slaves from Washington, in the District of Columbia, on the Night of the 15th of April, 1848; tried before Thomas H. Crawford, Judge of the Criminal Court of the District of Columbia. P. B. Key, District Attorney; Horace Mann and James M. Carlisle, Counsel for the Prisoner.

Gentlemen of the Jury;

I rise before you under circumstances rarely exceeded in embarrassment. I am an utter stranger to his honor, the judge, and to all of you, gentlemen, who compose the jury. Among all the eager faces in this crowded hall, there is not one with which I am familiar. I suppose there is not one man in this vast assembly who has any sympathy for my client or for me.

The case before us is acknowledged, on all sides, to be one of great moment. It directly affects human interests, — large pecuniary interests, — and these are among the most active and powerful of human impulses. It is a case which has given birth to great excitement. It has been narrated with formidable exaggerations in the public papers; it has been angrily discussed in both houses of Congress, and bruited over the land. From what has transpired in and about this court room, since the trial commenced, I perceive that each individual seems not only to be convinced that the prisoner at the bar has committed a great offence, but, like a light reflected from a multiplying glass, he sees that offence multiplied a thousand fold in the opinions and feelings of those around him. I cannot forbear to add, that it is a case, also, which, in some of its aspects, touches the deepest and tenderest sympathies of the human heart; for this prosecution not only deals with human beings as offenders, but with human beings and human rights, as the subject matters of the offence.

We have been called to trial, too, at an untimely hour. I have not had time for the preparation and investigation which so important a case demands. Added to this, my colleague, [Mr. Carlisle,] was taken ill on the day he was retained, and, until the evening immediately preceding the commencement of the trial, I had no opportunity for a single interview with him, and then but for an hour, in his sick chamber. During all this time, too, as some of you may know, my attention has been called away by official duties elsewhere.

Gentlemen, let me come a little closer to my relations to this case and to yourselves. I stand here, on this side of the table; you sit there, on the other side. Our *persons* are near to each other; but should I not greatly deceive myself, were I to suppose that our *opinions* were as near together as our persons? We are within shaking-hands' distance of each other; still, our convictions and sentiments on certain subjects may be wide asunder as the poles. On a subject of vast importance and gravity, — a subject reflected from every feature of this case, — I was born, and from my birth have been trained up, in one set of ideas; and I mean no discourtesy when I say that you have been born and trained in another set of ideas. Hence it is natural, yes, it is inevitable, — is it not? — that we should approach this subject with widely different views, and, as it were, from opposite points of the moral compass. I am admonished, then, in the outset, that your prepossessions are against me. The frame of your minds must be adverse to the reception of my views. We are in a position where the hearer, consciously or unconsciously, braces himself against the pressure of the speaker's arguments. And of all difficult positions in which advocate or orator was ever placed, the most difficult is that of encountering the honest antipathies of his hearers. The heart, secure in its own convictions, closes itself against the argument that would overthrow them, as a fond parent bars his doors against the foe that would carry away his children.

But, gentlemen, amid all these adverse circumstances, and amid these conflicts of hostile and perhaps irreconcilable feelings, is there not some common ground on which you and I can stand together, and greet each other as brethren? Is there not one spot where we can stand side by side, as friends, sympathize with each other, and act together in harmony? Yes, gentlemen, there *is* one such spot. *It is the ground of* DUTY. In this case, I have certain duties to perform; you, too, have certain duties to perform; and the feeling of a common duty is always creative of the feeling of brotherhood. We are called to these duties as by the voice of God; we are to perform them as under the eye of the Omniscient. Here we are embarked in a common cause. From this moment, then, let all feelings of alienation or repugnance be banished from between us.

Gentlemen, this prisoner has requested me to be his counsel; and I, perhaps unwisely, have acceded to his request. I have taken an oath to be true to him. This has imposed certain responsibilities upon me, which, before Heaven, I may not escape. In this I find my strength. With the fierce excitement, which blazed forth in this District when the prisoners of the "Pearl" were first arrested, still hot around me; with the generally adverse feelings which I suppose you entertain towards the side of the cause which I have espoused, and therefore against its advocate; with these thronged spectators, who show, at every turn and incident of the trial, what their feelings are towards the prisoner and his defenders, I should not be able to stand here one moment, were it not for the supporting, uplifting sentiment, glowing through every fibre of my frame, that I am here in the performance of a high and holy duty. In all else I may be weak; in this I am strong.*

So you, gentlemen, sit there to perform a duty. Swearing upon the Holy Evangelists, you have invoked the vengeance of Heaven upon your souls, if, consciously and wittingly, you swerve a hair's breadth from the line of rectitude; if you allow any partiality in favor of a cherished institution, or any prejudice against the prisoner, to close your eyes or blind your minds to any fact of evidence or rule of law which may be adduced in his behalf.

I might even add a consideration of a lighter nature leading to the same result. Your fortune and mine, for some days to come, I suppose to be settled. I know not how protracted this trial may be, but, gentlemen, we are in it, for longer or shorter, for better or worse; and while we are in it, we shall be obliged to come together from day to day, and live in each other's presence and company. Now, I trust you have too much philosophy about you to make bad worse. And so of myself. Were we fellow-travellers in the same stage-coach or steamboat, and were doomed to be so for a week or a fortnight, it would be most unwise to add to our inevitable discomforts that of striving to annoy each other; so, when packed together in this room, which seems to have been constructed for

* In attendance upon the trial, and stationing themselves as near as practicable to the counsel for the defence, were men who cocked pistols and drew dirks upon Drayton, in the mob that pursued him.

creatures that do not breathe, and with the thermometer above ninety degrees, I trust any icy feelings we may have had towards each other will speedily melt away. In a word, I heartily concur, and I trust you will do the same, in the opinion of the old man who declared, according to the anecdote, that after the experience of a long life, he had found it best to submit to what he could not possibly help.

What, then, is the business before us? Daniel Drayton is set here at the bar charged with a grave offence, and you are impanelled to try him. And who is Daniel Drayton? We shall prove to you that he is a man of sober and industrious life, against whose character, as a just, upright, exemplary citizen, no charge was ever before preferred. Whatever may have been his errors in regard to the transaction which has brought him before you, he has, in consequence of it, passed through scenes which must move your sympathy. He has been torn from his family and immured in a loathsome cell. From feeling that sense of security from lawless violence, which every man, whether guilty or innocent, is entitled to feel, he has been in imminent danger of being torn in pieces by an infuriated mob. Yes, gentlemen, on Tuesday, the eighteenth day of April last, this man, this fellow-citizen of ours, in this capital of the nation, within sight of Congress, and of the President's house, and within hearing of them, too, was pursued by a mob, from near the river's side on the south of us to the very doors of the jail on the north, — a mob estimated to consist of from four to six thousand people, — many of them armed with deadly weapons; the thrusts of a dirk knife, which was drawn upon him, coming within an inch of his body; amid wrathful cries of "Hang him!" "Lynch him!" accompanied by all the profanities and abominations of speech which usually issue from the foul throat of that hideous monster — A MOB. Arrived at the jail, the mob besieged him there. When afterwards, and while under examination before magistrates of the city, a distinguished gentleman and member of Congress, [the Hon. Joshua R. Giddings, of Ohio,] appeared at his request and in his defence, the mob surrounded the gates of the jail, demanding the immediate expulsion of the counsel; and the jailer, to save bloodshed, insisted upon his departure. The storm swept beyond the prison and the prisoner. It assailed all who were supposed to sympathize with him. The office of a newspaper in this city, (the National Era,) was threatened with demolition. At a mob meeting, votes were passed, — without any great scrutiny, I presume, into the qualifications of the voters, — that the paper should be discontinued. Its editor was waited upon at night, or at midnight, by a mob-elected committee, and a peremptory demand was made upon him to remove his establishment beyond the District, or to abandon it.

But I will not dwell longer upon these details, so disgraceful to the capital of a republic that calls itself *free*, and so abhorrent to the feelings of every right-minded man. Were I to enumerate all the perils, the indignities, and the privations to which my client has been subjected, the day would be too short for the narration.

After Drayton's examination, he was held to bail. And what, think you, was the amount of the bail demanded? Seventy-six thousand dollars! and seventy-six thousand dollars also for each of the other prisoners, — $228,000 for the seventy-six alleged slaves, when the common market value of such slaves in this neighborhood would not, I suppose, be more than three or four hundred dollars apiece; — and though all of them, too, had been returned, and were in possession of their claimants at the time. Has the fact never yet come to the knowledge of the magistrates of the District of Columbia, that the constitution of the United States declares that "excessive bail shall not be required"?

But, gentlemen, these are not the only hardships and oppressions to which my client has been subjected. How many, at the most, are the offences against the laws of this District which he has committed? He came here on the 13th of April, in the schooner Pearl. He departed on the 15th. On the 17th, he was arrested near the mouth of the Potomac, with a company of alleged slaves on board his vessel. Was not this all one transaction? Can it be divided and separated into a multitude of distinct offences? Can this one deed be made an offence against different laws? If not, then there is another clause in the constitution set at nought, — that clause which declares that no person shall be "subject for the same offence to be twice put in jeopardy of life or limb."

And yet, gentlemen, what do we find on the records of this court? One hundred and fifteen indictments against this prisoner for this one act; and one hundred and fifteen indictments also against each of the other prisoners for engaging in the same. Three hundred and forty-five indictments! Reams of indictments for a single deed! Nor is this the only injustice. Each of the prisoners is indicted for having violated, by this one act, separate and distinct laws. There is an old law of Maryland against stealing slaves, and another law against transporting them out of the jurisdiction; and these laws are claimed, by virtue of an act of Congress, to be in force in this District. Now, if the prisoner stole the slaves, he is not guilty of the separate offence of transporting. If he is guilty of transporting, he is not guilty of stealing. That the two offences should have been committed by one and the same act, is a legal impossibility. If the grand jury first found the prisoner guilty of the offence of stealing the slaves, they thereby declared that he was not guilty of the different offence of transporting. Or, if they first found him guilty of the offence of transporting, they thereby declared that he was not guilty of the separate offence of stealing. To proceed, therefore, after a finding for one offence, to charge the prisoner with the other, was not only a legal absurdity, but a grievous injustice.

Besides, if these slaves were stolen, as is alleged, from forty-one different masters, the whole might have been charged in different counts in the same indictment, and the prisoner might be found guilty upon as many of the counts as law and evidence would warrant.

So there was but one act of transportation. Even, therefore, if it were just to charge the prisoner with the breach of two different laws for the same act, still, as the transportation of the whole was but one, it should have been charged only in one indictment.

See how fatal to any man must such a course of proceeding be. If the stealing were charged in one indictment, it would be tried by one jury; and the evidence being to a great degree the same, the whole trial might be brought within a limited period of time. But with forty-one indictments, there must be forty-one trials, before forty-one different juries; for neither government nor prisoner would consent that a jury, who had given an adverse verdict, should try another of the cases. Now, gentlemen, I care not for the enormous expense of such a proceeding, — ten dollars on each indictment, enuring to the benefit of the district attorney, —

Here Mr. KEY, the district attorney, interrupted and said: If Mr. Mann thinks I am to have ten dollars on each of these indictments, he is mistaken; and in my argument to the jury I shall deny it.

Mr. CARLISLE. Mr. Mann is not mistaken in the general statement, that the district attorney receives ten dollars on each indictment. He receives ten dollars on each, until the income of his office amounts to six thousand dollars a year. It is only when the emoluments of the office reach that sum that he ceases to draw his ten dollars on each indictment.

Mr. MANN. I was saying, gentlemen, that I care comparatively nothing for the amount of expense incurred in consequence of these three hundred and forty-five indictments. Far graver consequences than the mere expenditure of money are involved. Who can maintain or survive a contest against such a host of indictments, sustained by all the power and resources of the government? Were a man rich as Crœsus, it would exhaust his means. Were he brave as a martyr, it would outweary his endurance. Were he innocent as a child unborn, still, on the mere doctrine of chances, he might fail in some one case, out of such a multitude. Were he in the prime of life, its setting sun might go down in darkness and sorrow before the final verdict of acquittal could be pronounced in his favor. Under such a practice with regard to indictments, coupled with such a practice in regard to bail, an accusation would be as fatal as crime itself, however innocent the accused might be. The law provides a statute of limitations as to offences. Could it have foreseen such an abuse as this, it would have provided a statute of limitations against the number of prosecutions for a single offence; for the government might as well try a man, on a separate indictment, for each hair of a horse he had stolen, and hold him, on each of them, to separate bail. The English courts, gentlemen, have provided a remedy for the beginnings of this injustice. They have decided, again and again, that when even two indictments are found against a man for the same offence, they will compel the prosecutor to make his election between them, — to proceed upon one and abandon the other. 2 Leach's Cr. Cas., 608, *Rex* vs. *Doran*. 3 Carr. & P. 412, *Rex* vs. *Smith*.

Ib. ***Rex*** vs. ***Flower***, 413. 3 T. R. *Young* vs. *The King*, (*in error*,) 106. See, also, in support of the same principle, New York Revised Statutes, vol. 2, part 4, ch. 2, § 42, where provision is made that "if there be at any time pending against the same defendant two or more indictments for the same offence, or two indictments for the same matter, although charged as different offences, the indictment first found shall be deemed to be superseded by such second indictment, and shall be quashed."

But, gentlemen, there is another aspect of this case, which presents, in a manner still more glaring, the enormity of the proceeding to which we are subjected. Under each of the forty-one indictments against this prisoner for stealing, he is liable, if convicted, to be sentenced to twenty years' imprisonment, which would make an aggregate imprisonment of more than eight hundred years. Methuselah himself must have been caught young, in order to survive such a sentence. The very shortest time which the court, in its discretion, could imprison, after a conviction on all these indictments, would be two hundred and eighty-seven years! Did the law ever contemplate so cruel and revengeful a proceeding? Did the law ever suppose that the court, after having sentenced a man to eight hundred years' imprisonment, or even to two hundred and eighty years' imprisonment, should go on, and sentence him to twenty years, or even to seven years more? — when the court must know that it would be imposing sentences to be executed centuries after the prisoner would be dead, and after he would have left his prison, not to return to this world, but to go to another.

But even this is not all. Behind these forty-one indictments for stealing stand drawn up, in battle array, against this same prisoner, seventy-four other indictments for transporting the very slaves whom he is charged to have stolen. The penalty for each of these offences is a fine of two hundred dollars, with imprisonment till paid. The aggregate of these fines would be $14,800. But a penalty not inflicted by the statute, but superadded by this unwarrantable proceeding of the government, is the defence of seventy-four successive cases, under which the wealthiest, the strongest, and the most innocent man must break down, and be swept to ruin.

Corresponding with the oppressive character of all these preliminaries was the manner of the prosecutor, in his opening argument. He has seen fit to use language against the prisoner the most vehement and denunciatory. He has imputed to him every base motive that can actuate a depraved heart, and showered upon him the coarsest epithets that can describe a villain. Now if it shall turn out that my client is innocent, then all these criminations are unjust and cruel; and even should it be proved that he is guilty, it is no part of his punishment to be compelled to sit here in enforced silence, hour after hour, and hear himself denounced and vilified in language as unfitted to his character as to the sobriety of judicial proceedings.

Gentlemen, the representative of the government, like the government itself, should be dispassionate and calm. Majesty is one of the attributes of sovereignty, and serenity is inseparable from majesty. The government is not a being of wrath, of ferocity, of vindictiveness; and the exhibition of such passions is as unsuitable to the representative of the government as to the government itself. Though the image of justice may be represented as holding the sword of power in one hand, yet she is also represented as holding the balance of equity in the other; but when the government assumes the guilt of the prisoner, before it has been found, and denounces him in bitterest epithets as criminal, while as yet the law presumes him to be innocent, — the only proper emblem of such a government is an image which, a few years ago, might have been seen surmounting the dome of the court house in Taunton, in the county of Somersetshire, in England, to which the artist had originally given both the balance and the sword; but a storm, careering through the sky, had swept the balance away, so that nothing but the avenging sword was left; and there the hateful figure stood aloft, an image of wrath untempered by equity.

But, gentlemen, let me trust that the prisoner has at length escaped from the turbulent and perilous scenes which have hitherto destroyed his peace and threatened his life. Let me trust that the fell spirits which prompted the proposal, made by one of his captors while he was yet on board the steamboat, and previous to his return to this city, that he should be brought up and hung at the yard-arm, — as was testified to by the government's witnesses, — is at length exorcised; let me trust that the demoniac cry of vengeance which was shouted by the mob, and the thirst for blood which their conduct betokened, while the prisoner, bound and defenceless, was conducted from the river to the jail, has found no welcoming response in your bosoms. Let me trust, also, that the violence of manner and the bitterness of language which have been so freely employed in the opening of this case, have not disturbed the balance of your minds, or so ruffled their serenity that the images of truth shall be distorted as they are reflected from them.

Gentlemen, the spot on which a jury are seated should be a place separate and apart from the rest of the world; sacred, and inaccessible to the passions and prejudices that move the community without. It should be a place consecrated to the inquiry, "What is truth?" and to the application of its conclusions to the conduct of men. When you took your seats in that place, you were severally asked by the court whether you had formed any opinion respecting the guilt or innocence of the prisoner, and you severally answered in the negative. The final opinion, then, which shall be expressed in your verdict, must be an opinion which you have formed *since* that time, and from the law and testimony here introduced. Into that opinion, no other element must be allowed to enter. The prejudged guilt of the prisoner, as manifested by repeated attempts to take his life; the demand which may exist, and which I suppose does exist, out of doors, that he shall be convicted, innocent or guilty; the anticipation that you are to meet an angry community, if you acquit him; — all these considerations, if they obtrude upon your minds, must be sternly rebuked and banished. The record of your verdict will survive these temporary excitements. It should be a verdict, therefore, which you can look upon, at the close of life, with conscientious satisfaction. It must be one which your children can look at with a filial and honorable regard for their fathers' uprightness. In a case which has excited so much attention, both here and throughout the country, you, too, must expect to be put on trial; your verdict will go into the great record of history, to be passed upon by your country and by posterity.

Once, gentlemen, in the state to which I belong, a case arose in which the deepest and holiest feelings of the community were intensely excited. One of the preludes to the great drama of the American revolution was the slaughtering, in the year 1770, of five American citizens, in the streets of Boston, by the British soldiery. The supposed offenders were brought to trial for the homicide. They were defended by John Adams and Josiah Quincy, — illustrious names! The public breast throbbed with excitement. The sight of butchered countrymen made the blood seethe in the hearts of their fellow-citizens. If there ever could be a case where the law might be wrested to meet the popular outcry for redress; if there ever could be a case where the evidence might be strained and distorted to bring the facts within strained and distorted law, so as to visit a high outrage with a moral, if not a legal penalty, the "Boston Massacre" of 1770 supplied all its conditions. That cause was tried, and the prisoners were acquitted. The storm of popular disaffection soon cleared away, and now twelve purer and fairer names are not inscribed on the roll of fame than the names of those twelve jurymen, who dared to brave public opinion, and to perform an act of arduous, if not of perilous justice. Noble and illustrious bravery of the soul, which, when the yelling fiends of popular passion and prejudice beset the ascending pathway of virtue, can look to conscience, to posterity, and to God, and defy them all! Follow their example, gentlemen, and, whatever fierce sounds of public condemnation may be now rung in your ears, you will have the same glorious reward, and your children, and all the good men of your country, will honor your memories.

Gentlemen, in the vehement appeals which were made to you by the government's counsel, for the condemnation of the prisoner, you were told that he had "invaded this District, and ruthlessly carried away more than a hundred thousand dollars' worth of its property;" and you were warned that, if you let such a man escape, you might as well abandon at once all property in slaves. But it so happens, gentlemen, that you are sworn to try this prisoner for stealing John and Sam, two slaves of one Andrew Hoover, of the alleged value of fourteen hundred dollars only. Is each of these forty-one cases against the prisoner to be inflamed and exasperated by charging him with plundering the District to the amount of more than a hundred thousand dollars? A pretty strong effort of fancy, is it not?

to work up the fourteen hundred dollars of the indictment into more than four millions in the argument! Is this to be another of the oppressive consequences of multiplying the one alleged offence of the prisoner into forty-one separate offences? Is the government's counsel to botch up any sort of nefarious charge against the prisoner, and then call upon you to find him guilty on these strained and overwrought exaggerations of his conduct? No, gentlemen! This would be to suppose that you sit there to administer the worst kind of Lynch law, — a kind that has all its injustice, while screening itself from the odium of its violence. The object of civil society is to protect rights and to redress wrongs. For these great purposes laws are enacted, courts are established, juries are instituted, and rules of evidence are framed. Without civil society, each man would have a right to preserve his own rights and to redress his own wrongs. Civil society takes away something from a man's rights, but it adds immensely to his powers; it makes him stronger than any individual oppressor, and, on the whole, it protects its members far better than they could protect themselves. But civil society, like every thing human, is imperfect. Once out of ten times, or once out of twenty times, it may fail to accomplish the end for which it was established. The very instruments it has framed may sometimes be the cause of its failure. What then? We do but fail in each tenth, or each twentieth case, when, without the social organization, failure might have been the general rule. And, therefore, even if a guilty person does sometimes escape, all we can say is that civil society has not done its work infallibly. It has done well, though it has not done all. But suppose this very civil society, wielding as it does the combined and terrible strength of the whole community, should turn its collected force against an innocent man, and crush him, then in what an utter and hopeless ruin is he overwhelmed! How much better for him had its powerful machinery never existed, than that he should be ground to powder beneath its wheels! Now, such might be the case with every prisoner, if juries were to act without strict obedience to law, and a strict observance of the forms of law. Any appeals, therefore, made to you, that because this prisoner may have committed *some* offence against law, you are, therefore, to discard all scruples and find him guilty of *this* offence, I regard as treason against justice, as a monstrous perversion of judicial proceedings; yes, as a thousand times worse than any guilt of the prisoner, even supposing the distorted features of the picture, drawn by the government's counsel, to be genuine. It would be nothing less than Lynch law, perpetrated by twelve picked and sworn men, instead of a mob.

Gentlemen, the district attorney in his opening has not deigned to tell us on what law he proceeds. He has accused the prisoner of stealing often enough, but has read no statute, and referred to no decision, which creates or describes any such offence. Hence a task which clearly belonged to him is devolved upon me.

After the District of Columbia was ceded to the United States, Congress passed a general law, adopting the laws of Maryland, for that part of the District which had been ceded by Maryland. This trial, therefore, must proceed upon laws originally passed by Maryland. By the act of 1737, ch. 2, § 4, it is provided that any person "who shall steal any negro or other slave," "or who shall counsel, hire, aid, abet, or command any person or persons" to do so, shall suffer death as a felon. The punishment has since been changed to imprisonment in the United States prison, for a term of not less than seven, nor more than twenty years. [Here comments were made at length on the preamble of the statute, and the class of cases to which the law was intended to apply.]

This act was designed to prevent slaves from being *stolen*. But a man might lose a slave without his being stolen. The slave might be enticed or persuaded to run away. Experience, doubtless, made the masters aware of this. Hence, fourteen years afterwards, by the act of 1751, ch. 14, § 10, it was provided that "if any person shall entice and persuade any slave within this province to run away, and who shall actually run away from the master," &c., he shall be punished, &c.

But there was still another way of depriving a master of the service of his slave. Hence the act of 1796, ch. 67, § 19, made it a separate and distinct offence for any person to be guilty of "the transporting of any slave or person, held to service," from the state.

Now, here, gentlemen, are four distinct legal provisions, all designed to protect slave property. By these provisions, four distinct legal offences are created. The law, by creating and defining these offences, has authoritatively declared that one of them is not either of the others of them. "Stealing" is one thing. "Counselling, hiring," &c., a man to steal, is not stealing itself. "Enticing and persuading" a slave to run away from his master is not stealing. "Transporting" a slave out of the jurisdiction is not stealing. The inquiry for you, therefore, is whether the prisoner is guilty of any of these offences, and if of any, then, of which.

Now, gentlemen, let me take advantage of a map which is lying here accidentally before me, to illustrate this case. Four states, — Pennsylvania, Maryland, Virginia, and North Carolina, are here represented. The boundaries between them are distinctly marked. Pennsylvania is not Maryland, nor either of the others. Maryland is not Virginia, nor either of the others; and so of the rest. Just so it is with the offences created by these statutes. Any one of them is not either of the others. It is as plain that the offence of "transporting" a slave out of the jurisdiction is as different from the offence of stealing a slave, as this geographical shape of Maryland is different from this geographical shape of Pennsylvania. As, therefore, if the geographical metes and bounds of the State of Maryland were shown to you, you could not say, upon your oaths, that it was a description of the State of Pennsylvania; so, if the offence of "transporting" be proved to you, you cannot say, on your oaths, that it is the offence of stealing.

Or take an illustration from other things. The object of a sun-dial, a watch, a clock, and a chronometer is the same. All are made for the measurement of time, as all these laws were made for the protection of slave property. But could you, therefore, on your oaths, convict a man of stealing a chronometer, when he had only taken a clock or a watch? No, you could find him guilty only of the thing proved to have been done.

Or, again, suppose a law should be made to protect a man's property in his books; and the stealing of books, generally, should be punishable by five years' confinement in the penitentiary. Such a general law would include all books. Suppose a subsequent law should inflict a lighter penalty for stealing an octavo volume, and a still lighter one for a duodecimo. Then it would be necessary, in an indictment, to set out the kind of book stolen, and no man could be lawfully punished for the weightier offence who had only committed the lighter. So here, the first law punished "stealing," the next "enticing," and the next "transporting."

Now, gentlemen, I maintain that, at most, nothing but the offence of "transporting" has been proved against this prisoner. But he is arraigned for *stealing*. What then, let us inquire, are the ingredients which constitute the offence of stealing, — which are indispensable to its perpetration? They are, 1. That the property shall be taken by the thief from the possession of the owner. 2. That it shall be taken into the possession of the thief, — that is, that the taker shall exercise some act of control or ownership over it. And, 3. That this taking by the thief, from the possession of the owner, and into his own possession, shall be for the felonious purpose of converting the said property to his own use.

Now, I think it is not too much to say, that neither one of these three indispensable ingredients of larceny has been proved in this case.

1. It is not proved that the prisoner took the two slaves mentioned in the indictment *from the possession* of Andrew Hoover. Could not some other person besides the prisoner have put it into the heads of these slaves to leave their master? There are white men in this city hostile to the institution of slavery, and desiring the freedom of all slaves. Could they not have said to Hoover's slaves, "Here is a schooner at the wharf; it is to sail at such a time; be there, and you may escape to a free state"? Here, too, are thousands of free negroes, or colored persons, in this District, with whom the slaves are in daily and open communication. Could they not have infused into the mind of these slaves the idea of liberty? Is it not a thousand times more probable that it was done by some citizen in the District, or by some colored acquaintance or friend of theirs, enjoying the means of constant communication with them, than that it was done by an entire stranger to them, as the prisoner was? Can aught be conceived more absurd or preposterous than that the prisoner should go round the streets of Washington, picking up a slave here and there, to complete his cargo, as the driver of a stage-coach goes round picking up passengers? Should he accost a colored man in the streets, and ask him if he were a slave, the

chances are three to one that the person addressed would turn out to be a freeman; for I suppose the proportion, in this District, of the free colored persons to the slaves to be as great as this. If the fourth man or woman he might meet should prove to be a slave, how could he know but what he might be addressing one so attached to the place, to his home and relatives, and to his master, that even the sweets of freedom would not tempt him to leave; and that the consequence would be an immediate reporting of the interview, and sudden detection and punishment? But a person on the spot would know who were slaves, and what slaves were discontented with their condition; he could select the occasion when a slave had been punished by his master, when his body was smarting, and his mind was fired with indignation against him, and then sow the seeds of discontent and the hopes of escape in a fruitful soil. If, then, the slaves were, in fact, instigated to leave their master's possession, the probabilities are a thousand to one that they were so instigated by some other person or persons resident here, and not by the prisoner. If this were so, and they came on board the prisoner's schooner, after having absconded from their master, then he did not take them from Hoover's possession, and so is not guilty of the first ingredient in the crime of larceny.

But is there not still another way in which slaves may be induced to leave the possession of their master? Though we may call men slaves, yet are they not human beings? — degraded from the natural dignity of manhood, it is true, and dwarfed in their mental stature, but still human beings; subject to the passions of our common nature, animated by its hopes, inflamed by its resentments, and shrinking and flying through fear from the uplifted rod. As human beings, could not the desire of escape from their master's possession have originated with themselves? — prompted by the inward and instinctive longings for liberty, which spring perennial in the human breast.

The attorney for the government, in his opening, dwelt long and earnestly on the value of this species of property. He described it as the most valuable kind of property known in the District, and therefore most vigilantly to be guarded. Doubtless it has a certain pecuniary value ; and, as it increases in intelligence, activity, and skill, its value is greatly enhanced. But with this enhanced value comes a *per contra.* With increased intelligence and mental development, the desires natural to manhood spring up ; — the longing for liberty, and for the possession of free agency ; the desire of selecting one's own field of labor, and means of enjoyment ; the desire of commanding the rewards of one's own toil. So that, as the value of a slave increases, the strength of the tenure by which he is held becomes less secure. It is a weight of gold suspended by a cord. The master wishes to increase the mass. He adds little by little, until the weight snaps the cord, and he loses the whole.

Hoover says he had been offered $1400 for the two slaves mentioned in the indictment, and had refused the offer. Their services were probably worth to him a dollar a day each. One of them was employed in driving a cart about the city. As he saw a handful of money paid to his master every week, or every month, for his own earnings, think you he never asked himself, why that money could not be his ? When three out of every four colored men whom he met, from day to day, were receiving their own earnings, and making those earnings minister to their comforts and their pleasures, might not Hoover's slaves have said, " Why are not our earnings our own ? and, if we cannot possess them here, why should we not go to a country where the laborer is deemed, in the language of Scripture, to be worthy of his hire ? " and so have fled of their own accord? for, though we are prone to apply the precepts of the gospel to others rather than to ourselves, yet this is a passage which they would be likely to take home.

But this is not all, gentlemen. In this capital of a nation so boastful of its freedom, the common air is vocal with the accents of liberty. Many of the colored people can read. Who knows but some of them have read the Declaration of American Independence; and, *in their blindness and simplicity of mind*, applied its immortal truths to themselves? "All men are created equal!" and among their "inalienable rights" "are life, LIBERTY, and the pursuit of happiness!" Who knows but that they may have seen these doctrines, with a constellation of names subscribed to them as glorious as any that ever shone in history's firmament? If such ideas once got possession of a man's mind, do you think that fire or water could ever burn them or drown them out? Those who cannot read, can hear; and if you are to keep from them the perpetually recurring sights and sounds which must awaken the quick instincts of liberty, you must extinguish their eyes, and seal up their ears in everlasting silence. The last spring was one of peculiar "refreshing" to the ardent lovers of liberty. The recent events of Europe were the theme of every tongue. Not only in the market-place, in the street, and in after-dinner conversations, was the emancipation of Europe the subject of discussion, but stormy eloquence rushed forth from the capital of the nation, like winds from the cave of Æolus, and roared and raved till all but the dead must have heard it. Nay, more, gentlemen, one of the witnesses identified the day when the defendant's schooner, the Pearl, came to anchor in the waters of this city, because he remembered it as the day of the "torchlight procession." And what was the "torchlight procession"? You all know;—

drums beating, music playing, bonfires blazing, the house of the President and of high official dignitaries illuminated, the trees of the avenue fancifully lighted up with many-colored lanterns; men, women, children, and slaves, all out, and all agog to see and to hear of the wonderful things which "liberty" had done, or had *not* done, on the other side of the Atlantic. There, too, moved in long procession men who were elected for the occasion, from among the nation's elect, — heads of departments, senators, and representatives, — men distended almost to bursting with eloquence for regenerated Europe, who must speak or die! They marched to an open space on Pennsylvania Avenue, where, on an extempore rostrum, they eased themselves of their repletion of patriotism; while people of all kinds, conditions, and colors stood below, empty and agape, to receive what the upper divinities might send down. And now let me read to you, gentlemen of the jury, some of the precious things that were said on that memorable evening, — only two nights before the escape of the slaves in the schooner Pearl, — and see, after you have tasted of the yeast, if you can wonder at the fermentation: —

"—— Events which hold out *to the whole family of man* so bright a promise of *the universal establishment of* CIVIL *and religious liberty*, and the general destruction of monarchical power throughout the world."

"New and endearing ties" — "between the people of liberated France, and *the twenty millions of freemen* who dwell, in all the plenitude of social and political happiness, between the great seas which water the eastern and western shores of this vast continent."

"I feel authorized to declare that there is *not one* in this vast multitude whose sympathies are not deeply enkindled in behalf of France and Frenchmen."

"—— Such has been the extraordinary course of events in France, and in Europe, within the last two months, that the more deliberately we survey the scene which has been spread out before us, and the more rigidly we scrutinize the conduct of its actors, the more confident does our conviction become that the *glorious work* which has been so well begun cannot possibly fail of complete accomplishment; that the age of TYRANTS AND SLAVERY is rapidly drawing to a close; and that the happy period to be signalized by the *universal emancipation of man* from the *fetters of civil oppression*, and the recognition *in all countries* of the great principles of *popular sovereignty*, *equality*, *and* BROTHERHOOD, is, at this moment, visibly commencing."

[Here Judge CRAWFORD broke in, with great sharpness, and said, "Mr. MANN, such inflammatory language cannot be allowed in this court. We have institutions that may be endangered by it. The court thinks it its duty to interfere. The counsel cannot be allowed to proceed with such inflammatory language."

Mr. CARLISLE here rose, and, for the space of ten or fifteen minutes, with the crowded audience hushed to a grave-like silence, he interspersed resistless logic with noble sentiments, in a strain of eloquence rarely, if ever, surpassed. He vindicated every word his colleague had said, both as to matter and manner, and obtested Heaven to preserve American tribunals of justice from following the examples of the worst times of English judicial tyranny, when the basest minions of the crown were elevated to the bench, that they might overawe and abash counsel in their defence of prisoners whom the king had foredoomed to punishment.

Judge CRAWFORD. (Trembling with emotion.) Mr. MANN's course of argument was perfectly legitimate. It was the inflammatory language that I objected to. It was the language, and not the argument, that was objectionable.]

Mr. MANN. Gentlemen of the jury, as the interdict against the line of argument I was pursuing, — now acknowledged to be just and proper, — has been withdrawn, I take it up where I left it, and proceed.

Mr. KEY, district attorney. I demand to know from what paper the gentleman reads.

Mr. MANN. (Holding up the paper and pointing to its heading.) From Mr. Ritchie's Washington Union, of April 20th. Isn't that good authority on this subject?

Mr. KEY. From whose speech does the gentleman read?

Mr. MANN. From the speeeh of the Hon. Henry

S. Foote, a senator in Congress from the State of Mississippi.

Mr. KEY. The gentleman cannot read a paper to the jury, unless he expects to prove it.

Mr. MANN. I deny that as a principle; but, if required, will call Mr. Foote to swear to his speech.

Judge CRAWFORD. Mr. Mann knows Mr. Foote did not mean his language for *our* slaves. (A suppressed laugh around the bar.)

Mr. MANN. May it please your honor, while nothing, on the one hand, will ever deter me from doing my duty to a client, yet, on the other hand, I am moved to say that I have been trained from my youth to such respect for a court of justice, that I would say nothing to it or before it which should not be fitting and appropriate, as apples of gold in pictures of silver. Let me then restate my argument, that we may see whether, and by whom, this rule has been departed from. I reiterate, then, if slaves are property, they are a peculiar kind of property. They are instinct with the common desires of humanity, and among them one of the deepest and strongest is the love of liberty. And just in proportion as their value is increased by intelligence and development, just in that proportion is the bond weakened by which they are held. In all places slaves hear something, but in this place they hear much, of what is said in behalf of human liberty and of human rights. If they hear this, and are above the condition of brutes, they will apply it to themselves. Every Fourth of July oration, if understood, is a torch to light up another St. Domingo. If they hear the word "*slave*" used in reference to those who have been deprived of their natural rights in other countries, they will apply that word to their own condition in this. If they hear the word "*tyrants*" used in reference to one who deprives others of their rights, for "*tyrants*" they will read "*masters;*" and no mortal power, or law, or art, can help it, but by blotting out all that is human within them. The slaves in this city are constantly hearing what must remind them that they are slaves; and therefore they are constantly incited to escape from their bondage. The torchlight procession, with its speeches and parade, was *one* among ten thousand of these incitements. The slaves, therefore, who went on board the Pearl, might have obtained the idea of escape from some other person than from the prisoner, — from some orator who lays down rules for the meridian of Europe, which do not quite suit the meridian of America. Hence they might have gone and applied to the prisoner for a passage. To this he might have assented. And if so, then his offence can be nothing beyond the offence of "transporting," and is not the offence of *stealing*, as charged in this indictment.

And, as to the inflammatory language which the court charges me with having used: every word which was uttered by me, and which the court characterizes and denounces as "inflammatory," and thinks not proper to be spoken in this court room, because it may endanger the institutions of this city, was the exact language of the Hon. Mr. Foote, senator in Congress from the State of Mississippi, uttered by him from the rostrum, on Pennsylvania Avenue, the most public place in this city, on the evening of the 13th of April last, to thousands of people there assembled, men, women, children, negroes and all.

I had marked, may it please the court, several other passages, — for this purpose most pungent and piercing, — in the speeches of that evening, to be read on this occasion; but as I think both court and jury are already pretty well apprised of the pertinency and force of my argument under this head, I shall content myself with reading one passage more. It is from the speech of the Hon. Frederick P. Staunton, representative in Congress from Tennessee, delivered on the same occasion, and printed in the same paper:—

"It has been truly said here this evening, that our example has been of essential service to France. Who can doubt it? How different would have been the struggle for liberty to be secured by republicanism, if there had been no example of a stable republican government to which the patriot could point, for the encouragement of his people! It is said we are propagandists. We do not, indeed, propagate our principles with the sword of power; but there is one sense in which we are propagandists. We cannot help being so. Our example is contagious. In the section of this great country where I live, on the banks of the mighty Mississippi river, we have the true emblem of the tree of liberty. There you may see the giant cottonwood spreading his branches widely to the winds of heaven. Sometimes the current lays bare his roots, and you behold them extending far around and penetrating to an immense depth in the soil. When the season of maturity comes, the air is filled with a cotton-like substance, which floats in every direction, bearing, on its light wings, the living seeds of the mighty tree. They lodge upon every bank of sand which emerges from the bosom of the receding tide, and soon a young forest is seen to lift its head from the surface of the barren waste. Thus the seeds of freedom have emanated from the tree of our liberties. They fill the air. They are wafted to every part of the habitable globe. And even in the barren sands of tyranny they are destined to take root. The tree of liberty will spring up every where, and nations shall recline in its shade."

And thus, gentlemen of the jury, I say that while some of the seeds of liberty which we scatter are wafted to a foreign realm, and fall upon a foreign soil, others will drop upon the hearts of bondmen and bondwomen at home, and will there fructify and mature into *their* appropriate harvest.

Such, gentlemen, are the considerations that lead me to believe that the slaves found on board the schooner Pearl left the possession of their masters of their own accord, or at the private suggestion of some friend, and not at that of the prisoner; or because they were publicly incited thereto by that boastful spirit amongst us which is forever shouting the praises of liberty, while restricting the application of its principles. I therefore infer that the prisoner has not committed the act which forms the first ingredient in the offence of larceny, — the taking of property from the possession of the owner.

2. To constitute the offence of larceny, the prisoner must have taken the slaves into his own possession. Now, of this there is not a particle of evidence. For aught that appears, the slaves might have been passengers, on board his schooner, for a fare. They themselves might have paid this fare, or others might have paid it for them. In either case, they were no more in possession of the prisoner than you or I are in possession of a railroad corporation, when we travel in its cars.

3. The third question is, whether, even if the prisoner did take the slaves named in this indictment from the possession of Andrew Hoover, and into his own possession, he did so for the felonious purpose of converting them to his own use.

The act of stealing, gentlemen, springs from the impulse to acquire property, as a means of gratification. This impulse or desire to obtain the means of enjoyment is universal. The law denounces its penalties against stealing, in order to repress the excesses of this propensity, and to confine it to honest acquisitions. Hence one man may interfere with the property of another in a thousand ways, without being guilty of stealing. It is not the mere taking of another man's property, therefore, which constitutes stealing, but the taking of it *in order to convert it to the use of the taker*, and so to save himself the labor of earning it. Hence I may take a man's plough from his field, or his wagon from his barn, and use them temporarily; but if I return them again to the owner, it is not stealing, but only a trespass. So, according to the books, I may take a man's horse from his stable, ride him thirty miles, in order to flee from justice, and then, if I abandon the horse, it is not stealing. It is only a trespass.

The doctrine, gentlemen, which I wish to enforce upon your minds, is, that every act of taking another man's property is not stealing. When a wag, riding with a clergyman to church, took his sermon from his pocket, for the purpose of enjoying his embarrassment when he should get into the pulpit, and find himself in the presence of the enemy without any ammunition, such taking was not stealing ; for doubtless the rogue had no intention of appropriating either the sermon or its morals to his own use.

So it is related of Sir Walter Scott, that, when he was a boy at school, he got within one of the head of his class. But the boy at the head never made a mistake, and so he stood there, as perseveringly as the letter A stands at the head of the alphabet. But Sir Walter observed that, when his classmate was reciting, his fingers always fumbled with a button on his jacket, and, watching his opportunity at their next romping on the playground, he cut off the button from his rival's jacket ; and, at the very next lesson, the boy, being disconcerted at not finding the button, missed his answer, and Sir Walter rose to the head. But surely this was not stealing.

The reason why, in each of these cases, one would not be guilty of stealing, is, that he does not mean to make the article taken his own. He gets a temporary advantage from it, but does no act that proves a design of permanent or unlimited ownership. Hence there is the broadest and most striking difference between stealing and malicious mischief. If one man takes the property of another, merely to destroy or annihilate it, out of ill will or revenge towards the owner, this is malicious mischief only, and not stealing. It is not punished as stealing. Morally, it may be as wrong, — perhaps worse than stealing itself. But this impulse which prompts to the *destruction* of another man's property is vastly weaker than that which leads to its *appropriation.* The latter is gratified a thousand times where the former is once, and therefore the law visits the former with the milder penalty. If taking property from its owner from revenge, and for the malicious purpose of destroying it, be not stealing, but only malicious mischief, then surely taking the property for the benevolent purpose of doing a kindness to the property itself, — as to a slave, — is not stealing.

Take an illustration. Wild animals are the property of no one. The undomesticated hares that run over my fields, the pigeons that fly over my house, or the fishes that swim in my streams, are not my property so that they can be the subjects of larceny. If a man takes them, he is liable in trespass for entering my grounds, and that is all. But if I confine hares in a warren, or pigeons in a cote, or fishes in a seine, then they are my property, and are the subjects of larceny, because I have reduced them to possession. Under such circumstances, if a man shoots or catches them for his table, — that is, to convert them to his own use, — he steals them; but if a man merely releases them from their confinement, breaks open their enclosures to let them go free, he is at most only guilty of malicious mischief. The English nobility send to France for foxes. These are caught in the Pyrenees or other mountains, brought across the English channel, and placed in the parks of noblemen preparatory to the barbarous amusement of a fox-hunt. Now, if one lord should take a fox from the park of another lord, for the pleasure of hunting him down, on his own premises, this would be stealing; but if he should only assist a fox to escape out of the park, for the benevolent

10 *

purpose of restoring him to his natural liberty, this would not be stealing, but only a trespass. In such a case, the man who enlarges the fox does not do it in order to save himself the labor or expense of catching a fox; that is, he does not convert the fox to his own use.

Let me give you another illustration, which I select for the beauty of the language in which it is conveyed, and for the nobleness of the sentiments that accompany it. In the "Sentimental Journey" of Sterne, the following incident is related: —

"I was interrupted, in the heyday of this soliloquy, with a voice which I took to be of a child, which complained, it could not get out. I looked up and down the passage, and seeing neither man, woman, nor child, I went out without further attention.

"In my return back through the passage, I heard the same words repeated twice over, and looking up, I saw it was a starling, hung in a little cage. 'I can't get out, I can't get out,' said the starling.

"I stood looking at the bird, and to every person who came through the passage, it ran fluttering to the side which they approached, with the same lamentation of its captivity, — 'I can't get out,' said the starling. God help thee! said I, but I'll let thee out, cost what it will; so I turned about the cage to get at the door. It was twisted and double twisted so fast with wire, there was no getting it open without pulling the cage to pieces. I took both hands to it.

"The bird flew to the place where I was attempting his deliverance, and, thrusting his head through the trellis, pressed his breast against it as if impatient. I fear, poor creature, said I, I cannot set thee at liberty. 'No,' said the starling, 'I can't get out. I can't get out,' said the starling.

"I vow I never had my affections more tenderly awakened."

And then he bursts out into that apostrophe to Slavery, which has thrilled the hearts of all his readers in times past, and will continue to thrill the heart of every reader in all time to come: —

"Disguise thyself as thou wilt, still, Slavery, still thou art a bitter draught! and, though thousands in all ages have been made to drink of thee, thou art no less bitter on that account. 'Tis thou, thrice sweet and gracious goddess, LIBERTY, whom all in public or in private worship, whose taste is grateful, and ever will be so till Nature herself shall change. No *tint* of words can spot thy snowy mantle, or chemic power turn thy sceptre into iron. With thee to smile upon him as he eats his crust, the swain is happier than his monarch, from whose court thou art exiled. Gracious Heaven! grant me but health, thou great Bestower of it, and give me but this fair goddess as my companion, and shower down thy mitres, if it seems good unto thy divine providence, upon those heads which are aching for them."

Had Sterne released that bird, and sent it abroad to rejoice in its native fields of air, would his myriads of readers, who have been delighted at the story, have convicted him of *stealing?*

Now for the application. These slaves, by the law of nature, were as free as you or I. By the law and force of man, they have been subjected to bondage. If the prisoner took them, and took them either to sell them or to use them himself, then he took them, in the language of the law, for the felonious purpose of converting them to his own use; and such taking would be larceny according to the law. But if he took them for the purpose of carrying them to a free state, and of thus restoring them to their natural liberty, then he did not intend to convert them to his own use, and is not guilty of stealing.

There is another view of this case. The harshest doctrines in favor of slavery only claim, that a master has a right to the *services* of his slave. He has not a right to his flesh and bones, so that he can cut up the former for dog's meat, and grind the latter for compost. To constitute larceny, then, of this kind of property, the prisoner must have deprived the master of the *services* of his slaves, with the intent, with the felonious intent, to use *those services* himself, or to sell them to another, which would be the most effective act of use. But no evidence of any such intent has been adduced in this case. I therefore maintain, that neither of the three ingredients necessary to constitute the offence of larceny has been proved by the government.

And now, gentlemen, in closing, I will narrate to you the worst of the prisoner's case. I will make confession for him of the length and breadth of his offence. There resides in this city a man named Daniel Bell, who was once held as a slave, but who purchased his own freedom. He had a family, consisting of his wife and eight or ten children. These were manumitted by their master, when he was brought to that most searching of all earthly tribunals, — the death bed. After the master's decease, his heirs attempted to reclaim the property; for the living and the dying have very different views on the subject of slavery. Their ground of claim was, that the master was not of sound and disposing mind when he made the deed of manumission. But the magistrate who prepared the deed, and before whom it was executed and acknowledged, set that pretence aside by his own knowledge of the grantor's sanity; and so the family of Bell passed as free, and were treated as free, for years. At length this magistrate died, and immediately the attempt to reduce the family to bondage was renewed. A trial was had, and through default of the now deceased magistrate's testimony, a verdict against them was obtained. But new evidence was discovered, and one of the most respectable counsellors of this court, Joseph H. Bradley, Esq., made oath as to his belief in the sufficiency of that evidence, and moved for a new trial. It was while these proceedings were pending, in behalf of the wife and children, that they became alarmed lest they should be clandestinely sent to the south, and there be plunged into irredeemable slavery. Believing themselves free, and fearing bondage, they did send to Philadelphia for assistance, (I tell you the worst of it,) in being rescued from such a fate. This defendant, Drayton, being led also to believe that they were free, did come to assist them. Drayton might have said to himself, "Men go to assist Poles and Hungarians, and even Texans, and get glory for it; and why should I not assist free women and children in imminent danger of bondage?" He arrived here on Thursday evening, the 13th of April, and, having no other special business, prepared to sail from here, and did so sail, on Saturday evening, the 15th. Bell's family knew the place where the defendant's vessel was anchored, and the time fixed for its departure. Drayton, expecting to meet them there at the time appointed, was not at his vessel during the whole evening. But one thing happened which he did not expect, and had not provided against. Bell's family had a few friends whom they thought they could take with them. They did not propose any spoiling of the Egyptians, but thought the escape of a few Israelites lawful. But these friends had *their* friends, and they still another circle; and so, while the defendant was absent from his vessel on Saturday evening, and without his knowledge or consent, they flocked down and stowed themselves in the hold; so that, — and I say now, gentlemen, what I religiously believe to be true, — when these slaves were ordered to come on deck after the capture, the prisoner was as much astonished as any body at the number of fishes that had got into his net.

These, gentlemen, are the facts, and, as I believe, all the important facts pertaining to this case; and on these facts we claim that you must acquit the prisoner of the offence of larceny.

NOTE. This case and one or two others were tried, and, in consequence of a series of most extraordinary rulings by the court, a verdict of "*guilty*" was rendered.

Every lawyer knows that in the course of a trial, when counsel can have no time for examination or reflection, they take exceptions, wherever an objection to the decision of the judge seems probably, or even plausibly good. A clew, therefore, will be given to the course which the court pursued throughout these trials, when the fact is stated, that, on appeal to the Superior Court, *seventeen* out of *twenty-four* of the rulings of the judge to which exception had been taken were set aside.

The cases for larceny were remanded to be tried anew, when a verdict of "not guilty" was rendered in them all.

Drayton, the captain, and Sayres, his mate, were afterwards convicted of "transporting" the slaves, and were fined.

English, the "boy," though indicted in one hundred and fifteen indictments, was discharged without a trial.

Part of Bell's free family were ransomed; the rest were sold and sent to the South.

Although the facts pertaining to the mob, the repeated attempts upon Drayton's life, the besieging of the jail, and the expulsion of Drayton's counsel from it when engaged in his defence, all came out before the grand jury that found these scores and hundreds of indictments, and though it was notorious who some of the ringleaders of the mob were, yet no bill of indictment was ever found against any of them.

LETTER

To the Whig Convention, (and also to the Free Soil Convention, *mutatis mutandis*,) accepting their respective Nominations for the Thirty-first Congress.

[*One paragraph of this Letter is omitted, as referring to a subject unconnected with the object of the present volume.*]

West Newton, Sept. 23, 1848.

Gentlemen;

I have received with lively emotions of gratitude a copy of the resolutions passed at a district convention, held at Dedham, on the — inst.; from one of which it appears that I was unanimously nominated by the convention, as their candidate for the Thirty-first Congress of the United States.

. . . .

The convention you have the honor to represent was pleased to refer to my views respecting the institution of slavery. Some of these views were partly expressed in the remarks made by me in the House of Representatives, on the 30th of June last; in the letter to my constituents before referred to; and in my arguments before the *Criminal* Court of the District of Columbia, in the "Pearl" cases. These, and kindred views, I shall improve all fitting opportunities that I may ever enjoy to enlarge upon and enforce; and had I the tongue of an angel, or the pen of inspiration, I believe I could use them on no holier theme than in kindling abhorrence at the wrongs suffered by the slave, and in melting the universal heart of humanity into pity for his lot; for I hold it to be impossible for the soul of a slave, — benighted, strangled, and buried alive as it is, — ever fully to know and feel the joys of that spiritual liberty wherewith Christ maketh his disciples free.

Be pleased, gentlemen, to accept my thanks for the very kind manner in which you have made known to me the decision of the convention you represent, and believe me,

Very truly and sincerely, yours, &c., &c.,

HORACE MANN.

SPEECH

Delivered in the House of Representatives of the United States, February 23, 1849, on Slavery and the Slave Trade in the District of Columbia.

Mr. Chairman;

There is a bill upon the speaker's table which provides for abolishing the slave trade in the District of Columbia. For three successive days we have tried in vain to reach it, in the order of business. Its opponents have baffled our efforts. Our difficulty is not in carrying the bill, but in reaching it. I am not without apprehension that the last sands of this Congress will run out, without any action upon the subject. Even should the bill be taken up, it is probable that all debate upon it will be suppressed by that sovereign silencer, — the previous question. Hence I avail myself of the present opportunity, as it is probably the only one I shall have, during the present session, to submit my views upon it.

I frankly avow, in the outset, that the bill provides for one part only of an evil, whose remedy, as it seems to me, is not only the object of a reasonable desire, but of a righteous and legal demand. The bill proposes the abolition, not of slavery, but only of the slave trade, in the District of Columbia. My argument will go to show, that, within the limits of this District, slavery ought not to exist in fact, and does not exist in law.

Sir, in the first place, let us inquire what is the state of things in this District on this subject. The gentleman from Indiana, [Mr. R. W. Thompson,] who addressed us a few days since, used the following language: —

"What is the slave trade in the District of Columbia? I have heard a great deal said about 'slave pens,' — about slaves sold at auction, — and about stripping the mother from the child, and the husband from the wife. These things may exist here, but I do not know of them. Since I have been in the habit of visiting the District, — which is from my boyhood, — I have never seen a negro sold here, — I have never seen a band of negroes taken off by the slave trader. I do not remember that I have ever seen the slave trader himself. I know nothing of the 'slave pen' that is so much talked about. It may be here, however, and these things may happen every day before the eyes of gentlemen who choose to hunt them up; but for myself, I have no taste for such things."

Now, sir, if the gentleman means to say that he has no personal knowledge of "slave pens" and of the slave traffic in this District, that is one thing; but if he means to deny or call in question the existence of the traffic itself, or of the dens where its concentrated iniquities make up the daily employment of men, that is quite another thing. Sir, from the western front of this Capitol, from the piazza that opens out from your congressional library, as you cast your eye along the horizon and over the conspicuous objects of the landscape, — the President's Mansion, the Smithsonian Institution, and the site of the Washington Monument, you cannot fail to see the horrid and black receptacles where human beings are penned like cattle, and kept like cattle, that they may be sold like cattle, — as strictly and literally so as oxen and swine are kept and sold at the Smithfield shambles in London, or at the cattle fair in Brighton. In a communication made during the last session, by the mayor of this city, to an honorable member of this House, *he* acknowledges the existence of slave pens here. Up and down the beautiful river that sweeps along the western margin of the District, slavers come and go, bearing their freight of human souls to be vended in this market-place; and after they have changed hands, according to the forms of commerce, they are retransported, — the father of a family to go, perhaps, to the rice fields of South Carolina, the mother to the cotton fields of Alabama, and the children to be scattered over the sugar plantations of Louisiana or Texas.

Sir, it is notorious that the slave traders of this District advertise for slaves in the newspapers of the neighboring counties of Maryland, to be delivered in any numbers at their slave pens in this city; and that they have agents, in the city and out of it, who are engaged in supplying victims for their shambles. Since the gentleman from Indiana was elected to this Congress, and, I believe, since he took his seat in this Congress, one coffle of about sixty slaves came, chained and driven, into this city; and at about the same time another coffle of a hundred. Here they were lodged for a short period, were then sold, and went on their returnless way to the ingulfing south.

Sir, all this is done here under our own eyes, and within hearing of our own ears. All this is done now, and it has been done for fifty years, — ever since the seat of the national government was established in this place, and ever since Congress, in accordance with the constitution, has exercised "*exclusive* legislation" over it. But the gentleman from Indiana, though accustomed to visit this District from his boyhood, has "never seen a negro sold here;" — he has "never seen a band of negroes taken off by the slave trader;" he does not remember "to have seen the slave trader himself;" he knows "nothing of the 'slave pen' that is so much talked about." Sir, the eye sees, not less from the inner than from the outer light. The eye sees what the mind is disposed to recognize. The image upon the retina is nothing, if there be not an inward sense to discern it. The artist sees beauty; the philosopher sees relations of cause and effect; the benevolent man catches the slightest tone of sorrow; but the insensate heart can wade through tears and see no weeping, and can live amidst groans of anguish, and the air will be a non-conductor of the sound. I know a true anecdote of an American gentleman who walked through the streets of London with a British nobleman; and being beset at every step of the way by squalid mendicants, the American, at the end of the excursion, adverted to their having run a gantlet between beggars. "What beggars?" said his lordship; "*I have seen none.*"

But the gentleman from Indiana says, "But for myself, I have no taste for such things." His taste explains his vision. Suppose Wilberforce and Clarkson to have had no "taste" for quelling the horrors of the African slave trade. Suppose Howard and Mrs. Fry to have had no "taste" for laying open the abominations of the prison-house, and for giving relief to the prisoner. Suppose Miss Dix to have had no "taste" for carrying solace and comfort and restoration to the insane. Suppose the Abbé L'Epée to have had no "taste" for teaching deaf mutes; or the Abbé Hauy for educating the blind; or M. Seguin and others for training idiots, and for educing docility and decency, and a love of order from those almost imperceptible germs of reason and sense, that barely distinguish them from the brutes! Suppose these things, and in what a different condition would the charities and the sufferings of the world have been! Herod had no "taste" for sparing the lives of the children of Bethlehem, and of all the coasts thereof; and doubtless he could have said, with entire truth, that he never heard the voice, in Rama, of lamentation and weeping and great mourning; nor saw, among all the mothers of Syria, any Rachel weeping for her children and refusing to be comforted, because they were not. But, sir, just in proportion as the light of civilization and Christianity dawns upon the world, will men be found who have a "taste" for succoring the afflicted and for righting the wronged. It was the clearest proof of the Great Teacher's mission, that he had "a taste" for going about doing good.

During the last fifty years, and especially during the last half of these fifty years, the world has made great advances in the principles of liberty. Human rights have been recognized, and their practical enjoyment, to some extent, secured. There is not a government in Europe, even the most iron and despotical of them all, that has not participated in the ameliorations which characterize the present age. A noble catalogue of rights has been wrested by the British commons from the British nobility. France and Italy have been revolutionized. Even the Pope of Rome, whose power seemed as eternal as the hills on which he was seated, has sunk under the shock. Prussia, and all the Germanic powers, with the exception of Austria, have been half revolutionized; and even the icy despotisms of Austria and Russia are forced to relent under those central fires of liberty which burn forever in the human heart, as the central fires of the earth burn forever at its core. Great Britain has abolished African slavery throughout all her realms. France has declared that any one who shall voluntarily become the owner of a slave, or shall voluntarily continue to be the owner of a slave cast upon him by bequest or inheritance, shall cease to be a citizen of France. Denmark has abolished slavery wherever it existed in her possessions. The Bey of Tunis, acting under the light of the Mahometan religion, has abolished it. The priests of Persia declare the sentiment to have come by tradition from Mahomet himself, "that the worst of men is the seller of men." Not only all civilized nations, but the half civilized, the semi-barbarous, are acting under the guidance of the clearer light and the higher motives of our day. But there is one conspicuous exception; there is one government which closes its eyes to this increasing light; which resists the persuasion of these ennobling motives; which, on the grand subject of human liberty and human rights, is stationary and even retrogrades, while the whole world around is advancing; sleeps while all others are awaking; loves its darkness while all others are aspiring and ascending to a purer air and a brighter sky. This government, too, is the one which is most boastful and vain-glorious of its freedom; and if the humiliating truth must be spoken, this government is our own. In regard to slavery and the slave trade in this District, where we possess the power of exclusive legislation, we stand where we stood fifty years ago. Not a single ameliorating law has been passed. In practice, we are where we were then; in spirit, there are proofs that we have gone backward.

There are now on the surface of the globe two conspicuous places, — places which are attracting the gaze of the whole civilized world, — whither men and women are brought from great distances to be sold, and whence they are carried to great distances to suffer the heaviest wrongs that human nature can bear. One of these places is the coast of Africa, which is among the most pagan and benighted regions of the earth; the other is the District of Columbia, the capital and seat of government of the United States.

As far back as 1808, Congress did what it could to abolish the slave trade on the coast of Africa. In 1820 it declared the foreign slave trade to be piracy; but on the 31st of January, 1849, a bill was introduced into this House to abolish the domestic slave trade in this District, — here, in the centre and heart of the nation, — and seventy-two representatives voted against it, — voted to lay it on the table, where, as we all know, it would sleep a dreamless sleep. This was in the House of Representatives. It is well known that the Senate is still more resistant of progress than the House ; and it is the opinion of many that, even if a bill should pass both House and Senate, it would receive the Executive veto. By authority of Congress, the city of Washington is the Congo of America.

But, still more degrading than this, there is another contrast which we present to the whole civilized world. The very slaves upon whom we have trodden have risen above us, and their moral superiority makes our conduct ignominious. Not Europeans only, not only Arabians and Turks, are emerging from the inhumanity and the enormities of the slave traffic ; but even our own slaves, transplanted to the land of their fathers, are raising barriers against the spread of this execrable commerce. On the shores of Africa, a republic is springing up, whose inhabitants were transplanted from this Egypt of bondage. And now, look at the government which these slaves and descendants of slaves have established, and contrast it with our own. They discard the institution of slavery, while we cherish it. A far greater proportion of their children than of the white children of the slave states of this Union are at school. In the metropolis of their nation, their flag does not protect the slave traffic, nor wave over the slave mart. Would to God that the very opposite of this were not true of our own! Their laws punish the merchandise of human beings; our laws sanction and encourage it. They have erected, and are erecting, fortifications and military posts along the shores of the Atlantic, for seven hundred miles, to prevent pirates from invading the domain of their neighbors, and kidnapping people who, to them, are foreign nations. We open market-places here, at the centre of the nation, where, from seven hundred miles of coast, the sellers may come to sell, and where buyers may come to buy, and whence slaves are carried almost as far from their birthplace as Africa is from America. The governor of Liberia has lately made a voyage to England and France, and entered into treaties of amity and commerce with them; and he has obtained naval forces from them, to abolish this traffic in human beings. At the same time, we are affording guaranties to the same traffic. Virginia and Maryland are to the slave trade what the interior of Africa once was. The Potomac and the Chesapeake are the American Niger and Bight of Benin; while this District is the great government barracoon, whence coffles are driven across the country to Alabama or Texas, as slave ships once bore their dreadful cargoes of agony and woe across the Atlantic. The very race, then, which were first stolen, brought to this country, despoiled of all the rights which God had given them, and kept in bondage for generations, at last, after redeeming themselves, or being restored to their natural liberty in some other way, have crossed the ocean, established a government for themselves, and are now setting us an example which should cause our cheeks to blister with shame.

Sir, there is an idea often introduced here and elsewhere, and made to bear against any restriction of slavery, or any amelioration of the condition of the slave, which I wish to consider. It was brought odiously and prominently forward the other day, by the gentleman from Pennsylvania, [Mr. Charles Brown.] The idea is, that the slaves are in a better condition in this country than they would have been at home. It is affirmed that they are brought under some degree of civilizing and humanizing influences amongst us, which they would not have felt in the land of their fathers.

Let us look, first, at the philosophy of this notion, and then at its morality. All those who use this argument as a defence or a mitigation of the evils of slavery, or as a *final cause* for its existence, *assume* that if the present three million slaves, who now darken our southern horizon, and fill the air with their groans, had not been here in their present state of bondage, they would have been in Africa, in a state of paganism. Now, the slightest reflection shows that this assumption has no basis of truth. Not one of them all would now have been in existence, if their ancestors had not been brought to this country. And, according to the laws of population operative among barbarous nations, there are now just as many inhabitants,—pagans, cannibals, or what you please,—in Africa, as there would have been if the spoiler had never entered their home, and ravished and borne them into bondage. Among savage nations, or nomadic tribes, the population equals the means of subsistence. Take away two, three, or four per cent. of the consumers, and the vacuum is immediately filled. The population keeps up to the level of the production. Among such people, there is always a tendency to increase faster than the means of living increase. Take away a part of them, and this tendency to increase takes effect by its own vigor,—it executes itself. It is like a bow that unbends, or a spring that uncoils, as soon as an external pressure is removed. Dam up a fountain, and the weight of the accumulating strata will eventually check the outflow from the spring. So it is of a savage population. Of them, the Malthusian theory is true.

And how infinitely absurd and ridiculous is the plea that the slaves are better off here "*than* THEY *would have been in Africa*"! Go out into the streets of this city, and take the first one you meet,—perhaps he is a mulatto. But for being here, he would have been a mulatto in the middle of Africa, would he? Take them all,—mulatto, mestizo, zambo, and all "the vast variety of man," so far as color is concerned,—and if they had not their existence here, they would have had it in Africa! This is the doctrine. Would they have had the same American names also? Would they have spoken the same language, and worn cotton grown on the same fields? The last is just as certain as the first. It is all more silly than the repinings of the silly girls who grieved because their mother had not married a certain rich suitor, whose addresses in early life she had rejected; for then, said they, how rich *we* should have been! No, not one of these three millions of men, women, and children, would have been in existence in Africa. All the crime of their kidnapping; all the horrors of the middle passage; all their sufferings for two centuries, or six generations; and all the calamities that are yet to grow out of their condition, — all these crimes and agonies are gratuitous crimes and agonies. There is no recompense or palliation for them. They have been added unnecessarily and remorselessly to the amount of human guilt and suffering for which the white race must answer in the day of account. The idea, then, of sending the slaves back to *their* country is an egregious fallacy. If they were to be sent *back* whence they came, it would not be to Africa, but to nonentity.

If the ancestors of the present three millions of slaves had never been brought here, — if their descendants had never been propagated here, for the supposed value of their services, their places would have been supplied by white laborers, — by men of the Caucasian race, — by freemen. Instead of the three million slaves, of all colors, we should doubtless now have at least three million white, freeborn citizens, adding to the real prosperity of the country, and to the power of the Republic. If the south had not had slaves to do their work for them, they would have become ingenious and inventive like the north, and would have enlisted the vast forces of nature in their service, — wind, and fire, and water, and steam, and lightning, the mighty energies of gravitation and the subtle forces of chemistry. The country might not have had so gaudy and ostentatious a civilization as at present, but it would have had one infinitely more pure and sound.

But admit the alleged statement, absurd and false as it is; admit that these three millions of slaves would have belonged to Africa if they had not belonged to America, — that they would have been born of the same fathers and mothers there as here, so that those of them who are American mulattoes would have been Ethiopian mulattoes; and admit, further, that their present condition is better than the alternative condition alleged, — and what then? Is your duty done? Is it enough if you have made the condition of a man or of a race a little better, or any better, if you have not made it as much better as you can? What standard of morals do gentlemen propose to themselves? If a fellow-being is suffering under a hundred diseases, and we can relieve him from them all, what kind of benevolence is that which boasts of relieving him from one, and permits him to suffer under the other ninety and nine? By the law of nature and of God, the slave, like every other man, is entitled "to life, liberty, and the pursuit of happiness;" he is entitled to his earnings, — to the enjoyment of his social affections, — to the development of his intellectual and moral faculties, — to that cultivation of his religious nature which shall fit him, not merely to feel, but reason of righteousness, temperance, and a judgment to come; — he is entitled to all these rights, of which he has been cruelly despoiled; and when he catches some feeble glimmering of some of them, we withhold the rest, and defend ourselves and pride ourselves that he is better off than he would have been in some other country or in some other condition. Suppose the Samaritan had bound up a single wound, or relieved a single pang of the bleeding wayfarer who had fallen among thieves, and then had gone to the next inn and boasted of his benevolence. He would only have shown the difference between a "good Samaritan" and a "bigot Samaritan." The thieves themselves might have done as much.

But there is another inquiry which the champions of slavery have got to answer before the world and before Heaven. If American slaves are better off than native Africans, who is to be thanked for it? Has their improved condition resulted from any purposed plan, any well-digested, systematized measure, carefully thought out, and reasoned out, and intended for their benefit? Not at all. In all the southern statute books, and legislative records, there is no trace of any such scheme. Laws, judicial decisions, the writing of political economists, — all treat the slave as a thing to make money with. Agricultural societies give rewards for the best crops. Horse-jockey societies improve the fleetness of the breed for the sports of the turf. Even the dogs have professional trainers. But not one thing is done to bring out the qualities of manhood that lie buried in a slave. Look through the southern statute books, and see what Draconian penalties are inflicted for teaching a slave to read, — see how he is lashed for attending a meeting to hear the Word of God. On every highroad patrols lie in wait to scourge him back if he attempts to visit father, mother, wife, child, or friend, on a neighboring plantation. By day and by night, at all times and every where, he is the victim of an energetic and comprehensive system of measures, which blot out his senses, paralyze his mind, degrade and brutify his nature, and suppress the instinctive workings of truth, generosity, and manhood in his breast. All the good that reaches him, reaches him in defiance of these privations and disabilities. If any light penetrates to his soul, it is because human art cannot weave a cloud dense and dark enough to be wholly impervious to it. There are some blessings which the goodness of God will bestow in spite of human efforts to intercept them. It is these only which reach the slave. And after having built up all barriers to forbid the access of improvement; after having sealed his senses by ignorance, and more than half obliterated his faculties by neglect and perversion, the oppressor turns round, and because there are some scanty, incidental benefits growing out of the very deplorableness of his condition, he justifies himself before the world, and claims the approval of Heaven, because the slave is better off here than *he* would be in Africa. Sir, such an argument as this is an offence to Heaven. I consider it to be as much worse than atheism as Christianity is better. And when such an argument comes from a gentleman belonging to a free state; when it comes from the gentleman from Pennsylvania, [Mr. Brown,] from a representative of the city of William Penn; when he, without motive, without inducement, offers such a gratuity to the devil, I can account for it only on the principle of the man who, having a keen relish for the flesh of swine, said he wished he were a Jew, that he might have the pleasure of eating pork and committing a sin at the same time.

But the subject presents a still more painful aspect. How are slaves made better, and from what motives are they made better, in this country? It is no secret that I am about to tell. There are certain virtues and sanctities which increase the pecuniary value of certain slaves; and there are certain vices and debasements which increase the market price of others. If a master wishes to repose personal confidence in his slave, he desires to have him honest and faithful to truth. But if he desires to make use of him to deceive and cajole and defraud, then he wishes to make him cunning and tricky and false. If the master trains the slave to take care of his own children, or of his favorite animals, then he wishes to have him kind; but if he trains him for a tasker or a field overseer, then he wishes to have him severe. Now, it is in this way that some of the

Christian attributes of character, being directly convertible into money or money's worth, enhance the value of a slave. Hence, it is said in advertisements that a slave is pious, and, at the auction block, the hardened and heartless seller dwells upon the Christian graces and religious character of some slaves with the unction of an apostle. The purchaser sympathizes, and only desires to know whether the article be a real or a sham Christian. If mere bones and muscles compacted into human shape be worth five hundred dollars, then, if the auctioneer can warrant the subject to have the meekness of Moses and the patience of Job, the same article may be worth seven hundred. If the slave will forgive injuries, not merely seventy times seven, but injuries inflicted all his life long, then an additional hundred may be bid for him. If he possesses all the attributes of religion and piety, the endurance of a hero, the constancy of a saint, the firmness of a martyr, the trustingness of a disciple, — all except those which go to make him feel like a man, and believe himself a man, — then that which as mere bone and muscle was worth five hundred dollars, is now worth a thousand. Sir, is not this selling the Holy Spirit? Is not this making merchandise of the Savior? Is not this the case of Judas selling his Master over again, with the important exception of the remorse that made the original culprit go and hang himself? But suppose the case to be that of a woman; suppose her ability to work and capacity for production to be worth five hundred dollars; suppose, in addition to this, she is young and sprightly and voluptuous; suppose the repeated infusion of Saxon blood has almost washed the darkness from her skin; and suppose she is not unwilling to submit herself to the libertine's embrace; then, too, that which before was worth but five hundred dollars, will now bring two thousand. And thus infernal as well as celestial qualities are coined into money, according to the demands of the market and the uses of the purchaser.

Now, it is only in some such incidental way, and with regard to some individuals, that it can be said, that their condition is better here than it would be in Africa. And this improvement, where it exists, is not the result of any system of measures designed for their benefit, but is the product of selfish motives, turning godliness into gain ; and where more gain or more gratification can be obtained by the debasement, the irreligion, the pollution of the slave, there the instincts of chastity, the sanctity of the marriage relation, the holiness of maternal love are all profaned to give security and zest to the guilty pleasures of the sensualist and debauchee. There are individual exceptions to what I have said, — exceptions which, amid surrounding iniquity, shine "like a jewel in an Ethiop's ear," but they are exceptions. Laws, institutions, and the prevailing public sentiment are as I have described.

I regard the argument, therefore, of the gentleman from Pennsylvania, [Mr. Brown,] not only as utterly unsound and false in its premises, but as blasphemous in its conclusions. Common blasphemy seldom reaches beyond exclamation. It is some fiery outburst of impious passion, that flashes and expires. But the gentleman reasons it out coolly. His is argumentative blasphemy, borrowing the forms of logic that it may appear to have its force, and transferring it from the passions to the intellect, to give it permanency.

But the gentleman from Pennsylvania retorts upon Massachusetts, and refers to certain things in her history which he regards as disreputable to her. In this he has been followed by the gentleman from Virginia, [Mr. Bedinger,] who has poured out a torrent of abuse upon my native state, and who has attempted to fortify his own intemperate accusations from a pro-slavery pamphlet which has been profusely scattered about this

House within a few days past, and which is not merely full of falsehoods, but is composed of falsehoods; so that if one were to take the false assertions and the false arguments out of it, there would be nothing but the covers left.* Sir, I am very far from arrogating for Massachusetts all the merits and the virtues which she ought to possess. I mourn over her errors, and would die to reform, rather than spend one breath to defend them. The recital of her offences can fall more sadly upon no ear than upon my own. But it is as true of a state as of an individual, that repentance is the first step towards reformation. Massachusetts has committed errors; but when they were seen to be errors, she discarded them. She once held slaves; but when she saw that slavery was contrary to the rights of man and the law of God, she emancipated them. She was the first government in the civilized world, — in the whole world, ancient or modern, — to abolish slavery, wherever she had power to do so. This is an honor that no rival can ever snatch from her brow. Once, — I say it with humiliation, — she was engaged in the slave trade. But all the gold that could be earned by the accursed traffic, though spent in the splendors of luxury and the seductions of hospitality, could not save the trader himself from infamy and scorn; and I am sure I am right in saying that the slave trade ceased to be conducted by Massachusetts merchants, and to be carried on in Massachusetts ships, from Massachusetts ports, before it was abandoned by the merchants and discontinued in the ships and from the ports of any other commercial state or nation in the world. This, too, is an honor, which it will be hers, through all the immortality of the ages, alone to wear. But Massa-

* Lecture on the North and South. Delivered in College Hall, January 16, 1849, before the Young Men's Mercantile Library Association of Cincinnati. By Ellwood Fisher.

chusetts, it is still said, has her idolaters of Mammon in other forms. It is charged upon her that many of her children still wallow in the sty of intemperance; that her spiritualism runs wild in religious vagaries; and that something of the old leaven of persecution still clings to her heart. In vindicating what is right, I will not defend what is wrong. I cannot deny, — would to God that I could, — that we still have vices and vicious men amongst us. There are those there, as elsewhere, who, if they were to hear for the first time of the River of Life flowing fast by the throne of God, would instinctively ask whether there were any good mill sites on it. There are those there, as elsewhere, whose highest aspirations for heaven and for happiness, whether for this life or for another, are a distillery and a sugar-house, with steam machinery to mix the products. There, as elsewhere, there are religionists who are quick to imitate the Savior when he strikes, but despise his example when he heals.

But, sir, let me say this for Massachusetts, that whatever sins she may have committed in former times, — whatever dissenters she may have persecuted, or witches she may have hanged, or Africans she may have stolen and sold, — she has long since abandoned these offences, and is bringing forth fruits meet for repentance. And is a state to have no benefit from a statute of limitations? Is a crime committed by ancestors to be forever imputed to their posterity? This is worse than non-forgiveness; it is making punishment hereditary. Sir, of these offences, Massachusetts has repented and reformed; and she is giving that noblest of atonements or expiations, which consists in repairing the wrong that has been done; and where the victim of the wrong has himself passed away, and is beyond relief, then in paying, with large interest, the debt to humanity which the special creditor is no longer present to receive, by seeking out the objects of want and suffering wherever they may be found. Sir, our accusers unconsciously do us the highest honor, when, in their zeal to malign us, they seek for historical reproaches. If they could find present offences wherewith to upbraid us, they would not exhume the past. But they condemn themselves, for they show that even the resuscitation of the errors of the dead gives them more pleasure than a contemplation of the virtues of the living. One thing is certain: the moment the other states shall imitate our present example, they will cease to condemn us for our past offences. The sympathy of a common desire for improvement will destroy the pleasure of crimination.

And where, I ask, on the surface of the earth, is there a population of only eight hundred thousand, who are striving so earnestly, and doing so much, to advance the cause of humanity and civilization, as is doing by the people of Massachusetts? Where else, where universal suffrage is allowed, is a million of dollars voted every year, by the very men who have to pay it, for the public, free education of every child in the state?

Where else, by such a limited population, is another million of dollars voluntarily voted and paid each year for the salaries of clergymen alone? Where else, where the population is so small, and natural resources so few and scanty, is still another million of dollars annually given in charity? — the greater portion of which is sent beyond their own borders, flows into every state in the Union, and leaves not a nation on the globe, nor an island in the sea, unwatered by its fertilizing streams. Look into the statute book of Massachusetts, for the last twenty years, and you will see how the whole current of her legislation has set in the direction of human improvement; — for succoring disease or restoration from it, for supplying the privations of nature, for reclaiming the vicious, for elevating all,

— a comprehensiveness of scope that takes in every human being, and an energy of action that follows every individual with a blessing to his home. When others will abandon their offences, then let the remembrance of them be blotted out.

But, sir, I think it proper to advert to the fact that I have had other proofs, during the present session of Congress, of the same spirit of crimination and obloquy which was so fully developed in the speeches of the gentleman from Pennsylvania, [Mr. Brown,] and the gentleman from Virginia, [Mr. Bedinger.] Through the post-office of the House of Representatives, I have been in the regular receipt of anonymous letters, made up mainly of small slips cut from newspapers printed at the north, describing some case of murder, suicide, robbery, or other offence. These have been arranged under the heads of different states, — Ohio, Pennsylvania, New York, Connecticut, &c., and accompanied, in the margin, with rude drawings of a school-book or a schoolhouse, and all referred to Common Schools, as to their source. Two only, of the whole number thus collected, originated in Massachusetts, and one of these was a case of suicide committed by a man who had become insane from the loss of his wife. Which of these events, in the opinion of my anonymous correspondent, constituted the crime, — whether the bereavement that caused the insanity, or the suicide committed in one of its paroxysms, — I am unable to say. Now, what satisfaction even a bad man could have in referring offences against law and morality to the institution of public schools, when he must have known that the very existence of the offences only proves that education has not yet done its perfect work, I cannot conceive. And what spite, either against an educational office which I once held, or against an institution which is worthy of all honor, could be so mean and paltry as to derive gratification from referring me to long lists of offences, only one of which was committed in my native state, I must leave for others to conjecture. Surely the author of these letters must have known little of Common Schools, and profited by them as little as he has known. Had he referred to any considerable number of crimes perpetrated in Massachusetts, I would take his letters home and carry them into our public schools, and make them the text for a sermon, in which I would warn the children to beware of all crimes, and especially of the meanness and the wickedness which feels a complacency in the crimes of others, or can give a false paternity to them. And, sir, I should be sure of a response; for out of those schools there is going forth a nobler band of young men and women than ever before conferred intelligence, virtue, refinement, and renown upon any people or community on the face of the globe.

But whatever may be said in mitigation or in condemnation of slavery elsewhere, there are special reasons why it should be discontinued in this District. This District is the common property of the nation. Having power of exclusive legislation over it, we are all responsible for the institutions in it. While slaves exist in it, therefore, it can be charged upon the north that they uphold slavery. This is unjust to us, because it places us before the world in the attitude of sustaining what we condemn. It wounds our moral and religious sensibilities, because we believe the institution to be cruel towards men, and sinful in the sight of Heaven; and yet we are made apparently to sanction it. It is like that species of injustice where a man is compelled by a tax to support a religion which he disbelieves, and to pay a hierarchy whom his conscience compels him to denounce. But the existence of slavery here is not necessary to the faith or the practice of our southern brethren. If they believe it to be a useful and justifiable institution, then they evince the sincerity of that belief by sustaining and perpetuating it at home. For this purpose, there is no necessity of a crusade to propagate it, or sustain it elsewhere.

Look at the relation which we bear to it, in another respect. I have been taught from my earliest childhood that "all men are created equal." This has become in me not merely a conviction of the understanding, but a sentiment of the heart. This maxim is my principle of action, whenever I am called upon to act; and it rises spontaneously to my contemplations when I speculate upon human duty. It is the plainest corollary from the doctrine of the natural equality of man, that when I see a man, or a class of men, who are not equal to myself in opportunities, in gifts, in means of improvement, or in motives and incitements to an elevated character and an exemplary life, — I say, it is the plainest corollary that I should desire to elevate those men to an equality with myself. However far my own life may fall below the standard of Christianity and gentlemanliness, yet I hold it to be clear, that no man is a Christian or a gentleman, who does not carry about an habitual frame of mind which prompts him, as far as he has the means to do it, to instruct all the ignorance, to relieve all the privations, to minister to all the pains, and to supply all the deficiencies of those with whom he meets in the daily walks of life; and, so far as he is a man who wields influence, possesses authority, or exercises legislative power, he is bound to exert his gifts and his prerogatives for the amelioration and the improvement of his fellow-men. This is the lowest standard of duty that any one who aspires to be a Christian or a gentleman can set up for his guidance. Now take the case of a man from the north, who has incorporated these views, or any similitude of these views, into his character, and who has occasion to visit this District. Suppose him to be elected and sent here as a member of Congress, or to be appointed to a post in some of the departments, or to visit this city on public business, or to come here from motives of curiosity; what is the sight which is inflicted upon him when he first sets his foot within this common property of the nation, — when he first enters this household, where the head of the nation resides and directs? Sir, when he first alights from the cars that bring him within your limits and your jurisdiction, he beholds a degraded caste, — a race of men whom God endowed with the faculties of intelligence, but whom man has despoiled of the power of improving those faculties, squalid in their garb, betraying ignorance in every word they utter, uncultivated in their manners and their tastes, fawning for a favor, instead of standing erect like men who are conscious of rights; or, if they have outgrown servile and sycophantic habits, then erring on the side of impudence and insolence as much as they erred before on that of cringing and servility. He repairs to his lodgings, and there, too, all his moral sensibilities are shocked and outraged, by seeing a class of men and women hopelessly degraded, cut off by law and custom from all opportunity of emerging from their debasement; whom no talent, taste, or virtue can ever redeem to the pleasures and the rights of social intercourse. He sees men and women who are not degraded on account of the services they perform, — for "honor and shame from no condition rise," — but degraded by the motive and spirit from which the services are performed; men and women who have no inducements to industry and frugality, for their earnings will all be seized by another; who have no incentives to self-respect, for they can never emerge from their menial condition; who are bereaved of all the wonders and glories of knowledge, lest under its expansions their natures should burst the thraldom that enslaves them; and all whose manly qualities, all whose higher faculties, therefore, are irredeemably and hopelessly crushed, extinguished, obliterated, so that nothing but the animal, which the master can use for his selfish purposes, remains.

Mr. Brodhead, [of Pennsylvania.] Would you advance the slaves to an equal social and political condition with the white race?

Mr. Mann. I would give to every human being the best opportunity I could to develop and cultivate the faculties which God has bestowed upon him, and which, therefore, he holds under a divine charter. I would take from his neck the heel that has trodden him down; I would dispel from his mind the cloud that has shrouded him in moral night; I would remove the obstructions that have forbidden his soul to aspire; and having done this, I would leave him, as I would leave every other man, to find his level, — to occupy the position to which he should be entitled by his intelligence and his virtues. I entertain no fears on the much dreaded subject of amalgamation. Legal amalgamation between the races will never take place, unless, in the changed condition of society, reasons shall exist to warrant and sanction it; and, in that case, it will carry its own justification with it. But one thing I could never understand, — why those who are so horror-stricken at the idea of *theoretic* amalgamation, should exhibit to the world, in all their cities, on all their plantations, and in all their households, such numberless proofs of *practical* amalgamation. I never could see why those who arraign and condemn us at the north so vehemently, because, as they say, we obtrude our prying eyes into what they call a "domestic" or "fireside" institution, should have no hesitation in exhibiting to the world, through all their borders, ten thousand, and ten times ten thousand, living witnesses, that they make it a bedside institution.

Multitudes of the slaves of the south bear about upon their persons a brand as indelible as that of Cain; but the mark has been fastened upon them, not for their own crimes, but for the crimes of their fathers. In the complexion of the slave, we read the horrid history of the guilt of the enslavers. They demonstrate that the one race has been to the other, not the object of benevolence, but the victim of licentiousness.

But to resume. When the visitor to this city from the north leaves his lodgings, and goes into the public streets, half the people whom he meets there are of the same degraded class. Their tattered dress and unseemly manners denote congenital debasement. Their language proclaims their ignorance. If you have occasion to send them on an errand, they cannot read the direction of a note, or a sign on a shopboard. Their ideas are limited within the narrowest range. They speak the natural language of servility, and they wear the livery of an inferior condition. The conviction of their deplorable state is perpetually forced upon the mind. You do not need their color to remind you of their degradation. Color, sir! They are oftentimes almost as white as ourselves. Sir, there is not a member of Congress who has not frequently seen some of his fellow-members, in the spring of the year, with a jaundiced skin more sallow and more yellow than that of many a slave who is bought and sold and owned in this city. I have seen members of this House to whom I have been disposed to give a friendly caution to keep their "free papers" about their persons, lest suddenly, on the presumption from color, they should be seized and sold for runaway slaves. A yellow complexion here is so common a badge of slavery, that one whose skin is colored by disease is by no means out of danger. To enjoy security, a man must do more than take care of his life; he must take care of his health. It is not enough to take heed to the meditations of his heart; he must see also to the secretions of his liver.

But, sir, the stranger from the north visits the courts of justice in this city; he goes into halls set apart and consecrated, even in the dark and half-heathenish periods of English history, to the investigation of truth and the administration of justice; but if he sees any specimens of the colored race there, he sees them only as menials. They cannot go there as witnesses. However atrocious the wrongs they may suffer in their own person and character, or in the person and character of wife or children, they cannot appeal to the courts to avenge or redress them. If introduced there at all, it is as a bale of goods is introduced, or as an ox or a horse is brought within their purlieus, for the purpose of trying some disputed question of identity or ownership. They go not as suitors, but as sacrifices. In the courts of law; in the temples with which all our ideas of justice, of right between man and man, are associated; where truth goes to be vindicated, where innocence flies to be avenged, — in these courts, an entire portion of the human race are known, not as men, but as chattels, as cattle. Where, for them, is the Magna Charta that the old barons wrested from King John? Is a whole race to be forever doomed to this outlawry? Are they forever to wear a "wolf's head," which every white man may cut off when he pleases? Sir, it cannot be that this state of things will last forever. If all the rights of the black race are thus withheld from them, it is just as certain as the progress of time that they, too, will have their Runnymede, their Declaration of Independence, their Bunker Hill, and their Yorktown.

Such, sir, are the sights that molest us when we come here from the north, — that molest us in the hotels, that molest us in the streets, that molest us in the courts, that molest us every where. But the week passes away, and the Sabbath comes, — the day of rest from worldly toils, the day set apart for social worship, when men come together, and, by their mutual presence and assistance, lift up the hearts of each other in gratitude to God. But where now are the colored population, that seemed to be so numerous every where else? Have they no God? Have they no interest in the Savior's example and precepts? Have they no need of consolation, of faith in the Unseen, to help them bear up under the burdens and anxieties of life? Is their futurity so uncertain or so worthless that they need no guide to a better country, or that they can be turned off with a guide as ignorant and blind as themselves?

We go from the courts and the churches to the schools. But no child in whose skin there is a shadow of a shade of African complexion is to be found there. The channels are so cut that all the sacred and healing waters of knowledge flow, not to him, but by him. Sir, of all the remorseless and wanton cruelties ever committed in this world of wickedness and woe, I hold that to be the most remorseless and wanton which shuts out from all the means of instruction a being whom God has endued with the capacities of knowledge, and inspired with the divine desire *to know*. Strike blossom and beauty from the vernal season of the year, and leave it sombre and cheerless; annihilate the harmonies with which the birds of spring make vocal the field and the forest, and let exulting Nature become silent and desolate; dry up even those fountains of joy and gladsomeness that flow unbidden from the heart of childhood, and let the radiant countenance of youth become dull and stony like that of age; — do all this, if you will, but withhold your profane hand from those creative sources of knowledge which shall give ever-renewing and ever-increasing delight through all the cycles of immortality, and which have the power to assimilate the finite creature more and more nearly to the infinite Creator. Sir, he who denies to children the acquisition of knowledge works devilish miracles. If a man destroys my power of hearing, it is precisely the same to me as though, leaving my faculty of hearing untouched, he had annihilated all the melodies and harmonies of the universe. If a man obliterates my power of vision, it is precisely the same to me as though he had blotted out the light of the sun, and flung a pall of darkness over all the beauties of the earth and the glories of the firmament. So, if a usurper of human rights takes away from a child the faculties of knowledge, or the means and opportunities to know, it is precisely the same to that child as though all the beauties and the wonders, all the magnificence and the glory, of the universe itself had been destroyed. To one who is permitted to know nothing of the charms and sublimities of science, all science is non-existent. To one who is permitted to know nothing of the historical past, all the past generations of men are a nonentity. To one whose mind is not made capacious of the future, and opened to receive it, all the great interests of futurity have less of reality than a dream. I say, therefore, in strict, literal, philosophical truth, that whoever denies knowledge to children works devilish miracles. Just so far as he disables and incapacitates them from knowing, he annihilates the objects of knowledge; he obliterates history; he destroys the countless materials in the natural world that might, through the medium of the useful arts, be converted into human comforts and blessings; he suspends the sublime order and progression of Nature, and blots out those wonderful relations of cause and effect that belong to her unchangeable laws. Nay, there is a sense in which such an impious destroyer of knowledge may be said to annihilate the attributes of the

Creator himself, for he does annihilate the capacity of forming a conception of that Creator, and thus prevents a soul that was created in the image of God from ever receiving the image it was created to reflect. Such a destroyer of knowledge dims the highest moral splendor of the universe. God is more to me than a grand and solitary Being, though refulgent with infinite perfections. Contemplated as enthroned in the midst of his works, his spiritual offspring in all the grand circuit of the worlds he has formed become a multiplying glass, reflecting back the Original in the profusion and countlessness of infinity. But when the wickedness of man cuts off entire generations and whole races from the capacity of reflecting back this radiant image of the Creator, then all that part of the universe where they dwell becomes black and revolting, and all that portion of the Mirror of Souls which was designed to reproduce and rekindle the glories of the Eternal absorbs and quenches the rays which it should have caught and flamed with anew, and multiplied and returned. And still further, sir, I affirm, in words as true and literal as any that belong to geometry, that the man who withholds knowledge from a child not only works diabolical miracles for the destruction of good, but for the creation of evil also. He who shuts out truth, by the same act opens the door to all the error that supplies its place. Ignorance breeds monsters to fill up all the vacuities of the soul that are unoccupied by the verities of knowledge. He who dethrones the idea of law, bids chaos welcome in its stead. Superstition is the mathematical complement of religious truth; and just so much less as the life of a human being is reclaimed to good, just so much more is it delivered over to evil. The man or the institution, therefore, that withholds knowledge from a child, or from a race of children, exercises the awful power of changing the world in which they are to live, just as much as though he should annihilate all that is most lovely and grand in this planet of ours, or transport the victim of his cruelty to some dark and frigid zone of the universe, where the sweets of knowledge are unknown, and the terrors of ignorance hold their undisputed and remorseless reign. Sir, the laws recorded in the statute books of the free states, providing the means of education, and wooing the children to receive the blessedness of true knowledge, are worthy to be inscribed as emblems and hieroglyphics upon the golden gates of heaven; but those laws which deform the statute books of the slave states of this Union, making it a penal offence to educate human beings, and dooming immortal souls to perpetual ignorance, would make the most appropriate adornment wherewith to embellish with inscription and bas-relief the pillars of the council hall of Pandemonium.

Sir, if there is any thing for which I would go back to childhood, and live this weary life over again, it is for the burning, exalting, transporting thrill and ecstasy with which the young faculties hold their earliest communion with knowledge. When the panting and thirsting soul first drinks the delicious waters of truth; when the moral and intellectual tastes and desires first seize the fragrant fruits that flourish in the garden of knowledge; then does the child catch a glimpse and foretaste of heaven. He regales himself upon the nectar and ambrosia of the gods. Late in life, this zest is rarely if ever felt so keenly as at the beginning. Such ought not to be the fact; but our bodies are so systematically abused by transgressions of the laws of health and diet, that the sympathizing soul loses the keenness of its early relish. Even then, however, age has its compensations. The old may experience the delights of learning, anew, in the reflex pleasure of seeing children learn. But these lofty and enduring satisfactions, — this pleasure, — it is no extravagance to say, this bliss of knowledge, both for parent and child, is withheld, cruelly, remorselessly withheld, from the slave. We know all this; we see its imbruting consequences; and we are compelled to see them, because the government will uphold slavery here.

Such, sir, is the spectacle which is presented to all northern men, whenever for duty, for business, or for pleasure, they visit this metropolis. Wherever we go, wherever we are, the odious, abhorred concomitants of this institution are forced upon our observation, and become a perpetual bitterness in the cup of life. The whole system, with all its adjuncts, is irreconcilably repugnant to our ideas of justice. We believe it to be a denial of the rights of man; we believe it to be contrary to the law of God. Whether these feelings wear away by the lapse of time, and the indurating power of custom, I know not; but, for one, I hope never to become hardened and callous to the sight; for it is a case where I could experience no mitigation of my pains, without a corresponding debasement of my nature.

Now, in all sincerity, and in all kindness, I ask our southern brethren what there is to them so valuable and desirable in retaining slavery here, as to be a compensation for all the pain and evil which its existence inflicts upon the north? Surely its abandonment here would be a small thing to them, while its continuance is a great thing to us. It is a great thing to us, because we are held responsible for it by the whole civilized world. This District is the common possession of the nation. Congress has power of exclusive legislation over it. Congress, therefore, is responsible for its institutions, as a man is responsible for the condition of his house, and the customs of his family. The general government is not responsible for the local institutions of Massachusetts or of Mississippi. Each of them has supreme control over its own domestic concerns. They may honorably discharge their debts or repudiate them; they may build up institutions of charity, of learning, and of religion; or they may suffer inhumanity and violence, ignorance and paganism, to prevail; and we, here, cannot help it, and therefore are not responsible for it. But it is wholly otherwise with regard to the institutions that prevail in this District; their honor, or their infamy, attaches to us. We are judged by them the world round. We of the Northern States feel it at home; we are made to feel it still more deeply abroad. Throughout every nation in Europe, it is the common language and the common sentiment, that an institution which exists in one half of the states of this Union is in flagrant contrast and contradiction to the theory of our government. When we are reminded of this, — whether in a kindly and expostulatory manner by our friends, or in an offensive and taunting one by our enemies, — we of the north can say, at least, that we are not responsible for it. We can explain why we are no more amenable for the local laws of Arkansas or Missouri than we are for the Catholic religion in Mexico, or for the revolutions in the South American republics. This is our answer. But they still retort upon us, and say, There is one spot for which you are responsible, — the District of Columbia. You could abolish slavery there if you would; you do not; and therefore the sin of its continuance is yours, as much as if it existed in New York or Massachusetts. Now I ask southern gentlemen how it is consistent with magnanimity and honor, with a fraternal feeling towards the north, for them to force the odium of this inconsistency upon us? Surely they gain no credit, no character by it; we lose both credit and character. The existence of slavery here is no benefit to them; it is of unspeakable injury to us. They would lose nothing by surrendering it; we suffer every thing by its continuance. A change would work them no injury; it would be invaluable to us. I ask them, on principles of common fairness and good neighborhood, that they should courteously and voluntarily yield us this point, which would allay so much bitterness and heart-burning at the north, and which, according to their view of the matter, would fill the south with the sweet savor of a generous deed.

I know, sir, that some southern gentleman profess to see a principle in such a course that debars them from adopting it. They say that if slavery in this District should be surrendered, it would only be giving the adversary a vantage ground, on which he could plant himself to attack slavery in the states. I dissent from this view entirely. Has not the gentleman from Ohio, [Mr. Giddings,] who is supposed to represent the extreme anti-slavery views which exist in this House, — has he not declared here, a hundred times over, that he disclaims all right, that he renounces all legal authority and pretext, under the constitution, to lay the hands of this government, for the purpose of freeing him, on a single slave in the slave states? But clearly the principle is different in regard to slaves in this District, where we possess the power of "exclusive legislation." But if gentlemen at the south see a principle which debars them from surrendering slavery in this District, we at the north see a principle which prompts us, and will prompt us, until the work is accomplished, to renewed exertions. On the same ground on which slavery in this District has been defended for the last fifty years, it can be defended for the next fifty, or the next five hundred years; it can be defended forever. This idea of perpetual slavery in the very household of a republic of freemen is not to be tolerated, and cannot be tolerated. But I will not dwell on this topic further. I close this branch of my argument with a proposition which seems to me but fair and equitable. The south has held this metropolis as a slave capital for fifty years. Let it now be held as a free capital for fifty years; and if, at the end of this period, adequate reasons can be shown, before any nation, civilized or uncivilized, upon the face of the earth, for restoring it to slavery again, I, for one, should have no fears of entering into an engagement upon such a condition, that it should again become "a land of Egypt and a house of bondage."

Notwithstanding I have dwelt so long upon the social and moral aspects of this subject, I am still tempted not to forego that which was my principal object in rising, namely, to submit an argument on the question of the legality or constitutionality of slavery in this District. I have bestowed much careful attention upon this subject, with the sincerest desire of arriving at true, legal, and constitutional results. I submit my views with deference, because I know they are in conflict with the views of others, for whose knowledge and abilities I have a profound respect.

The legality of slavery in the District of Columbia has been assumed, and practically acquiesced in, for fifty years. Had the question of its validity been raised, and argued on the principles of the constitution, immediately after the creation of the District, I believe this territory would have been declared free soil. In my conscientious opinion, slavery exists in this District only by original usurpation and subsequent acquiescence. If so, Congress cannot be too speedily invoked to abdicate the power it has usurped.

1. The first position I take is this: *That slavery has no legal existence any where, unless by force of positive law.*

If any man claims authority over the body, mind, and soul of one of his fellow-men, and claims this authority not only for the whole life of his victim, but a like authority over all his descendants, there is no part of the civilized world where he will not be required to show some positive law, authorizing the power and the bondage. If the claimant says, "I am stronger, or I am wiser than he;" or, "I have an Anglo-Saxon brain, while he has only an African brain;" or, "my skin is white, and his skin is not white;" or, "I descended from Shem, and he from Ham; and, therefore, he is my slave," — there is not a court in Christendom, which, though it may admit the fact, will ratify the inference. If the claimant affirms that it is *morally* right for him to seize his fellow-man and reduce him to slavery; if he brings the Bible into court as his law book, and cites Abraham and Isaac, and Jacob and Paul, as his authorities; still, I say, there is not a court in Christendom that will not deny the validity of the title, and rebuke the arrogance of the demand.* Positive law, then, is the only foundation of slavery. The authorities are numerous, if not numberless, to establish this position. I shall not encumber this argument by citing many of them. The few which I shall cite will contain a reference to the rest.

The grand reason against slavery given by Lord Mansfield, in Somerset's case, was, "that it is so intrinsically wrong that it is incapable of being introduced

* An anecdote, which I have on the best authority, is not inappropriate. A few years ago, a citizen of the State of Connecticut absconded, leaving a wife behind him. He went to the State of Mississippi, where he took a colored woman as his concubine, had children by her, acquired property, and died. The wife and heirs in Connecticut claimed the property acquired in Mississippi. The claim was contested. The honorable HENRY S. FOOTE, now a senator from that state, conducted the defence. He denied the title of the wife in Connecticut, affirmed that of the concubine and her children in Mississippi, and cited the case of Abraham and Sarah and Hagar, to prove the legality and the propriety of the concubinage, and the divine authority for it. And surely, if the Bible argument in favor of slavery is sound, Mr. FOOTE's argument in favor of concubinage is equally so.

into any country, on any reasons moral or political, and can only stand on positive law. 20 State Trials, 1.

Chief Justice Marshall says, " That it [slavery] is contrary to the law of nature, will scarcely be denied. That every man has a natural right to the fruits of his own labor, is generally admitted; and that no other person can rightfully deprive him of those fruits and appropriate them against his will, seems to be the necessary result of this admission." Antelope, 10 Wheat., 120.

" The first objection," says Mr. Justice Best, in the case of Forbes and Cochrane, " which occurs to me, in this case, is that it does not appear, in the special case, that the right to slaves exists in East Florida. *That right is not a general but a local right;* it ought, therefore, to have been shown that it existed in Florida, and that the defendants knew of its existence. Assuming, however, that those facts did appear, still, under the circumstances of this case, this action could not be maintained.

" The question is, Were these persons slaves at the time when Sir G. Cockburn refused to do the act which he was desired to do? I am decidedly of opinion that they were no longer slaves. The moment they put their feet on board of a *British* man-of-war, not lying within the waters of East Florida, (where undoubtedly the laws of that country would prevail,) those persons who had before been slaves were free. . . . . . Slavery is a local law, and, therefore, if a man wishes to preserve his slaves, let him attach them to him by affection, or make fast the bars of their prison, or rivet well their chains; *for the instant they get beyond the limits where slavery is recognized by the local law, they have broken their chains, they have escaped from their prison, and are free.*" 2 Barn. & Cres. 466–7; *Forbes* vs. *Cochrane*, S. C., 3 Dowl. & Ryland, 679.

"I am of opinion," says Holroyd, J., in the same

case, "that according to the principles of the English law the right to slaves, even in a country where such rights are recognized by law, must be considered as founded, not upon the law of nature, but upon the particular law of that country."

"The law of slavery is a law *in invitum; and when a party gets out of the territory where it prevails*, and out of the power of his master, and gets under the protection of another power, without any wrongful act done by the party giving that protection, the right of the master, *which is founded on the municipal law of the particular place only*, does not continue, and there is no right of action against a party who merely receives the slave in that country, without doing any wrongful act."

The definition of slavery given by the Roman law implies that it is local: *Servitus est constitutio juris gentium, qua quis dominio alieno,* CONTRA NATURAM, *subjicitur. Commonwealth* vs. *Aves*, 18 Pick. Rep., 193; *Lunsford* vs. *Coquillon*, 14 Martin's Rep. 402. "The relation of owner and slave is a creation of the municipal law." *Rankin* vs. *Lydia*, 3 Marshall, 470, Ky.; *Butler* vs. *Hopper*, 1 Wash. C. C. Rep. 499; *Ex parte Simmons*, 4 Wash. C. C. 296; *Marie Louise* vs. *Marot et al.*, 9 Curry's Louisiana Rep. 473.

This point may be presented in another light. By the law of nature all men are free. But in some governments the law of the state, upheld by the power of the state, overrides the law of nature, and enslaves a portion of the people. The law of nature recedes before this legalized violence; but it recedes no farther than the legalized violence drives it back. Within the jurisdictional limits of such states, then, slavery is made *legal*, though it is not made *right*. But if a slave passes out of the jurisdiction where violence overpowers right, into a jurisdiction where right is superior to violence, he is then free; not because there is any change in the man, but because there is a change in the laws to which the man is subject.

There may, however, be some further positive law which, though it does not authorize the buying or selling of a slave, still does provide that an escaped or escaping slave may be recaptured and redelivered into bondage. Such is the third paragraph of the second section of the fourth article of the constitution of the United States. Such, too, is the act of Congress of February 12, 1793, providing for the recapture of fugitive slaves. This, however, would not be without positive law.

The debates in all the conventions for adopting the constitution of the United States, proceed upon the ground that slavery depends upon positive law for its existence. If it did not, — if a man who has a legal right to a slave in Virginia, has a legal right to him anywhere, — then the provision in the constitution, and the act of 1793 for recapturing fugitive slaves, would have been unnecessary.

On the south side of a boundary line, then, slavery may exist by force of positive law; while, on the north side, in the absence of any such law, slavery is unlawful. A slave passing out of a jurisdiction where slavery is legalized, into a jurisdiction where it is not, becomes free. It is as though a man should migrate from one of those South Sea islands, where cannibalism is legalized, and where the public authorities, according to the reports of travellers, not only condemn and execute a criminal, *but dine on him, after he is executed*, — it is, I say, as though the subject of such a government should migrate into one where cannibalism is not lawful, and where, therefore, though he should be condemned and executed for crime, it would be no part of the sentence or the ceremony that he should be eaten by his judges. He is out of cannibal jurisdiction.

The right of freedom is a natural right. It is a positive existence. It is a moral entity. Like the right to life, it pertains, by the law of nature and of God, to every human being. This moral right continues to exist until it is abolished. Some act abolishing this freedom, then, must be proved; it must be proved affirmatively, or else the fact of freedom remains. This is the solid and indestructible ground of the maxim, that slavery can exist only by positive law; that it is a *local* institution; that the right of freedom must first be abolished before slavery can exist.

2. My second position is this: *That a man's legal condition may be changed by a change in the government over him, while he remains in the same place, just as effectually as it can be changed by his removal to another place, and putting himself under another government.* The inhabitants of the North American colonies did not change their place of residence when they passed from under the government of Great Britain, and came under the government of the confederation. The Mexicans, inhabiting the then states of California and New Mexico, did not change their place of residence, when, on the thirtieth day of May last, they ceased to be citizens of the Mexican republic, and became citizens, or *quasi* citizens of the United States. Their political relations were changed, not by their removal from under the canopy of one government and placing themselves under the canopy of another government, but by the withdrawal of one government from over them, and by the extension to them of certain *political* rights and capacities under another government. Before this thirtieth day of May, they could have committed treason against Mexico, but not after it. Before it, they could not commit treason against the United States; but when they shall be citizens of the Union, they can. These vital changes in their relations are without any change in their residence. Within my recollection, an old gentleman died in Massachusetts,

who had lived in five different towns, but still remained where he was born, like one of the old oak trees on the homestead. The part of the original town where he was born had been set off and incorporated into a new town; and that part of the second town where he lived, into a third; and so on, until he died in the fifth town without any change of domicile. Now, this man lived under the jurisdiction and by-laws of five towns, as they were successively incorporated over him, just as much as though he had struck his tent five times, and placed himself, by successive migrations, under five different municipal jurisdictions.

A similar thing must have happened to thousands of our fellow-citizens of the Union. Some of them at first lived under a foreign government; then under one territorial government; then under another; and at last have become citizens of a state, without any change of domicile. Indeed, it would seem that nothing can be clearer than the proposition, whether regarded as a legal or a political one, that the laws and the jurisdiction may be changed over a man who continues to reside in the same place, just as effectually and as completely as a man may change the laws and jurisdiction over himself by removing to a different place. In many cases, the former works a more thorough change than the latter. The laws of Great Britain do not acknowledge the right of self-expatriation; while, at the same time, it is held, that the inhabitants of a foreign province, incorporated into the kingdom, change their allegiance without changing their residence.

3. My third proposition is this: *That the jurisdiction under which the inhabitants of what is now the District of Columbia lived, prior to the cession of the District by Maryland to the United States, was utterly and totally changed, at the moment of the cession, — at the moment when, according to the provisions of the constitution, they ceased to be citizens of the state of*

Maryland, and became citizens of the District of Columbia.

By the 17th paragraph, (Hickey's Constitution,) of the 8th section of the 1st article, it is provided that Congress shall have power "to exercise exclusive legislation in all cases whatsoever over such District, (not exceeding ten miles square,) as may, by cession of particular states, and the acceptance of Congress, become the seat of the government of the United States."

Congress, then, has the power of sole and exclusive legislation, "in all cases whatsoever," in regard to the District of Columbia. What is the meaning of the word "exclusive" in this connection? It cannot mean *absolute* and *uncontrolled;* for, if it did, it would make Congress as sovereign as the Russian autocrat. It means that no other government, no other body of men whatever, shall have concurrent power of legislation over the District; nor, indeed, any subordinate power, except what may be derived from Congress. Over every man who is a citizen of one of the United States, there are two jurisdictions, — the jurisdiction of the general government, and the jurisdiction of the state government. There are two governments that have the power to legislate for him; but there is only one power, — the Congress of the United States, — that can legislate for a citizen of the District of Columbia.

In *Kendall* vs. *The United States*, 12 Peters, 524, it is said, "There is in the District of Columbia no division of powers between the general and state governments. Congress has the entire control over the District, for every purpose of government."

So it has been held that a justice of the peace in the District of Columbia is an officer of the government of the United States, and is therefore exempt from militia duty. *Wise* vs. *Withers*, 3 Cranch, 331; 1 Cond. Rep. 552.

A citizen of the District of Columbia is not a citizen of any one of the United States. *Hebpurn et al.* vs. *Ellery*, 2 Cranch, 445 ; *Westcott's Lessee* vs. *Inhabitants* ——, Peters, C. C. R. 45.

Up to the time of the cession, the inhabitants of this District were under two jurisdictions—that of Maryland and that of Congress ; but after the cession, under that of Congress alone. Now, when the inhabitants of this District passed out of the jurisdiction of Maryland, and came under the exclusive jurisdiction of Congress, let us see what was the effect of such change of jurisdiction upon them.

In the act of Congress of 1790, c. 28, sect. 1, which was an act for establishing the seat of government of the United States, there is the following clause : " *Provided, nevertheless,* That the operation of the laws of the state [of Maryland] within such District shall not be affected by this acceptance, *until the time fixed for the removal of the government thereto, and until Congress shall otherwise by law provide.*"

Here, then, Congress *expressly* provided and contracted with the state of Maryland, that the laws of Maryland in this District should not be interfered with until the removal of the seat of government to this place ; and Congress likewise *impliedly* provided and contracted, that when the seat of government should be removed to this place, it would discharge the duty imposed upon it by the constitution of the United States, and would assume and exercise the " exclusive legislation" provided for in that instrument. This act of Congress was approved on the 16th of July, 1790.

By the Maryland laws of 1791, c. 45, sect. 2, that state ceded to the United States the territory which now constitutes the District of Columbia, and the words of the cession are these : " In full and absolute right, as well of soil as of person, residing or to reside thereon," &c. . . . provided that the jurisdiction of the laws of Maryland "shall not cease or determine *until Congress shall by law provide for the government thereof.*"

The state of the case, then, was simply this: 1. The constitution gave Congress power of "exclusive legislation" over such district as might be ceded for the seat of government. 2. Congress, by the act of 1790, above referred to, proposed to the state of Maryland to accept a portion of her territory for this purpose, but engaged not to interfere with her laws until after it had taken actual possession of the ceded territory. 3. Maryland accepted the proposition, rehearsing the condition in these words; namely, that "the laws of Maryland shall not cease or determine until Congress shall by law provide for the government thereof."

By the 6th section of the act of 1790, c. 28, Congress provided that it would remove to this District, and make this the seat of government, on the first Monday of December, 1800. It did so; and now its express duty under the constitution, and its implied promise to the state of Maryland, were to be fulfilled, by exercising "exclusive legislation" over this District.

In fulfilment of this duty and promise, Congress, on the 27th of February, 1801, by the act of 1801, c. 15, proceeded to legislate for the District of Columbia; and, in the first section of that act, it provided as follows: —

"*Be it enacted, &c.*, That the laws of the state of Virginia, as they now exist, shall be and continue in force in that part of the District of Columbia which was ceded by the said state to the United States, and by them accepted for the permanent seat of government; and that the laws of the state of Maryland, as they now exist, shall be and continue in force in that part of the said District which was ceded by that state to the United States, and by them accepted, as aforesaid."

By this act, then, Congress assumed to exercise, and did exercise, that exclusive legislation over the District of Columbia which had been provided for by the constitution.

That portion of the District which was ceded to Congress by Virginia, having been receded to that state by the act of Congress of July 9, 1846, (stat. 1846, c. 35,) all that relates to it may, for the purposes of this argument, be laid out of the question.

On the 27th day of February, 1801, then, the laws of Maryland, *as such*, were abrogated in this District. The legislative power of Congress was *de facto* exclusive. All legislative power previously possessed by Maryland over it, then ceased. The connection of Maryland with this District, as a part of its former territory, and occupied by its former citizens, was dissolved. It had no longer any more legislative power over the District than Maine or Georgia had. Historically, we may talk about the laws of Maryland, as they once existed here; but practically, and as a matter of strict law and fact, her laws were no longer known within the District. The laws which governed the people of this District after the 27th day of February, 1801, were the laws of Congress, and not the laws of Maryland.

To show that this part of the District passed out from under the government of Maryland, and came under the government of the United States, I refer to *Reilly, appellant*, vs. *Lamar et al.*, 2 Cranch, 344; 1 Cond. Rep. 322, where it is said, "By the separation of the District of Columbia from the State of Maryland, the residents in that part of Maryland which became a part of the District, ceased to be citizens of the state." It was held, in that case, that a citizen of the District of Columbia could not be discharged by the insolvent law of Maryland.

A citizen of the District of Columbia cannot maintain an action in the circuit court of the United States out of the District, he not being a citizen of the state within the meaning of the provision of the law of the United States regulating the jurisdiction of the courts of the United States. *Hepburn et al.* vs. *Ellzey*, 2 Cranch, 445; 1 Cond. Rep. 444. See also *Loughborough* vs. *Blake*, 5 Wheat. 317, and *Levy Court of Washington* vs. *Ringgold*, 5 Peters, 451.

4. The next point of inquiry is, *What is the legal force and effect, upon the subject of slavery, of the act of Congress of* 1801, *before cited?* Its words are, "That the laws of the state of Maryland, as they now exist, shall be continued in force in that part of said District which was ceded by that state to the United States," &c. And here, I acknowledge that the operation of this clause is precisely the same as though Congress had transcribed all the Maryland laws, word for word, and letter for letter, into its own statute book, with the clause prefixed, "Be it enacted by the Senate and House of Representatives of the United States of America in Congress assembled," and the President of the United States had affixed his signature thereto. I acknowledge further, that the laws of Maryland had legalized slavery within the state of Maryland, and had defined what classes of persons might be held as slaves therein.

But it by no means follows, because Congress proposed to reënact, in terms, for this District, all the laws of Maryland, that, therefore, it did reënact them. It does not follow, that because two legislatures use the same words, that the words must necessarily have the same effect. It makes all the difference in the world, whether words are used by one possessed of power, or by one devoid of power. Congress might pass a law in precisely the same words as those used by the Parliament of Great Britain, and yet the law of Congress be invalid and inoperative, while the act of Parliament would be valid and binding. We have a written constitution; Great Britain has no written constitution. The British Parliament, on many subjects, has an ampler jurisdiction than the American Congress. The law of Congress might be unconstitutional and void, while that of the British Parliament, framed in precisely the same language, might be constitutional and binding.

So the law of Maryland might be valid under the constitution of Maryland, and, therefore, binding upon the citizens of Maryland; while the law of Congress, though framed in precisely the same words, would be repugnant to the constitution of the United States, and therefore have no validity.

Now this is precisely the case before us. Congress, in attempting to reënact the Maryland laws, to uphold slavery in this District, transcended the limits of its constitutional power. It acted unconstitutionally. It acted in plain contravention of some of the plainest and most obvious principles consecrated by the constitution. If so, no one will dispute that its act is void. I do not deny, then, that Congress used words of sufficient amplitude to cover slavery; but what I deny is, that it had any power to give legal force to those words.

5. My next proposition, therefore, is this: That *as Congress can do nothing excepting what it is empowered to do by the constitution, and as the constitution does not empower it to establish slavery here, it cannot establish slavery here, nor continue it.*

Where is there any *express* power given to Congress by the constitution to establish slavery? Where is the article, section, or clause? I demand to have the title shown. Thousands of human beings are not to be robbed of all their dearest rights, and they and their children, forever, by strained constitutions, or apocryphal authority, doomed to bondage. Will those who say that Congress cannot establish a banking institution by construction, nor aid internal improvements, nor enact a tariff, — will they say that Congress can make a man a slave, and all his posterity slaves, by construction ?

Nor can any power to establish slavery be deduced from the 18th clause of the 8th section of the 1st article of the constitution, which gives Congress power "to make all laws which shall be necessary and proper for carrying into execution" the powers that are granted.

What power is granted to Congress, for the exercise of which the establishment of slavery in this District is a necessary means or a preliminary ? Congress has power to lay and collect taxes ; to borrow money ; to regulate commerce ; to establish uniform rules of naturalization ; to coin money ; to punish counterfeiters ; to establish post offices and post roads ; to promote the progress of science and the arts ; to establish courts ; to define and punish piracies on the high seas ; to declare war ; to raise and support armies ; to provide and maintain a navy ; to organize and maintain a militia ; and so forth, and so forth. But to what one of all these powers is the power to establish slavery in the District of Columbia a necessary incident ? If slavery in the District of Columbia were to cease to-day, could not the government continue to exercise every function which it has heretofore exercised ? If so, then the existence of slavery in this District is not "necessary" to the exercise of any of the expressly granted powers. I call upon any gentleman to name any one power of this government which cannot be exercised, which must necessarily cease, if slavery should cease to be, in this District of Columbia ? "I pause for a reply."

Well, then, if a power to establish slavery in this District is not among the granted powers, and if it is not necessary for the exercise of any one of the granted powers, then it is — no where ; — it does not exist at all. No power of Congress, then, exists, either for the creation or for the continuance of slavery in this District; and all the legislation of Congress upon this subject is beyond or against the constitution.

Let me illustrate this in another way. Suppose there had been a religious establishment in Maryland at the time of the cession; suppose, under the auspices of Lord Baltimore, the Catholic religion had been established as the religion of the state; and that, in order to punish heresy and secure conformity to the religion of the state, an inquisition had been founded, and that the seat of that inquisition had been within the limits of the District of Columbia, at the time of the cession; could Congress, in the absence of all express or implied authority on the subject of establishing a state religion, have upheld the Catholic religion here, and appointed the officers of the inquisition to administer it? The idea is abhorrent to the whole spirit of the constitution. But Congress had as much power to establish a national religion here, in the absence of all express or implied authority to do so, as to establish slavery here.

Congress, then, does not and cannot legalize slavery in this District. It found slavery in existence in the states; and it does not abolish it, or interfere with it, because it has no power of "exclusive legislation" in them. But Congress has as much right to go into any state and abolish slavery there, as any state, even Virginia or Maryland, has to come into this District with its laws and establish slavery here. I suppose that no jurist will contend that Congress could have passed the act of 1793, for the recapture of fugitive slaves, had it not been for the third clause in the second section of the fourth article of the constitution, which provides for the redelivery of a fugitive slave, on the claim of his master. By this article in the constitution, the case of *fugitive* slaves only is provided for. If a master voluntarily carries his slave into a free state, and the slave departs from his possession, he cannot reclaim him. Why not? Why cannot Congress pass a law, that if a man takes a dozen slaves to Boston, and they there see fit to strike for wages, and to leave his possession because their terms are not complied with, — why is it, I ask, that Congress cannot pass a law authorizing their seizure and delivery into the master's hands? The reason is, that the constitution has conferred upon Congress no such express power, nor is any such power implied as being necessary to the exercise of any power that is expressed. And if Congress cannot so much as restore a slave to a master, who has voluntarily carried him into a free state, how can it continue slavery in this District, after Maryland has ceded it to this government, whose fundamental, organic law gives it no power to create or continue slavery here?

Suppose Maryland had ceded her share of the District to Massachusetts, would not every slave in it have been instantaneously free by the constitution of Massachusetts? They would have been transferred to a free jurisdiction, — just as much as an individual owner of a slave transfers him to a free jurisdiction, when he voluntarily takes him to the north. The legal existence of slavery was annulled in this District when Congress exercised its "exclusive" power over it, just as much as the debtor's right to be discharged under the Maryland bankrupt law was annulled.

But I go further than this; and I say that the constitution not only does not empower Congress to establish or continue slavery in this District, but again and again, by the strongest implications possible, it prohibits the exercise of such a power.

In regard to this whole matter of slavery, the constitution touches the subject with an averted face. The abhorred word "*slave*" is nowhere mentioned in it. The constitution is ashamed to utter such a name. The country, coming fresh from that baptism of fire, — the American Revolution, — would not profane its lips with this unhallowed word. Hence, circumlocution is resorted to. It seeks to escape a guilty confession. Like a culprit, in whom some love of character still survives, it speaks of its offence without calling it by name. It uses the reputable and honorable word "persons," instead of the accursed word "slaves." As the Tyrian queen, about to perpetrate a deed which would consign her character to infamy, called it by the sacred name of "marriage," and committed it, —

"*Hoc prætexit nomine culpam ;*"

so the constitution, about to recognize the most guilty and cruel of all relations between man and man, sought to avert its eyes from the act, and to pacify the remonstrances of conscience against every participation in the crime, by hiding the deed under a reputable word.

But let us look to the prohibitions of the constitution; for I maintain that there is not only no power, express or implied, in the constitution authorizing Congress to create or continue slavery in this District, but that it is debarred and prohibited from doing so, again and again.

I suppose no one will deny that the positive prohibitions, against the exercise of certain enumerated powers, apply to Congress, when legislating for this District, just as much as when legislating for the union at large. This doctrine has recently been strongly asserted by Mr. Calhoun in the Senate of the United States; and, as I would gladly produce conviction in southern minds, I make use of this southern authority. He affirms that Congress, in legislating for the territories, "is subject to many and important restrictions and conditions, of which some are expressed and others implied. Among the former may be classed all the general and absolute prohibitions of the constitution; that is, all those which prohibit the exercise of certain powers under any circumstances. In this class is included the prohibition of granting titles of nobility; passing *ex post facto* laws and bills of attainder; the suspension of the writ of *habeas corpus*, except in certain cases; making laws respecting the establishment of religion, or its free exercise, and every other of like description."

Will any man say that Congress can pass an *ex post facto* law for this District, and defend itself by referring to its power of "exclusive legislation" over it? Can Congress pass a bill of attainder corrupting the blood of an inhabitant of this District, or repeal or suspend at any time his right to a writ of *habeas corpus*, or establish a religion here, or interdict the free exercise thereof? No jurist, no statesman, will pretend it.

But there is another prohibition in the constitution every whit as full and explicit as any of these. The fifth article of amendment declares that "no person shall be deprived of life, liberty, or property, without due process of law."

Here the constitution uses the word "person,"—the most comprehensive word it could find. "No **PERSON** shall be deprived of life, liberty, or property, without due process of law." Now, what does this word "person" mean? Or who, under the constitution, is such a "person" as cannot be deprived of life, liberty, or property, by virtue of an act of Congress, *without due process of law?* Let us take our definition of the word "*person*" from the constitution itself. "No *person* shall be a representative, who shall not have attained the age of twenty-five years," &c., (see 2d clause of the 2d section of the 1st article.) "Representatives and direct taxes shall be apportioned among the several states which may be included within this union, according to their respective numbers, which shall be determined by adding to the whole number of free *persons*, including those bound to service for a term of years, and excluding Indians not taxed, three fifths of all other *persons*." (3d clause of the same section.) "No *person* shall be a senator who shall not have attained the age of thirty years," &c. (1st art., 3d section, 3d clause.) "No *person* shall be convicted [of an impeachable offence, by the Senate] without the concurrence of two thirds." (1st art., 3d section, 6th clause.) "No *person* holding any office under the United States, shall be a member of either House, during his continuance in office." (1st art., 6th section, 2d clause.) "The migration or importation of such *persons* as any of the states now existing shall think proper to admit, shall not be prohibited," — "but a tax, or duty, may be imposed on such importation, not exceeding ten dollars for each *person*," &c. (1st art., 9th section, 1st clause.) "No *person* holding any office of profit or trust," "shall accept any present," &c. (1st art., 9th section, 8th clause.) "No *person* holding an office of trust or profit under the United States, shall be appointed an elector." (2d art., 1st section, 2d clause.) "The electors shall meet in their respective states and vote by ballot for two *persons*," &c. "The *person* having the greatest number of votes shall be the President," &c. "If no *person* have a majority," &c. "In every case, after the choice of the President, the *person* having the greatest number of votes of the electors, shall be Vice President." (2d art., 1st section, 2d clause.*) "No *person* except a natural born citizen," &c., "shall be eligible to the office of President; neither shall any *person* be eligible to that office, who shall not have attained the age of

* This clause in the constitution is annulled; but for all purposes of determining the true interpretation of words, it is as good as ever.

thirty-five years," &c. "No *person* shall be convicted of treason, unless on the testimony of two witnesses," &c. (3d art., 3d sect., 3d clause.) "A *person* charged in any state with treason," &c. (4th art., 2d section, 2d clause.) "No *person* held to service or labor," &c. (4th art., 2d section, 3d clause.)

Now, it will be seen from all this, that the word "*person*" is used in the constitution in the most comprehensive sense. It embraces Indians, if taxed; it embraces natives of Africa; it embraces apprentices and slaves, or those held to service or labor; and it embraces every citizen, from the humblest to the highest, from the most true to the most treasonable. It embraces all, from the slave to the President of the United States. And after having used the word to embrace all these classes and descriptions of men, it proceeds to say, in an amendment, that "*no* PERSON *shall be deprived of life, liberty, or property, without due process of law.*" (*Amendment, Article* 5.)

The law of Maryland ceded this District to Congress, "in full and absolute right, as well of soil as of *person*, residing, or to reside therein."

Now Congress, in attempting to legalize slavery in the District of Columbia, has provided in terms, by its adoption of the Maryland laws, that one man may hold another man in bondage in this District, "WITHOUT DUE PROCESS OF LAW," and indeed without any process of law; may hold him in bondage from his birth; may beget him, and still hold him and his posterity in bondage. "Process of law" means legal proceedings and a jury trial. It is a phrase that does not pertain to the legislature, but to the courts. It means the institution of a suit in civil matters; the finding of an indictment, or an information in criminal ones; the issuing of subpœnas for witnesses, &c., in both. (See *Art.* 6 *of Amendments to the Constitution.*)

Now, a slave is a *person* deprived of his liberty and

property, without any process of law. There has been no "due" process of law to reduce him to this miserable condition; there has been no process of law at all. A slave, therefore, in this District, is deprived of his liberty and property, in pursuance of the laws of Congress, without *any* legal process whatever, and therefore in flagrant contradiction of the fifth article of the Amendments to the Constitution of the United States. Hence, the act of Congress, purporting to continue the Maryland laws respecting slavery in this District, was, and is, and forever must be, until the constitution is altered, null and void.

There is a striking historical fact in regard to the phraseology of this fifth article of amendment. Its substance was proposed by several states. Virginia proposed it in the following words: "No *freeman* ought to be taken, imprisoned, or disseized of his freehold liberties, privileges, or franchises, or outlawed or exiled, or in any manner destroyed or deprived of his life, liberty, or property, but by the law of the land." (See 3 *Elliot's Debates*, 593—*Proceedings of June* 27, 1788. *Also*, 4 *Elliot's Debates*, 216, *for the same amendment, as proposed by the State of New York.*)

The Virginia amendment used the word "freeman." It proposed that no "freeman" should be deprived, &c. The New York amendment used the word "*person.*" And the amendment was adopted and ratified, almost in the words of the New York phraseology. The word *person* was chosen, and therefore Congress has no constitutional power to deprive of life, liberty, or property, *without due process of law*, any being embraced in the definition of that word. By its own selection of words it is debarred not merely from depriving a "*freeman*," but from depriving a "*person*" of this right.

When Congress attempted to legalize and perpetuate slavery in this District, it violated the fourth article of the Amendments, which declares "the right of the people to be *secure* in their persons, houses, papers, and effects, against unreasonable searches and seizures." If Congress cannot authorize domiciliary searches and seizures against a single individual, can it degrade a whole race of men to the condition of slaves, and then say that *because they are slaves*, they shall not be "secure;" but shall be at the mercy of any alleged master, in regard to their persons, — to be commanded and restrained, to be bought and sold? If Congress cannot authorize searches and seizures of houses, papers, and effects, can it get round the constitution, by saying we will create a class of persons who shall have no power of owning any houses, papers, or effects, to be searched or seized?

Again; Congress shall pass "no bill of attainder." What is a bill of attainder? It is a bill that works corruption of blood. It disfranchises its object. It takes away from him the common privileges of a citizen. It makes a man incapable of acquiring, inheriting, or transmitting property; incapable of holding office, or acting as attorney for others; and it shuts the door of the courts against him. These disabling consequences may descend to a man's children after him, though this is not necessary. Now, to pass such a bill is a thing which Congress cannot do. But when Congress undertook to legalize slavery in this District, it undertook to do all this, and worse than all this. It attainted, not individuals merely, but a whole race. A slave is an outlaw; that is, he cannot make a contract; he cannot prosecute and defend in court; property cannot be acquired by him, or devised to him, or transmitted through him. A white man may give his testimony against him, but he cannot give his testimony against a white man. He is despoiled of his *liberam legem*, — his birthright. He cannot own the food or clothes he has earned. What is his, is his master's.

And this corruption of blood, which the law of slavery works, does not stop with the first, nor with the second generation, — not with the tenth nor the ten thousandth; but by the theory of the law, goes on forever. Bills of attainder, during the history of the worst periods of the world, have applied to individuals only, or at most to a family. But here, Congress, in defiance of the constitution, has undertaken to establish a degraded caste in society, and to perpetuate it through all generations. Now, can any reasonable man for a moment suppose that the constitution meant to debar Congress from passing acts of attainder against individuals, but to permit it to pass wholesale, sweeping laws, working disfranchisement of an entire race, and entailing degradation forever?

Let us look at another general prohibition of the constitution: "No title of nobility shall be granted by the United States." (art. 1, § 9, clause 8.) "The distinction of rank and honors," says Blackstone, "is necessary in every well-governed state, in order to reward such as are eminent for their services to the public." But the framers of the constitution did not think so; the people of the United States did not think so; and therefore they incorporated a provision into their organic law that "no title of nobility should be granted." But it matters not whether the favored individual is called "Marquess" or "Master." If he is invested by the government with a monopoly of rights and privileges, in virtue of his title and its legal incidents, without any corresponding civil duties, he belongs to an order of nobility, — he is a nobleman. Mr. McDuffie defends the institution of slavery, on the ground that it establishes the highest of all ranks and the broadest of all distinctions between men. He says no nation has yet existed which has not in some form created the distinction of classes, — such as patrician and plebeian, or citizen and helot, or lord and commoner, — and that the institution of slavery stands here instead of these orders, and supersedes them all, by being equivalent to them all. Now, is it not inconceivable that the constitution should interdict the bestowment of special favors to distinguished individuals for meritorious services, and yet should authorize Congress to confer the highest of all earthly prerogatives, — the prerogative over property, liberty, and volition itself, upon one class of men over another class of men? Yet if Congress can create or legalize slavery, it can establish the worst order of nobility that ever existed. It can give to one class of men the power to own and to control, to punish and to despoil another class; to sell father, mother, wife, and children, into bondage. To prohibit Congress from doing one of these things, and to permit it to do the other, is straining at a gnat and swallowing a camel, — a whole caravan of camels!

But the same clause in the constitution which gives Congress the power of exclusive legislation over this District, also empowers it "to exercise like authority over all places purchased by the consent of the legislature of the state, in which the same shall be, for the erection of forts, magazines, arsenals, dock-yards, and other needful buildings." If, then, Congress has any constitutional power to legalize slavery in this District, it has the same power to legalize it, (that is, to create it,) in all places in the state of Massachusetts, or New York, or any other, where it may have obtained territory from a state for a fort, magazine, arsenal, dock-yard, or other needful building. Where it has obtained land in the middle of a city, — Philadelphia, New York, Boston, or Chicago, — for a custom-house, it may create slavery there. The power to do this is conferred in precisely the same words as the power by which it has been held that slavery can be established in the District of Columbia.

And now I will occupy the few minutes that are left me, in considering what seems to me the only plausible argument that can be urged in favor of the constitutionality of slavery in this District.

It may be said, that when a territory is obtained by one nation from another, whether by conquest or by treaty, the laws which governed the inhabitants at the time of the conquest or cession, remain in force until they are abrogated by the laws of the conquering or purchasing power. For this principle, the authority of Lord Mansfield, in the case of *Campbell* v. *Hall*, 1 Cowper, 208, may be cited. The decision of our own courts are to the same effect. (See *United States, appellant*, vs. *Juan Percheman*, 2 Gallison's Reports, 501 ; *Johnson* vs. *McIntosh*, 7 Peters, 51 ; 8 Wheat. 543.) I do not dispute the authority of this case. But it does not touch the question I am arguing ; or, so far as it bears upon it at all, it confirms the views I would enforce. The principle is, that the existing laws remain in force *until* they are abrogated. I agree to this. But in the case of the District of Columbia, there was a special agreement between Maryland and the United States, that as soon as the United States should legislate for the District, the laws of Maryland, *as such*, should cease to be operative here. On the 27th day of February, 1801, therefore, all the rights which the citizens of this District possessed, they possessed under the law of Congress, and not under the law of Maryland. On the day preceding, a citizen could have voted for governor or other state officers of Maryland ; but on the day following, he could no longer vote for any such officer. On the day preceding, he could have voted for electors of President and Vice President of the United States ; but on the day following, he was bereft of all such right of the elective franchise, and must accept such officers and legislators as the rest of the country might choose to elect for him. On the day preceding, he might, in the character of an insolvent debtor, have been discharged under the insolvent laws of Maryland; but on the day following, he could no longer be so discharged. On the day preceding, he might have been required, though a justice of the peace of the State of Maryland, to perform militia duty; but on the day following, if commissioned as a justice of the peace of the District of Columbia, he could not be compelled to perform militia duty, because he would, in such case, be an officer of the United States. On the day preceding, he might have sued in the circuit court of the United States, as being a citizen of Maryland; but, on the day following, he could not so sue, because he had ceased to be a citizen of a state. Thus the change of jurisdiction over him deprived him of some privileges, and relieved him from some burdens. It deprived him of these privileges, and relieved him from these burdens, notwithstanding the act of Congress had said, in unambiguous words, "the laws of the State of Maryland, AS THEY NOW EXIST, *shall be and continue in force* in that part of the said District which was ceded by that state to the United States." But the most momentous change which was wrought by the transfer of the citizen from the jurisdiction of Maryland to the jurisdiction of the United States, was that which made it impossible for him any longer to hold a slave. Under the laws of Maryland, he might have held his slave, for her statutes had legalized slavery; but under the constitution of the United States, he could not hold a slave; for that constitution had given Congress no power to legalize slavery in this District, and had gone so far as to make prohibitions against it. His right to hold slaves then expired, or fell, like his right to vote for United States' officers, or for state officers, or his right to be discharged under the Maryland insolvent law, or his right to sue in certain courts, &c., &c.

One point more, sir, and I have done. Why, says my opponent, did not the right to hold slaves continue after the change of jurisdiction, as well as the right to hold horses? For the plainest of all reasons, I answer: for the reason that a horse is *property* by the universal consent of mankind, by the recognition of every civilized court in Christendom, without any positive law declaring it to be the subject of ownership. But a *man* is not property, without positive law; without a law declaring him to be the subject of ownership. There was such a positive law in Maryland; but Congress, for want of constitutional authority, could not enact, revive, or continue it. And such I verily believe would have been the decision of the Supreme Court of the United States, had the question been carried before them immediately subsequent to the act of 1801. But now, as slavery has existed practically in this District for half a century, it is proper to pass a law abolishing it. It is better, under the present circumstances, that slavery should be abolished here by a law of Congress, than by the decision of a court; because Congress can provide an indemnity for the owners, and let the slaves go free. But should it be abolished by a legal adjudication, every slave would be hurried away to the south, and sold, he and his descendants, into perpetual bondage.

In justice, then, to the north, which ought not to bear the opprobrium of slavery in this capital of the nation; in justice to the slaves who are here held in bondage against legal, as well as natural right; and, in more than justice to the masters, whose alleged claims I am willing, under all the circumstances, to satisfy, let a law be forthwith passed for ascertaining and paying the market value of the slaves, and for repealing all laws which uphold slavery in this District.

SPEECH

Delivered in the United States House of Representatives, February 15, 1850, on the Subject of Slavery in the Territories, and the Consequences of a Dissolution of the Union.

Mr. Chairman ;

Ever since the organization of this House, — before its organization, and even in a preliminary caucus that preceded the commencement of the session, southern gentlemen have pressed the cause, not only of human slavery, but of slavery extension, upon us. From motives of forbearance, and not from any question as to our rights, we of the north have maintained an unbroken silence. The time has surely come when the voice of freedom should find an utterance. Would to God that on the present occasion it might find an abler defender than myself, although if my ability to defend it were equal to the love I bear it, it could ask no stronger champion.

I wish to premise a few words respecting the propriety and true significance of some of the epithets by which the parties to this discussion are characterized. The term "Free Soiler" is perpetually used upon this floor as a term of ignominy and reproach ; yet I maintain that in its original and legitimate sense, as denoting an advocate of the doctrine that all our territorial possessions should be consecrated to freedom, there is no language that can supply a more honorable appellation. It expresses a determination on the part of its disciples to keep free the territory that is now free ; to stand upon its frontiers as the cherubim stood at the gates of Paradise, with a flaming sword to turn every way, to keep the sin of slavery from crossing its borders. If, in any instance, the original advocates of Free Soil have abandoned their integrity, and have courted allies who had no sympathy with their principles, but were only eager to join them in a struggle for mere political ascendency, then, in my judgment, they have lost infinitely more in moral power than they have gained in numbers. They have ceased to be genuine and single-hearted Free Soilers, whom I love, and have become partisans, whom I condemn. For myself, I will engage in any honorable measure most likely to secure freedom to the new territories. I will resist any and every measure that proposes to abandon them to slavery. The epithet "Free Soiler," therefore, when rightly understood and correctly applied, implies both political and moral worth; and I covet the honor of its application to myself. But what does its opposite mean? What does the term "Slave Soiler" signify? It signifies one who desires and designs that all soil should be made to bear slaves. Its dreadful significancy is, that, after Magna Charta and the Petition of Right, in Great Britain, and after the Declaration of Independence, in this country, we should cast aside with scorn, not only the teachings of Christianity, but the clearest principles of natural religion and of natural law, and should retrograde from our boasted civilization, into the Dark Ages, — ay, into periods that the dark ages might have called dark. It means that this *Republic*, as we call it, formed to establish freedom, should enlist in a crusade against freedom.

And again; those of us at the north who resist slavery extension, who mean to withstand its spread beyond the limits where it now exists, are denounced as Abolitionists. This epithet is applied to us as a term of reproach and obloquy; as a brand and stigma upon our characters and principles. No distinction is made between those few individuals among us who desire to abolish the constitution of the United States, and that great body of the people, who, while their allegiance to this constitution is unshaken, mean also to maintain their allegiance to truth and to duty, in withstanding the hitherto onward march of slavery. Among the latter class, Mr. Collamer, the postmaster-general, is called an Abolitionist. Mr. John Quincy Adams was denounced as an arch-Abolitionist. Every man who advocates the Jefferson proviso, against the spread of slavery, is so called; and if an unspeakable abhorrence of this institution, and the belief that it is the second greatest enormity which the oppressor, in his power, ever committed against the oppressed, in his weakness, — being inferior only to that ecclesiastical domination which has trampled upon the religious freedom of man, — I say, if this abhorrence of slavery, and this belief in its criminality, entitle a man to be denominated an Abolitionist, then I rejoice in my unquestionable right to the name.

In my apprehension, sir, before we can decide upon the honor or the infamy of the term "Abolitionist," we must know what things they are which he proposes to abolish. We of the north, you say, are Abolitionists; but abolitionists of what? Are we abolitionists of the inalienable, indefeasible, indestructible rights of man? Are we abolitionists of knowledge, abolitionists of virtue, of education, and of human culture? Do we seek to abolish the glorious moral and intellectual attributes which God has given to his children, and thus, as far as it lies in our power, make the facts of slavery conform to the law of slavery, by obliterating the distinction between a man and a beast?

Do our laws and our institutions seek to blot out and abolish the image of God in the human soul? Do we abolish the marriage covenant; and instead of saying, with the apostle, that wives shall submit themselves to their husbands, command them to submit themselves to any body, and to their master as husband over all? Do we ruthlessly tear asunder the sacred ties of affection by which God has bound the parent to the child and the child to the parent? Do we seek to abolish all those noble instincts of the human soul, by which it yearns for improvement and progress; and do we quench its sublime aspirations after knowledge and virtue? A stranger would suppose, from hearing the epithets of contumely that are heaped upon us, that we were abolitionists of all truth, purity, knowledge, improvement, civilization, happiness, and holiness. On this subject, perversion of language and of idea has been reduced to a system, and the falsehoods of our calumniators exclude truth with the exactness of a science.

But if the word "Abolitionist" is to be used in a reproachful and contumelious sense, does it not more properly belong to those who would extend a system which in its very nature abolishes freedom, justice, equity, and a sense of human brotherhood? Does it not belong to those who would abolish not only all social and political, but all natural rights; who would abolish "liberty and the pursuit of happiness;" who would close up all the avenues to knowledge; who would render freedom of thought and liberty of conscience impossible, by crushing out the faculties by which alone we can think and decide; who would rob a fellow-man of his parental rights, and innocent children of the tenderness and joys of a filial love; who would introduce a foul concubinage in place of the institution of marriage, and who would remorselessly trample upon all the tenderest and holiest affections which the human soul is capable of feeling? After Mr. Jefferson, in the Declaration of Independence, had enumerated a few oppressive deeds of the British king towards his American colonists, he denominated him "a prince whose character was marked by every act that could define a tyrant." There are now as many slaves in this country as there were colonists in 1776. Compare the condition of these three million slaves with the condition of the three million colonists. The conduct of that sovereign who was denounced before earth and heaven as having committed all the atrocities that could "define a tyrant," was mercy and loving-kindness compared with the wrongs and privations of three millions of our fellow-beings, now existing among us. If the word "Abolitionist," then, is to be used in a reproachful sense, let it be applied to those who, in the middle of the nineteenth century, and in defiance of all the lights of the age, would extend the horrors of an institution which, by one all-comprehending crime towards a helpless race, makes it impossible to commit any new crime against them, — unless it be to enlarge the area of their bondage, and to multiply the number of their victims.

If we are abolitionists, then, we are abolitionists of human bondage; while those who oppose us are abolitionists of human liberty. We would prevent the extension of one of the greatest wrongs that man ever suffered upon earth; they would carry bodily chains and mental chains, — chains in a literal and chains in a figurative sense, — into realms where even the half-civilized descendants of the Spaniard and the Indian have silenced their clanking. We would avert the impending night of ignorance and superstition; they would abolish the glorious liberty wherewith God maketh his children free. In using this word, therefore, to calumniate us, they put darkness for light, and light for darkness; good for evil, and evil for good.

The constitutional right of Congress to legislate for the territories is still debated. Having presented my views on this subject before, I shall now treat it with brevity. In a speech, by General Cass, which has lately been published, that distinguished senator, in order to prove that Congress has no power to legislate on the subject of slavery in the territories, has attempted to prove that it has no right to legislate for the territories at all. I refer to the senator from Michigan, because he now stands before the country in the twofold character of being the head of the Democratic party, which goes for the "*largest liberty*," and also of the extreme pro-slavery party, which goes for the *largest bondage*. He would sever all diplomatic relations between this country and Austria, because she has robbed the Hungarians of *a part* of their liberties, while he is drawing closer the political ties which bind him to the south, which has despoiled three millions of the African race of *all* their liberties, and is now intent on propagating other millions for new despoliations. He claims, as the great bequest of the barons of Runnymede, that the inhabitants of the territories, under all circumstances of infancy, or poverty, or weakness, shall have the sole and exclusive right of governing themselves, when the practical result of this doctrine, so nicely timed, would be, that one part of those inhabitants would be crowned with power like so many King Johns, to lord it over their vassals. Under the name of liberty, he enters a path that terminates in bondage. Southern gentlemen had all admitted the power of Congress to legislate for the territories, though they denied the special inference, deducible from the general power, that they could legislate to prohibit slavery in them. But, seeing that the right to legislate on the subject of slavery flows irresistibly from the right to legislate on all other subjects, because no rule of interpretation, which concedes the power to make laws respecting political franchises, courts, crimes, officers, and the militia, can stop short at the subject of slavery; — seeing all this, General

Cass denies both inference and premises, *and places the general government in the relation of a foreign power to the territories which it owns*, and of which it possesses the acknowledged sovereignty. He reminds one of the man who denied the existence of future punishment, and, when pressed with arguments drawn from the deserts of men, and from the justice of God, he suddenly arrested his antagonist by denying the existence of a God!

When some immensely long speech made in the British House of Commons, was spoken of before Sheridan as being *luminous*, he expressed both a negative and an affirmative opinion respecting it, in a single word, by replying that it was *vo*-luminous. General Cass, in a speech that fills more than nineteen columns in the Washington *Union*, has reviewed the decisions of all the judges of the Supreme Court who have ever expressed any opinion on the subject of congressional power over territorial legislation; he has commented upon the views of all the jurists who have written upon it, and of most of the speakers in both Houses of Congress who have discussed it; he has surveyed the course of administration of all the Presidents we have ever had; and has come to the clear conclusion that all of them, — judges, jurists, legislators, and presidents, — have systematically violated the constitution of the United States, or commended its violation, on every practicable occasion for the last sixty years.

Omitting the hundred ways in which the absurdity of this conclusion can be exposed, let me subject it to one practical test. We have acquired territory from Mexico. General Cass voted to ratify the treaty of cession. Measures have been instituted for the formation of three separate governments in this Territory, — those of California, Deseret, [Utah,] and New Mexico. The boundaries marked out by California and Deseret overlay each other to the amount of thousands of square miles. If they have the exclusive right of self-government, as General Cass declares, and Congress none, then they must settle this question of boundary themselves. They may declare war against each other, make alliances with foreign powers, equip armies, build fleets ; while Congress can do nothing within their limits but — sell land.

But what renders the argument of General Cass still more extraordinary is the fact, that, according to his own doctrine, he has spent the greater part of his political life in violating the constitution, while constantly repeating his oath to support it. As marshal of Ohio, as governor of Michigan, as Indian agent, he has appointed officers and magistrates, and executed laws, when, according to his own showing, he was a mere interloper and usurper; he has met territorial legislatures, which had no more right to assemble than a mob; he has doubtless imprisoned, if not executed many alleged offenders, who had as good a legal right to execute or to imprison him ; and he has received salaries for more than twenty years, to which the khan of Tartary was as much entitled as he. Now, if he will refund the salaries he has unconstitutionally received ; make reparation for the penalties or forfeitures he has wrongfully extorted ; show some signs of contrition for the men whom he has unlawfully imprisoned or hung, it will remove the suspicions of many minds, in regard to the sincerity, if not the soundness, of his argument.

I mention these facts from no personal feelings in regard to the senator from Michigan ; but only to show to what desperate extremities men are driven in order to defend the right of spreading slavery from the Atlantic to the Pacific ocean ; and because this is the last reading of the constitution which has been invented for the purpose.

Since the last session of Congress, the condition of

a part of this territory has greatly changed. The unexampled velocity with which a living stream of men has poured into it within the last twelve months, has reversed its condition and decided its destiny. In other countries, *individuals* seek their fortunes by changing their residence. Under the vehement action of our enterprise, *cities* migrate. The new residents of California have framed a constitution, have applied for admission into this Union, and their application is now pending before us. Of their own accord, they have excluded slavery from their borders by their fundamental law. Until the discovery of gold in that country, and until all incredulity in regard to that remarkable fact had been overcome, it was confidently anticipated at the south, and intensely feared at the north, that the whole region would be overrun with slaveholders and with slaves. As far back as 1842, Mr. Wise, of Virginia, the administration leader in the House of Representatives, boldly declared that "*slavery should pour itself abroad without restraint, and find no limit but the Southern Ocean.*" The war with Mexico was waged for the twofold purpose of robbing that republic of its territory, and then robbing that territory of its freedom. Congressional orators and the southern press avowed that the object of acquiring territory was to extend the "divine institution." I could quote pages in proof of this assertion. The north had no hope, the south had no fear, if the territories were left without control, but that they would first be filled with slaveholders, and would then incorporate slavery into their organic law. While these prospects continued, the south insisted that the territories should be left untrammelled. Distinguished men in this House, Mr. Calhoun and other senators, the government organ, which was supposed to express the views of President Polk and his cabinet, all proclaimed that the territories should be left free to institute such government as they might choose.* But since California has formed a *free* constitution, what a sudden change has taken place in the convictions of

* In February, 1847, Mr. Calhoun offered a series of resolutions in the Senate of the United States, among which was the following: —

" *Resolved,* That it is a fundamental principle in our political creed, that a people, in forming a constitution, have the unconditional right to form and adopt the government which they may think best calculated to secure their liberty, prosperity and happiness; and, in conformity thereto, no other condition is imposed by the Federal Constitution on a state, in order to be admitted into this Union, except that its constitution shall be "republican;" and that the imposition of any other by Congress would not only be in violation of the constitution, but in direct conflict with the principle on which our political system rests."

In sustaining these resolutions, he said, —

" Sir, I hold it to be a fundamental principle of our political system that the people have a right to establish what government they may think proper for themselves; that every state ABOUT to become a member of this Union has a right to FORM ITS OWN GOVERNMENT AS IT PLEASES; and that, in order to be admitted, there is but one qualification, and that is, that the government shall be republican. There is no express provision to that effect, but it results from that important section which guaranties to every state in this Union a republican form of government."

Mr. Senator Downs, of Louisiana, offered the following resolution: —

Resolved, That it is competent and expedient, and not inconsistent with the practice of the government in some cases, to admit California, or such portion of it as Congress may deem proper, immediately into the Union, on an equal footing with the other states; and that the committee on ——— be instructed to report a bill for that purpose, for that portion of California which lies west of the summit of the Sierra Neveda mountains."

The doctrine of these resolutions was fully indorsed by the Washington *Union*, speaking, doubtless, (for it never spoke any thing else,) the sentiments of the then administration.

"The south denies that Congress has any jurisdiction over the subject of slavery, and contends that the *people of the territories alone*, when they frame a constitution, preparatory to admission into the Union, *have a right to speak and be heard on that matter*. This fact being settled, *it really seems to us that this exciting question might be speedily adjusted*, if calm counsels prevail. The south contends for her honor, and for the great principles of non-intervention and state men! Within the present week we have had three most elaborate speeches in this House, in which the admission of California, with her free constitution, is vehemently opposed on constitutional grounds. Yes, sir, did you know it? *the constitution of the United States has just been altered;* or, what is intended to produce the same effect, without the trouble of an alteration in the manner prescribed by itself, its interpretation has been altered. While California promised to be a slave state, all interference was unconstitutional. Now, as she desires to be a free state, it has become constitutional to interfere and repel her. Not only so, but, according to the gentleman from Alabama, (Mr. Inge,) in swearing to support the constitution we have sworn to perpetuate, and not only to perpetuate, but to *extend* slavery. "To those," he says, "who are disposed to resist my views, I commend a more attentive reading of that instrument. They will find that it not only guranties slavery, but provides for its extension." Or, as he says in another place, it makes provision "to extend the institution indefinitely." And, therefore, when a territory asks to be admitted as a free state, it is to be repulsed, and virtually told, "If you will incorporate slavery into your constitution, you shall be admitted; if not, not." Had the man who first uttered the adage that "circumstances alter cases," foreseen our times, he would have said, "circumstances alter *principles.*"

The same gentleman defends slavery by an appeal to the Bible. But if the Bible be authority for the principal, is it not authority for the incidents also? If

equality. *Why, then, cannot all unite, and permit California to come into the Union as soon as she can frame a constitution?* Then, according to the doctrines which prevail on both sides of Mason's and Dixon's line, she may constitutionally establish her domestic institutions on any basis consistent with republican principles. *The south could lose nothing by adopting this course. On the contrary, she would save all for which she contends.*"

an authority for the cruelties of bondage, is it not an equal authority for its mitigations? Is not the command to "hallow the fiftieth year," as a year of jubilee, and to "proclaim liberty throughout all the land unto all the inhabitants thereof," contained in the same code, and in the same chapter of the same code, with that oft-cited authority to buy bondmen and bondmaids of the heathen? If the Bible is your commission, why do you not follow the terms of the commission, observing its limitations as well as its powers? This is the fiftieth year of the century,—the very year of jubilee itself; and yet, instead of "returning every man unto his possession, and every man unto his family," this is the chosen year for subjugating new realms to bondage. It is not to be "hallowed," as a year of jubilee, but to be profaned as a year of captivity and mourning.

Sir, I must express the most energetic dissent from those who would justify modern slavery from the Levitical law. My reason and conscience revolt from those interpretations which

"Torture the hallowed pages of the Bible,
To sanction crime, and robbery, and blood,
And, in oppression's hateful service, libel
Both man and God."

Priests appealed to the Bible in Galileo's time, to refute the truths of astronomy. For more than two hundred years, the same class of men appealed to the same authority to disprove the science of geology. And now, this authority is cited, not to disprove a law of physical nature merely, but to deny a great law of the human soul,—a law of human consciousness,—a law of God, written upon the tablet of every man's heart, authenticating and attesting his title to freedom. Sir, let those who reverence the Bible beware how they suborn it to commit this treason and perjury against the sacred rights of man and the holy law of

God. Whatever they gain for the support of their doctrine, will be so much subtracted from the authority of the Scriptures. If the Bible has crossed the Atlantic to spread slavery over a continent where it was unknown before, then the Bible is a book of death, and not a book of life.

It is further objected to the admission of California, that its dimensions are too large for a single state. The force of this objection is somewhat abated when we reflect that it comes from men who were most strenuous for the admission of Texas. However, I shall not object very earnestly to the reduction of its limits. I will say, in frankness, that the southern portion of California is understood to be even more attached to freedom than the northern. The result may, therefore, be, if this objection is persisted in and a division made, that we shall soon have two free states instead of one. It was said by the last administration, that Mexico was to be dismembered, in order "to extend the area of freedom." The most just retribution for that diabolical irony is, to carry out the declaration literally.

But I now come to a more substantial part of this great question. The south rests its claims to the new territory upon the great doctrine of equality. There are fifteen slave states; there are only fifteen free states. The south contributed men and money for the conquest, not less than the north; hence, equal ownership and equal rights of enjoyment. This is the argument. In a long and most elaborate speech, delivered in the Senate this week by one of the most eminent jurists in the Southern States, (Judge Berrien,) he founds the whole claim of the south on this doctrine of equality.

Now, I admit this principle in its fullest extent, and without hesitation. That country is equally free to all the people of the United States. The government can sell the lands not already covered by valid titles; and any citizen who will comply with its terms can buy them. The people of each of the United States can go there and establish their domicile. The laws of Congress make no discrimination between them. The constitution makes no such discrimination. The law of nature and of nations makes none. The north has no privilege over the south, and the south has none over the north. If the north has any greater right there than the south, the equality is destroyed. If the south has any greater right there than the north, the equality is equally destroyed.

And now, practically, what right has the north, or what right is claimed by the north, which the south has not to an equal extent? What article of property can a citizen of Massachusetts carry there which a citizen of Georgia can *not* carry there? Can we carry any of our local laws there; even though all the inhabitants of the state should remove thither in a body? Certainly not. When we leave our state, we leave our local laws behind us. A citizen of Boston has a right to educate his children at school, at the public expense. In the Boston public schools, he can prepare his son to enter any college in this country, even though he is too poor to pay a cent for taxes, and never has paid a cent for taxes. Has he any such right on arriving at San Francisco? If the city of Boston debars him of this right of educating his son at the public charge, he can institute a suit against it and recover full damages. Can he do the same thing at San Francisco or San Jose? Certainly not. He has left the laws and institutions of Massachusetts behind him. But, it is said, we can carry our *property* there, and you cannot carry your *property* there. I think those who use this argument, like the old Roman augurs, must smile at each other askance, for the credulity or simplicity of those they beguile by it. Will not every man, even of the feeblest discernment, see the fallacy which is here covered up under the word "*property?*" What is meant by this deceptive term "*property?*" If you mean silver, or gold, or seeds, or grains, or sheep, or horses, cannot you carry these there as freely as we can? But you have special laws; local and peculiar laws, — laws contrary to the great principles of the common law, by which you call *men and women* property. And then, forsooth, because we can carry *property* there, when *property* means grain and cattle, you can carry property there when it means human beings, — perhaps your own brothers, or sisters, or children. Because we can carry our property there, when property means inanimate substances, you have only to call a human being *property*; — you have only to call a creature, formed in the image of God, *property*, and then he can be smuggled in under the new name. Why, sir, there is not a respectable village in the country, where, if a juggler or mountebank were to attempt to palm off upon his audience so flimsy a trick as this, he would not be hissed from the stage. There are certain kinds of property and rights which we can carry with us to the territories, and other kinds which we cannot. We can carry movable property, but not immovable, — a diamond or a library, but not a cotton factory nor a cotton field.

By the papers of this city, as I open them every morning, I see that lotteries are authorized by more or less of the Southern States. Their "schemes" are regularly advertised. I remember, when stopping for a day in one of the southern cities, that some half-official looking personages came into the hotel, cleared a large space in the public hall, set down a rotary machine, and proceeded to draw a lottery. Now, in Massachusetts, and in many of the Northern States, lotteries are prohibited, under severe penalties. With us, it is highly penal to advertise a lottery in any form, to placard one at the corners of the streets, or to exhibit any plan or emblem of one at a shop window. We act upon the well-known truth, that there is a much less number of persons who draw any considerable prize in a lottery, than there are who are killed by lightning; and therefore, whatever chance a ticket-holder has of drawing any considerable prize, we know that he has a much greater chance of being killed by lightning. Now, when a citizen of Virginia and a citizen of Massachusetts go to the new territories, does the former carry his right to establish and draw a lottery, or the latter carry his right to prosecute the other for doing so? Neither; certainly neither. Both have left the local law behind them. If any state in this Union had adopted polygamy as its peculiar institution, could an inhabitant of that state take a dozen wives with him into the new territories, and defend his claim to live with them there, because he could do so at home? Or, suppose, in pursuance of the "manifest destiny" principle, we should *re*-annex a part of China to this Union, could the Chinese, on removing to California, carry the practice of infanticide with them? Just as well, I answer, and on precisely the same legal ground that the south can carry slavery into New Mexico. The reason is that the law of slavery is a *local* law. Like lotteries, or polygamy, or infanticide, it can legally exist in no land where the principles of the common law prevail, until it is legalized and sanctioned by a special law. Then it is permitted on the simple ground that so much of the common law as secures liberty and property, the right of *habeas corpus* and freedom of speech to each individual, has been cut out and cast away. The constitution proceeds upon this doctrine when it provides for the recapture of fugitive slaves. Why did it not provide for the capture of a fugitive horse or ox? Why did it not provide that, if a horse or an ox should escape from a slave state into a free state, it should be delivered up, or be recoverable by legal process? Because horses and oxen are *prop-*

erty, by the common consent of mankind. It needed no law to make them property. They are property by the law of nations, by the English common law, by the law of every state in this Union, — *while men and women are not.* An escaped slave could not be recovered before the adoption of the constitution. The power to seize upon escaping slaves was one of the motives for adopting it. These considerations demonstrate that slaves are not *property*, within the meaning of this word, when it is affirmed that if the north can carry *its* property into the territories, so can the south. As the constitution, in terms, adopts the common law, it leaves slavery nothing to stand upon but the local laws of the states where it is established. Freedom is the rule, slavery is the exception. Judge Berrien's favorite doctrine of equality would, therefore, be destroyed, if the exception should prevail over the rule. For, if slavery can be carried into any of our territories by force of the constitution, it can into all of them; and if carried into all of them, the exception becomes the rule, and the rule perishes. Ay, the rule ceases to be even so much as an exception to that which was *its* own exception. It is wholly swallowed up and lost.

I know it is said that the *fact* of slavery always precedes the *law* of slavery; that *law* does not go before the institution and create it, but comes afterwards to sanction and regulate it. But this is no more true of slavery than of every other institution or practice among mankind, whether right or wrong. Homicide existed before law; the law came in subsequently, and declared that he who took an innocent man's life without law, should lose his own by law. The law came in to regulate homicide; to authorize the taking of human life for crime, just as we authorize involuntary servitude for crime; and it may just as well be argued that murder is a natural right because it existed before law, as that slavery is a natural right because it existed before law. *This argument appeals to the crime which the law was enacted to prevent, in order to establish the supremacy of the crime over the law that forbids it.*

There is another fallacy in the arguments which southern gentlemen use on this subject, which, though not as transparent as the preceding, is quite as unsound. They speak of the *rights* of the slaveholder in the new territories. They speak as though the collective ownership of the territories by the government, were the ownership of the people in severalty; as though each citizen could go there and draw a line round a "placer," and say *this is mine;* and then, *because it is his*, introduce his slaves upon it. But nothing is more clear than that there is no such *individual* right. The right of the government is, *first*, a right of sovereignty and jurisdiction; and *second*, the right of ownership of all lands, navigable waters, &c., which have not been conveyed away by the preëxisting government. Individuals retain their citizenship on going there, as they do on going to Great Britain, or France; but a slave has just as much right to a portion of the public lands in California, when he gets there, as his master.

Again; if the master carries into California the legal right to hold slaves, which he possessed at home, does not the slave also retain his legal rights when he is transferred there? The laws which govern slaves are as various as the states where they exist. In some states manumission is comparatively unobstructed. In Delaware, it is a penal offence even to sell a slave to a notorious slavedealer. In Georgia, the law forbids, or lately forbade, the importation of slaves for sale. Now, how can a Georgian import slaves into California from Georgia, when the very laws of his own state, under which he claims to hold slaves, and under which laws he claims to carry slaves with him, forbid their importation?

And further, political franchises or privileges are just as much a part of a man's rights as any tangible commodity. In South Carolina, the ownership of ten slaves constitutes a property qualification for being a member of the legislature. On removing to California, will the citizen of South Carolina, who owns ten slaves, carry an eligibility to the legislature of California with him? Nay, this political privilege in South Carolina goes further. It is a right in every owner of ten slaves, that no man who does not own ten slaves, (or some legal equivalent,) shall be a member of the legislature. The aspirant for office has a legal right in the limitation of the number of his competitors, as much as in any thing else. Can he carry *this* to California with him? The inference is inevitable, that if the inhabitants of the fifteen slave states can carry slaves into California by virtue of the laws of their respective states, then they must also carry all the incidents of slavery known to their respective codes. For, how can the incident be separated from the principal? You might, therefore, have, in a neighborhood of fifteen families, fifteen slave codes in operation at the same time, — a manifest absurdity.

The conclusion, then, is irresistible, that when you come to the boundary line between a slave state and a free state, you come to the boundary line of slavery itself. On one side of the line, down to the nadir and up to the zenith, the blackness of the slave code pervades all things; but, on the other side, as high above and as deep below, is the purity of freedom. Virginia cannot extend her laws one hair's breadth over the line into Pennsylvania or into Ohio, because their soil is beyond her jurisdiction. So neither Virginia, nor all the fifteen slave states combined, can extend their slave laws one hair's breadth into the new territories; and for the same reason, — the territories are beyond their jurisdiction.

As to the argument that the constitution of the United States recognizes slavery, and that, upon the cession of new territories, the constitution, by some magical and incomprehensible elasticity, extends itself over them, and carries slavery into them, I think I speak with all due respect when I say it does not come up to the dignity of a sophism. Where do strict constructionists, or even latitudinarian constructionists, find any clause, or phrase, or word, which shows that the constitution is any thing but a compact between *states?* Where do they find any thing that shows it to be a compact between territories, or between territories *and* states conjoined? On its very face, the constitution meets this pretension with a denial. The preamble declares, "We the people of the United States," — not the people of the territories, nor the people of the states *and* territories, — "in order to form a more perfect Union," — "do ordain and establish this constitution for *the United States* of America." If the constitution is a compact between the United States *and* the territories, then the people of the territories have all the rights under it which the people of the states have, — the right to choose electors for President and Vice-President, &c., and to be represented in Congress by a member who can vote as well as speak. The only way in which the constitution ever was extended, or ever can be extended over any part of the earth's surface outside of the "original thirteen," is this: The constitution in express terms authorizes the admission of new states, and therefore, when a new state is admitted, it becomes one of these "United States of America." The constitution does not extend over the territories, but Congress, being the creature of the constitution, is, when legislating for the territories, not only invested with constitutional powers, but is limited by constitutional restrictions.

It would have been a much more plausible pretension, when the purchase of Louisiana and Florida was made, that the constitution carried freedom into those territories; because the constitution was built upon the basis of the common law, and, in terms, adopts the common law for its legal processes and its rules of judicial interpretation; and every body knows that there is no principle more dear to the common law than that all treaties, statutes, and customs shall be construed in favor of life and in favor of liberty.

Having, as I trust, refuted the argument of the slaveholder, that the prohibition of slavery in the territories is an act of injustice to his rights, I will consider his next assertion, that it is an insult to his feelings. We are told that the exclusion of slavery from the territories is an affront to the honorable sensibilities of the south; and that acquiescence in this exclusion would involve their dishonor and degradation.

There are two answers to this complaint. The first is, that among gentlemen, no insult is ever offered where none is intended. There may be heedlessness of conduct, there may be an unintentional wounding of sensibilities; but there can be no affront where the design to affront is wanting. He is not a gentleman, but a poltroon and a braggart, who pretends he is insulted and proceeds to retaliate for the affront, when all insult and all affront are sincerely disclaimed. Now, it is infinitely far from the purpose of the north to offer any indignity to the south by excluding slavery from the territories. Their hostility to slavery grows out of an honest allegiance to what they believe to be the highest moral and religious duty; it is fortified by the opinions of mankind; and is perfectly compatible with the most fraternal feelings towards the south. They wish to expostulate, in regard to the wrong, in such a way as to arrest the wrong, and not, by inflaming the wrongdoer, to increase the evil. However erroneous, then, their language or their sentiments may be, they are not affrontive nor contumelious; and, when all such purpose is disavowed, those who aspire to stand on the footing of gentlemen cannot reiterate the charge.

But there is another consideration, — one which appertains to the party supposed to be insulted, rather than the party charged with the insult. In his "Theory of Moral Sentiments," Adam Smith maintains that it is the judgment of men, — the opinion of the bystanders, — that gives us the pleasure of being approved, or the pain of being disapproved, on account of our conduct. Now, in this contest between the north and the south, on the subject of extending slavery, who are the bystanders? They are the civilized nations of the earth. We, the north and the south, are contending in the arena. All civilized men stand around us. They are a ring of lookers-on. It is an august spectacle. It is a larger assemblage than ever witnessed any other struggle in the history of mankind; and their shouts of approbation or hisses of scorn are worthy of our heed. And what do these spectators say, in the alternations of the combat? Do they urge on the south to mightier efforts, to the wider spread of slavery, and the multiplication of its victims? Do they shout when she triumphs? When new chains are forged and riveted, when new realms are subdued by haughty taskmasters, and overrun by imbruted slaves, do their plaudits greet your ears and rouse you to more vehement efforts? All the reverse; totally the reverse. They are now looking on with disgust and abhorrence. They groan, they mock, they hiss. The brightest pages of their literature portray you, as covered with badges of dishonor; their orators hold up your purposes as objects for the execration of mankind; their wits hurl the lightnings of satire at your leaders; their statute books abound in laws in which institutions like yours are branded as crimes; their moralists, from their high and serene seats of justice, arraign and condemn you; their theologians find your doom of retribution in the oracles of God. England has abolished slavery. France, in one fervid moment of liberty, struck the chains from off all her slaves, as the bonds of Paul and Silas were loosed in the inner prison by the mighty power of God. Sweden has abolished it. More than twenty years ago, impotent, half-civilized Mexico did the same. Tunis, a Barbary state, and, I might add, a barbarous state, has abolished slavery. Mahometanism precedes Christianity, and sets it an example of virtue. Liberia, a republic of emancipated slaves, the very brothers and sisters of those whom you now hold in bondage, has been acknowledged as an independent sovereignty, and welcomed into the family of nations, by two of the most powerful governments on the globe. By this act, freedom secures a new domain on the eastern continent, while you are striving to give a new domain to bondage on the western. A monarchy hails the advent of a free nation in Africa, where slavery existed before; a republic is seeking to create ten thousand absolute despotisms in America, where freedom existed before.

Now, these are the bystanders and lookers-on in this grand and awful contestation. They are all agreed, as one man, in their opinions about it. They are unitedly visiting your course with execration and anathema. There is not a nation on the globe, that has a printing press and a people that can read, from which you can extort one token of approval. I would agree to submit the question now at issue between the north and the south to the arbitrament of any people on the face of the earth, not absolutely savage, and to abide its decision. Nay, the wild tribes of the Caucasus and of Upper India, who have defended themselves so nobly against aggression, would spurn your claim and deride its pretexts. And yet you say you are insulted, dishonored, disgraced in the eyes of mankind, if you are not permitted to bring down upon our heads, also, the curses they are pouring upon yours. So far is this from truth, that if you would promptly and cheerfully consecrate the new territories to freedom, every nation in the world would send their plaudits of your conduct to the skies.

But gentlemen of the south not only argue the question of right and of honor; they go further, and they tell us what they will proceed to do if we do not yield to their demands. A large majority of the southern legislatures have solemnly "resolved" that if Congress prohibits slavery in the new territories, they will resist the law "at any and at every hazard." And yet they say they do not mean to threaten us. They desire to abstain from all language of menace, for threats and menaces are beneath the character of gentlemen. Sir, what is the meaning of the terms "threats" and "menaces?" Mr. Troup, formerly governor of Georgia, speaking of us who are upon this floor, and of others who resist the extension of slavery, calls each of us a "fanatic." He says that it is only the dread of death that will stay our hands or stop our machinations; and then adds, "THAT DREAD YOU MUST PRESENT TO HIM IN A VISIBLE, PALPABLE FORM." "If," he says in another place, "the abolitionists resolve to force emancipation, or *to force dishonor upon the southern states by any act of Congress*, then it is my decided opinion that, with the military preparation here indicated, conjoined to a good volunteer instead of a militia system, THE STATE SHOULD MARCH UPON WASHINGTON AND DISSOLVE THE GOVERNMENT." The gentleman from North Carolina, [Mr. CLINGMAN,] forewarns us that if certain measures, — and they are legal and constitutional measures which he indicates, — are taken in order to carry on the business of legislation in this House, the House itself shall be the "Lexington" of a new revolution, and that "such a struggle would not leave a quorum to do business." I could occupy my hour in citing passages of a similar character from the southern press and from southern men. Now, if these are not threats, — threats most gross, flagrant, and offensive, — I know not the meaning of the word. Perhaps those who utter such sentiments are only practising an inversion of language equal to their inversion of ideas on this subject, and would call them "enticements;" like the sailor, who said he was enticed to join a mutiny, and being asked what arts had been used to entice him, said that the ringleader sprang at him with a handspike, and swore if he did not join it he would knock out his brains.

And do those gentlemen who make these threats soberly consider how deeply they are pledging themselves and their constituents by them? Threats of dissolution, if executed, become rebellion and treason. The machinery of this government is now moving onward in its majestic course. Custom-houses, post-offices, land-offices, army, navy, are fulfilling their prescribed circle of duties. They will continue to fulfil them until arrested by violence. Should the hand of violence be laid upon them, then will come that exigency expressly provided for in the constitution and in the President's inaugural oath, "TO TAKE CARE THAT THE LAWS BE FAITHFULLY EXECUTED." Mr. Chairman, such collision would be *war*. Such forcible opposition to the government would be *treason*. Its agents and abettors would be *traitors*. Wherever this rebellion rears its crest, martial law will be proclaimed; and those found with hostile arms in their hands must prepare for the felon's doom.

Sir, I cannot contemplate this spectacle without a thrill of horror. If the two sections of this country ever marshal themselves against each other, and their squadrons rush to the conflict, it will be a war carried on by such powers of intellect, animated by such vehemence of passion, and sustained by such an abundance of resources, as the world has never before witnessed. "Ten foreign wars," it has been well said, "are a luxury compared with one civil war." But I turn from this scene with a shudder. If, in the retributive providence of God, the volcano of civil war should ever burst upon us, it will be amid thunderings above, and earthquakes below, and darkness around; and when that darkness is lifted up, we shall see this once glorious union, — this oneness of government, under which we have been prospered and blessed as Heaven never prospered and blessed any other people, — rifted in twain from east to west, with a gulf between us wide and profound, save that this gulf will be filled and heaped high with the slaughtered bodies of our countrymen; and when we reäwaken to consciousness, we shall behold the garments and the hands of the survivors red with fratricidal blood.

And what is the object for which we are willing to make this awful sacrifice? Is it to redeem a realm to freedom? No! But to subjugate a realm to slavery. Is it to defend the rights of man? No! But to abolish the rights of man!

Mr. Bowdon. Does not the gentleman think that such a picture as he has drawn would induce the north to yield a portion of the new territories to the institution of slavery?

Mr. Mann. I trust that no pictures *and no realities* will ever induce us to extend slavery beyond its present limits. Beyond those limits, "No more slave territories, no more slave states," is the doctrine by which I, for one, shall live and die.

Now, sir, as this event of a dissolution of the Union is so frequently forced upon our contemplation, I propose to occupy the residue of my hour in considering some of its more obvious consequences. Southern papers and southern resolution writers have a favorite phrase, that if Congress shall pass any law against the extension of slavery, they will resist it "at any and every hazard." Let us inquire, soberly, what a few of these hazards are: —

First, as to the recovery, or non-recovery, of fugitive slaves, which is one of the alleged provocatives of dissolution. Take a map of the Southern States and spread it out before you. Although they cover an area of about nine hundred thousand square miles, yet it is a very remarkable fact, that only an insignificantly small portion of this vast extent lies more than two hundred and fifty miles from a free frontier; and those parts which do lie beyond this distance hold but few slaves. Those portions of North Carolina, South Carolina, Georgia, Alabama, and Tennessee, where their upper boundaries converge among the mountains, are a little more than this distance from a free border; but this territory is relatively insignificant in size, and sparsely populated with slaves. An outside belt or border region of the slave states, no part of which shall be more than one hundred miles from a free frontier, would embrace nearly one half of their whole area; and, as I suppose, much more than one half of their whole slave population. What is to prevent the easy escape of slaves living within these limits? While God sends nights upon the earth, nothing can prevent it. I venture to predict, that in such a state of things, slaves will become cheap, and horses will become dear. I am aware of your laws which forbid slaves to cross bridges or ferries, without a pass; but you can have no law against seasons of low water. The old adage says, "riches have wings." You will find that these riches have legs. The Mississippi and Ohio Rivers, where they border upon free states, will be alive as with shoals of porpoises. Remember there is no constitution of the United States now. That you have broken. The free states are therefore absolved from all obligation to surrender fugitives. The law of 1793 is at an end. No action can be maintained for aiding them to escape, nor for harboring or concealing them. The distinguished senator from Kentucky, [Mr. Clay,] said, in his late speech, that no instance had ever come to his knowledge where an action for harboring runaways had not been maintained in the courts of the free states, and damages recovered. But this remedy you will have annulled. The constitution of the United States, and the law of 1793, being at an end, the law of nature revives. By this law, every case of an escaping slave is but *the self-recovery of stolen goods.* When they cross the line into a free state, they are free, — as free as you or I. The states being separated, I would as soon return my own brother or sister into bondage, as I would return a fugitive slave. Before God, and Christ, and all Christian men, they are my brothers and sisters. As our laws make it piracy to kidnap slaves in Africa, or to ship them thence, so it shall be a felony, punishable with death, for any southern master to kidnap a colored man, in a free state, or transport him from it, on the ground of alleged ownership. You are fond of quoting Scripture to us, in justification of slavery. We will retort the Scripture, that "he that stealeth a man, and selleth him, or *if he be found in his hand*, he shall surely be put to death."

Here, then, is a free land frontier of about two thousand miles, and a free ocean frontier of about twenty-five hundred miles; and more than one half of all your slaves are within two days' run of it. More than one quarter of them are within one night's run of it. Thousands and tens of thousands can escape, even while you are dining. Canada, now so distant, is brought five hundred miles nearer. The under-ground railroad will be abandoned, and its stock so invested as to yield quicker returns. What facilities for escape, too, will the ocean present. Fleets of vessels are constantly passing and repassing within a few hours' sail of the coast. The day for the power and the triumph of those whom you hate as abolitionists will have arrived. Steamboats could lie out of sight of land in the day time, run in at night, and be out of sight again before the rising of the sun. To guard twenty-five hundred miles of coast is impossible. If you declare war in order to avenge your losses, then that war makes your coast lawfully accessible both by day and by night, and multiplies a hundred fold the opportunities and facilities for this self-recovery of stolen goods.

I know it is said that some of the Northern States are averse to the reception of blacks. Let us analyze this idea. There are now by estimation three millions of slaves. Say one half of these are either too old or too young to have the strength or the intelligence to escape. A million and a half are left; five hundred thousand of these will have attachments to their own parents or children, or to their masters, too strong to be broken; or they may be so degraded as to be contented with bondage; for their contentment is always one of the measures of their degradation. This would leave a million for fugitives, consisting wholly of the most able bodied and intelligent. The Northern States comprise a territory of five hundred thousand square miles. A million of escaped slaves would give but two to a square mile, and this surely would not be a formidable number, even where colorphobia is strongest. Suppose the case of a family of fourteen slaves, — two grandparents, too decrepit for labor, six athletic sons or daughters, and six grand children. What but affection should prevent the able-bodied and the profitable from escaping, and leaving the aged and the young on their masters' hands. Affection, indeed, would bind the parents to their children, but they know too well how often this bond is remorselessly broken by the master; and, besides, an enlightened affection would look to future children and their posterity forever, as well as to those they already have.

Will you make your laws horribly penal, in order to deter slaves from escaping by fear? Will you mutilate them, or scourge them till within a minute of death? Do so. All such punishments not only nourish the love of freedom, but breed the purpose of revenge; and it is a kind of lesson which a brutalized nature is always prone to retaliate with improvements. Will you make the act of escape a capital offence in a slave, and destroy the victim you cannot restrain? Do so. Though you may inflict death in a paroxysm of wrath, yet of all your penal dispensations it is the most merciful. It not only releases the slave himself, but is a prospective and perpetual amnesty, — a true act of oblivion, — for all his descendants. But this extremity of punishment is not likely to be resorted to. In looking over the criminal codes of the slave states, I think I have noted cases where the slave is not punished with death for an offence for which a white man is. The *value* moderates the vengeance. There are not many who, like Cleopatra, can afford to dissolve a pearl in the cup of revenge, and swallow it at a draught, when that pearl will command five hundred or a thousand dollars in the market-place.

Southern gentlemen, when they threaten disunion, cannot surely be so much at fault as to forget that slavery exists here as it never existed before in the world. In Greece there were slaves; — in some cases, highly intelligent and accomplished slaves. They could have escaped if they would; but where should they escape to? All coterminous nations, — the whole circle round, — were barbarians. These slaves, therefore, had no place to flee to, where better institutions and juster laws prevailed. So it was with Rome. Whither could her slaves fly but to barbarous Spain, or more barbarous Gaul, or to some nation whose language they did not understand. Ignorance of language is a more insuperable barrier than mountains or oceans. It is just the reverse here. The English language is spoken on all sides; and our slave land is encircled by free land or free ocean, — Jamaica, the Bermudas, and two thousand miles of northern frontier. And I have lately seen an estimate from a credible source, that if an inter-oceanic canal should be opened across the Isthmus of Darien, twelve hundred ships would annually pass through it; and, as they sail to and fro, they will skirt the whole of your gulf coast, and the whole of your Atlantic coast, a great part of the voyage being within sight, or within a day's sail, of your shores. Now, the ignorant slave knows but little of geography, but he would know of these avenues to freedom, and nothing but death could extinguish such knowledge and the hopes it would inspire. I say, sir, under such circumstances, slavery would melt away upon your borders like an iceberg in the tropics. The particles, that is, the individuals of the exposed surface, would disappear; and you might as well attempt to stop solar evaporation by statutory laws, as to prevent their escape. Perhaps a dissolution of the Union is the means foreordained by God for the extinction of slavery; and did I not foresee its doom before any very long period shall have elapsed, without the unspeakable horrors of a civil and a servile war, I cannot say to what conclusion the above considerations would lead my own mind.

Having shown how the "*redress*" of disunion will operate upon one of the grievances alleged as its motive and excuse, let us look at another of those "hazards," whose list, of indefinite length, the south is so willing to brave. In case of rebellion or secession, to whom will the territories belong? It is the rule of political as well as of municipal law, that whoever retires from a community, leaves its common property behind him. I have a direct interest and proprietorship in the church in my parish, in the schoolhouse in my town, and in the state-house and other public property belonging to my state. But if I expatriate myself, I leave all that interest and proprietorship behind me. If the county of Brooke, in Virginia, should secede from the State of Virginia, and should annex itself to Ohio or Pennsylvania, no one doubts that it would forfeit all its rights to whatever public property the State of Virginia possesses. In like manner, if the "*United States South*,"—as the new confederacy has already been named by the "Richmond Enquirer,"—should secede, they would, by the very act of secession, surrender and abandon all right, title, and interest in the new territories. By such secession, all their citizens become foreigners. They have no rights under the treaty with Mexico. The new Spanish citizen, whose allegiance was transferred by the treaty with Mexico, and whose citizenship is not yet two years old, would have a right to expel them. The "United States South," it is true, may declare war, and attempt the conquest of the territories by force; but in such a contest, the army and navy and military stores of the government, which, also, they have lost by secession, will be turned against them. But, I venture to prophesy, that if the slave states shall pass through one war, single-handed, they will afterwards be the most peaceable nation the world ever saw. To every frontier country and to every naval power, they have given three millions of hostages for their good behavior.

Let us look at a third grievance they mean to redress, and a third "hazard" they are ready to encounter. They complain of northern agitation on the subject of slavery, and northern instigation of the slaves themselves. On the subject of "agitation," I deny that the north has ever overstepped the limits of their constitutional rights. They have never agitated the question of slavery in the states. It has been only in regard to slavery in this District, or the annexation of Texas, or the acquisition of territory for the extension of slavery, or the imprisonment of her own citizens in southern ports, or a denial of the inviolable right of petition ; — it has been only on such subjects that the north has lifted up the voice of expostulation and remonstrance. Even these constitutional rights she has used forbearingly. She has never exerted force, nor threatened force, either to maintain the right of petition or to liberate her own citizens imprisoned in southern jails.

In regard to instigating slaves to escape, I acknowledge there have been some instances of it; but they have been few. The perpetrators have been tried and severely punished, and the north has acquiesced; for they acknowledge that, if a man will go into a slave state and violate its laws, he must be judged by them. But I have never known of a single case, — I believe there is no well-authenticated case on record, — where a northern man has instigated the slaves to rise in rebellion, and to retaliate upon their masters for the wrongs which they and their race have suffered. As I dread indiscriminate massacre and conflagration, I should abhor the perpetrator of such a crime. But will separation bring relief or security? No, sir; it will enhance the danger a myriad fold. Thousands will start up, who will think it as much a duty and an honor to assist the slaves in any contest with their masters, as to assist Greeks, or Poles, or Hungarians, in resisting their tyrants. Two things exist at the north which the south does not duly appreciate, — the depth and intensity of our abhorrence of slavery, and that reverence for the law which keeps it in check. The latter counterpoises the former. We are a law-abiding people. But release us from our obligations, tear off from the bond with your own hands the signatures which bind our consciences and repress our feelings, destroy those compensations which the world and which posterity would derive from a continuance of this Union, and well may you tremble for the result. I have seen fugitive slaves at the north, and heard from their own lips the dreadful recital of their wrongs: and if I am any judge of the natural language of men; if I can divine from the outward expression what passions are burning within, each one of them had a hundred conflagrations and a hundred massacres in his bosom. They felt as you and I should feel if we had been subjected to Algerine bondage. And do you doubt, sir, does any southern gentleman on this floor doubt, for one moment, that if he were seized by a Barbary corsair and sold into Algerine bondage, and carried a hundred miles into the interior, that he would improve the first opportunity to escape, though at every step in his flight he should crush out a human life, and should leave an ever-widening expanse of conflagration behind him? If agitation and instigation are evils now, woe to those who would seek to mitigate or to repress them by the remedies of disunion and civil war. Let men who live in a powder-mill beware how they madden pyrotechnists.

But it is said that if dissolution occurs, the "United States South" can form an alliance with Great Britain. And are there no instigators and abolitionists in England? Yes, sir, ten in England where there is one at the north. Frederick Douglass has just returned from England, where he has enjoyed the honors of an ovation. William Wells Brown, another fugitive slave, is now travelling in England. His journeys from place to place are like the "progresses" of one of the magnates of that land, — passing wherever he will with free tickets, and enjoying the hospitalities of the most refined and educated men. The very last steamer brought out an account of his public reception at Newcastle. An entertainment was given him which was attended by four hundred ladies and gentlemen. Men of high distinction and character adorned it by their presence. The ladies made up a purse of twenty sovereigns, which they gave him. It was presented in a beautiful purse that one of their number, — the successful competitor for the honor, — had wrought with her own hands. All their generosity and kindness they considered as repaid by hearing from his own lips the pathetic story of his captivity and the heroism of his escape. Sir, every man who has travelled in England knows that there are large, wealthy, and refined circles there, no member of which would allow a slaveholder to sit at his table or enter his doors. Not only churches, but moral and religious men, the world over, have begun to read slaveholders out of their communion and companionship. If the south expects to rid itself of agitation and abolitionism by rupturing its bonds with the north and substituting an alliance with Great Britain for our present constitution, they may envy the wisdom of the geese who invited the fox to stand sentinel over them while they slept. Northern interference will increase a hundred fold; and the whole power and wealth of British abolitionism, not only founded on moral principle but nursed by national pride, will be brought to bear directly upon them.

I said that the slave does not know much of geography; but he understands enough of it to know where lies the free frontier. The slave does not know much of astronomy; but there is one star in the firmament which is dearer to him than all the heavenly host were to the Chaldeans. He worships the north star with more than Persian idolatry. But let the south form commercial alliances with Great Britain; let the carrying trade be carried on in British vessels; and the slave will find a star in the east as beautiful to his eye, and as inspiring to his hopes, as the star in the north.

Is the case of the *Amistad* forgotten, where a few ignorant, degraded wretches, fresh from the jungles of benighted Africa herself, seized upon the vessel in which they were transported, and compelled the master, under peril of his life, to steer for the north star, — that light which God kindled in the heavens, and which he will as soon extinguish as he will extinguish the love of liberty which he has kindled in every human breast?

And will a slave, escaping to Great Britain, or to any of her colonial possessions, be reclaimable? Examine Somerset's case for an answer. No, sir. Neither the third clause of the second section of the fourth article of the constitution, nor the law of 1793, will ever be extended over the Three Kingdoms or their dependencies.

It surely is not beneath the dignity of the place or the occasion to look at another of those "hazards" which the south are invoking. They are proud of their past history, and I doubt not their reflecting and patriotic men are at least reasonably solicitous of their future fame. When they meet in august council to inaugurate the great event of establishing an independent confederacy of slave states, and of dissolving the political bands which now unite them with us, "a decent respect to the opinions of mankind" will "require them to declare the causes which had impelled them to the separation." And will they find a model for their manifesto in that glorious Declaration of American Independence which their own immortal

Jefferson prepared, and to which many of the greatest of all their historic names are subscribed? Alas, they will have to read that Declaration, as the devil reads Scripture, backwards! I know not what may be the rhetorical terms and phrases of the new Declaration, but I do know that its *historic* form and substance cannot be widely different from this: —

"We hold these truths to be self-evident, that men are not created equal; that they are not endowed by their Creator with inalienable rights; that white men, of the Anglo-Saxon race, were born to rob, and tyrannize, and enjoy, and black men, of the African race, to labor, and suffer, and obey; that a man, with a drop of African blood in his veins, has no political rights, and therefore shall never vote; that he has no pecuniary rights, and therefore whatever he may earn or receive, belongs to his master; that he has no judicial rights, and therefore he shall never be heard as a witness to redress wrong, or violence, or robbery, committed by white men upon him; that he has no parental rights, and therefore his children may be torn from his bosom, at the pleasure or caprice of his owner; that he has no marital rights, and therefore his wife may be lawfully sold away into distant bondage, or violated before his eyes; that he has no rights of mind or of conscience, and therefore he shall never be allowed to read or to think, and all his aspirations for improvement shall be extinguished; that he has no religious rights, and therefore he shall never read the Bible; that he has no heaven-descended, God-given rights of freedom, and therefore he and his posterity shall be slaves forever. We hold that governments were instituted among men to secure and fortify this ascendency of one race over another; that this ascendency has its foundation in force ratified by law, and in ignorance and debasement inflicted by intelligence and superiority; and when any people, with whom we are politically associated, would debar us from propagating our doctrines or extending our domination into new realms and over free territories, it becomes our duty to separate from them, and to hold them, as we hold the rest of mankind, — friends when they make slaves, enemies when they make freemen."

I say, sir, of whatever words and phrases the southern "Magna Charta" may consist, this, or something like this, must be its substance and reality.

So the preamble to their constitution must run in this wise: "We, the people of the 'United States South,' in order to form a more perfect conspiracy against the rights of the African race, establish injustice, insure domestic slavery, provide for holding three millions of our fellow-beings, with all the countless millions of their posterity, in bondage, and to secure to ourselves and our posterity the enjoyment of power, and luxury, and sloth, do ordain and establish this constitution for the 'United States South.'"

Sir, should a civil war ensue between the north and the south, (which may God in his mercy avert,) in consequence of an attempt to dissolve this Union, and the certain resistance which would be made to such an attempt, it would be difficult to exaggerate the immediate evils which would befall the interests of New England and some other parts of the north. Our manufactures and our commerce would suffer at least a temporary derangement. But we have boundless resources in our enterprise and our intelligence. Knowledge and industry are recuperative energies that can never long be balked in their quest of prosperity. The people that bore the embargo of 1807, and the war of 1812, when all their capital was embarked in commerce, can survive any change that does not stop the revolution of the seasons or suspend the great laws of nature. And, when the day of peace again returns, business will again return to its old channels. The south, notwithstanding any personal hostility, will be as ready to take northern gold as though it had come from the English mint; and they will employ those first, who will do their manufacturing or their commercial labor cheapest and best. Gold is a great pacificator between nations; and, in this money-loving age, mutual interests will, in the end, subdue mutual hostilities. Our share, therefore, of the calamities of a civil war, will be mainly of a pecuniary nature. They will not be intolerable. They will invade none of the securities of home; they will not associate poison with our daily food, nor murder and conflagration with our nightly repose; nor black violation with the sanctities of our daughters and our wives.

Even in a pecuniary point of view, a dissolution of our political ties would cause less immediate and intense suffering at the north than at the south. Our laws and institutions are all framed so as to encourage the poor man, and, by education, to elevate his children above the condition of their parents; but their laws and institutions all tend to aggrandize the rich, and to perpetuate power in their hands. Were it not for the visions of horror and of bloodshed which southern threats have so intimately associated with this controversy, one remarkable feature, which has hitherto been eclipsed, would have been most conspicuous.

With every philanthropic northern man, a collateral motive for keeping the new territories free is, that they may be a land of hope and of promise to the poor man, to whichever of all our states he may belong; where he may go and find a home and a homestead and abundance. But the south, in attempting to open these territories to the slaveholders, would give them to the rich alone, — would give them to less than three hundred thousand persons out of a population of six millions. The interests of the poorer classes at the south all demand free territory, where they can go and rise at once to an equality with their fellow-citizens, which they never can do at home. They are natural abolitionists, and unless blinded by ignorance, or overawed by their social superiors, they will so declare themselves. Every intelligent and virtue-loving wife or mother, at the south, when she thinks of her husband and her sons, is forced to be an abolitionist. The attempt, therefore, to subject the new territories to the law of slavery is not made in the name of one half of the people of the United States; it is not made for the six millions, more or less, who inhabit the slave states; but it is made for less than three hundred thousand slaveholders among more than twenty millions of people.

There is one other "hazard," sir, which the south invokes and defies, which to her high-minded and honor-loving sons, should be more formidable than all the rest. She is defying the Spirit of the Age. She is not only defying the judgment of contemporaries, but invoking upon herself the execrations of posterity. Mark the progress in the public sentiment of Christendom, within the last few centuries, on the subject of slavery and the rights of man. After the discovery of this continent by Columbus, the ecclesiastics of Spain held councils to discuss the question, whether the aborigines of this country had or had not souls to be saved. They left this question undecided; but they said, as it was possible that the nations of the new world might have an immortal spirit, they would send them the gospel, so as to be on the safe side; and the mission of Las Casas was the result. In the time of Lord Coke, only a little more than two centuries ago, the doctrine was openly avowed and held, in Westminster Hall, that the heathen had no rights; and therefore that it was lawful for Christians to drive them out of their inheritance, and to despoil them, as the Jews despoiled the Egyptians and drove out the

Canaanites. During the seventeenth century, all the commercial nations of Europe engaged in the African slave trade, without compunction or reproach. In the last, or eighteenth century, the horrors of that trade were aggravated and blackened by such demoniacal atrocities, as, were it not for some redeeming attributes among men, would have made the human race immortally hateful. Even when our own constitution was formed, in 1787, this dreadful traffic was not only sanctioned, but a solemn compact was entered into, by which all prohibition of it was prohibited for twenty years. Yet, in the year 1820, after the lapse of only thirty-three years, this very trade was declared to be piracy, — the highest offence known to the law, — and the felon's death was denounced against all principals and abettors. We are often reminded by gentlemen of the south, that, at the time of the adoption of that constitution, slavery existed in almost every state in the Union; and that some northern merchants, by a devilish alchemy, transmuted gold from its tears and blood. But can they read no lesson as to the progress of the age from the fact that all those states have since abjured slavery of their own free will; and that, at the present day, it would be more tolerable for any northern merchant, rather than to be reasonably suspected of the guilt of this traffic, to be cast into the fiery furnace of Nebuchadnezzar, seven times heated? In Europe, the tide of liberty, though meeting with obstructions from firm-seated dynasties and time-strengthened prerogative, still rises, and sweeps onward with unebbing flow. In France, revolutions follow each other in quicker and quicker succession. These revolutions are only gigantic struggles of the popular will to escape from oppression; and, at each struggle, the giant snaps a chain.

Great Britain, which in former times sent more vessels to the coast of Africa to kidnap and to transport its natives, than all the other nations of the earth together, now maintains a fleet upon the same coast to suppress the trade she so lately encouraged. Three times, during the present century, has that government escaped civil commotion by making large concessions to popular rights. Since the year 1814, written constitutions have been extorted by the people from more than three fourths of all the sovereigns of Europe. What a tempest now beats upon Austria, from all points of the compass, because, during the last season, she attempted only to half enslave the Hungarians, — because she attempted to do what, during the last century, she might have done without a remonstrance! The rights of individuals, not less than the rights of communities, have emerged from oblivion into recognition, and have become law. Penal codes have been ameliorated, and barbarous customs abolished. There are now but two places on the globe where a woman can be publicly whipped, — in Hungary and in the Southern States! And the universal scorn and hissing with which the rulers of the former country have been visited for their women-whipping, and their execution of those whose sole crime was their love of freedom, only foretoken that fiercer scorn and louder hissing with which, from all sides of the civilized world, the latter will soon be visited. Let the high-toned and chivalrous sons of the south, — those "who feel a stain upon their honor like a wound," — think of all this, as one in the long catalogue of "hazards" upon which they are rushing.

Sir, the leading minds in a community are mainly responsible for the fortunes of that community. Under God, the men of education, of talent, and of attainment, turn the tides of human affairs. Where great social distinctions exist, the intelligence and the wealth of a few stimulate or suppress the volition of the masses. They are the sensorium of the body politic, and their social inferiors are the mighty limbs, which, for good or for evil, they wield. Such is the relation in which the three hundred thousand, or less than three hundred thousand slave owners of the south, hold to their fellow-citizens. They can light the torch of civil war, or they can quench it. But if civil war once blazes forth, it is not given to mortal wisdom to extinguish or control it. It comes under other and mightier laws, under other and mightier agencies. Human passions feed the combustion ; and the flame which the breath of man has kindled, the passions of the multitude,—stronger than the breath of the hurricane,—will spread. Among these passions, one of the strongest and boldest is the love of liberty, which dwells in every bosom. In the educated and civilized, this love of liberty is a regulated but paramount desire; in the ignorant and debased, it is a wild, vehement instinct. It is an indestructible part of the nature of man. Weakened it may be, but it cannot be destroyed. It is a thread of asbestos in the web of the soul, which all the fires of oppression cannot consume.

With the creation of every human being, God creates this love of liberty anew. The slave shares it with his master, and it has descended into his bosom from the same high source. Whether dormant or wakeful, it only awaits an opportunity to become the mastering impulse of the soul. Civil war is that opportunity. Under oppression it bides its time. Civil war is the fulness of time. It is literal truth that the south fosters within its homes three millions of latent rebellions. Imbedded in a material spontaneously combustible, it laughs at fire. Has it any barriers to keep the spirit of liberty, which has electrified the Old World, from crossing its own borders, and quickening its bondmen into mutinous life?—not all of them, but one in ten thousand, one in a hundred thousand of them. If there is no Spartacus among them, with his lofty heroism and his masterly skill for attack and defence, is the race of Nat Turners extinct, who, in their religious musings, and their dumb melancholy, take the impulses of their own passions for the inspiration of God, and, after prayer and the eucharist, proceed to massacre and conflagration? In ignorant and imbruted minds, a thousand motives work which we cannot divine. A thousand excitements madden them, which we cannot control. It may be a text of Scripture, it may be the contents of a wine vault; but the result will be the same,—havoc wherever there is wealth, murder wherever there is life, violation wherever there is chastity. Let this wildfire of a servile insurrection break out in but one place in a state; nay, in but ten places, or in five places in all the fifteen states; and then, in all their length and breadth, there will be no more quiet sleep. Not Macbeth, but the angel of retribution, will "murder sleep." The mother will clasp her infant to her breast, and, while she clasps it, die a double death. But, where will the slaves find arms? "*Furor arma ministrat.*" Rage will supply their weapons. Read the history of those slaves who have escaped from bondage; mark their endurance and their contrivance, and let incredulity cease forever. They have hid themselves under coverts; dug holes and burrowed in the earth for concealment; sunk themselves in ponds, and sustained life by breathing through a reed, until their pursuers had passed by; wandered in "Dismal Swamps," far away from the habitations of men; almost fasting for forty days and forty nights, like Christ in the wilderness; crushed themselves into boxes, but of half a coffin's dimensions, to be nailed up and transported hundreds of miles, as merchandise; and, in this horrible condition, have endured hunger and thirst, and, standing upon the head, without a groan or a sigh;—and, will men, who devise such things, and endure such things, be balked in their purposes of hope and of revenge, when the angel of destruction, in the form of the angel of liberty, descends into their breasts?

The state of slavery is always a state of war. In its deepest tranquillity, it is but a truce. Active hostilities are liable at any hour to be resumed. Civil war between the north and the south, — any thing that brings the quickening idea of freedom home to the mind of the slave; that supplies him with facilities of escape, or immunities for revenge, — will unleash the bloodhounds of insurrection. Can you muster armies in secret, and march them in secret, so that the slave shall not know that they are mustered and marched to perpetuate his bondage, and to extend the bondage of his race? Was not Major Dade's whole command supposed to be massacred through the treachery of a slave? A foray within your borders places you in such a relation to the slave that you are helpless without him, and in danger of assassination with him. He that defends slavery by war, wars against the eternal laws of God, and rushes upon the thick bosses of Jehovah's buckler. Such are some of the "hazards" which the leaders of public opinion at the south, the legislators and guides of men in this dark and perilous hour, are invoking upon themselves and their fellows; not for the interests of the whole, but for the fancied interests of the slaveholders alone, and against the real interest of a vast majority of the people. May God give that wisdom to the followers which he seems not yet to have imparted to the leaders.

Sir, in these remarks, I have studiously abstained from every thing that seemed to me like retaliation or unkindness. I certainly have suffered no purposed word of crimination to pass my lips. If I have uttered severe truths, I have not sought for severe language in which to clothe them. What I have said, I have said as to a brother sleeping on the brink of a precipice, where one motion of his troubled sleeping, or of his bewildered awaking, might plunge him into remediless ruin.

In conclusion, I have only to add, that such is my solemn and abiding conviction of the character of slavery, that under a full sense of my responsibility to my country and my God, I deliberately say, better disunion, — better a civil or a servile war, — better any thing that God in his providence shall send, than an extension of the bounds of slavery.

Upon the close of Mr. Mann's remarks,

Mr. Burt, of South Carolina, rose and said that he had not interrupted the gentleman from Massachusetts during his speech, but he presumed he did not wish to have any error go forth under the sanction of his name; and he therefore called upon him to retract what he had said in regard to slaves ever being exempted from capital punishment for crimes for which the whites were executed. He called upon him also to withdraw the imputation that the pecuniary value of the slave was a motive for any such difference in the laws respecting them. He remarked that, by the laws of the Southern States, such a distinction is not made. I know, said he, no instance in which it exists. On the contrary, slaves are punished capitally for offences that are not so punished when committed by white men. In South Carolina, slaves have never been admitted to the benefit of clergy for offences at common law; and thus a slave is punished capitally for maiming or grievously beating a white man. Mr. Burt was also understood to say that there were "six or eight," or "eight or ten," offences in South Carolina for which slaves were punished capitally, but for which white men were not.

Mr. Mann replied that he had stated what he believed to be true; but if he had fallen into any mistake, he should be most happy to be corrected. He was assured also by the gentleman from Georgia, on his left, [Mr. Toombs,] that no such distinction existed as he had supposed; and it was but reasonable to believe that those gentlemen were more conversant with the southern laws than himself.

Mr. Mann added that he, (Mr. Mann,) could not be expected to have the statute books of the Southern States before him, at that time, to meet so unexpected a denial. Neither could he be expected by any honorable gentleman to make a retraction until he had time to see whether the ground he had taken were tenable.

Note by Mr. Mann. On repairing to the Law library to ascertain which party was right in regard to the above difference of opinion, the second book I opened contained at least three cases, where the courts were authorized to sentence a slave to be transported for the commission of an offence, for which a white man must be unconditionally hung. See North Carolina Rev. Stat. vol. i. chap. 3, §§ 36, 37, 39. Of course, the reason of this difference is the pecuniary value of the slave. Hung, he would be worthless; transported to Cuba, he might bring five hundred dollars.

The law was formerly so in Mr. Burt's own state.

In the seventh volume of the Statutes at Large of South Carolina, No. 344, § 5, I find the following: "And *whereas*, it has been found by experience that the execution of several negroes for felonies of a smaller nature, by which they have been condemned to die, has been of great charge and expense to the public, and will continue, (if some remedy be not found,) to be very chargeable and burdensome to this province; *Be it therefore enacted*, by the authority aforesaid, that all negroes or other slaves who shall be convicted and found guilty of any capital crime, (murder excepted,) for which they used to receive the sentence of death, as the law directs, shall be transported from this province, by the public receiver for the time being, to any other of his majesty's plantations, or other foreign part, where he shall think fitting to send them, *for the use of the public*."

The slave condemned to transportation was to be appraised, and his master paid out of the public treasury, and this amount was, of course, to be reimbursed by what should be received from the foreign sale. From the statement of Mr. Burt, that no such law *now* exists in South Carolina, I suppose the above enactment must have been repealed.

The *fact* stated in the speech is therefore proved, although the instances may be fewer than I had supposed. As to the motive attributed, there can be no doubt. The cases are most numerous in the Southern States, where white men are merely *imprisoned* for offences for which slaves are whipped, branded, and cropped, or otherwise corporally punished. The slave's time is too valuable to be lost in a prison, but the white man's is not; the white man's skin is too sacred to be flayed or branded, but the slave's is not.

But laws which punish "*six or eight*," or "*eight or ten*," or any other number of offences with death, when committed by slaves, while the same offences receive a milder penalty when committed by whites; or laws denying the benefit of clergy, (where that relic of barbarism still prevails,) to a slave, while it is granted to a white man, are surely among the greatest atrocities recorded in the history of the race. Ponder for a moment upon the accursed fact. A freeman acting under all the motives to self-respect; moved by all the incentives to good conduct; enjoying all the means of education; inspired by all the influences of the gospel; and capable of comprehending all the powerful restraints and the sublime rewards connected with a hereafter, *exonerated* from the punishment of death; while death, in all the horrors with which ignorance and superstition can invest it, is inflicted upon men who are subjected to bondage; deprived of all motive for honorable conduct; debarred from every avenue to knowledge by cruel penalties; blinded to the light of the gospel; and, in a land of boasted Christianity, left in the darkness of heathenism! These are not the customs of a lawless banditti, of outcasts or renegades, but solemn enactments of state legislatures, devised by talent and eminence, enforced and preserved by the oligarchical few, by the virtual nobility and flower of populous communities. Such laws demand a return of five talents, under penalty of death, where only one talent had been confided; they absolve him who had received five talents, though he brings none of them back. Such laws make the Scriptures read, that the servant who knoweth his lord's will, but doeth it not, shall be beaten with but few stripes; but the servant who did not know it, whom his very master debarred from knowing it, shall be beaten with many stripes; for unto whomsoever much is given, but little shall be required; but to whom men have committed much, of him little shall be asked. What shall be thought of a system, AND OF EXTENDING A SYSTEM, which so perverts the hearts of men, otherwise clear-headed, high-minded, and generous!

What more fitting theme could be conceived, were the arch-enemy of mankind to compose a *burlesque*, in ridicule of *Republics*, to be represented in that Theatre which is all "*Pit*"?

It is not, however, the *existence* of slavery, but its *extension*, we now intend to avert.

The last paragraph in the foregoing speech gave rise to the following correspondence, which was published in the National Intelligencer: —

LETTER FROM MR. MANN.

Messrs. Editors; Your paper of this morning contains a portion of a speech of the Hon. Mr. Badger, of North Carolina, delivered in the Senate on the 19th instant, in which he comments upon some remarks lately made by me in the House of Representatives. The respect which, (without any personal acquaintance,) I have long entertained for this distinguished senator, would deter me from noticing any such miscontructions of my remarks as a candid mind might inadvertently commit; but the misrepresentations which the senator has made are so gratuitous and gross, that I am constrained to notice them. I therefore ask the favor of a place in your paper, where he can answer me, if he pleases, though he chose a place for his animadversions where he knew I could not answer him.

The following is a passage in his speech: —

"Nor, Mr. President, must I forget that, in considering the effect which this proviso is likely to have upon the condition of the southern mind, we must look to what has been said by northern gentlemen in connection with this subject. Permit me to call the attention of the Senate to a very brief extract from a speech delivered in the other end of the capitol: —

"'In conclusion, I have only to add, that such is my solemn and abiding conviction of the character of slavery, that, under a full sense of my responsibility to my country and my God, I deliberately say, better disunion, bettet a civil or a servile war, better any thing that God in his providence shall send, than an extension of the bounds of slavery.'

"Several Senators. Whose speech is that?

"A Senator. Mr. Mann's.

"Mr. Badger. We have heard much, Mr. President, of the violence of southern declamation. I have most carefully avoided reading the speeches of southern gentlemen who were supposed to be liable to that charge. I happened, however, in the early part of this session, and before the other House was organized, to be in that body when there were some bursts of feeling and denunciation from southern gentlemen, which I heard with pain, mortification, almost with anguish of mind. But, sir, these were bursts of feeling; these were passionate and excited declarations; these had every thing to plead for them as being spontaneous and fiery ebullitions of men burning at the moment under a sense of wrong. And where, among these, will you find any thing equal to the cool, calm, deliberate announcement of the philosophic mind that delivered in the other House the passage which I have read: 'Better disunion, better a civil or a servile war, better any thing that God in his providence shall send, than an extension of the bounds of slavery.'

"In other words, it is the deliberate, settled, fixed opinion of the honorable gentleman who made that speech, that rather than the extension of slavery *one foot,* — yes sir, there is no qualification, *one foot,* — he would prefer a **disunion of these states**; he would **prefer all the horrors of civil war, all the** monstrous, untold, and almost inconceivable atrocities of a servile war; he would pile the earth with dead; he would light up heaven with midnight conflagrations; all this, yea, and more, — all the vials of wrath which God in his providence might see fit to pour down upon us, he would suffer, rather than permit, not one man who is now free to be made a slave, — that would be extravagant enough, — but rather than permit one man who now stands upon the soil of North Carolina a slave, to stand a slave upon the soil of New Mexico:

"Yes, sir, here is a sacrifice of life and happiness, and of all that is dear to the black and white races together, to a mere idealism, — a sacrifice proposed by a gentleman who claims to be a philosopher, and to speak the language of calm deliberation, — a sacrifice of our glorious Union proposed by a patriot, — not rather than freemen should be made slaves, — not rather than the condition of even one human being should be made worse than it now is, — but rather than one man shall remove from one spot of the earth to another without an improvement of his condition, without passing from slavery to freedom. Sir, after that announcement, thus made, which I beg to say, sir, I did not seek, — for the speech I have never read; the extract I found in one of the newspapers of the day, — after that announcement, talk not of southern violence, talk not of southern egotism, talk not of our disposition to sacrifice to our peculiar notions and our peculiar relations, the peace and happiness, the growing prosperity, and the mutual concord of this great Union. Now, sir, if that announcement goes abroad into the southern country, attended by the wanton application of this Wilmot proviso, an irritating commentary upon that patriotic announcement, what can be expected? What but the deepest emotions of indignation in the bosoms of those born and brought up where slavery exists, and taking totally different views of the institution from those which are taken by the honorable gentleman who has placed himself upon this cool and deliberate, humane and philosophical position."

By his own confession, Mr. Badger had not read my speech. He takes up a single sentence, therefore, for comment, without the justice of looking at the context. He is like the man who should declare that the Scriptures say "there is no God," when it is the fool, and not the Bible, that makes the declaration. My speech discussed the question of extending slavery over our territories and the proposed southern remedy for prohibiting that extension, namely, the disunion of the states. The conclusion to which I came was, that the north had better submit to the application of the southern remedy, than to surrender the new territories to all the horrors of bondage. Beyond our present limits "no more slave territories and no more slave states," was the exact ground I took. But Mr. Badger represents me as saying that I would "prefer a disunion of these states," and all the other evils in his long and labored catalogue, "rather than the extension of slavery *one foot;* "yes," he repeats with emphasis, "*one foot.*" Now, I never made such a declaration as this. I never said any thing to give countenance or color to such a declaration. Many persons, seeing the statement of the honorable senator, and relying upon his character for fairness and veracity, have believed that I did. But he has led them into the error. My argument and conclusion had reference to new slave territories, or to *a* new slave territory. Mr. Badger construes, or rather misconstrues this to mean "*one foot.*" If my speech is fairly susceptible of this construction, I wish so far to retract it. He shall have my consent to a "*one foot*" territory, and to as many slaves as he can hold on it under the *local law.*

Mr. Badger further charges me with invoking all the calamities he enumerates, "rather than permit one man who now stands upon the soil of North Carolina a slave, to stand a slave upon the soil of New Mexico." This statement is not merely forced, but fabricated. Surely I said no such thing. I intimated nor hinted at, nor thought of such a thing. There may be little choice whether any one man who now "stands a slave," shall "stand a slave" in one place or in another, *if that be all.* In a national point of view, and looking at the subject as a statesman, the sentiment imputed to me is simply ridiculous. But this wrongful imputation of such a sentiment, without substance or semblance to justify it, is far worse than ridiculous; it becomes unjust and ungenerous; and is none the less so for being made in a place where he knew I could not repel it. The whole scope and stress of my argument went against yielding any such portion of our new acquisitions to slavery as would form either a state or a territory. The eight or ten southern legislatures, the eight or ten governors of southern states, the southern Senators and Representatives in Congress, and the confederates in getting up the Nashville Convention, have never, to my knowledge, proposed a compromise on the platform of a "*one foot*" territory, or expressed their readiness to spare the Union if "one man who stands a slave in North Carolina," is permitted to "stand a slave in New Mexico." When such an issue is brought forward seriously, it will be met seriously. But the real issue on this point is, (and the senator must know it,) whether the victims of slavery shall be indefinitely multiplied by the addition to its domain of regions now free. That the creation of a new slave territory will increase the victims of slavery, is a proposition too plain to be argued. To deny this, is to assert that if slavery had been confined to the State of Virginia, or to the settlement at Jamestown, where the first cargo of slaves was landed, the present number of slaves in this country would be no less than it now is; or, in other words, there would now be three millions of slaves within the limits of Virginia, or within the limits of Jamestown.

I have made this reply to the honorable senator from North Carolina with great reluctance, and from no motive of personal unkindness. I have long been accustomed to regard his character with respect, and his opinions with deference; and I am happy in an opportunity to express a feeling of personal gratitude for his former endeavors to avert from the councils of the nation the subject-matter of this most lamentable contention.

Very truly, yours, &c., HORACE MANN.

WASHINGTON, March 28, 1850.

P. S. Another point in the honorable senator's speech, in which he attempts to vindicate the penal slave code of North Carolina and of the other Southern States from the taint of cupidity, may be safely left without comment to intelligent men. Every student of the *criminal* legislation of the Southern States in regard to slaves, knows that their laws are replete with proofs where the sensibilities of a man are sacrificed to the spirit of gain.

MR. BADGER'S REPLY.

To the Editors of the National Intelligencer;

A communication in your paper of yesterday, from the Hon. Horace Mann, of the House of Representatives, seems to require a brief notice from me.

The honorable gentleman accuses me of having treated him with gross injustice in a recent speech, in which I referred to the closing paragraph of a speech of his, and made some comments thereupon.

Now, in what consists the injustice? I quoted that paragraph from his speech, and he does not deny that it was quoted truly. There is not a word or syllable attributed to him, not a word or syllable alleged or insinuated to have been spoken by him, except that paragraph, and that he admits was spoken and printed by him just as I quoted it. Then, in the statement of his language, I have done him no injustice.

In my comments, I gave "in other words," — in my own words, — what I deemed a true interpretation of his; and, as I attributed to him no language which he did not use; as every thing to which he objects is, and upon the face of my remarks plainly purports to be, merely my own commentary upon the single quotation correctly taken from the gentleman's speech, it is very obvious that I have "fabricated" nothing. Whether the interpretation given to the honorable gentleman's language be correct or incorrect, a just carrying of it out to its true results, or an unfair exaggeration, intelligent men will be able to decide from the reading of my speech, which presents together both the text and the commentary, and to them I am willing to leave it.

But the gentleman says that in his speech he "discussed the question of extending slavery over our territories," and that "no more slave territories and no more slave states was the exact ground" he took. And what has that to do with the matter of his complaint against me? I referred not to his discussion, or the grounds taken in it. I was not considering the course or validity of his reasoning, but the conclusion at which he arrived. That was set down in his speech in these words: —

"In conclusion, I have only to add, that such is my solemn and abiding conviction of the character of slavery, that, under a full sense of my responsibility to my country and my God, I deliberately say, better disunion, — better a civil or a servile war, — better any thing that God in his providence shall send, than *an extension of the bounds of slavery.*"

Here is no reference to any particular degree, kind, or manner of extending slavery. He speaks not of the "proposed or desired extension," of "extension into our territories," or even of "*the* extension," but he speaks of "an extension of the bounds of slavery," without a reference to any thing in the speech or elsewhere by which the generality of his language might be modified or explained. To refer, therefore, to the speech in order to understand the import of this general conclusion, is idle. If the reasoning in the speech be particular, and the deduction general, there would be the logical defect of a conclusion too large for the premises, but the *meanings* of the conclusion would remain, and the want of reasoning to support it would not abate aught of its unmitigated and sweeping generality.

It is evident, then, that, whether supported by any reasoning, particular or general, the gentleman's conclusion remains, that disunion, civil war, servile war, with certain undefined judgments of Heaven besides, are preferable to "an extension of the bounds of slavery;" but the indefinite article "an" is here exactly equivalent to "any," and therefore whatever amounts to "any extension," however small, — a square mile, or acre, or foot, — is strictly within the meaning of the language which he has thought proper deliberately to retain in his printed speech.

But I accept willingly the explanation now given of his meaning, and only regret that, when writing out his speech, he did not then give the explanation which converts his general into a particular proposition. By this explanation I learn that, in his conclusion, he meant to speak not of any extension, however small, but of an extension of slavery in our territories.

Then the gentleman's conclusion, as modified by himself, will be thus: "Better disunion," [the dissolution of our government and destruction of the Union formed by our fathers;] "better a civil or a servile war," [the most disastrous, ferocious, and cruel of all wars;] "better any thing that God in his providence shall send," [for example, pestilence and famine;] "than an extension of the bounds of slavery" over our territories!

I cheerfully submit to all "intelligent men," if they are at the same time humane and patriotic, to pass upon such a sentiment. To his own intelligent, patriotic, and humane constituents, I submit it, with entire confidence that it will not meet their approval; but, on the contrary, that they will regard the honorable gentleman as having been betrayed by the pervading excitement on the slavery question, into an extravagant, — I will not say fanatical, — declaration, which he is not able to defend, or willing, as yet, to retract or qualify.

I had believed that the honorable gentleman had, under the exciting influence of discussion, unconsciously done injustice to my own state, but a remark added to his communication would perhaps justify me, if inclined to judge unkindly, in supposing that the wrong was wilful. But I am not so inclined, and draw no such conclusion. I infer, rather, that the bewildering excitement under which the speech was made has not yet passed away, but still continues to influence unfavorably the otherwise clear understanding and fair and upright purposes of the honorable gentleman.

GEO. E. BADGER.

WASHINGTON, March 30, 1850.

MR. MANN'S REJOINDER.

Messrs. Editors; Your paper of this morning contains a communication from the Hon. Mr. Badger, in reply to mine of the 29th ultimo. I ask your indulgence while I briefly answer him.

My complaint was, that he had taken half a dozen lines from my speech, and had attributed a meaning to them, in some respects odious, in other respects ridiculous, and in all respects unwarrantable. By his own admission, too, he had done this without reading the speech itself; when, had he accorded to me the justice of hearing me before he condemned me, he would have found that both subject-matter and context confuted his interpretation.

His first reply is, that he did not "attribute" to me "a word" nor "a syllable" which I did not use; and, repeating himself, he adds, that he did not "allege" or "insinuate" a "word" nor "a syllable" that I now deny. In view of this he asks, with an air of triumph, "In what consists the injustice?"

I answer, as before; the injustice consists in giving a false meaning to true "words" and "syllables," — a meaning which both the subject-matter and context of my speech repudiate. I do not see that it is less unjustifiable to attach false meanings to words correctly quoted, than to forge quotations. Surely, the honorable senator is too good a lawyer to be ignorant of the maxim, "*qui hæret in litera*," &c.; and too good a theologian not to have read that "the letter killeth" if divorced from the spirit. When Beaumont and Fletcher were closeted together to devise the plan of one of their joint plays, in which a king was to be killed, they were severally overheard to say, "I will kill the king," and "I will kill the king;" whereupon they were arrested, transported to London, and arraigned for conspiring the death of the reigning sovereign. Suppose them to have been convicted of treason and gibbeted; could not the perjured informer, with a charming and childlike simplicity, have used the exact language of Mr. Badger, and said, I testified to the exact "*words*" and "*syllables*." "In what consists the injustice?"

But the honorable senator goes on to say, that he had no concern with my *speech*, but only with my *conclusion*. His language is, "I was not considering the course or validity of his reasoning, but the conclusion at which he arrived." He then repeats the quotation, and adds, "To refer, therefore, to the speech in order to understand the import of this conclusion, is idle."

With all deference to the senator, — and mine is unfeignedly great, — I submit that this is false logic and worse ethics. As well may one declare the judgment of a court to be legal or illegal, merciful or tyrannous, without looking back to the allegations and proofs on which it is founded. As well may one affirm or deny the "Q. E. D."

of the geometer, without reference to the problem or demonstration to which it is subjoined. When a discussion exists respecting "*an extension of the bounds of slavery*," (and these were my words,) and I say that I would prefer certain enumerated evils rather than the extension in controversy, it surely becomes all-important to know whether that extension is to embrace the whole earth and to extend through all time, or whether it is only the addition of one atom or granule to existing slave territory, or of one respiration, or one heart-beat of an existing slave, on territory now free. I affirm, then, that a knowledge of the premises *is* indispensable to a judgment on the conclusion.

But he accepts my explanation, and then appeals from me to what he is pleased to call, (and I thank him for the justice that prompted the well-deserved compliment,) my "intelligent, patriotic, and humane constituents," — "with entire confidence that it will not meet their approval." I gladly join in this appeal. As "*intelligent*" men, my constituents foresee that the extension of slavery over our territories will not only be an unspeakable crime in itself, but will be converted into the means of future unspeakable crimes in further extensions. As "*patriotic*" men, they prefer to bear any calamity that may come upon themselves, rather than to devolve accumulated calamities, growing out of their own dereliction from duty, upon their posterity. As "*humane*" men, they would deprecate and forefend that greatest of inhumanities, the dooming of increased thousands and millions of their fellow-men to the dreadful inheritance of bondage. And as religious men, — as men who "tremble when they reflect that God is just, and that his justice will not sleep forever," — they mean to use all constitutional means to arrest the slave-creating and slave-extending policy of this government, let the two or three hundred thousand slaveholders among our twenty millions of people do what they will.

That the bearings of the subject may be rightly understood, it should be remembered that my speech was made on the 15th of February, after ten weeks of threatened disunion on certain specified and not improbable contingencies. "My conclusion," therefore, was not *aggressive*, but *submissive*. I only declared which branch of their proffered alternative I should prefer.

The closing paragraph of the respected senator's communication alludes to the *motives* of those wide and painful differences which are made between the whites and the slaves in the *criminal* legislation of the Southern States. Nothing could be more edifying, as to the demoralizing nature of slavery and its effects upon men, who, like the senator, are otherwise honorable and generous, than a comparison of the two codes of law and the two systems of jurisprudence which the rulers have respectively established for themselves and for their bondmen. The laws or customs known to civilized men and to barbarians are not more diverse. It would be rash and reckless in me to encounter the distinguished senator on any other subject; but on this I would say, as was said by a knight in an old tournament, that he had such confidence in the justness of his cause that he would give his adversary the advantage of sun and wind.

HORACE MANN.

WASHINGTON, April 1, 1850.

LETTERS

On the Extension of Slavery into California and New Mexico; and on the Duty of Congress to provide the Trial by Jury for alleged Fugitive Slaves.

Hon. Horace Mann;

Dear Sir,—Having learned that you are spending a few days at home, and approving the course you have pursued in Congress, in maintaining so ably the sentiments and convictions which we maintain and cherish on the great national questions of the day, we respectfully request you, before returning to Washington, to give your constituents an opportunity of hearing somewhat more at length than the hour rule would allow, your views and opinions upon the question of the immediate admission of California, and other questions now before Congress, arising out of the acquisition of territory by the treaty with Mexico.

Should you comply with our request, please name some day which will be convenient for you, that we may give seasonable notice through your district.

Dedham.

James Richardson, I. Cleveland, John Gardner.

Roxbury.

David A. Simmons, John J. Clarke, Francis Hilliard,
G. R. Russell, Jos. N. Brewer, Daniel Jackson,
Joseph H. Billings, Wm. A. Crafts, J. B. Kettell.
L. M. Sargent, Wm. Capen,

Brookline.

Charles Wild, Wm. Dearborn, David Wilder, Jr.,
Marshall Stearns, G. Griggs, G. F. Homer.

Dorchester,

E. Sharpe, N. F. Safford, J. G. Nazro.

Brighton, J. Breck. *Randolph*, J. Wales. *Stoughton*, J. Smith.
Foxboro', A. Hodges. *Quincy*, L. Richards. *Milton*, J. Reed.
Walpole, A. Bigelow. *Franklin*, L. Harding. *Cohasset*, Geo. Beal.

Newton.

E. C. Dyer, R. E. Patterson, W. S. Whitwell.

Hingham.

C. W. Cushing.

April 23d, 1850.

LETTER I.

West Newton, May 3, 1850.

To the Hon. James Richardson, I. Cleveland, and John Gardner, of Dedham; Hon. D. A. Simmons, John J. Clarke, Francis Hilliard, and George R. Russell, of Roxbury, &c., &c.

Gentlemen;

Having been called home on account of sickness in my family, I have just received, at this place, your kind invitation to meet and address my constituents of the 8th Congressional District, and to give them my "*views and opinions upon the question of the immediate admission of California, and other questions now before Congress, arising out of the acquisition of territory by the treaty with Mexico.*"

A request from so high a source has almost the force of a command. Yet I dare not promise to comply. I am liable at any moment to be recalled, and, instead of speaking here, to vote there, upon the questions to which you refer. I might be summoned to return on the day appointed for us to meet. The only alternative, therefore, which is left me, is to address you by letter. This I will do, if I can find time. I shall thus comply with your request, in substance, if not in form.

On many accounts, I have the extremest reluctance to appear before the public on the present occasion. My views, on some vital questions, differ most materially from those of gentlemen for whom I have felt the profoundest respect; and for some of whom I cherish the strongest personal attachment. But I feel, on the other hand, that my constituents, having intrusted to me some of their most precious interests, are entitled to know my "views and opinions" respecting the hopes and the dangers that encompass them. I shall not, therefore, take the responsibility of declining.

I will premise further, that my relations to political parties, for many years past, have left me as free from all partisan bias "as the lot of humanity will admit." For twelve years I held an office whose duties required me to abstain from all active coöperation in political conflicts; and that duty was so religiously fulfilled, that, to my knowledge, I was never charged with its violation. During the Presidential contest of 1848, those obligations of neutrality still rested upon me. For a year afterwards, I was not called upon to do any official act displeasing to any party amongst us. This interval I employed in forming the best opinion I could of public men and measures, and their influence upon the moral and industrial interests of the country. I had long entertained most decided convictions in favor of protecting American labor, in favor of cheap postage, and of security to the lives and property of our fellow-citizens engaged in commerce. But a new question had arisen, — the great question of freedom or slavery in our recently acquired territories, — and this question I deemed, for the time being, to be, though not exclusive of others, yet paramount to them. Or rather, I saw that nothing could be so favorable to all the last-named interests, as the proper adjustment of the first. He who would provide for the welfare of mankind, must first provide for their liberty.

Sympathizing, then, on different points with different parties, but exclusively bound to none, I stood, in reference to the great question of territorial freedom or slavery, in the position of the *true* mother in the litigation before Solomon, preferring that the object of my love should be spared in the hands of any one, rather than perish in my own.

Our present difficulties, which, as you well know,

have arrested the gaze of the nation, and almost suspended the legislative functions of Congress, pertain to the destiny of freedom or of slavery, to which our new territories are to be devoted. After the acquisition of Louisiana, and Florida, and Texas, for the aggrandizement and security of the Slave-power; after the aboriginal occupants of the soil of the Southern States have been slaughtered, or driven from their homes, at an expense of not less than a hundred millions of dollars, and at the infinite expense of our national reputation for justice and humanity; and after the area of the slave states has been made almost double that of the free states, while the population of the free is about double that of the slave; the reasons seem so strong that they can hardly be made stronger, why the career of our government, as a slavery-extending power, should be arrested. On the other hand, the oligarchy who rule the south, seeing that, notwithstanding their rich and almost illimitable domain, they are rapidly falling behind the north in all the distinctive elements of civilization and well being, — industry, temperance, education, wealth, — not only defend the Upas that blasts their soil, as though it were the tree of life, but seek to transplant it to other lands. With but about three slaves to a square mile, — three millions of slaves to nearly a million of square miles, — they say they are too crowded; that they feel a sense of suffocation, and must have more room, when all their weakness and pain proceed, not from the limited quantity, but from the malignant quality of the atmosphere they breathe. Hence the war with Mexico, commenced and prosecuted to add slave territory and slave states to the southern section. Hence the refusal to accept propositions of peace, unless territory *south* of latitude 36′ 30°, (the Missouri cômpromise line, so called,) should be ceded to us. Hence, when the Mexican negotiators proposed to insert a prohibition of slavery in the treaty of cession, and declared that the inquisition would not be more odious to the American people than the reinstitution of slavery to them, our minister, Mr. Trist, told them he would not consent to such a prohibition though they would cover the soil a foot deep with gold. And hence, also, the determination of a portion of the southern members of Congress to stop the whole machinery of the government, to sacrifice all the great interests of the country, and assail even the Union itself, unless slavery shall be permitted to cross the Rio Grande and enter the vast regions of the west, as it heretofore, in its aggressive march, crossed the Mississippi and the Sabine.

Even in 1846, when the war against Mexico was declared, all men of sagacity foresaw the present conflict. Could that question have been decided on its merits, or could the institutions to be planted upon the territory we might acquire have been determined by the unbiased suffrages of the American people, no war would have been declared, and no territory acquired. But the great political leaders of the south expected to make up both for their numerical weakness and for the injustice of their cause, by connecting the question of slavery extension with that of future presidential elections and with the strife of parties. They promised themselves that they could draw over leading northern men to their support, by offering them the Tantalus cup of presidential honors; and then, by the force of party cohesion and discipline, insure the support of the vast descending scale of office expectants. Early in the present session of Congress, it was distinctly declared from a high southern source, that the south must do most for those northern men who would do most for them. A few words will make it apparent how faithfully this plan has been adhered to, and how successful it may become.

No northern Democrat, opposed to slavery extension,

could expect the support of the southern democracy. Hence, General Cass stepped promptly forward, and declared, in his Nicholson letter, that Congress had no power to exclude slavery from the territories. This has been technically called his "bid," or his "first bid." It was deemed satisfactory by the south; for, according to their philosophy, the relation of master and slave is the natural or normal relation of mankind; and therefore, where no prohibition of it exists, slavery flows into free territory as water runs down hill. This avowal of General Cass was rendered more signal and valuable to the south, because, for the greater part of his political life, he had taken oaths, held offices, and administered laws, in undeniable contradiction to the declaration then made. The ordinance of 1787 was expressly recognized by the first Congress held under the constitution, [see ch. 8.] It was modified in part, and confirmed as to the rest; and in holding offices under this, General Cass had laid the foundation of his honors and his fortune. His declaration, therefore, against all interdiction of slavery, made under circumstances so extraordinary and in contradiction to the whole tenor of his past life, was hailed with acclamation by the south, and he was unanimously declared, at Baltimore, to be the accepted candidate of the democracy, for the office of President. The common notion is, that a man shows his love for a cause by the amount of sacrifice he will make for it; and as consistency, honor, and truth, are the most precious elements in character, he showed his devotion to the south by sacrificing them all.

To the honor of the Whig party be it said, there was not a northern man to be found, who, to gain the support of the south, would espouse its pro-slavery doctrines, or invent any new reading of the constitution to give them a semblance of law. Hence, at the Philadelphia Convention, no northern Whig received even so much as a complimentary vote. The judicial eminence of Judge McLean, the military eminence of General Scott, were passed contemptuously by; and Mr. Webster, acknowledged to be the greatest statesman of the age, received but fourteen votes out of almost three hundred; and twelve of these were from Massachusetts. Mr. Webster had spoken more eloquent words for liberty than any other living man, and this distinguished neglect was doubtless intended to teach him the lesson, that the path to presidential honors did not lie through an advocacy of the rights of man. General Taylor was nominated and chosen. He was understood to take neutral ground. Discountenancing the veto power, if the House of Representatives, who are chosen directly from and by the people, and the Senate, who are chosen by the states, will pass a territorial bill, either with or without a prohibition of slavery, he will approve it. This is the common opinion, and I have no doubt of its correctness.

Under these circumstances, a most desperate effort was made at the close of the last Congress to provide a government for the territories with no prohibition of slavery. Had General Cass been elected, no such effort would have been necessary, for he was pledged to veto a prohibition. General Taylor was supposed to be pledged to an opposite course; and hence the struggle. The facts must be so fresh in the recollection of all, that they hardly need to be recounted. The House performed its duty to the country and to freedom, by sending territorial bills to the Senate containing the prohibitory clause. The Senate, equalling the northern by its southern votes, and far outnumbering the Whigs by its Democrats, left those bills to sleep the sleep of death upon its table. But during the closing hours of the session, it foisted a provision for the government of the territories into the general appropriation bill; and held out the menace that this bill should not pass at all, unless the territorial clause should pass with it. The flagitiousness of this proceeding it is difficult to comprehend and impossible to describe. The appropriation bill is one on which the working, and even the continuance of the government, depend. Without it, the machinery of the state must cease to move. Contracts by the government to pay money must be violated. Officers cannot obtain their salaries. Families must be left without subsistence. If long continued, all judges would resign, and courts be broken up; and when justice should cease to be administered, violence, robbery, and every form of crime would run riot through the land.

Besides, an appropriation bill and a bill for the government of territories have no congruity with each other. They are not relevant. Neither is germane to the other. Every one knows it to be a common parliamentary rule that when a proposition is submitted which is susceptible of a division, any *one* member has a right to demand it. All bills, too, for raising revenue, must, by the constitution, originate in the House; and the House has as much right to interfere to prevent the Senate from ratifying a treaty, as the Senate has to obstruct the passage of a revenue bill by adding to it extraneous provisions. It was this effort on the part of the Senate to incorporate into the appropriation bill a provision most unrighteous in itself and most odious to the free sentiments of the north, which led to the protracted session on the night of the 3d of March, 1849. The course of the pro-slavery leaders, on that occasion, resembled that of a madman who should seize a torch and stand over the magazine of a ship, and proclaim that he would send men and vessel to destruction, unless they would steer for his port. A portion of the House confederated with the majority of the Senate in this unprincipled machination; but the larger number stood undaunted, and after perils, such as so precious an interest never before encountered, the pro-slavery amendment was stricken out, and its champions were foiled. Through that memorable night the friends of freedom wrestled like Jacob with the angel of God, and though the session did not close until the sun of a Sabbath morning shone full into the windows of the capitol, yet a holier work never was done on that holy day.

It was with a joy such as no words can ever express, that I saw the territories rescued from the clutch of slavery by the expiration of the Thirtieth Congress. I felt confident that when the Thirty-first Congress should assemble, it would be under better auspices, and with a stronger phalanx on the side of freedom. In regard to California, those hopes have been fulfilled; but I proceed to state how they have been nearly extinguished in regard to the residue of the territory.

Our first disaster was the election of a most adroit, talented, and zealous pro-slavery speaker. A better organ for the accomplishment of their purposes the friends of slavery could not have found; nor the friends of freedom a more formidable opponent. Whilst the pro-slavery champions of the south, almost without distinction of party, exulted over this triumph, it has been the occasion of most lamentable criminations and recriminations at the north. Southern men abandon all distinctions of Whig or Democrat for the cause of slavery. Would to God we could do as much for the cause of freedom.

The choice of a pro-slavery speaker was immediately followed by the appointment of most ultra pro-slavery committees. Some Free-Soil members, it is true, were placed upon these committees; but in this, the speaker only carried out more fully his own purposes and those of his party, by putting, what they considered as insane men, into close custody, instead of letting them run at large. He showed, however, either a want of courage in himself, or of confidence in his chosen guards; for, on the District of Columbia committee he detailed a file of five, on the judiciary committee a file of four, and on the territorial committee a file of six strong pro-slavery men, for the safe keeping of one Free-Soiler.

Within an hour after the House was organized, Mr. Root, of Ohio, submitted a resolution, instructing the committee on territories to report territorial bills prohibiting slavery. Many true friends to freedom believed this movement to be ill timed and unfortunate; and though the House then refused, by a handsome vote, to lay the resolution on the table, yet when it came up for consideration again, the first decision was reversed by about the same majority. There is abundant proof that the latter vote did not express the true sentiment of the House. Not a few voted against the resolution avowedly because of its paternity, — thus spiting a noble son on account of its obnoxious father. Others repented of their votes as soon as they came to reflect that the record would go where their explanation could not accompany it.

But unfortunately it was too late. There stands the record, to survive through all time and to be read of all men. The champions of slavery seized upon this vote as a propitious omen. They derided and scouted the proviso with a fierceness unknown before. They shouted their threats of disunion with a more defiant tone, should any attempt at what they called its resurrection, be made. A speech was delivered by Mr. Clingman, of North Carolina, in which a massacre of a majority of the House was distinctly shadowed forth, so that not "a quorum should be left to do business." The effect of that vote was almost as bad as though it meant what it said.

At a later day, when a bill for the admission of California was presented, the tactics of delay were resorted to, and midnight found us calling the yeas and nays, for more than the thirtieth time, on questions whose frivolousness and vexatiousness cannot be indicated by numbers.

The proceedings in the Senate, however, are those which now threaten the most disastrous consequences. Early in the session, in order to bring his northern friends up to the doctrine that it is unconstitutional to legislate against slavery in the territories, General Cass made a speech, in which he denies that Congress has *any* power, under *any* circumstances, to pass *any* law respecting their inhabitants. According to that speech, the United States stands in the relation of a foreign government to the people of its own territories; and if they set up a king or establish a religion, we cannot help it; for we have no more power or right to control them than we have the subjects of Great Britain or the citizens of France. It has been said that the doctrine of General Cass and that of General Taylor, on this subject, are identical; but there is this all-important difference between them: — General Taylor maintains the right of Congress to legislate for the territories, and will doubtless approve any bill for the prohibition of slavery in them; but General Cass, denying this right in Congress, would, if President, veto such a bill. He, therefore, would leave the territories open to be invaded and possessed by slavery; and in southern law and practice possession is more than nine points.

Next came Mr. Clay's compromise resolutions, so called. By these, California was to be admitted as a state; the territories organized without any restriction upon slavery; the south-western boundary of Texas to be extended to the Rio Grande; a part of her ten or twelve million debt to be paid by the United States, on condition of her abandoning her claim to a part of New Mexico lying east of the Rio Grande; the abolition of the slave trade in the District of Columbia, and the inviolability of slavery in the District during the good pleasure of Maryland and of the inhabitants of the District; more effectual provision for the restitution of fugitive slaves, and free traffic in slaves forever between the states, unless forbidden by themselves.

A compromise is a settlement of difficulties by mutual concessions. Let us examine the mutuality of the concessions which Mr. Clay's resolutions propose.

In the first place, California is to be permitted to remain free if the territories of New Mexico and Utah may be opened to slavery. But California is free already; free by her own act; free without any concession of theirs, and without any grace but the grace of God. It is mainly occupied by a northern population, who do their own work with their own hands, or their own brains. Fifty hardy gold diggers from the north will never stand all day knee deep in water, shovel earth, rock washers, &c., under a broiling sun, and see a man with his fifty slaves standing under the shade of a tree, or having an umbrella held over his head, with whip in hand, and without wetting his dainty glove, or soiling his japanned boot, pocket as much at night as the whole of them together. Or, rather, they will never suffer institutions to exist which tolerate such unrighteousness. California, therefore, is free; as free as Massachusetts; and Mr. Clay might as well have said in terms, that whereas Massachusetts is free, therefore New Mexico and Utah shall be slave, or run the hazard of being so.

The next point of Mr. Clay's compromise is, that Texas shall extend her south-western boundary from or near the Nueces to the Rio Grande, and shall receive, probably, some six or eight millions of dollars for withdrawing her claim to that part of New Mexico which lies east of the last-named river. Now, Texas has no rightful or plausible claim to a foot of all this territory. But suppose it to be a subject of doubt, and therefore of compromise. The mutuality, then, consists in dividing the whole territory claimed by Texas, and then giving her a valid title to one portion of it, and paying her for all the rest. Texas, or, —what in this connection is the same thing,—slavery surrenders absolutely nothing, gets a good title to some seventy thousand square miles of territory, and pay for as much more!

But what renders it almost incredible that any man could soberly submit such a proposition and dare to call it a compromise, is this: All that part of New Mexico which Texas claims, and which lies between the parallels of 36° 30′ and 42°, is, by the resolutions of annexation, to be forever free. I shall consider the constitutionality of these resolutions by and by; I now treat them as valid. Now the compromise proposes to buy this territory, so secured to freedom, and annex it to New Mexico, which is to be left open to slavery. We are to peril all the broad region between 36° 30′ and 42°, and pay Texas some six or eight millions of dollars for the privilege of doing so! Mr. Clay is not less eminent for his statesmanship than for his waggery. Were he to succeed in playing off this practical joke upon the north, and were it not for the horrible consequences which it would involve, a roar of laughter, like a *feu de joie*, would run down the course of the ages. As it is, the laughter will be "elsewhere."

The next point pertains to the abolition of the slave trade, and the perpetuity of slavery, in the District of Columbia. This District has an area of about fifty square miles; and Mr. Clay proposes, in consideration of transferring its slave marts to Alexandria, on the Virginia side, or to some convenient place in Montgomery or Prince George's county, on the Maryland side, to divest Congress forever of its right of "exclusive legislation" over it. Should this plan prevail, the perpetuity of slavery in the District will be defended by more unassailable and impregnable barriers than any other institution in Christendom. The President has a veto upon Congress; but two thirds of both Houses may still pass any law, notwithstanding his dissent. Mr. Clay proposes to give, both to Maryland and to the citizens of the District, a veto on this subject;—an absolute veto, not a qualified one, like that of the President of the United States, but one that will control, not majorities merely, but an absolute unanimity in both branches of Congress. By his plan, therefore, three separate, independent powers are to have a veto upon the abolition of slavery in the District of Columbia. And not only so, but while it will require their *joint* or *concurrent* action to abolish the institution, any one of them can preserve it. The laws of the Medes and Persians had no such guaranties for perpetuity as this.

Mr. Clay's last point is really too facetious. So solemn a subject does not permit such long-continued levity, however it may be masked by sobriety of countenance. It is, that Congress shall make more effectual provision for the capture and delivery of fugitive slaves; and, as an equivalent for this, it shall bind itself never to interfere with the inter-state traffic in slaves. We are to catch the slaves of the South, and, as though this were a grateful privilege to us, we are to allow them free commerce in slaves, coastwise or inland. By this means, slaves can be transported to the mouth of the Rio Grande, and some hundreds of miles up that river, towards New Mexico, instead of being driven in coffles across the country. The compromise is, that for every slave we catch, we are to facilitate the passage of a hundred into New Mexico.

Such is the mutuality of Mr. Clay's compromises They are such compromises as the wolf offers to the lamb, or the vulture to the dove. They make the rightful admission of California into the Union, with her free constitution, contingent upon opening the new territories to slavery; they ratify one part of the predatory claim of Texas, and propose to give her millions for the other part; they give an unconditional veto to the state of Maryland and to the citizens of the District of Columbia, over a unanimous vote of both Houses of Congress, even when approved by the President; in connection with Mr. Butler's bill and Mr. Mason's amendments, they expose our white citizens to grievous penalties and imprisonments for not doing what the Supreme Court of the United States has decided we are not bound to do, in relation to fugitive slaves, and they offer our colored citizens to be kidnapped and spirited away into bondage; and they foreclose, in favor of the south, the disputed question of the inter-state commerce in slaves. In one particular only do they appear to concede any thing to northern rights, or northern convictions, or northern feelings. They propose to transfer the District of Columbia slave trade across an ideal line into Virginia or into Maryland, so that the slave planter or slave trader, when he comes to our American Congo to replenish his stock of human cattle, shall be obliged to go a mile or two, to the slave marts, instead of walking down Pennsylvania Avenue. I deem this to be no concession. If it is honorable to produce corn and cotton, it is honorable to buy and sell them,—and if it is honorable to hold beings created in God's image in slavery, it is honorable to stand between the producer and consumer, and to make merchandise of the bodies and the souls of men. Let this Light of the Age be set upon a hill, that all nations may behold it.

I will refer to Mr. Bell's resolutions no further than to say, that they propose the formation of three slave states out of what is now claimed by Texas, one of which is to be admitted into the Union forthwith as an offset to California.

Mr. Buchanan has not regarded the movements of his rival, General Cass, with indifference. He has spent a considerable portion of the winter in Washington, and it is understood that he holds out the Missouri compromise line, from the western boundary of Missouri to the Pacific Ocean, as his lure to the south, for their favorable regards in the ensuing presidential contest.

In a chronological order, I must now consider some vitally important views, which have been submitted by some members in the House, and by Mr. Webster and others in the Senate. In mentioning the name of this great statesman, and in avowing that I am one among the many whom his recently expressed opinions have failed to convince, it is due to myself, however indifferent it may be to him or to his friends, that I should express my admiration of his powers, my gratitude for his past services, and the diffidence with which I dissented, at first, from his views. But I have pondered upon them long, and the longer I have pondered the more questionable they appear. I shall therefore venture upon the perilous task of inquiring into their correctness; and while I do it with the deference and respect which belong to his character, I shall do it also with that fidelity to conscience and to judgment that belong to mine. He is great, but truth is greater than us all.

I shall confine myself mainly, and perhaps wholly, to Mr. Webster's views, because he has argued the cause of the south with vastly more ability than it has been argued by any one among themselves. If his conclusions, then, be not tenable, their case is lost.*

Mr. Webster casts away the "Proviso" altogether.

* All my quotations from Mr. Webster are taken from the edition of his speech which he dedicated to the "PEOPLE OF MASSACHUSETTS," March 18, 1850. Among the numerous readings which have appeared, I suppose this to be the most authentic.

He says, "*If a resolution or a law were now before us to provide a territorial government for New Mexico, I would not vote to put any prohibition into it whatever.*" (p. 44.) The reason given is, that slavery is already excluded from "California and New Mexico" "by the law of nature, of physical geography, the law of the formation of the earth." (p. 42.) "California and New Mexico are Asiatic in their formation and scenery. They are composed of vast ridges of mountains of enormous height, with broken ridges and deep valleys." (p. 43.)

Now, this is drawing moral conclusions from physical premises. It is arguing from physics to metaphysics. It is determining the law of the spirit by geographical phenomena. It is undertaking to settle by mountains and rivers, and not by the Ten Commandments, a great question of human duty. It abandons the second commandment of Christ and all bills of rights enacted in conformity thereto, and leaves our obligations to our "neighbor" to be determined by the accidents of earth and water and air. To ascertain whether a people will obey the Divine command, and do to others as they would be done by, it looks at the thermometer. What a problem would this be: "Required the height above the level of the sea at which the oppressor 'will undo the heavy burdens and let the oppressed go free, and break every yoke,'—to be determined barometrically." Alas! this cannot be done. Slavery depends, not upon climate, but upon conscience. Wherever the wicked passions of the human heart can go, there slavery can go. Slavery is an effect. Avarice, sloth, pride, and the love of domination, are its cause. In ascending mountain sides, at what altitude do men leave these passions behind them? Different vegetable growths are to be found at different heights, depending also upon the zone. This I can understand. There is the altitude of the palm, the altitude of the oak, the altitude of the pine, and, far above them all, the line of perpetual snow. But, in regard to innocence and guilt, where is the *white line?* How high up can a slaveholder go and not lose his free agency? At what elevation will the whip fall from the hand of the master, and the fetter from the limbs of the slave? There is no such point. Freedom and slavery on the one hand, and climate and geology on the other, are incommensurable quantities. We might as well attempt to determine a question in theology by the cube root, or a question in ethics by the black art. Slavery, being a crime founded upon human passions, can go wherever those passions are unrestrained. It has existed in Asia from the earliest ages, notwithstanding its "formation and scenery." It labors and groans on the flanks of the Ural mountains now. There are to-day forty-eight millions of slaves in Russia, not one rood of which comes down so low as the northern boundary of California and New Mexico.

Had Mr. Webster's philosophy been correct, then California was at superfluous pains when she incorporated the ordinance of 1787 into her constitution. Instead of saying that "slavery and involuntary servitude, (except for crime,) shall be forever prohibited," she should have said, "Whereas, by a law of nature, of physical geography, the law of the formation of the earth," "slavery cannot exist in California," therefore we will not "reaffirm an ordinance of nature, nor reenact the will of God."

Should it be said that slavery will not go into the new territories, because it is unprofitable; I ask, Where is it profitable? Where is ignorance so profitable as knowledge? Where is ungodliness gain, even for the things of this life? How little is the hand worth at one end of an arm, if there is not a brain at the other! Do not Maryland, Virginia, North Carolina, and other states, furnish witnesses by thousands and tens of thousands that slavery impoverishes? Yet with what enthusiasm they cherish it! Generally, ignorance is a necessary concomitant of slavery. Of white persons, over twenty years of age, unable to read and write, there were, according to the last census, 58,787 in Virginia, 56,609 in North Carolina, 58,513 in Tennessee, and so forth. I have a letter before me, received this morning, dated in Indiana, in which the writer says, he removed from North Carolina in 1802, when he was fourteen years old, and at that time he had never seen a newspaper in his life. Can there be genius, the inventive talent, or profitable labor, where ignorance is so dense? Can the oppression that tramples out voluntary industry, enterprise, intelligence, and the desire of independence, conduce to riches? Yet this is done wherever slavery exists, and is part and parcel of its working. Is any other form of robbery profitable? Yet individuals and communities have practised it and lived by it, and we may as well rely upon a "law of physical geography" to arrest the one as the other. It is not poetry, but literal truth, that the breath of the slave blasts vegetation, his tears poison the earth, and his groans strike it with sterility. It would be easy to show why the master does not abandon slavery, even amid the desolation with which it has surrounded him. There is a combination of poverty and pride, which slavery produces, *on the doctrine of natural appetence*, and which, therefore, it exactly fits. The helplessness of the master in regard to all personal wants seems to necessitate the slavery that has begotten it. All moral and religious principles are lowered till they conform to the daily practice. Custom blinds conscience, until, without any attempt to emancipate or ameliorate their victims, men can preach and pray and hold slaves, as Hamlet's grave digger jests and sings while he turns up skulls.

But slavery cannot go into California or New Mexico, because their staple productions are not "tobacco, corn, cotton, or rice." (p. 44.) These are agricultural products. But is slave labor confined to agriculture? Suppose that predial slavery will not become common in the new territories. Cannot menial? If slaves cannot do field work, cannot they do house work? There is an opening for a hundred thousand slaves to-day in the new territories, for purposes of domestic labor. And beyond this, let me ask, who possesses any such geologic vision that, at a distance of a thousand miles, he can penetrate the valleys and gorges of New Mexico, and say that gold will not yet be found there as it is in California, — not in sand and gravel only, but in forty-eight-pounders and fifty-sixes? This is the very kind of labor on which slaves, in all time, have been so extensively employed, — the very labor on which a million of slaves in Hispaniola lost their lives, within a few years after its discovery by Columbus. Gold deposits are now worked within twenty-five miles of Santa Fe. The last account which I have seen, of a company of emigrants passing from Santa Fe to California by the River Gila, announces rich discoveries of gold upon that river. A fellow-citizen of mine has just returned home, who says he saw a slave sold at the mines in California, in September last. As yet, the distant regions of the Gila and the Colorado cannot be worked, because of the Apaches, the Utahs, and other tribes of Indians. But admit slavery there, and the power of the government will be invoked to exterminate these Indians, as it was before to exterminate the Cherokees and Seminoles, — not to drive them beyond the Mississippi, but beyond the Styx. A few days since a letter was published in the papers, dated on board a steamer descending the Mississippi, which stated that a considerable number of slaves were on board, bound for California, under an agreement with their masters that they should be free after serving two years at the mines. We know, too, that the reason assigned for incorporating a provision in the constitution of California, authorizing its legislature to pass laws for the exclusion of free blacks from the state, was, that slaves would be brought there under this very form of agreement, and by and by the country would be overspread by people of color who had bought their freedom. The sagacious men who framed the California constitution came from all parts of the territory, and, being collected on the spot, having surveyed all its mountains, having breathed its air at all temperatures, and turned up its golden soil, — these men had never discovered any "law of physical geography" which the fell spirit of slavery could not transgress. Slaves were carried into Oregon, ten degrees of latitude higher up. Its colonists reënacted the ordinance of 1787 before Congress gave them a territorial government. In the territorial government that was given them, the prohibition was inserted; and President Polk signed the bill, with an express protest, that he ratified this exclusion of slavery only because the country lay north of the Missouri compromise line; but declared that, had it embraced the very region in question, he would have vetoed the bill.

General Cass never took the ground that slavery *could not* exist in the new territories; and no inconsiderable part of the opposition made to him in Massachusetts and in other free states, was placed expressly upon the ground that he would not prohibit it. Mr. Webster, in his Marshfield speech, September 1, 1848, opposed the election of General Cass, because, through his recreancy to northern principles, slavery would invade the territories. This was expressed with his usual clearness and force, as follows:—

"He, [General Cass,] will surely have the Senate; and with the patronage of the government, with every interest that he, as a northern man, can bring to bear, coöperating with every interest that the south can bring to bear, we cry safety before we are out of the woods, *if we feel that there is no danger as to these new territories.*"

Yet Mr. Webster now says, that to support the "Proviso," would "do disgrace to his own understanding." (p. 46.)

During the same campaign, also, the Hon. Rufus Choate, one of the most eloquent men in New England, and known to be the personal friend of Mr. Webster, delivered a speech at Salem, in which the following passage occurs: —

"It is the passage of a law to say that California and New Mexico shall remain forever free. That is, fellow-citizens, undoubtedly an object of great and transcendent importance; for there is none who will deny that we should go up to the very limits of the constitution itself, and with the wisdom of the wisest, and zeal of the most zealous, should unite to accomplish this great object, and to defeat the always detested, and forever to be detested object of the dark ambition of that candidate of the Baltimore convention, (General CASS,) who has ventured to pledge himself in advance that he will veto the future law of freedom; and may God avert the madness of all those who hate slavery and love freedom, that would unite in putting him in the place where his thrice accursed pledge may be redeemed! . . . . Is there a Whig upon this floor who doubts that the strength of the Whig party next March will insure freedom to California and New Mexico, if by the constitution they are entitled to freedom at all? Is there a member of Congress that would not vote for freedom? You know there is not one. Did not every Whig member of Congress from the free states vote at the last session for freedom? You know that every man of them returned home covered with the thanks of his constituents for that vote. Is there a single Whig constituency, in any free state in this country, that would return any man that would not vote for freedom? *Do you believe that Daniel Webster himself could be returned if there was the least doubt upon the question?*"

Mr. Choate then adds: "Upon this question alone, we always differ from those Whigs of the south; and on that one, we *propose simply to vote them down.*" Mr. Webster now says he will not join in voting them down.

Under such circumstances, is it frivolous or captious to ask for something more than a dogmatic assertion that slavery cannot impregnate these new regions, and cause them to breed monsters forever? On a subject of such infinite importance I cannot be satisfied with a dictum; I want a demonstration. I cannot accept the prophecy without inquiring what spirit inspired the prophet. As a revelation from Heaven, it would be most delightful; but, as it conflicts with all human experience, it requires at least one undoubted miracle to attest the divinity of its origin.

According to the last census, there were more than eight thousand persons of African blood in Massachusetts. Abolish the moral and religious convictions of our people, let slavery appear to be in their sight not only lawful and creditable, but desirable as a badge of aristocratic distinction, and as a "political, social, moral, and religious blessing," and what obstacle would prevent these eight thousand persons from being turned into slaves, on any day, by the easy, cheap, and short-hand kidnapping of a legislative act? Africans can exist here, for the best of all reasons, — they do exist here. A state of slavery would not stop their respiration, nor cause them to vanish "into thin air." Think, for a moment, of the complaints we constantly hear in certain circles, of the difficulty and vexatiousness of commanding domestic service. If no moral or religious objection existed against holding slaves, would not many of those respectable and opulent gentlemen who signed the letter of thanks to Mr. Webster, and hundreds of others indeed, instead of applying to intelligence offices, or visiting emigrant ships for "domestics," as we call them, go at once to the auction room and buy a man or a woman with as little hesitancy or compunction as they now send to Brighton for beeves, or go to Tattersall's for a horse? If the cold of the higher latitudes checks the flow of African blood, or benumbs African limbs, the slaveholder knows very well that a trifling extra expense for whips will make up for the difference.

But suppose a doubt could be reasonably entertained about the invasion of the new territories by slavery. Even suppose the chances to preponderate against it. What then? Are we to submit a question of human liberty over vast regions and for an indefinite extent of time, to the determination of chance? With all my faculties I say, *No!* Let me ask any man, let me respectfully ask Mr. Webster himself, if it were his own father and mother, and brothers and sisters, and sons and daughters, who were in peril of such a fate, whether he would abandon them to chance, — even to a favorable chance. Would he suffer their fate to be determined by dice or divination, when positive prohibition was in his power? And by what rule of Christian morality, or even of enlightened heathen morality, can we deal differently with the kindred of others from what we would with our own? He is not a Christian whose humanity is bounded by the legal degrees of blood, or by general types of feature.

But Mr. Webster would not "taunt" the south. Neither would I. I would not taunt any honorable man, much less a criminal. Still, when the most precious interests of humanity are in peril, I would not be timid. I would not stop too long to cull lovers' phrases. Standing under the eye of God, in the forum of the world and before the august tribunal of posterity, when the litigants are freedom and tyranny, and human happiness and human misery the prize they contest, it should happen to the sworn advocate of liberty, as Quintilian says it did to Demosthenes, "not to speak and to plead, but to thunder and to lighten." Mr. Webster would not taunt the south; and yet I say the south were never so insulted before as he has insulted them. Common scoffs, jeers, vilifications, are flattery and sycophancy compared with the indignities he heaped upon them. Look at the facts. The south waged war with Mexico from one, and only one, motive; for one, and only one, object, — the extension of slavery. They refused peace unless it surrendered territory. That territory must be south of the abhorred line of 36° 30′. The same President who abandoned the broad belt of country on our northern frontier, from 49° to 54° 40′, to which we had, in his own words, "an unquestionable title," would allow no prohibition of slavery to be imposed upon the territory which Mexico ceded, though she would bury it a foot deep in gold. The Proviso had been resisted in all forms, from the beginning. Southern Whigs voted against the ratification of the treaty, foreseeing the struggle that was to follow. Desperate efforts had been made, at the close of the last session of Congress, to smuggle in an unrestricted territorial government, against all parliamentary rule and all constitutional implication. The whole south, as one man, claimed it as a "describable, weighable, estimable, tangible," and most valuable "right" to carry slaves there. Calhoun, Berrien, Badger, Mason, Davis, — the whole southern phalanx, Whig and Democrat, pleaded for it, argued for it, and most of them declared themselves ready to fight for it; and yet Mr. Webster rises in his place, and tells them they are all moonstruck, hallucinated, fatuous; because "an ordinance of nature and the will of God" had settled this question against them from the beginning of the world. Mr. Calhoun said, immediately after this speech, "Give us free scope and time enough, and we will take care of the rest."

Mr. Mason said, —

"We have heard here from various quarters, and from high quarters, and repeated on all hands, — repeated here again to-day by the honorable senator from Illinois, [Mr. Shields,] that there is a law of nature which excludes the southern people from every portion of the state of California. I know of no such law of nature, — none whatever; but I do know the contrary, that if California had been organized with a territorial form of government only, and for which, at the last two sessions of Congress, she has obtained the entire southern vote, the people of the Southern States would have gone there freely, and have taken their slaves there in great numbers. They would have done so, because the value of the labor of that class would have been augmented to them many hundred fold. Why, in the debates which took place in the convention in California which formed the constitution, and which any senator can now read for himself, after the provision excluding slavery was agreed upon, it was proposed to prohibit the African race altogether, free as well as bond. A debate arose upon it, and the ground was distinctly taken, as shown in those debates, that if the entire African race was not excluded, their labor would be found so valuable that the owners of slaves would bring them there, even though slavery were prohibited, under a contract to manumit them in two or three years. And it required very little reasoning, on the part of those opposed to this class of population, to show that the productiveness of their labor would be such as to cause that result. An estimate was gone into with reference to the value of the labor of this class of people, showing that it would be increased to such an extent in the mines of California, that they could not be kept out. It was agreed that the labor of a slave in any one of the states from which they would be taken, was not worth more than one hundred or one hundred and fifty dollars a year, and that in California it would be worth from four to six thousand dollars. They would work themselves free in one or two years, and thus the country would be filled by a class of free blacks, and their former owners have an excellent bargain in taking them there."

Yet Mr. Webster stands up before all this array, and

says, "Gentlemen, you are beside yourselves. You have eaten 'of the insane root.' You would look more in character should you put on the 'cap and bells.' In sober sense, in seeing his object clearly and in pursuing it directly, Don Quixote was Doctor Franklin, compared with *you*. The dog in the fable, who dropped his meat to snap at his shadow, is no allegory in your case. I see two classes around me,—wise men and fools; *you* do not belong to the former. The chancellor, who keeps the king's idiots, should have custody of you." Such is a faithful abstract of what Mr. Webster said to southern senators, and, through them, to all the south.

Here certainly was a reflection upon the understanding and intelligence of the south, such as never was cast upon them before. But the balm went with the sting. They bore the affront to their judgments, because it was so grateful to their politics and pockets. I think it no injustice to those senators to say, that they would have nearly torn Mr. Webster in pieces for such a collective insult, had it not promised to add, what Mr. Mason called "many hundred fold," to their individual property, and to secure and perpetuate their political ascendency.

To help our conceptions in regard to Mr. Webster's course on this subject, let us imagine a parallel case,—or, rather, an approximate one, for there can be no parallel. Suppose a contest between the north and the south, on the subject of the tariff, to have been raging for years. The sober blood of the north is heated to the fever point. The newspapers treat of nothing else. Public meetings and private conversations discuss no other theme. Hundreds of delegates wait upon Congress to add, if it be but a feather's weight, to the scale which holds their interests. Petitions flow in, in thousands and tens of thousands. It is announced that Mr. Calhoun will pour out his great mind on the subject. Expectation is on tiptoe. All eyes, from all sides of the country, are turned towards Washington, as the Moslem's to Mecca. The senate chamber is packed, and the illustrious senator rises. After an historic sketch of existing difficulties, after reading from the speeches which he made in 1832 and in 1846, he proceeds to say that he withdraws all opposition to a tariff, — to any tariff! He will not offend the delicate nerves of northern manufacturers by further hostility. Were a bill then before him, he would not oppose it. "Take the schedules," says he, scornfully, to northern senators, "and fill up the blanks from A to Z with what per centages you please. For *ad valorem* rates, put in minimums and maximums at your pleasure. I will 'taunt' you no longer. I am for peace and the glorious Union. I have discovered an irrepealable and irreversible law of nature, which overrules all the devices of men. You cannot make one yard of woollens or cottons in New England. There, water has no gravity, steam has no force, and wheels will not revolve. In Vermont and New York, wool will not grow on sheep's backs. I have penetrated the geology of Pennsylvania, and through all its stratifications there is not a thimble full of coal, nor an ounce of iron ore; and, if there were, combustion would not help to forge it; for oxygen and carbon are divorced. As Massachusetts contributed one third of the men and one third of the money to carry on the revolutionary war, I am willing to compensate her for her lost blood and treasure to the amount of hundreds of millions of dollars, with which she may fertilize the barrenness of her genius, and indulge her insane love for churches and schools." Had the great southern senator spoken thus, I think that even idolatrous, man-worshipping South Carolina, — a state which Mr. Calhoun has ruled and moved for the last twenty-five years, as a puppet showman plays Punch and Judy, — would have sent forth, through all her organs, a voice of unanimous dissent.

As much as freedom is higher than tariff, so much stronger than their dissent should be ours.

Mr. Webster's averment that he would not "reäffirm an ordinance of nature, nor reënact the will of God," (p. 44,) has been commented on more pungently than I am able or willing to do. It has been well said that all law and all volition must be in harmony with the will of the Good Spirit, or with that of the evil one; and if we will not reënact the will of the former, then, either all legislation ceases, or we must register the decrees of the latter. But one important and pertinent consideration belongs to this subject, which I have nowhere seen developed. It is this: Endless doubts and contradictions exist among men, as to what is the will of God; and on no subject is there a wider diversity of opinion than on this very subject of slavery. Whose law was reënacted by the ordinance of 1787? whose, when the African slave trade was prohibited? whose, when it was declared piracy? True, it is useless to put upon our statute books an astronomical law, regulating sunrise, or high tides; but that is physical and beyond the jurisdiction of man, while slavery belongs to morals, and is within the jurisdiction of man. Cease to transcribe upon the statute book what our wisest and best men believe to be the will of God in regard to our worldly affairs, and the passions which we think appropriate to devils will soon take possession of society. In regard to slavery, piracy, and so forth, there are multitudes of men whose fear of the penal sanctions of another life is very much aided by a little salutary fine and imprisonment in this. Look at that noble array of principles which is contained in the Declaration of Rights in the constitution of Massachusetts. Is it not a most grand and beautiful exposition of "the will of God," — a transcript, as it were, from the Book of Life? So of the amendments to the constitution of the United States. Yet our fathers thought it no tampering with holy things to enact them; and, in times of struggle and peril, they have been to many a tempted man as an anchor to the soul, sure and steadfast.

I approach Mr. Webster's treatment of the Texas question with no ordinary anxiety. Having been accustomed from my very boyhood to regard him as the almost infallible expounder of constitutional law, it is impossible to describe the struggle, the revulsion of mind, with which I have passed from an instructed and joyous acquiescence in his former opinions to unhesitating dissent from his present ones.

I must premise that I cannot see any necessary or beneficial connection between the subject of new Texan states and the admission of California and the government of the territories. The former refers to some indefinite future, when, from its fruitful womb of slavery, Texas shall seek to cast forth an untimely birth. In this excited state of the country, at this critical juncture of our affairs, when there is sober talk of massacring a majority of the House of Representatives on their own floor, and a senator, instead of merely threatening to hang a brother senator on the highest tree, provided he could catch him in his own state, now draws a revolver of six barrels on another brother senator, on the floor of the Senate, in mid-session; at such a time, I say, when, however few Abels there may be at work in the political field, there are Cains more than enough, would it not have been well to have acted upon the precept, "Sufficient unto the day is the evil thereof"?

As the basis of his argument, Mr. Webster quotes the following resolution for the admission of Texas, passed March 1, 1845:—

"New states of convenient size, not exceeding four in

number, in addition to said State of Texas, and having sufficient population, may hereafter, by the consent of the said state, be formed out of the territory thereof, which shall be entitled to admission under the provisions of the federal constitution. And such states as may be formed out of that portion of said territory lying south of 36° 30′ north latitude, commonly known as the Missouri compromise line, shall be admitted into the Union with or without slavery, as the people of each state asking admission may desire; and in such state or states as shall be formed out of said territory north of said Missouri compromise line, slavery or involuntary servitude, (except for crime,) shall be prohibited."

Note here, first, that only "*four*" states are to be admitted in "addition to said state of Texas;" and second, that "such state or *states*," (in the plural,) as shall be formed from territory north of 36° 30′, *shall be free*. If *two*, or only *one* free state is to exist on the *north* side of the line, then how many will be left for the *south* side? I should expose myself to ridicule were I to set it down arithmetically, *four* minus *one*, equal to *three*. Yet Mr. Webster says, "The guaranty is, that new states shall be made out of it, [the Texan territory,] and that such states as are formed out of that portion of Texas lying south of 36° 30′, may come in as slave states, to *the number of* FOUR, in addition to the state then in existence, and admitted at that time by these resolutions." (p. 29.)

Here Mr. Webster gives outright to the south and to slavery, one more state than was contracted for, — assuming the contract to be valid. He makes a donation, a gratuity, of an entire slave state, larger than many a European principality. He transfers a whole state, with all its beating hearts, present and future; with all its infinite susceptibilities of weal and woe, from the side of freedom to that of slavery, in the leger book of humanity. What a bridal gift for the harlot of bondage!

Was not the bargain hard enough, according to its

terms? Must we fulfil it, and go beyond it? Is a slave state, which dooms our brethren of the human race, perhaps interminably, to the vassal's fate, so insignificant a trifle, that it may be flung in, as small change on the settlement of an account? Has the south been so generous a copartner as to deserve this distinguished token of our gratitude?

Why, by parity of reasoning, could he not have claimed all the four states, "in addition to said state of Texas," as free states? The resolutions divide the territory into two parts, one north and one south of the line of 36° 30′. Could not Mr. Webster have claimed the four states for freedom, with as sound logic and with far better humanity than he surrendered them all to slavery? When Texas and the south have got their slave states "*to the number of four*" into the Union, whence are we to obtain our one or more free states? The contract will have been executed, and the consent of Texas for another state will be withheld.

Notwithstanding all this, Mr. Webster affirms the right of slavery to four more states, in the following words: "I know no form of legislation which can strengthen this. I know no mode of recognition that can add a tittle of weight to it." Catching the tone of his asseveration, I respond that I know no form of statement, nor process of reasoning, which can make it more clear, that this is an absolute and wanton surrender of the rights of the north and the rights of humanity.

But I hold the Texan resolutions to have been utterly void; and proceed to give the reasons for my opinion.

I begin by quoting Mr. Webster against himself. In an address to the people of the United States, emanating from the Massachusetts Anti-Texas state convention, held January 29th, 1845, the subjoined passage, which is understood, or rather, I may say, is now well known, to have been dictated by Mr. Webster himself, may be found : —

"But we desire not to be misunderstood. According to our convictions, there is no power in any branch of the government, or all its branches, to annex foreign territory to this Union. We have made the foregoing remarks only to show, that, if any fair construction could show such a power to exist any where, or to be exercised in any form, yet the manner of its exercise now proposed is *destitute of all decent semblance of constitutional propriety.*"

Thus cancelling the authority of Mr. Webster in 1850 by the authority of Mr. Webster in 1845, I proceed with the argument.

Though the annexation of Texas was in pursuance of a void stipulation, yet it is a clear principle of law, that when a contract void between the parties, has been *executed* by them, it cannot then be annulled. If executed, it becomes valid, not by virtue of the contract but by virtue of the execution. I bow to this legal principle, and would fulfil it. But any independent stipulation which remains unexecuted, remains invalid. Such is that part of the annexation resolutions which provides for the admission of a brood of Texan states. The resolutions themselves say, in express terms, that the new states are to be admitted "under the provisions of the federal constitution;" and the federal constitution says, "New states may be admitted *by the Congress* into this Union." By what Congress? Plainly, by the Congress in session at the time when application for admission is made; and by no other. The fourth Texan state may not be ready for admission for fifty years to come; and could the Congress of 1845 bind the Congress of 1900? The Congress of 1900, and all future Congresses, will derive their authority from the constitution of the United States, and not from any preceding Congress. Put the case in a negative form. Could the Congress of 1845 bind all future Congresses *not* to admit new states, and thus, *pro tanto*, annul the constitution? Positive or negative, the result is the same. No previous Congress, on such a subject, can enlarge or limit the power of a subsequent one. Whenever, therefore, the question of a new Texan state comes up for consideration, the Congress *then in being* must decide it on its own merits, untrammelled by any thing their predecessors have done; and, especially, free from a law which, while similar in spirit, is a thousand times more odious in principle than statutes of mortmain.

Admitting that a future Congress, on such a subject, might be bound by a *treaty*, I answer that there was no treaty; while the fact that a treaty clause was introduced into the resolutions, in the Senate, for the sake of obtaining certain votes that would never otherwise have been given in their favor, and under an express pledge from the Executive that the method by treaty should be adopted, which pledge was forthwith iniquitously broken by the President, leaves no element of baseness and fraud by which this proceeding was not contaminated. In the name of the constitution, then, and of justice, let every honest man denounce those resolutions as void alike in the forum of law and in the forum of conscience; and, admitting Texas herself to be in the Union, yet, when application is made for any new state from that territory, let the question be decided upon the merits it may then possess.

And was not Mr. Webster of the same opinion, when, in Faneuil Hall, in November, 1845, after the resolutions of annexation had passed, he made the following emphatic, but unprophetic, declaration: —

"It is thought, it is an idea I do not say how well founded, that there may yet be a hope for resistance to the consummation of the act of annexation. I can only say for one, that *if it should fall to my lot to have a vote on such a question,* AND I VOTE FOR THE ADMISSION INTO THIS UNION OF ANY STATE WITH A CONSTITUTION WHICH PROHIBITS EVEN THE LEGISLATURE FROM EVER SETTING THE BONDMEN FREE, I SHALL NEVER SHOW MY HEAD AGAIN, DEPEND UPON IT, IN FANEUIL HALL."

There is another objection to any future claim of Texas to be divided into states, which grows out of her own neglect to fulfil the terms and spirit of the agreement. In the "territory north of the Missouri compromise line, slavery or involuntary servitude, (except for crime,) shall be prohibited." So reads the bond. But if Texas suffer slavery to be extended over that part of her territory, then, when it becomes populous enough for admission, and is overspread with slavery, a new state may present a free constitution, be admitted by Congress, and before the slaves have time to escape, or to carry the question of freedom before the judicial tribunals, *presto!* this free constitution will be changed into a slave constitution, under the alleged right of a state to decide upon its own domestic institutions; and thus the word of promise, which was kept to the ear, will be broken to the hope. If Texas meant to abide by the resolutions of annexation, and to claim any thing under them, it was her clear and imperative duty forthwith to pass a law, securing freedom to every inhabitant north of the compromise line. In this way only can the resolutions be executed in their true spirit. That territory is now in the condition of an egg. It is undergoing incubation. From it a state is hereafter to be hatched; but before promising to accept the chick, it would be agreeable to know whether a viper had impregnated the egg.

There is a still further objection, of whose soundness I have no doubt; but should I be in error in regard to it, the mistake will not invalidate any other argument. The parties to that agreement stipulated on the ground of mutuality, without which all contracts are void. Some states were to be admitted to strengthen the hands of slavery, and some of freedom. A line of demarcation was drawn. Now, on investigation, I believe it will most conclusively appear that there is not an inch of Texan territory north of the stipulated line. It all belongs to New Mexico, as much as Nantucket or Berkshire belongs to Massachusetts. It was a mistake on the part of the contracting parties; if, on the part of Texas, it was not something worse than a mistake. The mutuality, then, fails. The contract is *nudum pactum.* Texas can give nothing for what she was to receive; and is, therefore, entitled to receive nothing but what she has got.

In regard to "the business of seeing that fugitives are delivered up," Mr. Webster says, "My friend at the head of the judiciary committee, [Mr. BUTLER, of South Carolina,] has a bill on the subject now before the Senate, with some amendments to it, which I propose to support, with all its provisions, to the fullest extent."

Here is Mr. Butler's bill, with Mr. Mason's amendments: —

A BILL

To provide for the more effectual execution of the 3d clause of the 2d section of the 4th article of the Constitution of the United States.

Be it enacted by the Senate and House of Representatives of the United States of America in Congress assembled, That when a person held to service or labor in any state or territory of the United States, under the laws of such state or territory, shall escape into any other of the said states or territories, the person to whom such service or labor may be due, his or her agent or attorney, is hereby empowered to seize or arrest such fugitive from service or labor, and take him or her before any judge of the circuit or district courts of the United States, or before any commissioner, or clerk of such courts, or marshal thereof, or any postmaster of the United States, or collector of the customs of the United States, residing or being within such state wherein such seizure or arrest shall be made, and upon proof to the satisfaction of such judge, commissioner, clerk, marshal, postmaster, or collector, as the case may be, either by oral testimony or affidavit taken before and certified by any person authorized to administer an oath under the laws of the United States, or of any state, that the person so seized or arrested, under the laws of the state or territory from which he or she fled, owes service or labor to the person claiming him or her, it shall be the duty of such judge, commissioner, clerk, marshal, postmaster, or collector, to give a certificate thereof to such claimant, his or her agent or attorney, which certificate shall be a sufficient warrant for taking and removing such fugitive from service or labor to the state or territory from which he or she fled.

SEC. 2. *And be it further enacted*, That when a person held to service or labor, as mentioned in the first section of this act, shall escape from such service or labor, as therein mentioned, the person to whom such service or labor may be due, his or her agent or attorney, may apply to any one of the officers of the United States named in said section, other than a marshal of the United States, for a warrant to seize and arrest such fugitive, and upon affidavit being made before such officer, (each of whom for the purposes of this act is hereby authorized to administer an oath or affirmation,) by such claimant, his or her agent, that such person does, under the laws of the state or territory from which he or she fled, owe service or labor to such claimant, it shall be, and is hereby made, the duty of such officer, to and before whom such application and affidavit is made, to issue his warrant to any marshal of any of the courts of the United States to seize and arrest such alleged fugitive, and to bring him or her forthwith, or on a day to be named in such warrant, before the officer issuing such warrant, or either of the officers mentioned in said first section, except the marshal to whom the said warrant is directed, which said warrant or authority the said marshal is hereby authorized and directed in all things to obey.

SECT. 3. *And be it further enacted*, That upon affidavit made as aforesaid by the claimant of such fugitive, his agent or attorney, after such certificate has been issued, that he has reason to apprehend that such fugitive will be rescued by force from his or their possession, before he can be taken beyond the limits of the state in which the arrest is made, it shall be the duty of the officer making the arrest to retain such fugitive in his custody, and to remove him to the state whence he fled, and there to deliver him to said claimant, his agent or attorney. And to this end, the officer aforesaid is hereby authorized and required to employ so many persons as he may deem necessary to overcome such force, and to retain them in his service so long as circumstances may require. The said officer and his assistants, while so employed, to receive the same compensation and to be allowed the same expenses as are now allowed by law for transportation of criminals, to be certified by the judge of the district within which the arrest is made, and paid out of the treasury of the United States : *Provided*, That, before such charges are incurred, the claimant, his agent or attorney, shall secure to said officer payment of the same, and in case no actual force be opposed, then they shall be paid by such claimant, his agent or attorney.

SEC. 4. *And be it further enacted*, When a warrant shall have been issued by any of the officers under the second section of this act, and there shall be no marshal or deputy marshal within ten miles of the place where such warrant is issued, it shall be the duty of the officer issuing the same, at the request of the claimant, his agent or attorney, to appoint some fit and discreet person, who shall be willing to act as marshal, for the purpose of executing said warrant; and such person so appointed shall, to the extent of executing said warrant, and detaining and transporting the fugitive named therein, have all the power and authority, and be, with his assistants, entitled to the same compensation and expenses provided in this act in cases where the services are performed by the marshals of the courts.

SEC. 5. *And be it further enacted*, That any person who shall knowingly and willingly obstruct or hinder such claimant, his agent or attorney, or any person or persons assisting him, her, or them, in so serving or arresting such fugitive from service or labor, or shall rescue such fugitive from such claimant, his agent or attorney, when so arrested, pursuant to the authority herein given or declared, or shall aid, abet, or assist such person so owing service or labor to escape from such claimant, his agent or attorney, or shall harbor or conceal such person, after notice that he or she was a fugitive from labor, as aforesaid, shall, for either of the said offences, forfeit and pay the sum of one thousand dollars, which penalty may be recovered by and for the benefit of such claimant, by action of debt in any court proper to try the same, saving, moreover, to the person claiming such labor or service, his right of action for, or on account of, the said injuries, or either of them.

SEC. 6. *And be it further enacted*, That when said person is seized or arrested, under and by virtue of the said warrant, by such marshal, and is brought before either of the officers aforesaid, other than the said marshal, it shall be the duty of such officer to proceed in the case of such person, in the same way as he is directed and authorized to do when such person is seized and arrested by the person claiming him, or by his or her agent or attorney, and is brought before such officer under the provisions of the first section of this act.

AMENDMENTS

Intended to be proposed by Mr. Mason to the bill (Senate, 23) to provide for the more effectual execution of the third clause of the second section of the fourth article of the Constitution of the United States.

At the end of section 5, add:

And any person or persons offending against the provisions of this section, to be moreover deemed guilty of a misdemeanor, or of obstructing the due execution of the laws of the United States, and upon conviction thereof shall be fined in the sum of one thousand dollars, one half whereof shall be to the use of the informer; and shall also be imprisoned for the term of twelve months.

At the end of section 6, add:

And in no trial or hearing under this act shall the testimony of such fugitive be admitted in evidence.

It will be observed that the first section of the bill after constituting the judges of the courts, the seventeen thousand postmasters, the collectors, &c., tribunals, *without appeal*, for the delivery of any body, who is sworn by any body, any where, to be a fugitive slave, refers to the before-mentioned officers in the words "residing or *being* within such state where such seizure or arrest is made." That is, the judge, postmaster, collector, &c., need not be an inhabitant of the state, or hold his office in the state where the seizure is made; but it is sufficient if he is such officer any where within the United States. Mr. Butler or Mr. Mason, therefore, may send the postmaster of his own city or village into Massachusetts, with an agent or attorney, who brings his affidavit from South Carolina or Virginia, in his pocket; the agent or attorney may arrest any body, at any time, carry him before his accomplice, go through with the judicial forms, and hurry him to the south; the officer, after his judicial functions are discharged, turning bailiff, protecting the prey and speeding the flight!

Still further; this bill derides the trial by jury, secured by the constitution. A man may not lose a horse without a right to this trial; but he may his freedom. Mr. Webster spoke for the south and for slavery; not for the north and for freedom, when he abandoned this right. Such an abandonment, it would be impossible to believe of one who has earned such fame as defender of the constitution; it would be more reasonable to suppose the existence of some strange misapprehension, had not Mr. Webster, with that precision and strength which are so peculiarly his own, declared his determination to support this hideous bill, "with all its provisions to the fullest extent," when, at the same moment, another bill, of which he took no notice, was pending before the Senate, introduced by Mr. Seward, of New York, securing the invaluable privilege of a jury trial.

I disdain to avail myself, in a sober argument, of the popular sensitiveness on this subject; and I acknowledge my obligations to the constitution while it is suffered to last. But still I say, that the man who can read this bill without having his blood boil in his veins, has a power of refrigeration that would cool the tropics.

I cannot doubt that Mr. Webster will yet see the necessity of reconsidering his position on this whole question.

Mr. Webster says, "It is my firm opinion, this day, that within the last twenty years as much money has been collected and paid to the abolition societies, abolition presses, and abolition lecturers, as would purchase the freedom of every slave, man, woman, and child, in the State of Maryland, and send them all to Liberia."

The total number of slaves in Maryland, according to the last census, amounted to 89,405. At $250 apiece, — which is but about half the value commonly assigned to southern slaves by southern men, — this would be $22,373,750. Allowing $30 each for transportation to Liberia, without any provision for them after their arrival there, the whole sum would be $25,058,600,— in round numbers, twenty-five millions of dollars! more than a million and a quarter in each year, and about thirty-five hundred dollars per day. I had not supposed the abolitionists had such resources at their command!

I have dwelt thus long upon Mr. Webster's speech, because in connection with his two votes in favor of Mr. Foote's committee of compromise, which votes, had they been the other way, would have utterly defeated the committee, it is considered to have done more to jeopard the great cause of freedom in the territories, than any other event of this disastrous session. I have spoken of Mr. Webster by name, and, I trust, in none but respectful terms. I might have introduced other names, or examined his positions without mentioning him. I have taken what seemed to me the more manly course; and if these views should ever by chance fall under his eye, I believe he has magnanimity enough to respect me the more for the frankness I have used. If I am wrong, I will not add to an error of judgment the meanness of a clandestine attack. If I am right, no one can complain; for we must all bow before the majesty of truth.

I have now noticed the principal events which have taken place in Congress, and which have led to what military men would call the "demoralization" of many of the rank and file of its members. Some recent movements have brought vividly to mind certain historical recollections in regard to the African slave trade, now execrated by all civilized nations. When the immortal Wilberforce exposed to public gaze the secrets of that horrid traffic, his biographer says, "The first burst of generous indignation promised nothing less than the instant abolition of the trade, but *mercantile* jealousy had taken the alarm, and the defenders of the West India system found themselves strengthened by the independent alliance of *commercial* men." —*Life of Wilberforce*, vol. i. p. 291.

Again; opposition to Wilberforce's motion "arose amongst the Guinea *merchants*," — "reënforced, however, before long by the great body of West India planters." — *Ibid.*

The corporation of Liverpool spent, first and last, upwards of £10,000 in defence of a traffic which even the gravity and calmness of judicial decisions have since pronounced "infernal."

"Besides printing works in defence of the slave trade and remunerating their authors; paying the expenses of delegates to attend in London and watch Mr. Wilberforce's proceedings, they pensioned the widows of

Norris and Green, and voted plate to Mr. Penny, for their exertions in this cause." — *Ibid.* p. 345.

It is said, that the corporation of Liverpool, at this time, "believed firmly that the very existence of the city depended upon the continuance of the traffic." Look at Liverpool now, and reflect what greater rewards, even of a temporal nature, God reserves for men that abjure dishonesty and crime.

All collateral motives were brought to bear upon the subject, just as they are at the present time. The Guinea trade was defended "as a nursery for seamen." — *Ibid.* p. 293.

Even as late as 1816, the same class of men, in the same country, opposed the abolition of "white slavery" in Algiers, from the same base motives of interest. It was thought that the danger of navigating the Mediterranean, caused by the Barbary corsairs, was advantageous to British commerce; because it might deter the merchant ships of other nations from visiting it. After Lord Exmouth had compelled the Algerines to liberate their European slaves, he proceeded against Tunis and Tripoli. In giving an account of what he had done, he defends his conduct "upon general principles," but adds, "as applying to our own country, [Great Britain,] it may not be borne out, *the old mercantile interest being against it.*" — *Osler's Life of Exmouth*, p. 303.

So after Admiral Blake, in the time of Cromwell, had attacked Tunis, he says, in his despatch to Secretary Thurloe, "And now seeing it hath pleased God soe signally to justify us herein, I hope his highness will not be offended at it, nor any who regard duly the honor of the nation, *although I expect to have the clamors of* INTERESTED MEN." — *Thurloe's State Papers*, vol. ii. p. 390.

And is commerce, the daughter of freedom, thus forever to lift her parricidal hand against the parent that bore her? Are rich men forever to use their "thirty pieces of silver," or their "ten thousand pounds sterling," or their hundreds of thousands of dollars, to reward the Judases for betraying their Savior? Viewed by the light of our increased knowledge, and by our more elevated standard of duty, the extension of slavery into California or New Mexico, at the present time, or even the sufferance of it there, is a vastly greater crime than was the African slave trade itself, in the last century; and I would rather meet the doom of posterity, or of heaven, for being engaged in the traffic then, than for being accessory to its propagation now.

Let those who aid, abet, or connive at slavery extension now, as they read the damning sentence which history has awarded against the actors, abettors, and connivers of the African trade, *but change the names*, and they will be reading of themselves. Should our new territories be hereafter filled with groaning bondmen, should they become an American Egypt, tyrannized over by ten thousand Pharaohs, it will be no defence for those who permitted it, to say, "We hoped, we supposed, we trusted, that slavery could not go there;" Nemesis, as she plies her scorpion lash, will reply, "*You might have made it certain.*"

On this great question of freedom or slavery, I have observed with grief, nay, with anguish, that we, at the north, break up into hostile parties, hurl criminations and recriminations to and fro, and expend that strength for the ruin of each other, which should be directed against the enemies of liberty; while, at the south, whenever slavery is in jeopardy, all party lines are obliterated, dissensions are healed, enemies become friends, and all are found in a solid column, with an unbroken front. Are the children of darkness to be forever *so much* wiser than the children of light? In the recent choice of delegates for the Nashville convention, I have not seen a single instance where Whig and Democrat have not been chosen as though they were Siamese twins, and must go together. But here it often happens, that as soon as one party is known to be in favor of one man, this preference alone is deemed a sufficient reason why another party should oppose him. Why can we not combine for the sacred cause of freedom, as they combine for slavery? No thought or desire is further from my mind than that of interfering with any man's right of suffrage; but if, (which is by no means impossible, nor perhaps improbable,) the fate of New Mexico should be decided by one vote, and my vote should have been the cause of a vacancy in any Congressional district that might have sent a friend to freedom, I should say, with Cain, "My punishment is greater than I can bear."

On the subject of the present alienation and discord between the north and the south, I wish to say that I have as strong a desire for reconciliation and amity as any one can have. There is no *pecuniary* sacrifice within the limits of the constitution, which I would not willingly make for so desirable an object. Public revenues I would appropriate, private taxation I would endure, to relieve this otherwise thrice-glorious republic from the calamity and the wrong of slavery. I would not only resist the devil, but if he will flee from me, I will build a bridge of gold to facilitate his escape. I mention this to prove that it is not the value, *in money*, of territorial freedom, for which I contend, but its value *in character, in justice, in human happiness.* While I utterly deny the claim set up by the south, yet I would gladly consent that my southern fellow-citizens should go to the territories and carry there every kind of property which I can carry; I would then give to the Southern States their full share of all the income ever to be derived from the sales of the public lands, or the leasing of the public mines;

and whatever, after this deduction, was left in the public treasury, should be appropriated for the whole nation, as has been the practice heretofore. That is, in consideration of excluding slavery from the territories, I would give the south a double share, or even a threefold share, of all the income that may ever be derived from them. Pecuniary surrenders I would gladly make for the sake of peace, but not for peace itself would I surrender liberty.

It would be to suppose our merchants and manufacturers void of common foresight, could they believe that concession now will bring security hereafter. By yielding the moral question, they jeopard their pecuniary interests. Should the south succeed in their present attempt upon the territories, they will impatiently await the retirement of General Taylor from the executive chair, to add the "State of Cuba," with its 500,000 slaves, its ignorance and its demoralization, to their roll of triumph. California will be a free-trade state, by the most certain of all biases. They will have nothing to sell but gold; they will have every thing to buy, — cradles and coffins, and all between. If New Mexico is slave, it will also be free trade; and Cuba as certainly as either, — though in that island facilities for smuggling will reduce the difference between tariff and free trade to nothing. A surrender, therefore, by our northern business men, will be most disastrous to the very business that tempts them to surrender. Will they take no warning from the fact that their apathy in regard to Texas repealed the tariff of 1842? This is a low motive, I admit; but it may be set as a back-fire to the motive by which some of them appear to be influenced. There was no need, not a shadow of need, of perilling any principle, nor any interest. Had the north stood firm, had they been true to the great principles they have so often and so solemnly proclaimed, the waves of southern violence would have struck harmless at their feet. He is not learned in the weather who does not know that storms from the south, though violent, are short. We are assailed now because we have yielded before. The compromise of 1820 begat the nullification of 1832; the compromise of 1832 inspired the mad exploit of compassing Texas, which our greater madness made sane. The moral paralysis which failed to oppose the Mexican war, has given us the territories. If the territories are now surrendered, we shall have Cuba, and an indefinite career of conquest and of slavery will be opened on our southwestern border. Every new concession transfers strength from our side to the side of our opponents; and if we cannot arrest our own course when we are just entering the rapids, how can we arrest it when we come near the verge of the cataract? The south may rule the Union, but they cannot divide it. Their whole Atlantic seaboard is open to attack, and powerless for defence; and the Mississippi River may as easily be divided physically as politically into independent portions. With these advantages, let us never aggress upon their rights, but let us maintain our own.

Fellow-citizens, I would gladly relieve the darkness of this picture by some gleams of light. There are two hopes which, as yet, are not wholly extinguished in my mind. Beyond all question, a compromise bill will be reported by the committee of thirteen, in which free California will be made to carry as great a burden of slavery as she can bear. It is still *possible* that the House will treat, as it deserves, this adulterous union. A single vote may turn the scale, and Massachusetts may give that vote. Not improbably, too, the fate of the bill may depend upon the earnestness and decision with which northern constituencies make their sentiments known to their representatives, whether by petitions, by private letters, or by public resolutions. Let every lover of freedom do his best and his most.

Should the north fail, I have still one hope more. It is, that New Mexico will do for herself what we shall have basely failed to do for her. If both these hopes fail, our country is doomed to run its unobstructed career of conquest, of despotism, and of infamy.

I have now, my fellow-citizens, given you my "Views and Opinions" on the present crisis in our public affairs. Had I regarded my own feelings, I should have spoken less at length; but the subject has commanded me. I trust I have spoken respectfully towards those from whom I dissent, while speaking my own sentiments justly and truly. I have used no asperity; for all my emotions have been of grief, and not of anger. My words have been cool as the telegraphic wires, while my feelings have been like the lightning that runs through them. The idea that Massachusetts should contribute or consent to the extension of human slavery! — is it not enough, not merely to arouse the living from their torpor, but the dead from their graves! Were I to help this, nay, did I not oppose it with all the powers and faculties which God has given me, I should see myriads of agonized faces glaring out upon me from the future, more terrible than Duncan's at Macbeth; and I would rather feel an assassin's poniard in my breast than forever hereafter to see "the air-drawn dagger" of a guilty memory. In Massachusetts, the great drama of the revolution began. Some of its heroes yet survive amongst us. At Lexington, at Concord, and on Bunker Hill, the grass still grows greener where the soil was fattened with the blood of our fathers. If, in the providence of God, we must be vanquished in this contest, let it be by force of the overmastering and inscrutable powers above us, and not by our own base desertion.

I am, gentlemen, your much honored, obliged, and obedient servant,

HORACE MANN.

LETTER II.

To the Editors of the Boston Atlas ;

Gentlemen ; Your semi-weekly of the 1st instant contains a letter of the Hon. Daniel Webster, to certain citizens of Newburyport, in which he has been pleased to refer to me, and particularly to a passage in the letter which I addressed to a portion of my constituents, on the 3d of May last, [the preceding Letter.] His reference to me is of so extraordinary a character, both as to manner and matter, that I wish to reply. To prevent all chance of mistake, I quote the following passages : —

" But, at the same time, nothing is more false than that such jury trial is demanded in cases of this kind by the constitution, either in its letter or in its spirit. The constitution declares that in all criminal prosecutions there shall be a trial by jury. The claiming of a fugitive slave is not a criminal prosecution.

" The constitution also declares that in suits at common law the trial by jury shall be preserved ; the reclaiming of a fugitive slave is not a suit at the common law ; and there is no other clause or sentence in the constitution having the least bearing on the subject.

" I have seen a publication by Mr. Horace Mann, a member of Congress from Massachusetts, in which I find this sentence. Speaking of the bill before the Senate, he says : ' This bill derides the trial by jury secured by the constitution. A man may not lose his horse without a right to this trial, but he may lose his freedom. Mr. Webster speaks for the south and for slavery, not for the north and for freedom, when he abandons this right.' This personal vituperation does not annoy me, but I lament to see a public man of Massachusetts so crude and confused in his legal apprehensions, and so little acquainted with the constitution of his country, as these opinions evince Mr. Mann to be. His citation of a supposed case, as in point, if it have any analogy to the matter, would prove that, if Mr. Mann's horse stray into his neighbor's field, *he cannot lead him back without a previous trial by jury to ascertain the right.* Truly, if what Mr. Mann says of the provisions of the constitution in this publication be a test of his accuracy in the understanding of that instrument, he would do well not to seek to protect his peculiar notions under its sanction, but to appeal at once, as others do, to that higher authority which sits enthroned above the constitution and above the law."

I must deny this charge of "personal vituperation;" nothing was further from my thoughts; and I regret that Mr. Webster, while disclaiming "annoyance" at what I said, should betray it. I believe every part of my "Letter" to be within the bounds of courteous and respectful discussion. There is nothing in it which might not pass between gentlemen, without interrupting relations of civility or friendship. Though full of regret at his novel position, and of dissent from his unwonted doctrines, yet it abounds in proofs of deference to himself. I must now, however, be permitted to add that the highest eminence becomes unenviable when it breeds intolerance of dissent, or bars out the humblest man from a free expression of opinion.

Mr. Webster "laments to see a public man of Massachusetts so crude and confused in his legal apprehensions, and so little acquainted with the constitution of his country, as these opinions evince Mr. Mann to be." Yet he points out no error of opinion. He specifies nothing as unsound. Judgment and condemnation alone appear. He seems to have taken it for granted that he had only to say I was guilty, and then proceed to punish. I protest against and impugn this method of proceeding, by any man, however high, against any man, however humble.

When Mr. Webster penned his "lamentations" over my crudeness, confusion, and ignorance, he doubtless meant to deal me a mortal blow. The blow was certainly heavy; but the question still remains, *whether it hit.* Polyphemus struck hard blows, but his blindness left the objects of his passions unharmed.

But wherein do those erroneous "opinions" consist, which Mr. Webster does not deign to specify, but assumes to condemn? Fortunately, in writing the sentence which he quotes for animadversion, I followed the precise meaning of Judge Story, as laid down in his Commentaries; and in regard to the only point which is open to a question, *I took the exact words* of that great jurist. He speaks of "the right of a trial by jury, in civil cases," as an existing right *before* the seventh article of amendment to the constitution, which *preserves this right* "in suits at common law," had been adopted. (3 Comm., 628.) Instead of transcribing Judge Story's words, "in civil cases," which present no distinct image to common minds, I supposed the every-day case of litigation respecting a horse, which is a "civil case;" and this difference of form is the only difference between my language and that of the learned judge. I can wish Mr. Webster no more fitting retribution, after reposing from this ill-tempered attack upon me, than to awake and find that it was Judge Story whom he had been maligning.

Does not the authority of Judge Blackstone also support my position? He says, —

"Recapture or reprisal is another species of remedy, by the mere act of the party injured. . . . But as the public peace is a superior consideration to any one man's private property; and as, if individuals were once allowed to use private force as a remedy for private injuries, all social justice must cease, the strong would give law to the weak, and every man would revert to a state of nature; for these reasons, it is provided that this natural right of recaption shall never be exerted, where such exertion must occasion strife and bodily contention, or endanger the peace of society. If, for instance, my horse is taken away, and I find him in a common, a fair, or a public inn, I may lawfully seize him to my own use; but I cannot justify breaking open a private stable, *or entering on the grounds of a third person, to take him*, should he be feloniously stolen; *but must have recourse to an action at law*." — *Comm.* 4, 5.

But the opinion expressed by me on this point does not need the authority of any name to support it; and the illustration which I gave is not only intelligible to every sensible man, but is also apposite. I said "a man may not lose his horse, [i. e. his property in a horse,] without a right to this trial." Mr. Webster's comment is, that this case, "if it have any analogy to the matter," means, that if a man's horse "*stray* into his neighbor's field, *he cannot lead him back without a previous trial by jury to ascertain the right*." Was ever the plain meaning of a sentence more exactly changed about, end for end? Mr. Webster may pitch somersets with his own doctrines, but he has no right to pitch them with mine. I said a man may not *lose* his horse, or his property in a horse, without a right to the trial by jury. He says I said, a man cannot *find* or *retake* a lost horse, without a previous trial! *Dulce est desipere in loco.* Or, it is pleasant to see a grave senator play upon words; — though there should be some wit to redeem it from puerility.

But the childishness of this criticism is not its worst feature. What is the great *truth* which Mr. Webster and his apologists attempt here to ridicule? It is this: While every man amongst us, in regard to any piece of property worth more than twenty dollars, of which violence or fraud may attempt to despoil him, has a right to a trial by jury; yet a man's freedom and that of his posterity forever, may be wrested from him, as our law now stands, without such a trial. Does not this hold a man's freedom to be of less value than twenty dollars? If two adverse claimants contest title to an alleged slave, whose market value is more than this sum, each is entitled to a jury to try the fact of ownership. But if the alleged slave declares, here, in Massachusetts, that he owns himself, he is debarred from this right. And this truth, or a common illustration of it, Mr. Webster and his apologists think a suitable topic for sneers or pleasantry! A French proverb says, that for a man to kill his mother *is not in good taste.* I trust the moral and religious people of Massachusetts have too much *good taste* to relish jokes on such a theme.

Again; I said that Mr. Butler's bill "derides" the trial by jury. By that bill every commissioner and clerk of a United States court, every marshal and collector of the customs, and the seventeen thousand postmasters of the United States, are severally invested with jurisdiction and authority in all parts of the United States, to deliver any man, woman, or child in the United States, into custody, as a slave, on the strength of an *ex parte* affidavit, made any where in the United States. This affidavit may have been made a thousand miles off, by no one knows whom, and certified to by a person who never saw or heard of the individual named in it. A forged affidavit, or a fictitious affidavit, would often answer the purpose as well; for how difficult, and in many cases, how impossible, to prove its spuriousness. Did oppression ever before conceive such a tribunal, so countless in numbers, so ample in jurisdiction, so terrible in power? Had a bill similar to this been proposed in the British Parliament, from 1763 to 1776, what would our fathers have said of it? Yet this bill, with some kindred amendments, heightening its features of atrocity, Mr. Webster promised "to support, with all its provisions, to the fullest extent."

What aggravates the wrong, is, that the cruelties of the measure will fall upon the poor, the helpless, the ignorant, the unfriended. The bill would have been far less disgraceful, had its provisions borne upon the men who should pass it; because, in such case, there would have been a touch of equality. Now, if this bill does not "*deride*" all guaranties for the protection of human liberty, it is only because my word of reprobation is too weak. It is only because one needs "to tear a leaf from the curse-book of Pandemonium" in order to describe it by fitting epithets.

Another remarkable feature of Mr. Butler's bill is, that it provides no penalty whatever for any one who shall abuse, or fraudulently use, the dangerous authority which it gives. It furnishes endless temptations and facilities for committing wrong: it imposes no restraints; it warns by no threats of retribution.

Mr. Webster calls me to account for some unspecified erroneous "opinion," expressed in relation to this bill. Can any opinion be so false to the constitution, as this bill to humanity? I deprecate error of all sorts; but hold it to be more venial to err in judgment than in heart.

I said that in promising to support Mr. Butler's bill, "with all its provisions, to the fullest extent," Mr. Webster "abandoned" the right to a trial by jury. I spoke of him as a senator, as one who, with his co-legislators, was bound, in fulfilment of his constitutional duty, to secure this form of trial to the alleged slave, or to a known freeman seized as a slave. Mr. Seward's bill, providing for the trial by jury, in such cases, was before him. He took no notice of it. He passed by "on the other side," while he bestowed his best encomium on Mr. Butler's bill, by promising to support it. Was not this an "abandonment," under any of the synonymes given in the dictionary?

Mr. Webster advises me, in a certain contingency, "to appeal to that higher authority which sits enthroned above the constitution and above the law." I take no exception to this counsel, because of its officiousness, but would thank him for it. My ideas of duty require me to seek anxiously for the true interpretation of the constitution, and then to abide by it, unswayed by hopes or fears. If the constitution requires me to do any thing which my sense of duty forbids, I shall save my conscience by resigning my office. I am free, however, to say, that if, in the discharge of my political duties, I should transfer my allegiance to any other power, I should adopt Mr. Webster's ironical advice, and go to the power "which sits enthroned above," rather than descend to that opposite realm, whence the bill he so cordially promised to support must have emerged.

I wish, however, to remark, that though I acknowledge the constitution to be my guide while under oath to support it, yet I do not relish this fling either at the powers above us, or at those who reverence them. I hold it to be not only proper, but proof of sound moral and religious feeling, to look to the perfect law of God for light to enable us more justly to interpret the imperfect laws of man. Especially, when we are proposing to make or amend a law, ought we to take our gauge of purpose and of action from the highest standard.

Noy, that Solomon of the law, thought it not improper to say, "The inferior law must give place to the superior; man's laws to God's laws." — *Maxims*, pp. 6, 7.

"The law of Nature," says Blackstone, "being coeval with mankind, and dictated by God himself, is, of course, superior in obligation to any other. It is binding all over the globe; in all countries, at all times. No human laws have any validity, if contrary to this;

and such of them as are valid, derive all their force and all their authority, mediately or immediately, from this original." — 1 *Com.* 41.

Fortescue, the Chancellor of Henry VI., in his *De Laudibus Legum Angliæ*, cap. 42, has the following passage, the consideration of which, in requital for Mr. Webster's advice to me, I respectfully commend to him : —

"That must necessarily be adjudged a cruel law, which augments slavery, and diminishes liberty. For human nature implores, without ceasing, for liberty. Slavery is introduced by man, and through his vice. But liberty is the gift of God to man. Wherefore, when torn from a man, it ever yearns to return ; and it is the same with every thing when deprived of its natural liberty. On this account, that man is to be adjudged cruel, who does not favor liberty. By these considerations the laws of England, in every case, give favor to liberty."

Having defended my own propositions, I shall now take the liberty to examine some of Mr. Webster's ; and, in so doing, I shall examine the constitutional provisions for trial by jury, and fortify my opinion by historical references. I shall consider,

I. *Where Congress has power to provide for such trial.*

II. *Where it is the duty of Congress to do so.*

Mr. Webster says "the constitution declares, that in all criminal prosecutions, there shall be a trial by jury ;" and that "in suits at common law the trial by jury shall be preserved." He then adds, "There is no other clause or sentence in the constitution having the least bearing upon the subject." Mark his words : "There is no other clause or sentence in the constitution, *having the least bearing on the subject.*" This I deny.

Here Mr. Webster virtually declares that, but for the above-named two provisions, the right of the trial by jury would not have been secured to us by the constitution *in any case.* Of course, in the absence of these provisions, Congress would have been under no obligation, nor would it, indeed, have had any power, to provide by law for such trials.

Were I to say that this assertion borders on the incredible, one might well ask, Which side of the line does it lie ?

The provision for a trial by jury, *in criminal prosecutions,* is in the third clause of the second section of the third article, and is repeated, and somewhat enlarged, in the fifth and sixth articles of amendment.

But the provision for trial by jury, *in suits at common law,* is in the seventh article of amendment ; and neither this provision, nor any semblance of it, is to be found, in express words, in any part of the constitution as it came from the hands of its framers, and was adopted by the states.

According to Mr. Webster, then, Congress was under no obligation, and had no power, to make a law providing for trial by jury, *except in criminal prosecutions,* until *after* the seventh article of amendment had been ratified ; for if they had any such power, or were under any such obligation, it must be by virtue of some clause or sentence in the constitution, *having a " bearing upon the subject."*

Now, the first session of Congress commenced March 4th, 1789, but this seventh article of amendment was not ratified, and did not become a part of the constitution, according to Hickey, (Hickey's Const. p. 36,) until December 15, 1791.

Until this time, therefore, according to Mr. Webster, the constitution had secured no right to a trial by jury, except in the case of *criminal prosecutions ;* because, until this time, there was no clause or sentence in it " having the least bearing on the subject " of jury trials in any but criminal cases.

Yet, on the 24th of September, 1789, *and more than two years previous to the adoption of the seventh amendment*, (by which alone, according to Mr. Webster, they had any power to act in the premises,) Congress did pass the judiciary act; by the ninth, twelfth, and thirteenth sections of which it is provided, that the trial of issues in fact, in the district courts, in the circuit courts, and in the supreme court, shall, with certain exceptions, be by jury.

The act also empowers the courts to grant new trials "for reasons for which new trials have usually been granted in the courts of law." In what courts of law? Did it not mean the courts in Westminster Hall, and those in this country formed after that ancestral model? And does not this show beyond question or cavil, that the principle of the jury trial, *in civil cases*, was incorporated into the constitution of the United States, originally; and that it was universally understood to be so by its framers, and by their contemporaries, the members of the first Congress?

From the constitution alone, then, and not from any power above it, or outside of it, did Congress derive its power, on the 24th of September, 1789, and more than two years before the seventh amendment was adopted, to pass the judiciary act, and to fill it full of the fact and the doctrine of jury trials in civil cases. And if Congress, at that time, had legislated on the subject of fugitive slaves, would it not have had the same power to provide the trial by jury, to determine the question, slave or free, as it had to provide for this mode of trial in other cases?

All the state conventions for adopting the constitution, whose debates are preserved, and all the leading men who figured in them, held, — contrary to Mr. Webster, — that the third article in the constitution, providing for courts, carried jury trials in civil cases with it. Mr. Marshall, afterwards Chief Justice Marshall said in the Virginia convention, "Does the word *court*, [in the constitution,] only mean the judges? Does not the determination of a jury necessarily lead to the judgment of the court? Is there any thing which gives the judges exclusive jurisdiction of matters of fact? What is the object of a jury trial? To inform the court of the facts. When a court has cognizance of facts, does it not follow that they can make inquiry by a jury? It is impossible to be otherwise." — 3 *Elliott's Debates*, 506.

The third article in the Virginia bill of rights was as follows: —

"In controversies respecting property, and in suits between man and man, the ancient trial by jury is preferable to any other, and ought to be held sacred."

This article being read in the convention, Judge Marshall said *the trial by jury was as well secured by the United States constitution, as by the Virginia bill of rights.* — Ib. 524. He said this in reference to civil cases.

In the Massachusetts convention, it was said, without a doubt's being expressed from any quarter, that "the word *court* does not, either by popular or technical construction, exclude the use of a jury to try facts. When people in common language talk of a trial at the court of common pleas, or the supreme judicial court, do they not include all the branches and members of such courts, the jurors as well as the judges? They certainly do, whether they mention the jurors expressly or not. Our state legislators have construed the word *court* in the same way." — 2 *Elliott's Debates*, 127.

Such was the doctrine maintained by the leading minds of the state conventions; by Christopher Gore, in Massachusetts; by Judge Wilson, and Chief Justice McKean, in Pennsylvania; by Chief Justice Marshall

Judge Pendleton, and Mr. Madison, in Virginia; by Judge Iredell, in North Carolina, and many other distinguished names.

In the Virginia convention, objection was made to the constitution because it did not *expressly* secure to the accused the privilege of challenging or excepting to jurors in criminal cases. But Mr. Pendleton, the President of the convention, and for so many years afterwards the highest judicial officer in the state, replied: "When the constitution says that the trial shall be by jury, does it not say that every incident will go along with it?" — 3 *Elliott's Debates*, 497.

So when the constitution provided for "courts," and defined their jurisdiction, it clearly contemplated the trial by jury, in regard to all such rights of the citizen as had been usually, theretofore, tried by a jury. Congress, indeed, might fail to perform its duty; but in such case, no provisions of the constitution, however express and peremptory. would secure the rights of the people.

It is perfectly well known to every student of the constitution, that the only reason why that instrument did not make *express* provision for the trial by jury, in civil cases, was the difficulty of running the dividing line between the many cases that should be so tried, and the few that should not. All were agreed that ninety-nine per cent. of all civil cases should be tried by jury; but they could not agree upon the classes of cases from which the remaining one per cent. should be taken.

In this connection, it is worth while to notice the heading or preamble of the joint resolutions for submitting certain proposed amendments of the constitution to the states, among which was the seventh. It is as follows: —

"The conventions of a number of the states having at the time of their adopting the constitution expressed a desire, in order to prevent misconstruction or abuse of its powers, that further declaratory or restrictive clauses should be added; and as the extending the ground of public confidence in the government will best insure the beneficent ends of its institution, RESOLVED," &c.

From this it appears that the first Congress only proposed to submit certain "*further declaratory and restrictive clauses*," which were "to prevent misconstruction or abuse of its powers." This heading or title, of course, does not enlarge or limit the meaning of the amendments; but it shows the view which their authors had of their scope and intendment. And what is the seventh amendment but a "declaratory and restrictive clause," securing the trial by jury, in cases at common law, "where the value in controversy shall exceed twenty dollars," and abandoning it where the value is less?

The phraseology of the amendment is full of significance: "The right of trial by jury shall be preserved." Not created, but preserved. Not instituted *de novo*, but continued. Will Mr. Webster tell me, how a right can be *preserved*, which does not already *exist?*

In speaking of the trial by jury, in criminal cases, Judge Story uses the same word. He says it was "preserved." In neither class of cases, civil or criminal, was it ever abandoned or lost, through the fault of the constitution. If not always enjoyed by the citizen, it has been through the dereliction of Congress in not passing the requisite laws.

The great men who submitted this seventh amendment to the states, treated the trial by jury, in civil cases, as a then subsisting constitutional right. They passed a law to put the practical enjoyment of this right into the hands of the people, well knowing that there is scarcely a right which we hold under the constitution which we can beneficially possess or use, without the intervention of some law, as its channel or medium.

Suppose this seventh amendment had never been adopted, on what ground would the trial by jury, in civil cases, have rested up to the present day? Could it have been taken from us all, in all cases except criminal ones, by any corrupt Congress?

In asserting, therefore, that, besides the references he has made, there is not another "clause or sentence in the constitution, *having the least bearing on the subject*" of jury trials, Mr. Webster is contradicted by the members of the general convention, by the state conventions, by the senators and representatives, who passed the judiciary act, by President Washington who signed it, and by all the judges who administered that act until the seventh amendment was adopted.

II. *Where it is the duty of Congress to provide for trial by jury.*

But another of Mr. Webster's assertions is still more extraordinary. He says "nothing is more false than that such jury trial, [a trial by jury for an alleged slave, or for a freeman claimed as a slave,] is demanded by the constitution, either in its letter or in its spirit."

I make a preliminary remark upon the grossness of the error embodied in the form of this proposition.

"*Nothing is more false;*" that is, if I, or any one, had affirmed that our constitution forbids trial by jury, in all cases, under penalty of death; or that it creates an hereditary despotism; or that it establishes the Catholic religion, with the accompaniment of an inquisition for each state; or that it does all these things together; it would not be more "*false*" to the "*spirit*" of the constitution, than to say that it demands the trial by jury, when a man who is seized as a slave, but who asserts that he is free, invokes its protection.

But this pertains to the *form* only of his assertion, and is immaterial to the argument. I proceed to inquire whether its substance be not as indefensible as its form.

In another part of Mr. Webster's letter, he says, that he sees "no objection to the provisions of the law" of 1793. Of course; for he sees no objection to Mr. Butler's bill, and its amendments; but prefers them to Mr. Seward's. And he now says, there is nothing in the letter or in the "spirit" of the constitution, which demands the jury trial for an alleged slave, or for a freeman captured and about to be carried away as a slave.

Feeble and humble as I am, great and formidable as he is, I join issue with him on this momentous question, and put myself upon the country.

Our constitution, as the present generation has always been taught, yearns towards liberty and the rights of man. The trial by jury, in the important cases of life, liberty, and property, is essential to these rights. The two, therefore, have such close affinity for each other, as to render it highly probable, if not morally certain, that the framers of the former would make provision for the latter; that they would lay hold of it, as by a law of instinct, to carry out their beneficent purposes. The trial by jury was necessary to the vitality of the constitution; and, I think, it would not be too strong an expression to say that the constitution, as it came from the hands of its founders, necessitated the trial by jury.

The object for which the constitution was framed, as set forth in its preamble, — namely, to "establish justice," "promote the general welfare," and "secure the blessings of liberty," to the people, — could never be accomplished without the trial by jury. The preamble is not appealed to as a source of power; but it touches, as by the finger, the objects which it contemplated; it suggests the means by which its beneficent purposes were to be fulfilled, and it indicates the rules of interpretation by which all its provisions are to be expounded.

And not only the objects for which the constitution professes to exist, but historical facts from the time of Magna Charta, and before that time; the practice of the English and of our Colonial and Provincial courts before the revolution and during the confederacy; — in fine, all analogies and tendencies of constitutional law, and whatever belongs to ideas of freedom, conspire to force the expectation upon us, that, in a matter of such vast concernment as the life-long liberty or bondage of a man and his offspring, it has *not* left us without the right of trial by jury.

The very first law "for the general good of the colony of New Plymouth," (1623,) was, "that all criminal acts, and also all matters of *trespasses* and DEBTS, between man and man, should be tried by the verdict of twelve honest men."

In that fearful array of crimes which the Declaration of Independence charges home upon the king of Great Britain, that sublime instrument enumerates the following as among the most flagitious: "For depriving us, in many cases, of the benefits of trial by jury," and "for protecting his troops, *by a mock trial*, from punishment for any murders which they should commit on the inhabitants of these states."

According to Blackstone, the right to a trial by jury had been held, "time out of mind," to be the birthright of Englishmen. The 29th chapter of the Great Charter guarantied this right, not only in cases of liberty, life, and limb, but in cases of property, real and personal.

In England, it has become a traditional saying, and drops from the common tongue, that the great object of king, lords, and commons, is to get twelve men into the jury box.

Judge Story says, "When our more immediate ancestors removed to America, they brought this great privilege with them, *as their birthright and inheritance*, as a part of that admirable common law which had fenced round, and interposed barriers on every side, against the approaches of arbitrary power. It is now incorporated into all our state constitutions, as a fundamental right; and the constitution of the United States would have been justly obnoxious to the most conclusive objection, if it had not recognized and confirmed it in the most solemn terms." — 3 *Com.* 652, 3.

Is it conceivable, then, that the heroes and sages of the revolution, who rose in resistance to the most formidable power on earth; so many of whom rose against their own kindred in the mother country, because they loved liberty better than father or mother, or brother or sister, and who endured the privations and horrors of a seven years' war; — is it conceivable, I say, that, when they had achieved their independence, and there was no longer any earthly power to control them, they should have framed a fundamental law, and should not have imbued that law with the "*spirit*" of the trial by jury, as its breath of life? As British subjects, they were entitled to this trial. As Americans, did they renounce it? Did they wage war for seven years in order to place themselves in a worse condition than they had been placed in by their "tyrant"? Mr. Webster says they did. He charges this infinite folly and blindness upon them, singly and collectively, one and all.

I will now fortify this historical view, by a reference to some decisions of the supreme court which explain and define the meaning of the seventh amendment.*

What is the true meaning of those descriptive words, "suits at common law"? Has not Mr. Webster, relying on his high reputation, disposed of this matter a little too summarily? He says, "The constitution

* This argument may be found repeated and enlarged upon in a subsequent part of the present volume, p. 409, *et seq.* It is retained here only to preserve the logical and legal symmetry of the letter.

ieclares that in suits at common law, the trial by jury hall be preserved;" but he adds, "The reclaiming of fugitive slave is not a suit at common law."

But the supreme court of the United States has urnished us with an authoritative interpretation of the vords of the constitution bearing on this subject. In he case of *Cohens* vs. *Virginia*, 6 Wheaton, R. 407, hey define what is meant by a "suit." These are heir words: —

"What is a *suit?* We understand it to be the prosecution, r pursuit, of some *claim*, demand, or request. In law language, it is the prosecution of some demand in a court of ustice. 'The remedy for every species of wrong is,' says udge Blackstone, 'the being put in possession of that right vhereof the party injured is deprived.' The instruments vhereby this remedy is obtained are a diversity of *suits* and ctions, which are defined by the Mirror to be 'the lawful denand of one's right;' or, as Bracton and Fleta express it in he words of Justinian, '*jus prosequendi in judicio quod ilicui debetur*,' — (the form of prosecuting in trial, or judgnent, which is due to any one.) Blackstone then proceeds to lescribe every species of remedy by suit; and they are all cases where the party suing claims to obtain something to which he has a right.

"To commence a suit is to demand something by the institution of process in a court of justice; and to prosecute the suit is, according to the common acceptation of language, to continue that demand."

According to the supreme court, then, a *suit* is the prosecution of some *claim*, demand, or request. Now, he proceedings for a fugitive slave, according to the very letter of the constitution, are instituted to prosecute a *claim*. The person held to service or labor is o be delivered up, "on *claim* of the party to whom such service or labor may be due."

Still further, in a decision bearing directly on the ight to a trial by jury, the supreme court have defined he term "common law" in special reference to its meaning in the amendment to the constitution, which secures this right "in suits at common law." These are their words: —

"It is well known that in civil causes, in courts of equity and admiralty, juries do not intervene; and that courts of equity use the trial by jury only in extraordinary cases, to inform the conscience of the court. When, therefore, we find that the [7th] amendment requires that the right of trial by jury shall be preserved, in suits at common law, the natural conclusion is, that this distinction was present to the minds of the framers of the amendment. By *common law* they meant what the constitution denominated in the third article 'law;' not merely suits which the *common* law recognized among its old and settled proceedings; but suits in which *legal* rights were to be ascertained and determined, in contradistinction to those in which equitable rights alone were recognized, and equitable remedies were administered, or in which, as in the admiralty, a mixture of public law, and of maritime law and equity, was often found in the same suit. Probably there were few, if any, states in the Union, in which some new legal remedies, differing from the old common law forms, were not in use; but in which, however, the trial by jury intervened, and the general regulations in other respects were according to the course of the common law. Proceedings in cases of partition, and of foreign and domestic attachment, might be cited as examples variously adopted and modified. *In a just sense, the amendment, then, may well be construed to embrace all suits, which are not of equity or admiralty jurisdiction,* WHATEVER MAY BE THE PECULIAR FORM WHICH THEY MAY ASSUME TO SETTLE LEGAL RIGHTS." — *Parsons* vs. *Bedford*, 3 *Peters's Rep.* 456, 7.

The last sentence I have underscored. In this sentence, the supreme court plainly say, that, if the subject matter of the litigation, or the object of the proceeding, be to determine a "legal right" which was formerly determined by a "suit at common law," then such proceeding is embraced in the seventh amendment, and either party in interest has a right to the trial by jury. Now, is it not clear that any proceeding which determines whether a man owns himself, or is owned by another man, and which delivers one man into the custody of another, as his slave, or refuses so to deliver him, is, "whatever peculiar form it may assume," a proceeding "to settle a legal right," — the highest legal right? It is not a right in equity, in admiralty, or under the maritime law; but strictly and exclusively a *legal right*, and nothing else. According to the doctrine of the supreme court, then, in the above-cited case, the parties to such a proceeding have a right, under the seventh amendment, to a trial by jury. At least, is not such the "*spirit*" of the amendment?

But there is another well-known fact, which gives pertinence and stringency to the above view. At common law, the writ *de homine replegiando*, — the writ of personal replevin, or for replevying a man, — was an original writ; a writ which the party could sue out of right; one to be granted on motion, without showing cause, and which the court of chancery could not supersede. It was, according to the very language of our supreme court, recognized by the common law "among its old and settled proceedings." The form of it is found in that great arsenal of common law writs, the *Registrum Brevium*. A man, says Comyn, may have a *homine replegiando* for a negro; or for an Indian brought by him into England and detained from him; or it may be brought by an infant against his testamentary guardian; *or by a villein against his lord.* (Dig., Title Imprisonment, L. 4.)

If it could be brought by a villein against his lord, then it was the very writ for an alleged slave against an alleging owner. It was the mode provided by the common law for the determination of the *legal right* asserted in a human being. I have always understood that, before the revolution, and before the framing of our constitution, Comyn's Digest was a work of the highest authority. It must have been well known to all the lawyers in the convention. Did they expect, then, that when an alleged slave, or a known freeman, should be seized, that he should be hurried into bondage without any right to this ancient muniment of the subject's liberties ?

But "the reclaiming of a fugitive slave," says Mr. Webster, "is not a suit at the common law." The proceedings provided for by the statute of 1793, to which he "sees no objection," have no analogy to the writ *de homine replegiando.* But can you destroy the right to a jury trial by changing the process ? A sand-hiller from Georgia or North Carolina cannot come to Massachusetts and eject Mr. Webster from his Marshfield farm without being compelled to submit the question of title to a jury. But suppose Congress should say, in effect, that any one of the seventeen thousand postmasters in the United States might be brought into Massachusetts, (and, among so numerous a body, it is no libel to say there are some reckless men,) and that the said sand-hiller might go before the said imported postmaster, and after proof "to his satisfaction," "either by oral testimony or by affidavit," — an affidavit, be it remembered, taken any where in the United States, — then the claimant shall be put into immediate possession of the said farm, with a right to recover costs ; and suppose Mr. Webster should spurn the authority of this illegitimate court, and demand an observance of the ancient forms of law, and a trial by jury under the seventh amendment ; then the claimant has only to borrow Mr. Webster's own words, and say, "This is not a suit at the common law :" — suppose all this, I say, and I would then ask if such a proceeding would be satisfactory to the last-named gentleman ? The common sense of mankind is authority good enough to answer such a question ; but we have high legal authority in addition.

In *Baker* vs. *Riddle*, Mr. Justice Baldwin, one of

the judges of the supreme court of the United States, held that it was not in the power of Congress to take away the right of trial by jury, secured by the seventh amendment, either, — "1. By an organization of the courts in such a manner as not to secure it to suitors;" or, — "2. By authorizing the courts to exercise, or their assumption of, equity or admiralty jurisdiction over cases at law." "This amendment," says he, "preserves the right of jury trial against any infringement by any department of the government." — *Baldwin's Rep.* 404.

Now, what was Mr. Butler's bill but "a new organization of the courts," or, rather, a new creation of some twenty thousand courts, "in such a manner as not to secure [the right of trial by jury] to suitors?" It was, indeed, a violation of both of the principles laid down by Judge Baldwin. It was the creation of tribunals unknown to the common law, and authorizing those tribunals to decide upon rights not belonging to either "equity or admiralty jurisdiction."

In this connection, I will refer to the case of *Lee* vs. *Lee*, 8 *Peters's Rep.* 44.

By act of Congress of April 2, 1816, it was declared that no cause should be removed from the circuit court of the District of Columbia to the supreme court by appeal or writ of error, "unless the matter in dispute shall be of the value of one thousand dollars or upwards." The plaintiffs in error were claimed as slaves. Their petition for freedom in the court below had been decided against them; and from this decision they appealed. The defendant in error took the objection that they, — their bodies and souls, — were not worth one thousand dollars, and therefore that they had no right to appeal. But the court said, —

"The matter in dispute, in this case, is the freedom of the petitioners. The judgment of the court below is against their claims to freedom; the matter in dispute is, therefore, to the plaintiffs in error, the value of their freedom, ***and this is not susceptible of a pecuniary valuation.*** Had the judgment been in favor of the petitioners, and the writ of error brought by the party claiming to be the owner, the value of the slaves as *property* would have been the matter in dispute, and affidavits might be admitted to ascertain such value. But affidavits estimating the value of freedom are entirely inadmissible ; and no doubt is entertained of the jurisdiction of the court."

Now, if the supreme court of the United States, in construing a law, felt constrained by their oaths to hold the freedom of a man, — of any man, though he might be a drivelling idiot, or stretched upon his death bed, with only another hour to breathe, — to be worth more than a thousand dollars, how can a senator of the United States say, that in passing a law, under which human liberty may be retained or lost, he is not bound at least by the "*spirit*" of the constitution, if not by its letter, to hold that human liberty to be of greater value than twenty dollars, and therefore to provide the trial by jury for its protection ? What can prove more strikingly that Mr. Webster violates the whole "spirit" of the constitution, when the framers and ratifiers of this amendment covenanted for and decreed the trial by jury, for such a paltry sum of money ; and when the judges of the supreme court held human liberty to be worth more than any nameable sum of money, while he regards it as a thing to be disposed of by any corrupt postmaster, which any corrupt administration may corruptly appoint. Yet he says, "Nothing can be more false than that a jury trial is demanded in cases of this kind by the constitution, either in its letter, *or in its spirit.*"

I wish I could find, or felt at liberty to coin some milder word ; but for want of a better, I must say that Mr. Webster seems to me, throughout this whole matter, to *dogmatize.* He makes strong assertions without offering even weak reasons. Of this character was his annunciation of the discovery of a new law, — "the law of physical geography," — which was to suspend moral agency, and take from man his power to commit crime against his brother; as though in ascending hill-sides, freedom and slavery lie in different atmospherical strata, and are bounded by each other impassably; as though there were any mountain so "exceeding high," to whose top even Jesus Christ could go, that Satan could not go there to tempt him. This does not strike the common mind like a true discovery; — like the law of gravitation, for instance, discovered by Newton, or the existence of the planet Neptune, by Leverrier. It is rather like that earliest pretended discovery on record, which was designed to seduce, and did seduce, the first parents of us all. *Ye may eat of the forbidden tree, for ye shall* NOT *surely die.* So Mr. Webster says, Let slaves be driven in coffles, or carried in ships' holds to the new territories; they cannot live there. Will not the results of the two experiments bear a lively analogy to each other, and be likely to reflect similar credit upon their authors?

So, too, when he tore some of the brightest pages from the New Testament, by proclaiming that "there is to be found no injunction against that relation [of slavery] between man and man, in the teachings of the gospel of Jesus Christ, or of any of his apostles"! Upon how many Christian hearts did this sentiment fall like an anathema against all truth. He does not say any *express* injunction, but "no injunction;" — none of any kind. No *positive* injunction against slavery in the New Testament! — a book designed to regulate our life and condition for two worlds; yet, altogether, not so large as many a congressional report; less voluminous than the ordinances of many of our city governments; — a book, therefore, which, from the necessity of the case, must deal with great and immortal principles, and could not descend into specification and detail; — and because such a book as this contains no *express* injunction against slavery, therefore slavery is not forbidden by it, but has the implied approval of its silence! Surely, never was there a more sinister, unsound, unchristian argument uttered by infidel or pagan. Is there any *express* injunction "in the teachings of the gospel of Jesus Christ, or of any of his apostles," commanding us to declare the African slave trade piracy? Is there any *express* injunction "in the teachings of the gospel of Jesus Christ, or of any of his apostles," against cannibalism? Do they any where say, "Ye shall not eat one another?" Yet what enormity and flagitiousness would it be to infer, that, therefore, men and women may turn ogres and ogresses, and eat human flesh as they do mutton and sirloin. The inference in the latter case is every whit as warrantable and as sound, as in the former. Yet I consider that this theological argument does not violate the "spirit" of the gospel, any more than his constitutional argument violates the "spirit" of the constitution. John Wesley, who had lived amid slavery, denominates it the "sum of all villanies," and if Christ came into this world and left it, without permeating and saturating all his teachings with injunctions against the injustice, cruelty, pride, avarice, lust, love of domination, and love of adulation, which are the inseparable accompaniments of slavery, then I think the Christian world will cry out, that so far as this life is concerned, his mission was substantially fruitless.

> "O, star-eyed Science! hast thou wandered there,
> To bring us back these tidings of despair?"

So, if the constitution of the United States contains not even any *implied* security for the liberty of all the colored population in the free states and territories, and for the trial by jury as the only adequate means of securing that liberty, then would it not be more creditable to its framers never to have put their signatures to it?

Let me here compare the relative value of life or property on the one side, with liberty on the other, and see what inference must be drawn in favor of affording as great a protection to the latter as to the former.

The fifth article of amendment declares that "no person shall be deprived of life, liberty, or property, without due process of law." The commentators say that these words, "due process of law," are the equivalent of the phrase "the law of the land," in the 29th chapter of Magna Charta; and hence that "this clause in effect affirms the right of trial according to the process and proceedings of the common law;" that is, by jury. (See Story's Comm. 661; 2 Inst. 50, 51; 2 Kent's Comm. 10; 1 Tucker's Black. App. 304.)

Now, consider that the general right of trial by jury, in cases of *life*, was expressly secured by the constitution as originally adopted; that, somewhat more than three years afterwards, the same right was expressly secured for *property*, in suits at common law, whenever the value in controversy should exceed twenty dollars; and then say whether there is not the strongest implication in favor of the same right, in cases of human liberty, which is so much more precious than life and property combined. I do not here say it is an implication that binds the courts in administering a law. That is not the point under discussion. But is it not an implication that binds the *legislator*, so that when legislating on the subject, he cannot consciously and wilfully abandon it without infidelity to his oath? I do not believe that many men from the free states will ever be found in Congress who will not take this view of the subject. Indeed, not a few of the best lawyers and jurists have held that the implication binds the courts; and therefore that the statute of 1793 is unconstitutional.*

Mr. Webster treats the two cases, of fugitives from justice and fugitives from service, alike; although one can almost adopt his own language, and say that "nothing is more false" than that they are alike. In regard to the first class, the constitution says, a person "*charged*" with treason, &c.; but in regard to the second class, it says no person "*held*," &c.

According to the obvious intent of this language, the alleged fugitive must be *proved* to be *held*, *bound*, *obligated*. It is not enough that he be *charged* to be "held" to service, though it is enough that a man be "*charged*" with crime. To bring the first case within the legal category of the second, its terms should be, "a person *guilty* of treason," &c., shall be delivered up. Were such the phraseology, would any one doubt that proof of guilt should precede delivery, and that there could be no other foundation for it?

Mr. Webster says, "perhaps the only insuperable difficulty" to a trial by a jury, "has been created by the states themselves." Suppose this to be so, I would ask whose duty is it to act first, — that of Congress to provide the trial, or that of the states to remove the impediment? Shall the states repeal their laws first, and leave the liberty of the citizens in jeopardy; or shall not Congress legislate first, and secure that liberty? Which is of the greater importance, that the owner should recover his slave, or that the citizen should retain his freedom? I answer according to the language which the criminal law uses respecting guilt and innocence, that it is better that nine hundred and ninety-nine, that is, an indefinite number of slaves should escape, than that one free man should be delivered into bondage.

* See an elaborate opinion of Chancellor Walworth, 14 Wend. 507, *Jack* vs. *Martin*.

Besides, I think no state legislated on the subject for the protection of its own citizens, until 1842. This was after Congress had neglected, for more than fifty years, to do its duty. Why, then, should Mr. Webster cast the blame upon the states which forbore for more than fifty years to act protectively for themselves, when Congress, of which he had been a leading member for nearly forty years, had endangered, instead of securing, the liberty of their citizens? When he said that "every member of every northern legislature is bound by oath to support the constitution of the United States," why did not the retort suddenly rise to his mind that *he* was bound by oath not less than they; and that his oath embraced the men that owned freedom, not less than the men that owned slaves? Besides, he charges only a *part* of the free states with being guilty of unjust legislation. Shall the innocent states suffer because of the others' offence? Rather shall not Congress first supply the means of protection to the citizens of all?

It seems to me, too, that the fourth amendment has an important "*bearing upon the subject*," because it shows that the master-thought of our fathers, in forming the constitution, was to secure the liberties of the citizen. It provides against "unreasonable seizures" of "persons." I suppose the main idea of this amendment was to secure the citizen against "unreasonable seizure," even in cases where he should afterwards, and at *some time*, be brought to trial according to the forms of the common law. But what "seizure" can be more "unreasonable," than one whose object is, not an ultimate trial, but bondage forever, without trial? Can mortal imagination conceive of any seizure less entitled than this to be called "reasonable?" With what indignation did our fathers frown because they were transported beyond seas *to be tried;* yet, by our present law, and by the law which Mr. Webster promises to support, a free man may be transported, if not beyond seas, at least beyond lands, and beyond states, *not to be tried*, but to be held in slavery forever without trial. If a free citizen of Massachusetts should be seized and plunged into a Massachusetts prison, to be kept there for life; and his children, as a consequence of his fate, were put into the same, or into other prisons, as fast as they were born, to be also kept for life; and such was the original object and avowed purpose of the seizure, would not this conflict a little with the "*spirit*" of the fourth amendment? And does this proceeding conflict with this "*spirit*" any the less, because the prison is a southern rice swamp, or cotton field, where the nearest door or outlet of escape is more than a hundred miles from the spot of confinement? In common law actions, trover, detinue, replevin, &c., &c., the trial is to be in the vicinage, except there is some overpowering reason for changing the venue, or place of trial. But here is a transfer of the party, not for a trial, but for evading a trial.

I submit, then, to the public, that here are three provisions of the constitution, each one of which does have "*a bearing on the subject.*" Each strengthens the other. They form a triple implication, if not a *trinoda necessitas*, which no man, however powerful he may be, can break.

The argument which the lawyers call *ab inconvenienti*, — the argument from inconvenience, — has been pressed into the service of the slaveholder to endanger the liberties of the citizen. I answer, there are two sides to this argument; nor was it wise in the slaveholder, or his northern friends, to suggest it. It seems to me quite as *inconvenient* for a free man to lose his liberty, as for a slaveholder to lose his slave. If a southern man sues a northern one for the value of a bale of cotton or a barrel of rice, must not the plaintiff await the next term of the court before he can enter his action, abide by the rules of the court respecting continuances, and submit to the order of business in taking his turn before a jury? To obviate this inconvenience, has any legislature or any court ever proposed to set aside or annul, at once, all the securities by which we hold property and life? And how stands the question respecting evidence or proof? If difficult for a slave claimant, from Texas, to prove title to his slave in Massachusetts, how infinitely more difficult for a citizen of Massachusetts to prove title to himself in Texas. But Mr. Webster says there are independent courts at the south, "always open and ready to receive and decide upon petitions or applications for freedom." Suppose this to be true; how is a man or a woman, whose master knows that he or she is free, to get to the courts? Mr. Webster seems to think that as soon as a kidnapping slave dealer shall transport his human prey to the south, he will at once take him to, or allow him to go before a court of justice, or will sell him to some brother Samaritan who will do so. Does not every body know that any man, who is capable of the enormous guilt of seizing or buying a freeman, will make it impossible for that freeman to regain his birthright?

Mr. Webster says, persuasively, that the alleged slave "is only remitted, for inquiry into his rights, to the state from which he fled." But suppose he had never "fled," but was demeaning himself as a peaceable citizen, under the solemnly pledged protection of the government, on the soil where he was born! This is the false idea that underlies the whole of Mr. Webster's seductive letter, that under such a bill as Mr. Butler's, nobody but a slave would ever be arrested.

I have no doubt that what Mr. Webster says about southern courts being "fair and upright," is very generally and extensively true; but I have had a little personal knowledge of southern courts, and I have no hesitation in saying that there has been one, at least, before which, if a slave were suing for his freedom, and any popular clamor against him should exist, he would have no more hope of obtaining his liberty through the "fairness" of the court, than, if thrown overboard in the middle of the Atlantic ocean, he would have of saving his life by swimming ashore.

Mr. Webster holds Massachusetts up to the ridicule of the world, because, as he says, she "grows fervid on Pennsylvania wrongs;" and he has deemed it his duty to inquire how many seizures of fugitive slaves have occurred in New England within our time. Is this the Christian standard by which to estimate the evil of encroachments upon the most sacred rights of men? If I repose in contentment and indifference, because my own section, or state, or county, is as yet but a partial sufferer, why should I not continue contented and indifferent while I myself am safe? In providing for the liberties of the citizen, under a common government, I think Massachusetts worthy of all honor and not of ridicule, because she does "grow fervid on Pennsylvania wrongs," and on the wrongs of an entire race, whether in Pennsylvania or California, or any where within the boundaries of our own country. I see no reason why my sympathies as a man, or the obligations of my oath as an officer, in regard to the nearer or the remoter states, should be inversely as the squares of the distances. Even with regard to foreign countries, did Mr. Webster think so, in those better days, when his eloquent appeal for oppressed and bleeding Greece roused the nation, like the voice of a clarion. Did Mr. Webster deem it necessary to make inquisitions through all the New England States, to learn how many Hungarian patriots they had seen shot at the tap of drum, or how many noble Hungarian women had been stripped and whipped in their market places, before he thrilled the heart of the nation at the wrongs of Kossuth and his compatriots, and invoked the execrations of the world upon the Austrian and Russian despots? I see no difference between these cases, which is not in favor of our *home interests*, of our own *domestic rights*, except the difference of their bearings upon partisan politics and presidential rivalries. Mr. Webster quotes and commends Mr. Bissell, who said that those southern states which had suffered the least from loss of slaves, made the greatest clamor. That statement of a fact was well put by Mr. Bissell; but was it well applied by Mr. Webster? In the statement, it was a question as to the loss of property. In the application, it is a question as to the loss of liberty. The latter is not, therefore, the "counterpart" of the former. Blindness to the distinction between the value and the *principle* of property, and the value and the *principle* of liberty, could alone have permitted the comparison.

But I have extended this communication greatly beyond my original purpose. Several other topics contained in Mr. Webster's speech, or growing out of what has since happened in relation to it, and hardly less important than those already considered, must await another opportunity for discussion; unless, indeed, some disposal of the question shall render further discussion unnecessary.

I am not unmindful of the position in which I stand. I am not unaware that circumstances have placed me in an antagonist relation to a man whose vast powers of intellect the world has long so vividly enjoyed and so profoundly admired. I well know that a *personal* contest between us seems unequal, far more than did the impending combat between the Hebrew stripling and that champion of the Philistines who had a helmet of brass upon his head, and greaves of brass upon his legs, and the staff of whose spear was like a weaver's beam. But the contest is not between *us*. It is between truth and error; and just so certain as the spirit of Good will prevail over the spirit of Evil, just so certain will Truth ultimately triumph. In such a case as this, there is one point of view in which Mr. Webster is a desirable antagonist; for the thick and far-beaming points of light which he has left all along his former course of life, cannot fail to expose, to all eyes but his own, the devious path into which he has now wandered.

HORACE MANN.

WASHINGTON, June 6, 1850.

Several editions of the preceding Letters having been exhausted, another was printed, under date of July 8, 1850, with Notes.

NOTES

TO THE PRECEDING LETTERS.

I HAD hoped not to be required to say more on the subject discussed in the above Letters; but, during the last week, Mr. Webster has issued, in a pamphlet form, a speech made by him in the Senate on the 17th ult., accompanied by his letter, dated on the same day, to some gentlemen on the Kennebec River. In this letter, Mr. Webster has referred to me again; and I regret exceedingly to say, that he seems to have given himself full license to depart from all the rules of courtesy belonging to a gentleman, and to disobey the obligations of truth belonging to a man.

That I may not be supposed to make any over-statement respecting the character of Mr. Webster's language towards me, as expressed in this letter, I quote a specimen or two from it.

"A pamphlet has been put into circulation," says he, referring to the first of the above two letters, "in which it is said that my remark is 'undertaking to settle by mountains and rivers, and not by the Ten Commandments, the question of human duty.' 'Cease to transcribe,' it adds, 'upon the statute book what our wisest and best men believed to be the will of God, in regard to our wordly affairs, and the passions which we think appropriate to devils will soon take possession of society.'" He then adds, "One hardly knows which most to contemn, the nonsense or the dishonesty of such commentaries on another's words. I know no passion more appropriate to devils than the passion for gross misrepresentation and libel," &c., &c.

The angry and reproachful language, in which Mr. Webster has here indulged himself, releases me from all further obligation to treat him with personal regard. Yet I do not mean to avail myself of this release. Under our present relations, however, I do feel at liberty to use considerable plainness of speech.

1. Let me first refer to a misrepresentation by Mr. Webster of a plain matter of fact. In professing to quote, from

his 7th of March speech, a passage on which I had made a criticism, he alters the passage so as to evade the criticism, and then condemns me for making it. The original passage in his speech read as follows: "I would not take pains to reäffirm an ordinance of Nature, nor to reënact the will of God." This was the sentiment I criticized. It appears in these words in the *National Intelligencer*, in the *Washington Union*, in the *Republic*, in the *Globe*, and in the pamphlet edition of his speech, which he dedicated to the people of Massachusetts. But in the Kennebec letter, in order to elude the point of my criticism, he has interpolated a word into the sentence, which changes its whole meaning. Affirming that he quotes himself, he says, "I would not take pains USELESSLY to reäffirm an ordinance of Nature, or to reënact the will of God." By foisting in the word which I have underscored, he changes the entire character of the sentiment advanced. As now stated, nobody can dissent from it; for who would announce, in a distinct proposition, that he would *uselessly* do any thing? But, as originally stated, nobody can assent to it. This alteration of his language, after my criticism upon it was made, is not only unjust towards me, but it contains a latent confession that he knew he was wrong, but thought this surreptitious changing of his doctrine to be a less evil than a frank acknowledgment of his error. Had he truly quoted the original false sentiment, the world would have seen that I was right; but, in his dilemma, he falsely interpolated a true sentiment, not only to evade the force of my criticism upon him, but to make occasion for an unfounded imputation against me.

I shall not undertake to define or describe a proceeding like this in words of my own. But I may be permitted, without discourtesy, to use a sentiment advanced by himself, and leave its application to be made by its author. It is in the same connection that Mr. Webster makes the following remark: "I know no passion more appropriate to devils than the passion for gross misrepresentation and libel." Can any mortal specify a grosser instance of "gross misrepresentation and libel" than when one of the parties to a public discussion has uttered an obnoxious sentiment, and when this sentiment has met with very general reprobation, and when, in the progress of the discussion, the guilty party professes to restate the case, that he should then expunge the false sentiment he originally advanced, foist a trite and common-place one in its stead, then apply the criticism made on the suppressed sentiment to the forged one, and proceed to condemn his critic for "nonsense" or "dishonesty"? Is it not as palpable a case of alteration, as to change the date of a note of hand in order to take it out of the statute of limitations, or to obliterate the description of the premises in a deed, and put a more valuable estate in its place? This proceeding is worse, if possible, than the former "misrepresentation and libel" of my argument and myself, contained in the Newburyport letter. But the subject is painful, and I leave it.

2. Following up his attack upon me, Mr. Webster proceeds to say:

"In classical times, there was a set of small but rapacious critics, denominated *captatores verborum*, who snatched and caught at particular expressions; expended their strength on the *disjecta membra* of language; birds of rapine which preyed on words and syllables, and gorged themselves with feeding on the garbage of phrases, chopped, dislocated, and torn asunder by themselves, as flesh and limbs are by the claws of unclean birds."

May I most respectfully ask Mr. Webster on what authority he says there was, "in classical times," any such "set" of "small but rapacious critics," as he here speaks of — or exemplifies? In my ignorance, I have always supposed the "*captator*" of classical times, to be a kind of "genius" the very opposite of what Mr. Webster describes. Horace, Juvenal, and Livy represent him as a selfish, sycophantic gift-seeker, or fortune-hunter; not a twister, torturer, or interpolator, even, of words and phrases. If *captator* meant a cavilling, cynical critic, then *captatrix* should mean a scold, a vixen, or virago; but its true meaning was "a fawning gossip," or "mean flatterer."

No mistake could well be greater than that the old *captatores* "expended their strength on the *disjecta membra* of language," or "gorged themselves with the garbage of phrases, chopped, dislocated, and torn asunder, by themselves." On the contrary, they were "gentle as a sucking dove." The accompanying words descriptive of the "*captator*" were not *torve*, *ringi*, and so forth; but *callide*, *blande*, or *blandicule*. There was nothing like the harpy about them, as Mr. Webster seems to suppose, in this remarkable description of his, which is as rhetorically unsavory as it is classically untrue.

So far from there being any "set" of critics, in classic times, denominated and known as *captatores verborum*, I doubt whether even the abstract noun "*captatio*" occurs half a dozen times, in all the classics, in connection with the genitive of his pretended appellation. He could hardly have made a greater or more ludicrous mistake. It is exceedingly to be regretted, after the numerous instances we have lately had of Mr. Webster's bad logic, and bad humanity, and bad discoveries of natural law, that he should now offend the classical taste of the country, and bring discredit upon the New England colleges, by his bad Latin. This whole anti-classical paragraph about "*disjecta membra*," and "chopping," and "gorging," and "uncleanness," is an unclean conception of his own; not a pure but an impure invention, and seems more epigastric than intellectual in its origin.*

3. I will now give a specimen or two of Mr. Webster's errors in geography, and of his false citation of authorities. It will then be seen that his geographical statements are worthy to be placed side by side with his classical. In the same letter, he says the extent of New Mexico, north and south, on the line of the Rio Grande, "can hardly be less than a thousand miles." This makes a little more than *fourteen* degrees of latitude. Now, as its northern boundary is in 42°, its southern must be as low as 28°. This is *four* degrees below El Paso del Norte. Yet Mr. Webster, on the

* The above criticism on Mr. Webster's latinity aroused many self-supposed scholars, or at least fair proficients in the Latin grammar, to take up the pen in his defence. But unluckily, the quills they seized were plucked, not from the Roman eagle, but from the wings of some of those "unclean birds," to which Mr. Webster had introduced them. Among the most conspicuous of these defenders of Mr. Webster's ludicrous blunder, was Professor Felton, of Harvard College. If any person wishes to see one of the most neat, elegant, and at the same time thorough cases of *deplumation*, any where to be found in literary history, in which an individual who strutted on to the stage as a *peacock*, was soon obliged to leave it as a *daw*, he has only to read Dr. Beck's articles in "The Literary World," in which the fabricated quotation of Mr. Webster, and Professor Felton's defence of it, are shown to be exceedingly bad as Latin, and much worse as logic.

13th of June last, declared himself in favor of fixing the northern boundary of Texas at or near El Paso, and more than four degrees of latitude north of what he here says is the southern boundary of New Mexico. He also supported that part of the compromise bill which proposes to give Texas, not only these four degrees of latitude, but millions of money also, for taking what, as he now says, belongs to New Mexico and the United States. How can these views stand together?

In his 7th of March speech, Mr. Webster declared it to be a natural impossibility that African slavery could ever exist "in California or New Mexico." (p. 42.) He now defines the southern boundary of New Mexico. It can hardly be less, says he, than "a thousand miles" from the forty-second degree of north latitude. This places it four degrees south of El Paso. He is in favor of that part of the bill which gives these four degrees to Texas. According to him, therefore, should Texas get possession of these four degrees of what is now New Mexican territory, slavery will exist, as far up as the old southern boundary line of New Mexico, by virtue of the laws of Texas, but beyond this line, although within the bounds of Texas, it will not exist, because forbidden by the "will of God." Hence the extraordinary spectacle will be exhibited, of the existence of slavery coming plump up to the south side of an imaginary line, by the laws of Texas, while on the north side of the said imaginary line, its existence will be cut square off by the "will of God," although both sides are within the same political jurisdiction. This will be a miracle, compared with which the supposed miraculous preservation of the Jewish feature and complexion, for two thousand years, will be unworthy to be mentioned. It remains to be seen, however, whether this miracle will be vouchsafed to Mr. Webster, as a proof of the divine favor.

On the 5th of June, Mr. Webster voted against incorporating the "Proviso" into the governments for New Mexico and Utah, because slavery was already prohibited there by "Asiatic scenery" and the law of "physical geography." On the next day, too, he voted against the following amendment, offered by Mr. Walker: "And that peon servitude is forever abolished and prohibited." Whether he so voted because this species of slavery, (which is an existing institution at the present time,) was prohibited by "scenery" and "geography," does not appear.

But on the 17th of June, Mr. Webster, in the Senate, suggested a qualification of his doctrine as laid down on the 7th of March, viz., that "every foot of territory of the United States has a fixed character for slavery." An uncertainty as to the boundary line between New Mexico and Texas, gave rise to this qualification. "Let me say to gentlemen," said Mr. Webster, "that if any portion which they or I do not believe to be Texas, should be considered to become Texas, then, so far, that qualification of my remark is applicable." (*Cong. Globe*, 31st Cong., 1st session, p. 1239.) That is, if the compromise bill should so establish the boundary line between New Mexico and Texas, as that "any portion [of New Mexico] which they or I [other gentlemen or Mr. Webster,] do not believe to be Texas, should be considered to become Texas," then *as Texan territory*, it might lose its "fixed character," and become slave territory, notwithstanding the "ordinance of Nature" and the "will of God," to the contrary. But, strange to say, on this same 17th of June, the Kennebec letter was written, which carries the southern boundary of Mexico, on the east side of the Rio Grande, four degrees below El Paso, and, of course, includes all that region within New Mexico, and therefore within the "ordinance of Nature" and the "will of God!" So that, after all, he acknowledges that the "ordinance of Nature" and the "will of God," as he expounds them, may be overridden by the laws of Texas; — in which view he is undoubtedly right.

But his citation of authorities is among the most surprising of all his aberrations from fact. He first quotes Major Gaines, who, as he says, "traversed a part of this country during the Mexican war." By "this country," I suppose he means New Mexico. If he does not mean New Mexico, then the citation has no relation to the subject. If he does mean New Mexico, then he asserts what is untrue. Major Gaines did not go within four or five hundred miles of New Mexico during the war; and if the quotation from him was designed to create the belief that, in what Major Gaines said, he was speaking of New Mexico, it was as gross an imposition as could well be made.

The next citation is from Colonel Hardin. Two sentences are taken. I transcribe the first with Mr. Webster's italics.

"*The whole country is miserably watered; large districts have no water at all. The streams are small, and at great distances apart.* One day we marched on the road from Monclova to Parras, *thirty-five miles, without water*; a pretty severe day's march for infantry."

And what country does this describe?

"From Monclova to Parras, thirty-five miles"! says Colonel Hardin. And where is Monclova? Away down south, in Coahuila, hundreds of miles from any part of New Mexico.

I submit the following notes, one from the colonel of the regiment in which Mr. Gaines was a major; and the other from a major in the regiment of which Mr. Hardin was colonel. Both letters are from gentlemen who are now members of Congress.

House of Representatives, June 27, 1850.

Sir; In reply to your note of this date, I state that Major Gaines did not, during the Mexican war, travel though any part of New Mexico. Major Gaines entered Mexico at Camargo, on the Rio Grande; was engaged near Saltillo, until he was captured and taken to the city of Mexico; and thence he returned to the United States by the way of Vera Cruz.

I am, sir, very respectfully, &c., HUMPHREY MARSHALL.

P. S. In reply to your verbal inquiry, whether Colonel Hardin was in New Mexico, I state, that Colonel Hardin was attached to General Wool's command, and passed from San Antonio de Bexar, by the Presidio de Rio Grande, Monclova, and Parras, to Saltillo; so that he did not enter New Mexico. H. M.

Hon. H. Mann.

House of Representatives, June 28, 1850.

Hon. H. Mann. Sir; In reply to your note of this date, I have the honor to say, that I was an officer of the first regiment, Illinois volunteers, commanded by Colonel J. J. Hardin, during the Mexican war, and that during the time Colonel Hardin was in command of the regiment he was not in New Mexico. His nearest point to New Mexico was Monclova or Parras, which was several hundred miles distant. In my opinion, Colonel Hardin was never in New Mexico; he certainly was not in that country during the Mexican war.

Respectfully, W. A. RICHARDSON.

Now what possible excuse can be offered for these misleading citations? What information would be given of the soil of the Genesee valley of New York, by proving the condition of the sands of Cape Cod?

Mr. Webster next quotes, for the second time, the letter of Hugh N. Smith, Esq. This letter, if taken by itself, would render it improbable, in Mr. Smith's opinion, that slavery would go into New Mexico; but it by no means proves the physical impossibility of its existence there. But what different language has Mr. Smith since held in his address to his constituents in New Mexico itself? I will quote a few passages from this address to show its general drift and intent.

"Your state, [New Mexico,] is threatened with dismemberment, and *what is yet more fatal, the introduction of slavery into its bosom.*" (p. 1.)

"The most formidable part of this combination against you is that which originates in the slave interest. It not only rallies against you the whole slaveholding south, but all the influence of selfish, venal, and ambitious men in the north, *looking to speculations in discredited bonds and land jobbing, or to the political honors which the combined vote of the south may promise.*" (p. 2.)

"The doctrine of the slaveholding states, in regard to their domestic institutions, is non-intervention; but with regard to yours, it is *instant intervention,* to set at nought the prohibition of slavery, which you brought with you into the Union," &c. *Ib.*

"I am myself a native of the section, [Mr. Smith is a Kentuckian,] whose fate I deplore, and if my duty did not require, I would be the last to advert to the malady that preys upon its life. . . . . . The schemes of those who would bind you to the destiny of the slave states, render it necessary that your representative should be excluded from the halls of Congress." (p. 3.)

"*You are left prostrate, that Texas may dismember and divide New Mexico, and subject her to southern influence; that negro slavery may be introduced into the remnant of territory that may not be appropriated to Texas; and, finally, that the region thus secured to southern policy may become the stock on which to graft new conquests from Mexico.*" (p. 4.) [*These* are Mr. Smith's italics.]

"The first step in this process is to supplant the fundamental municipal institutions brought by New Mexico with her into the Union, by a territorial government, which, by omitting the inhibition against slavery in the Congressional act, failing to reserve that contained in the Mexican code, and preventing the people of the territory from legislating upon the subject of slavery, and from reënacting the prohibitory clause, will unquestionably abolish all protections against that institution; and, indeed, more effectual legislation for the extension of slavery into New Mexico could not be enacted." (p. 5.)

"The whole body of southern influence, now that mining is a mania, would combine to pour an immense colony of slaves into New Mexico. The consequence of this would be to level the whole population of New Mexico with the new caste brought into competition; and you, my Mexican fellow-citizens, who till your own soil with your own hands, would be compelled to fly your country, or be degraded from your equality of freemen, forfeiting your hopes of rising to the new elevation promised by your alliance with the great North American republic, and living only to witness the ruin of all that renders life desirable." (p. 6.)

This is what Mr. Smith says, when he writes home to his own people, who know all about their own country, and its danger of being invaded by slavery.

Now, let the reader suppose himself to have read from Mr. Smith's address, as much more of the same kind as the above, and then say how far his evidence goes to sustain Mr. Webster's discovery, that slavery can never go into New Mexico. Mr. Smith's address has been published for two months; it has been on the tables of members, published, and quoted from in the newspapers, and yet Mr. Webster continues to cite Mr. Smith as a witness in his favor. What influences were used to induce Mr. Smith to withhold, in the letter to Mr. Webster, the facts and views which he has so clearly brought out in the letter to his constituents?

The next and last citation is from an officer at Santa Fe. No name is given. We are informed neither of the character of the author nor of his means of information; and if this authority is as fallacious and deceptive as the preceding, it is a great deal worse than nothing. It would be like the testimony sometimes offered in court, which ruins the cause and dishonors the counsel.

4. In his Kennebec letter, Mr. Webster says, "I have studied the geography of New Mexico diligently, having read all that I could find in print, and inquired of many intelligent persons, who have been in the country, traversed it, and become familiar with it." He sets forth his knowledge in this confident tone, so that his impressions in favor of the *natural* prohibition of slavery may be more readily received. According to this statement, he must have read the letters of Mr. James S. Calhoun, Indian agent at Santa Fe, communicated to Congress by the President, on the 23d of January last. Speaking of the Navajoes, a tribe of 7,000 Indians, within the limits of what it is proposed to include in New Mexico, Mr. Calhoun says, that it is "not a rare instance for one individual to possess 5,000 to 10,000 sheep, and 400 to 500 head of other stock," (p. 184;) and that their country "is rich in its valleys, rich in its fields of grain, and rich in its vegetables and peach orchards." (p. 199.) "We encamped," says he, "near extensive cornfields, belonging to the Navajoes." (p. 197.) Their "soil is easy of cultivation, and capable of sustaining nearly as many millions of inhabitants as they have

thousands." (p. 202.) Look at this: A country owned by one tribe capable, according to Mr. Calhoun, of sustaining nearly 7,000,000 inhabitants, and yet, as Mr. Webster avers, inaccessible to slavery, on account of its barrenness!

Speaking of the Indians, (Pueblos,) on the Rio Grande, Mr. Calhoun says, "These people can raise immense quantities of corn and wheat, and have large herds of sheep and goats. The grazing for cattle generally is superior." (p. 206.) Of the more western Pueblos, he says, they have "an extent of country nearly four hundred miles square"; — more than twenty times as large as Massachusetts; — "they have rich valleys to cultivate, grow quantities of corn and wheat, and raise vast herds of horses, mules, sheep, and goats, all of which may be immensely increased by properly stimulating their industry, and instructing them in the agricultural arts." (p. 215.)

I might cite much more from the same authority, to the same effect; but I do not refer to Mr. Calhoun so much for the purpose of showing the agricultural capabilities of New Mexico, as of asking why Mr. Webster did not quote from this recent official work, which has been lying on the tables of members for months, instead of quoting descriptions from military officers respecting a country which he well knew they had never seen?

There is good reason to believe that there are wide tracts of fertile land lying between the Sierra de los Mimbres and the Sierra Nevada, on the east and west, and the 32d and 35th degrees of latitude. The waters at the mouth of a river give no doubtful indication respecting the country from which they flow. If the volume be large, we know it must drain an extensive region; for the waters of a great river cannot be supplied from a narrow surface. So if the water be muddy, as is said to be the case with that of the Colorado, it is proof that it courses through a diluvial country. But however this may be, all accounts concur in representing New Mexico to be rich in mines; and mines are the favorite sphere for slavery, as the ocean is for commerce.

In his late speech in the Senate, Mr. Davis, of Massachusetts, said, that however it might be with regard to employing slaves in New Mexico for raising crops of corn or cotton, there was still one purpose to which they might be applied,—

the most odious of all purposes, — to raising crops from themselves. From this "Southern Hive," the markets of Texas and Louisiana might be supplied with "vigintial" crops of human beings. It will be incumbent on Mr. Webster to invent some new "physical" law to meet this astute suggestion of his colleague. "Asiatic scenery" will hardly answer his purpose here.

Within the limits of the proposed territory of New Mexico, it is said, on the authority of Humboldt, that that powerful and comparatively civilized people, the Aztecs, once resided. Can any person for a moment believe that the Aztecs ever grew to opulence and power, in any such sterile and desolate region, as Mr. Webster's "diligent reading" portrays?

But what must satisfy every man whose blindness is not of the soul rather than of the senses, is the fact that the people of New Mexico, in the constitution which they have just framed, have embodied a prohibition of slavery in their fundamental law. Had slavery been forbidden there by any "Asiatic scenery," or by any "law of physical geography," who should know it better than they? They have had slavery amongst them heretofore, and therefore they know it can invade them again, and therefore they forbid it; and in the choice of senators to Congress under the new organization, should any candidate put forward the vagary, the phantasm, the fatuity, that slavery *cannot* exist among them, they would doubtless deem him a less fit subject for the Senate of the United States than for sanitary treatment.

How stands the evidence, then, on the question, whether "California and New Mexico," from their geology, their geography, or their Asiatic scenery, are inaccessible or not, to the invasion of slavery? It is well known that the war with Mexico was provoked, and violently precipitated upon the country, in order to extend the domain and the power of slavery. In negotiating for the cession of California and New Mexico, the Mexican commissioners strove to introduce a prohibition against slavery into the treaty. This demonstrates that they thought slavery could exist there. Our minister declared that he would assent to no such stipulation, though they would cover all the land a foot thick with gold. This shows the tenacity with which Mr. Polk's administration, and all its southern friends, adhered to their original purpose of obtaining new territory for slavery. In view of this, the House of Representatives again and again voted to apply the proviso to whatever territory should be obtained. When the treaty was ratified, many of the leading senators voted against the clause for acquisition, foreseeing the present controversy, and hoping to avert it. Even after the treaty was ratified, leading southern Whigs in the House voted against paying the first instalment under it, still clinging to the hope that the territory might be restored to Mexico, and this cause of dissension withdrawn. During all this period, fourteen of the northern legislatures, many of them again and again, voted that the proviso should be applied. The present six months' contest, in the Senate and House, between the north and the south, is conducted solely on the conviction that slavery *may* exist in the territories; and that it will or will not exist there, according as the law allows or forbids it. Otherwise it would be the most nonsensical and nugatory discussion ever engaged in out of a lunatic asylum. Once make it as clear as any law of physical nature, that slavery can never transgress the bounds of the new territories, and there is not a man so demented that he would any longer contend either for the proviso, or against it. Mr. Webster was always of the same opinion, and has declared it a hundred times. In his Marshfield speech, September 1, 1848, he said, "He [General Cass] will surely have the Senate, and with the patronage of the government, with every interest that he, as a northern man, can bring to bear, coöperating with every interest that the south can bring to bear, we cry safety before we are out of the woods, *if we feel that there is no danger* [of slavery] *as to these new territories.*" Up to the 7th of March, 1850, then, when he abandoned all the doctrines and sentiments he had ever before advocated on this subject, and when he incurred the public, hearty approval and encomiums of Mr. Calhoun, by his moral agility in springing, at one leap, from Massachusetts to South Carolina; — until this time, Mr. Webster had always held, that slavery would invade the new territories if not barred out of them by positive law. And what would be still more remarkable, if the doctrines of the 7th of March speech had the least shadow of soundness in them, is, that they have now been before the public for more than four months, and, so far as I know, not a single southern man has been converted by them. Are not Mr. Benton, Mr. Mason, Colonel Davis, and thousands of others, individually, as good judges, or as good witnesses, as he is? Since the speech, the people of New Mexico have prohibited slavery in their constitution, because they knew it to be possible among them. Before the speech, California did the same, and for the same reason. The Nashville convention has just resolved, "That California is peculiarly adapted for slave labor, and that if the tenure of slave property was by recognition of this kind secured in that part of the country south of 36° 30′, it would in a short time form one or more slaveholding states, to swell the number and power of those already in existence." Even those who seek to apologize for Mr. Webster, avow, at the same time, their disbelief in his doctrine. Such is the evidence, on the one side and on the other, as to the possibility or impossibility of slavery in the territories. Mr. Webster is against the whole world, and the whole world is against him, and this, too, on a question already settled by history and experience. He is just as much to be believed, as a man who looks up into the clear midnight sky, and denies the existence of the heavenly host, while all the stars of the firmament are shining down into his eyes.

To increase the overwhelming proof against Mr. Webster, I add the following: —

HOUSE OF REPRESENTATIVES, June 1, 1850.

HON. S. R. THURSTON, Delegate from Oregon.

DEAR SIR; In a speech delivered by you, in the House of Representatives, in March last, I understood you to say that you had been in the valley of the Great Salt Lake, and that you were acquainted, from personal observation, with a large part of the territory of California. Will you be so good as to give me your opinion, and the reasons for entertaining it, of the probability or improbability of the introduction of slave labor into any part of the territory recently acquired by the United States from Mexico; provided such introduction be not prohibited by law.

I wish to obtain your opinion in regard to other kinds of labor, as well as agricultural; because, as it seems to me, a most unwarrantable, if not a most disingenuous attempt has been made, to lead the public to believe that no form of slave labor will ever be introduced there, because, possibly, or probably, it may not be introduced for agricultural purposes.

A reply at your earliest convenience will much oblige

Yours, very truly,

HORACE MANN.

WASHINGTON, June 10, 1850.

HON. HORACE MANN;

I received a note from you some days ago, making certain inquiries, but which, up to this time, I have been unable to answer. I desire to take no part in the question now dividing the country; but as you have asked my judgment upon a matter which appears to be a disputed point, I cannot, consistently with the law of courtesy, refuse you an answer. That answer will be in conformity with what I have frequently said, heretofore, in private conversation with gentlemen on this subject.

The point of inquiry seems to be, whether slave labor could be profitably employed in Oregon, California, Utah, and New Mexico. If the nature of the climate and resources of these countries are such as to furnish a profitable market for slave labor, it appears to be conceded, on all sides, that it would be introduced, if left free to seek profitable investment, like other capital. The whole point at issue, then, is dependent, as it is conceived, upon the determination of the first point of inquiry. Hence, to that point, only, it is necessary for me to confine my answer.

I need not remind you of the law regulating the investment of capital. It will always go where, under all circumstances, it will yield the greatest return to the owner. Upon this principle I am very clear, that slave labor, if unrestricted, could be employed in Oregon, with at least double the profit to the owner of the slave that it now yields in any state of the Union. I am uninformed as to the usual price of slave labor in the states, but the price paid to Indians in Oregon during the past year, for labor, has ranged from two to three dollars per day. Domestic negro servants, whether male or female, who understand the business of housework, would command, *readily*, five or six hundred dollars a year. I recollect well that there was a mulatto man on board the vessel in which I took passage from Oregon to San Francisco, who was paid *one hundred and eighty* dollars per month for his services as cook. I will not stop to particularize further, in regard to the inducements Oregon would offer to unrestricted slave labor, but will simply add, that a very large number of slaves might now be employed in Oregon at annual wages sufficiently large to purchase their freedom. I think, therefore, that the point is settled so far as Oregon is concerned, and that slave labor, if it had been left free to seek profitable employment, would readily find its way to that territory.

As to California, I am equally clear. California will always be a mining country, and wages will range high. At present, slave labor in California would be more profitable than in Oregon. And I have always been of the opinion, that wherever there is a mining country, if not in a climate uncongenial to slave labor, that species of labor would be profitable. That it would be in the California mines, is evident. A good able-bodied slave would have commanded, in California, during the past year, from eight to ten hundred dollars per annum. When it is recollected that one hundred dollars per annum, upon an average, is considered a good compensation for their labor in the Southern States, it is idle, in my judgment, to contend that slaves would not be carried to the California market, if protected by law.

The greatest impediment which white labor has to encounter in the mines, is the intensity of the heat, and the prevalence of bilious disease. The one is almost insufferable, while the other is pestilential. Against both of these the negro is almost proof. Now, while white labor is so high, it is evident that no one can hire a white laborer, except at a rate that would consume his profit. Not so with negro labor. That species of labor might be obtained for half the amount which you would have to pay for white labor. The result would be a profit alike to the hirer and seller of slave labor. There is no doubt, in my judgment, that almost any number of slaves might be hired out in California, were the whites willing to allow it, at from eight to ten hundred dollars a year. This is pay so much above what their services command in the states, as to satisfy any one, that could this species of service be protected in California, it would rush to the Pacific in almost any quantity.

Let us next turn our attention to Utah and New Mexico. I have no doubt, from what knowledge I have of those countries, that they will turn out to be filled with the richest mines. I clip the following from a recent paper, containing the news from Texas and Chihuahua : —

"Mr. James was informed, by Major Neighbours and Mr. Lee Vining, that they had been shown by Major Stein, some gold washed out by his troops, on the Gila River, in a short excursion to that stream.

"It is reported, that, at the copper mines above El Paso, there are *about one hundred tons of pure copper lying upon the ground. This had* been got out by Mexicans, and abandoned when attacked by Indians.

"There are at El Paso, in the hands of different persons, several large amounts of silver ore, taken from the mines in that neighborhood. With guaranties of titles to lands, and protection from Indians, only a short time would elapse before all these mines would be well worked, and we would have large quantities of metal seeking a market through this place."

And if you consult Fremont's map, printed by order of the Senate in 1848, you will find, near the source of one of the branches of the Gila River, "copper and gold mines" laid down. And if I am not greatly mistaken, it will turn out that the Mormons are in possession of the richest kind of mines, east of the Sierra Nevada. It is known, too, that silver and copper mines have, for many years, been worked in New Mexico; and I am informed by Hugh N. Smith, Esq., that *there are, in that territory, gold, silver, copper, lead, and zinc mines* of the richest quality, and that the reason why they have not latterly been worked more extensively is, that it is prevented by the incursions of the Indians. He is of the opinion, and he is borne out by what history we can get on the subject, that when these mines shall come to be explored, their wealth will turn out to be enormous. When you have once cast your eye over the country lying west of the Rocky Mountains, and east of the Sierra Nevada, and are informed of the peculiarity of the gold bearing region, you at once become convinced that the United States is in possession of mineral wealth so vast, that ages will not be able to measure its extent. And when these mines shall begin to be developed, and their unquestionable richness known, population will set that way, attended with the usual consequences, high prices, and a demand for labor. If slave labor is like other capital, if it will go where it is best paid, then we have a right to say it will seek these mines, and become a part of the producing capital of the country where those mines are located. That these whole regions are filled with rich mines, is little less than certain, and that they can be profitably worked by slave labor is sure. Hence, were I a southern man, and my property invested in slaves, I should consider the markets of New Mexico, Utah, and California, for slave labor, worthy of an honorable contest to secure.

I am, sir, with due consideration, yours, truly,

SAMUEL R. THURSTON.

5. The Kennebec letter has another most extraordinary and discreditable passage. It is near the close. Mr. Webster quotes from a speech delivered by him in the Senate, March 23, 1848, says it was published in newspapers and circulated in pamphlet form, and that that speech contained the same doctrines in regard to the "legal construction and effect of the resolutions" for admitting Texas, as are contained in the speech of the 7th of March. He says nobody complained then, and he wonders that any body should complain now.

It is very remarkable that such a man as Mr. Webster should furnish, in the very quotation which he offers, the means of utterly confuting the assertion which he makes. I suppose this can be accounted for only on the ground, that he now occupies a position so antagonistic to that which he has abandoned that he can hardly refer to his former views without self-impeachment and self-conviction. Let passages from the two speeches be placed side by side, to show, not their identity, but their utter irreconcilability.

March 23, 1848.	March 7, 1850.
[*A passage quoted by himself.*] "It shall be *in the power* of Congress hereafter to make *four* other new states out of Texan territory."	"I wish it to be distinctly understood, to-day, that, according to my view of the matter, this government *is solemnly pledged by law and contract* to create new states out of Texas," &c. (p. 42.)

The first quotation only asserts a "power" in Congress to create new states; the last affirms an obligation, "by law and contract," to do so. How could Mr. Webster have expected that this broad distinction between *power* and *duty*, between *option* and *obligation*, could escape the attention of his readers?

But there is another discrepancy or contradiction still more remarkable:

MARCH 23, 1848.

"It shall be in the power of Congress hereafter to make *four* other new states out of Texan territory."

MARCH 7, 1850.

"——— the guaranty is, that new states shall be made out of it, and that such states as are formed out of that portion of Texas lying south of 36° 30′, may come in as slave states to the number of *four*, in addition to the state then in existence." (p. 29.)

The first speech speaks of the *power* of Congress, but the last of the *obligation* of Congress, to admit new states out of Texan territory. The first speaks of "four other new states;" but the last of the "guaranty" to admit "SLAVE states to the number of four." Yet the first speech is cited, to men who can read and write, as identical "in legal construction and effect" with the last. The motto under which Danton attempted to carry himself through his bloody career, was: "*L'audace, l'audace, toujours l'audace.*" "Audacity, audacity, always audacity."

But what else did Mr. Webster say, in his speech of the 23d of March, 1848? Referring to the debate which took place in December, 1845, on the final act for admitting Texas, Mr. Webster said: "And I added, that while I held, with as much faithfulness as any citizen of the country, to all the original arrangements and compromises of the constitution under which we live, I never could, and I never should, bring myself to be in favor of the admission of any states into the Union as slaveholding states."* This is what Mr. Webster reports himself to have said when the final vote on the admission of Texas was immediately to be taken, and when he commenced his speech by saying, "I am quite aware, Mr. President, that the resolution will pass,"—meaning the resolution for the admission of Texas. Mr. Webster's "never could and never should" covered the exact case of the then contemplated future slaveholding states to be formed out of Texas. While in the broadness of its terms it embraced all slaveholding states, whensoever, or whencesoever they might come, it had special and pointed application to any slave state to be thereafter formed out of Texan territory.

* Cong. Globe, 1st session 30th Congress, p. 533.

In the same speech of December 22, 1845, Mr. Webster spoke as follows : —

"It may be said that according to the provisions of the constitution, new states are to be admitted on the same footing as the old states. It may be so ; but it does not follow at all from that provision that every territory or portion of country may at pleasure establish slavery, and then say we will become a portion of the Union ; and will bring with us the principles which we may have thus adopted, and must be received on the same footing as the old states. It will always be a question whether the old states have not a right, (and I think they have the clearest right,) to require that the state coming into the Union should come in upon an equality ; and, if the existence of slavery be an impediment to coming in on an equality, then the state proposing to come in should be required to remove that inequality by abolishing slavery, or take the alternative of being excluded."

He also said, in the same speech, "I agree with the unanimous opinion of the legislature of Massachusetts."

And what was this "unanimous opinion of the legislature of Massachusetts"? Among many other things equally decisive, the Massachusetts legislature, on the 26th of March, 1845, — and, of course, long after the annexation resolutions had been passed, — declared as follows : —

"And whereas the consent of the executive and legislative departments of the government of the United States has been given, by a resolution passed on the 27th of February last, to the adoption of preliminary measures to accomplish this nefarious project, [the admission of Texas, with the stipulation to admit four more states out of its territory ;] therefore, be it

"*Resolved*, That Massachusetts hereby refuses to acknowledge the act of the government of the United States, authorizing the admission of Texas, as a legal act, in any way binding her from using her utmost exertions, in coöperation with other states, by every lawful and constitutional measure, to annul its conditions, and defeat its accomplishment.

"*Resolved*, That no territory hereafter applying to be admitted to the Union, as a state, should be admitted without a condition that domestic slavery should be utterly extinguished within its borders, and Massachusetts denies the validity of any compromise whatsoever, that may have been, or that may hereafter be, entered into by persons in the government of the Union, intended to preclude the future application of such a condition by the people, acting through their representatives in the Congress of the United States."

Such were the opinions which Mr. Webster then openly expressed, and such the resolutions of the legislature of Massachusetts, which he fully indorsed. Yet he now professes to wonder that any body can see any difference between the doctrine of those speeches and resolutions, and those of his speech delivered on the 7th of March.*

6. A reference to a few other misstatements of facts will close my remarks on this subject.

Mr. Webster says that, previous to writing his Newburyport letter, he made "diligent inquiry," of members of Congress from New England, to ascertain how many arrests of fugitive slaves had been made in their time; and he adds, "the result

* Professor Stuart, in a pamphlet entitled "Conscience and the Constitution," pp. 78, 9, steps in to defend Mr. Webster's position that we are bound, by contract with Texas, to admit from her territory, "slave states to the number of four;" and he incidentally refers to and combats my views on this subject.

I respectfully submit to the reverened and learned professor a single consideration, which I trust will convince him that I am not in error.

For argument's sake, admit the contract with Texas to be unimpeachable; although, if it be so, I see not why any one Congress may not absorb and exhaust all the power to admit new states, which the constitution contains, by making contracts for centuries to come, for all the new states that shall be admitted; and for all the applications for admission that shall be rejected. But, admitting the validity of the Texan contract, what does it purport? That "new states," "not exceeding four," "may be formed out of the territory thereof." Those south of 36° 30′, may be slave; that, or those, north of 36° 30′, shall be free; the whole "not exceeding four." Here, then, is an executory and mutual contract. It is executory; because it is not to be executed at the time of making, but *in futuro*. It is mutual, because, for the State of Texas, and for the one or more slave states, south of 36° 30′, there are to be one or more free states north of it.

Now, the principle is so clear that I think no one will for a moment dispute it, that when an executory and mutual contract is to be executed, say at four different times, each preceding act of execution must be such as to allow of the ultimate execution of the whole. Neither the first, second, nor third act of execution, must be so executed as to render the fourth impossible. Neither the first, second, nor third act, must be so executed in favor of either of the parties, as to render the execution of the fourth, in favor of the other party, impossible. But if Texas can have "*slave* states to the number of *four*," formed in succession out of her territory, then, as the whole number to be formed is not to exceed "four," there can be *no* free state formed, under the alleged contract.

It is not within my knowledge that such an interpretation of this supposed contract was ever suggested by any Texan citizen, or by any southern man. I suppose it to have been advanced, *first*, by a northern senator; and seconded, *first*, by a northern divine.

of all I can learn is this: No seizure of an alleged slave has ever been made in Maine."

Now, two such cases have happened in the State of Maine. One took place in the eastern part of the state, about 1835 or '36. The other happened at or near Thomaston, a little later. In this latter case, the fugitive came to Maine in a Thomaston vessel, whose master was afterwards demanded as a fugitive from justice. This demand gave rise to a prolonged correspondence, I think, with no less than three governors of Maine. This correspondence was extensively circulated through the newspapers, or referred to by them, and it would seem hardly possible that Mr. Webster should not have seen it. Since the Newburyport letter was published, this misstatement of fact has been noticed in the Maine newspapers, yet no retraction is made. The misstatement is allowed to be spread over the whole country, uncorrected by its author. Mr. Webster then adds, "No seizure of an alleged fugitive slave has ever been made in Vermont." Tradition, and, as I believe, authentic history, contradict Mr. Webster here. It is said by "members of Congress" from Vermont, that an alleged fugitive was carried before Judge Harrington of Vermont, in 1807, and on his being asked what evidence would satisfy him that the person was a slave, he replied, "A bill of sale from Almighty God."

But even if these statements of Mr. Webster, with regard to the New England States, were all true, it would avail him nothing; for, in the eye of patriotism, it matters not where such seizures are made. I refer to it only to show that Mr. Webster is not to be relied upon in these matters, either for the accuracy of his original positions, or for a retraction of them, when their error is pointed out by the public press. I wish not to be understood, *on this particular point*, as imputing to Mr. Webster an intentional misstatement; because he accompanied his original statement with a salvo. He confessed, — and he is entitled to the full benefit of the confession, — that his information might not be "entirely accurate," though he supposed it not to be "materially erroneous." It is "materially erroneous;" and though one error has been exposed in the Maine papers, he does not rectify it. Possibly he does not know it.

While holding Massachusetts up to reproach for "growing

fervid on Pennsylvania wrongs," Mr. Webster draws succor and encouragement from the Society of Friends, and especially from the Friends of Pennsylvania. He says that they remain "of sound and disposing minds and memories;" and he contrasts their wisdom and composure with the "vehement and empty declarations, the wild and fantastic conduct of both men and women which have so long disturbed and so much disgraced the commonwealth" of Massachusetts. He then adds, "I am misled by authority which ought not to mislead, if it be not true, that that great body, [of Friends,] approves the sentiments to which I gave utterance on the floor of the Senate." I will now show that this alleged approval by the Friends, though worthy of any price but truth, was too dearly bought.

It is well known that the Friends are divided into two great denominations. Each has its periodical, one now in its eighth, the other in its fourth year. In the numbers published since the appearance of the Newburyport letter, both these periodicals do not "approve," but repudiate and denounce the sentiments to which Mr. Webster gave utterance "on the floor of the Senate."

The *Friend's Intelligencer* deals at length with Mr. Webster's "sentiments" on the "Fugitive Slave Bill;" on the legislation of the north for the protection of its own citizens; on his pseudo discoveries in "physical geography;" and on the "legal construction and effect" of the Texas resolutions; and it condemns them all.

The *Friend's Review* dissents not less positively from Mr. Webster's positions; and both call him severely to account for the defamation of themselves, which his letter implies.

On his "sentiments" respecting fugitive slaves, the "*Review*" observes that they have yet to learn "that that part of his speech was approved by any member or professor of the society."

I wish I had space to quote from these able articles, but must forbear.

John G. Whittier, Esq., speaking for the Quakers of New England, gives "a peremptory denial" to Mr. Webster's statement. I quote the following paragraph from him: —

"Now, we undertake to say that there is not a member of the Society of Friends, in free or slave states, who, whether acting as a magistrate or as citizen, could carry out the provisions of this most atrocious bill, without rendering himself liable to immediate expulsion from a society whose character would be disgraced, and whose discipline would be violated, by such action. It has been, in times past, the misfortune of the Society of Friends to be villified, caricatured, and misrepresented; but we remember nothing, even in the old days of persecution, so hard to bear as the compliments of the Massachusetts senator. Whatever his 'authority' may have been, we do not hesitate to pronounce it unqualifiedly false to the last degree."

Now what shall be thought of a cause that requires such a series of fabrications as Mr. Webster is here proved to have made, or of the man that can make it!

There are many other points presented by Mr. Webster's speech of the 7th of March, or by what he has since said and written to defend it, which seem to me as unwarrantable in fact, and as reprehensible in principle, as any above enumerated. I shall close these notes, however, with one comment more; reserving others, — though sincerely hoping never to have occasion to use them.

Among the excoriations with which Mr. Webster amused himself and his southern new-born pro-slavery admirers, on the 7th of March last, he flayed nobody half so deeply or so complacently, as he did his old fellow-senators, Messrs. Dix, of New York, and Niles, of Connecticut. He scored them to the living flesh, and then soothed their smarting wounds by vitriol and caustic, as though he loved them. Their agency in the Texas swindle, he made odiously conspicuous. He taunted them with heart-piercing innuendo for their compulsory retirement from public life. And then he portrayed them as occupying their enforced vacation in attempting to rouse the people to save those regions from the curse of slavery, which, but for their sins, never would have been exposed to it. He worked up the scene so graphically, that every one mocked at their contemptible plight, and at the ridiculous contrast between the swiftness of their offence and the lameness of their expiation. The effect was dramatic. The pro-slavery part of the gallery and the floor responded with a shout of laughter. Yet devoted and long-tried friends of Mr. Webster were there, whom no darkness of blindness could prevent from seeing that his bitter sarcasm against the ex-senators, though calculated to make the "unskilful laugh," must make the "judicious grieve." They could not fail to see that he, Mr. Webster himself, at that very moment, was occupying precisely the same pro-slavery ground, which Messrs. Dix and Niles had occupied, when they brought in Texas and "reännexed" California and New Mexico. He was exerting all his great talents to do an act of precisely the same character which Messrs. Dix and Niles had done; — that is, to open new territory to slavery. And doubtless the first thought which arose in many a mind was the same melancholy one which spontaneously arose in my own, that should he succeed in arguing down, or laughing down the "*Wilmot*," as he twice scornfully called the great proviso of freedom; and should he then betake himself to penitence and prayer, and by years of effort, strive to stay back from slavery the regions he had doomed to it, he would only have elevated himself to the very "platform" on which Messrs. Dix and Niles stood ***when he made them the objects of his taunts and ridicule!***

LETTER

ANSWERING AN INVITATION TO CELEBRATE THE ANNIVERSARY OF THE ORDINANCE OF 1787, AT CLEVELAND, OHIO.

WEST NEWTON, July 9, 1849.

GENTLEMEN;

I have received your kind invitation to be present at Cleveland, on the 13th inst., to celebrate the anniversary of the great "Ordinance" which excluded slavery forever from, and secured freedom forever to the Northwestern Territory. If I could tell you how deeply I sympathize with you in this movement, and how much my soul desires, not merely to celebrate, but to hallow the event, you would then believe me when I say, that I have had a sharp struggle not to forego all considerations of business and of health, for the purpose of joining in your festival. I regard the Ordinance which redeemed a territory of more than *two hundred and sixty thousand square miles*, from the unspeakable sin and curse of slavery, and consecrated it to freedom, as one of the grandest moral events in the annals of mankind.

Without that Ordinance, the Declaration of Independence itself, in its application to that vast and fertile region, would have been deprived of its power to confer blessing and prosperity upon it; and it is a fact never to be forgotten, that the original Declaration and the original Ordinance were both drawn up by the same great champion of human rights, whose hatred of slavery grew strong and deep by his personal knowledge of its wrongs and its calamities.

Without the Ordinance, the Revolution itself, in its application to that territory, and the treaty of 1783, by which its ample domain was secured to the Union, would have been shorn of their glory, and robbed of their value.

Without the Ordinance, the discovery of this Western continent, so far as that territory constitutes a part of it, would have given us no occasion to remember the name of Columbus with gratitude.

Without the Ordinance, it would have been better, at the creation of the world, that all that part of it which now constitutes your five beautiful and flourishing states, with a residuum of space large enough for still another, had been left as a "Dead Sea," whose bitter and poisonous waters would not have allowed a live thing to swim beneath its surface, nor to fly above it, nor a green thing to grow by its shores.

And without the Ordinance, it is no irreverence to say, that even the omnipotent Spirit of God, working through natural laws, for human progress and human blessedness, would have met with bafflings and threatenings in its operations and influences for the redemption of the race.

Accept, gentlemen, the assurance of my sympathy and regard.

HORACE MANN.

Messrs. J. C. VAUGHAN, }
THOMAS BROWN, } Committee.

LETTER

ACCEPTING THE NOMINATION OF THE FREE SOIL CONVENTION FOR REPRESENTATIVE TO THE THIRTY-SECOND CONGRESS.

WEST NEWTON, Oct. 24, 1850.

HON. C. F. ADAMS;

Dear Sir, — Your favor of the 21st inst., is this day received. It informs me that at a convention, (over which you had the honor to preside,) held at Dedham, on the 16th inst., I was unanimously nominated as a candidate for Representative to the thirty-second Congress of the United States. For the kind terms in which your communication is expressed, be pleased to accept my thanks.

This nomination places me in no new relation to the friends of freedom and humanity, wherever they may be found. I believe my name was first suggested to the voters of this district, (now nearly three years ago,) on the ground of my supposed devotion to the rights of men. The resolutions passed at all the conventions by which I have been nominated, and especially those passed so repeatedly and unanimously by our state legislature, have been in the nature of instructions; or, at least, of urgent advice and solicitation, in regard to my course on the great questions which have since agitated the country. My own convictions of duty so fully and entirely corresponding with the injunctions thus laid upon me, it has been easy for me to act in full conformity to the wishes of the great majority of my constituents and of the state, as those wishes have been repeatedly expressed. This renders any detailed exposition of expectations on your part, or of assurances on mine, unnecessary. I know that the leading and most valued article in your creed is the sacredness and security of human freedom. You know that I embrace this same article of faith with my whole heart. Other matters may be very important, but still are subordinate. Peculiar forms of organization are comparatively non-essentials. They are but means to ends; and, in regard to them, a large allowance is to be made for honest differences of opinion. But the natural right of every human being to the liberty which God has given him, until forfeited by crime of his own; the duty of our government to save every part of this earth over which it has jurisdiction from the direst of all earthly curses and the greatest of all social crimes, — the curse and the crime of slavery; — these are among the first of the dread accountabilities that attach to rational and immortal creatures.

I believe it also to be the duty of government to provide for the economical or pecuniary welfare of the people; to encourage industry by securing the rewards of labor to the laborer, and to discourage the competitions into which those who rule and control the impoverished, degraded, and almost brutified laborers of other countries, are striving to enter with our own people, — competitions, which, if not prevented, will, to a great extent, reduce our laborers to the wretchedness and privation of theirs. I believe that the money, and the comforts purchasable with it, which such competitions take from the workman here, do not go to improve the condition of the workman there, but are intercepted and appropriated by others. I make this statement of my views all the more readily, because I do not wish to receive an unintelligent vote from any man, and I therefore abjure all disguises and reserves. From my past votes and speeches in Congress my constituents know upon what principles and to what ends I have acted. To them I refer, and deem it unnecessary to say more.

Those who have taken the trouble to read what I have said on the floor of the House, must have seen that, though I have endeavored to express some stern truths, on vital subjects, in unambiguous language, yet that I have never uttered a word designed to inflict unnecessary pain upon our political brethren of the south; or to wound feelings which men may erroneously call honorable. I desire to pursue the same course at all times and with all men. The cause of liberty is one in which the true object of ambition is to make great principles most clear, and not to use harsh expressions respecting the conduct or opinion of others. It is as necessary that the man whom I would convince should be in a calm state of mind, as that I should be in such a state myself. Exasperation paralyzes judgment. The great points on which men and parties so vehemently differ, can only be permanently settled at the tribunal of reason and conscience.

Several laws were passed at the last session of Congress, on which I desired and designed to speak, in the name and on behalf of my constituents. But I was obliged to act upon them, under the silence enforced by the previous question. One of them, in particular, was so hostile to all the principles which history and reason had ever taught me, and so wounding to all the sentiments which I had ever imbibed from benevolence and religion, that I resolved to seize the first opportunity that should be offered to portray some of its features. I refer to the Fugitive Slave act, so called; and I trust this will not be deemed an unfitting occasion to lay bare a portion of its enormities. I will remark, that I had prepared an amendment for the security of our free colored seamen in southern ports, but was shut out from all chance of offering it. It struck me that if new and oppressive measures were to be taken to carry back alleged slaves to bondage, something should also be done to restore freemen to liberty.

While the south were seeking new guaranties for men who claim to own other men, it was a time for the north to demand new guaranties for men who own themselves. But all debate was suppressed; property vanquished liberty; and a pure pro-slavery law was enacted, unadulterated by any alloy of freedom.

In regard to this Fugitive Slave act, is it not astonishing that men should ever ask the question, Does the constitution *demand* the trial by jury? instead of the question, Will the constitution *allow* it? The first is the tyrant's question, granting no more than he is compelled to give. The last is the republican's question, volunteering all that he can grant. In a free government, where the trial by jury is held to be the surest safeguard of personal liberty, the inquiry ought never to be, whether the constitution *secures or necessitates* this form of trial; for it is enough, if the constitution will *permit* or *tolerate* it. Instead of seeking evasions, and close constructions, and hunting among the musty precedents of darker times, in order to shut out the jury trial in cases of personal liberty, the true lover of freedom would ask only for an interpretation that would *warrant* it. It would not be among his last thoughts; he would not wait until a stern necessity forced such a construction upon him; but his first desire and effort would be to find some legitimate reason for conferring it. He would not ask, in how few cases he must, but in how many he might, admit it. Yet this matter has been discussed, and is still discussed, on one side, as though we were bound to avoid the jury trial if we could; not as though we were bound to grant it, if by fair interpretation we might. It has been discussed as though the jury trial, to protect a man's right to himself, were an evil; and as though the sudden seizure, "summary" adjudication, and speedy consignment of a fellow-being to bondage, were too precious a blessing to be put in jeopardy, by submission to twelve good and lawful men. Not how much may we do for freedom, but how much can we do for slavery, has been the tacit assumption of the argument. But I pass by this for graver objections.

The Fugitive Slave act purports to confer judicial power upon persons who are not judges. It provides for the creation of scores and hundreds of officers called "commissioners," and upon these, it is said on high authority, to confer *original* and *final* jurisdiction on questions of human liberty. The constitution declares in whom "the judicial power of the United States shall be vested." It shall be vested in "one supreme court, and in such inferior courts as Congress may from time to time establish." No commissioner, nor any number of commissioners, constitute one of these courts. "The judges, both of the supreme and inferior courts, shall hold their offices during good behavior." A commissioner can be made and unmade on any day. These judges are to "receive for their services a compensation, which shall not be diminished during their continuance in office." The commissioners are compensated by chance fees, and not by a fixed salary. The President nominates and the Senate confirms judges of the supreme and inferior courts. Commissioners are only the "inferior officers" who may be appointed by "the courts of law."

I need not enforce the position, that the power which this act purports to confer upon commissioners is *judicial.* It has all the attributes of judicial power. It is *original*, *final*, and *exclusive.* They are "to hear and *determine.*" The fourth section says they "shall have *concurrent* jurisdiction with the judges of the circuit and district courts of the United States." The attorney-general of the United States, in a written opinion, given by command of the President of the United States, says as follows: "These officers, [the commissioners,] and each of them, have *judicial* power, and jurisdiction to hear, examine, and decide the case." "The certificate to be granted to the owner is to be regarded as the act and judgment of a judicial tribunal having competent jurisdiction." "Congress has constituted a tribunal with exclusive jurisdiction to determine summarily, and without appeal, who are fugitives from service." "The judgment of the tribunal created by this act is conclusive upon all tribunals." The power of a commissioner, therefore, is *judicial* in the highest sense, — in the sense of the constitution. His decision cannot be reheard or reëxamined by any judge, or by any court, of any state, or of the United States. In no other case can a commissioner perform any judicial act, or issue any executive order, whose validity may not be reëxamined in the court for which he acts, or in some other. He cannot strike a blow, nor fine a dollar, nor punish by imprisonment for an hour. By appeal, by injunction, by mandamus or certiorari, the proceedings of inferior courts or magistrates can be reached, and their legality or constitutionality tested. But here a multitude of tribunals are established, over whose proceedings, not the supreme court of any state, no, not even the supreme court of the United States, has supervision. And what do these commissioners decide? That a man has no right to himself; that his body, limbs, faculties, are the *property* of another; that he *owes service.* Suppose the question were, whether the respondent owed the claimant a dollar. Could the commissioner give judgment and issue execution for it? Certainly not. But yet he is here authorized to decide questions infinitely more important than any amount of money. He is to decide that a man owes life-long service from himself, and from all the children of his loins.

But the surrender of an alleged fugitive from service

has been compared with the surrender of a fugitive from justice; and because the supreme executive of a state is required by the law of 1793 to surrender fugitives from justice, it is claimed that any commissioner may surrender fugitives from service, *without liability to question or reëxamination by any human authority.* But there is a world-wide difference between the cases. When the fugitive from justice is delivered up, he is delivered into the custody of the law. Legal process must have been commenced against him in the state from which he fled. He is returned, that the proceedings thus commenced may be consummated. He is never intrusted to private hands. The shield of the law is continued over him. After arrest, he is merely transferred from the hands of the law in one state to the hands of the law in another state. He is transferred, not to evade trial, but to have one. But the alleged slave is delivered up, not into the custody of the law, where his rights might be adjudicated upon, but into private hands; not into the hands of a neutral or indifferent person, but into the hands of a party interested to deprive him of all his rights; — if he be not a slave, then into the hands of a man-stealer. Mr. Clay saw this, and his plan provided that the alleged fugitive should be sent home *to be tried.* But the south grew bolder and bolder, until a law was passed, by which one class of men have less security for their freedom than another class have for their cattle.

It is nugatory to say, that when an alleged fugitive has reached his claimant's domicile, he may there petition for freedom. Should he do so, it would be an independent and original proceeding, instituted under *another* government. Not only would the jurisdiction be different, but the character of the litigants would be changed, — plaintiff for defendant, and defendant for plaintiff. The old case is not to be reheard, but a new one tried. Indeed, a very intelligent writer on this subject has queried whether the certificate of the commissioner may not be pleaded as an estoppel. I say, then, that, in effect, the commissioner, by this act, has *original*, *final*, and *exclusive* jurisdiction of a "case" "in law," "arising under the constitution and laws of the United States." This is the very function of judges and courts. This is the identical power which the constitution of the United States vests in judges who are to be nominated by the President, confirmed by the Senate, to hold office during good behavior, and to be compensated by fixed salaries.

Again, the act consigns a man to bondage, without crime, on evidence which he has had no opportunity to controvert. The claimant must prove three facts before the commissioner, — 1st, That the person named in the warrant owes the claimant service; 2d, That he has escaped; 3d, Identity.

Now, according to the act, the first two points, — the facts of owing service and of escaping, — may be proved behind the respondent's back. This proof may be procured against the alleged fugitive without any notice to him, actual or constructive; without the possibility of his encountering it, or disproving it, however false it may be. If this be not depriving a person of his "liberty" "without due process of law," what can be? Why not make the whole case provable behind the man's back, — in another state, — a thousand miles off, — and spurn the forms of justice, after having spurned its substance? This binding of a man by evidence obtained without his knowledge, is unknown to the common law, and abhorrent to it. It is never permitted, not even to deprive the worst man of the humblest right. Our laws save the rights of all parties under disability. Who is under so great a disability as he who knows nothing, and can know nothing, of what is going on against him? Notwithstanding the constitution declares that "full faith and credit shall be given in each state to the public acts, records, and judicial proceedings of every other state," yet it has been held that a judgment obtained in another state, without notice, shall not prejudice the party against whom it was rendered. Such an act violates the first principles of justice. All securities for the life, liberty and property of us all, are swept away if such principles can be established.

Once more: The act says the certificate "shall be conclusive of the right of the person or persons in whose favor granted, to remove such fugitive to the state or territory from which he escaped, and shall prevent all molestation of such person or persons, by any process issued by any court, judge, magistrate, or any other person whomsoever." According to this, the certificate is a talisman which protects its holder against all law, all evidence, and all judicial power. A kidnapper may seize a free man in Boston, buy evidence that he owes this mysterious *debt of service*, obtain the requisite certificate against his victim, and then neither the mother who bore him, nor the elder brothers and sisters who grew up with him, nor the neighbors who have known him from his cradle, nor the minister who baptized him, can testify that he is free; nor can all the judges and courts in the commonwealth stop the man who is bearing away one of their fellow-citizens to a bondage worse than death, to inquire into his title. He is in a charmed circle that neither law nor justice can enter. Do you ask where is that old, time-honored writ of *habeas corpus*, for which martyrs have died and rivers of blood have flowed, and which the constitution declares SHALL NOT be suspended "unless when in cases of rebellion or invasion, the public safety may require it"? The answer is, that the writ of *habeas corpus* is nothing but a "process issued" by a court, and the act declares that the holder of the certificate shall be exempt from all "molestation," "by any process issued by any court." In one word, the law contains a provision that its own constitutionality shall not be brought into question; at least, until its victim reaches the place of his bondage, and is beyond the reach of rescuing hands.

Now, even if this act does not commit such gross infractions of the constitution that the courts will set it aside, yet it would seem as though no sane man could help seeing that it wars upon all our ideas of justice; that it repudiates and scorns all the great securities for freedom which wise and good men, for centuries past, have given their labors, and their lives, to establish; and that it converts the vast machinery of the social state, not into the means of protecting, but of assailing, the liberties of the citizen. As to the appointment of commissioners, it gives us none of the constitutional securities that improper men will not be invested with these high prerogatives against our dearest rights; and as to the manner in which evidence may be procured, it resembles the missives which the inquisition, in olden times, sent forth against heretics, to seize without law, to try without defence, and to punish without mercy or hope. It resembles the *lettres de cachet*, which, before the great revolution, the despots of France gave, *in blank*, to villain courtiers, and villain courtesans, to be filled up with the names of those persons whose perdition they would compass.

There are other points in this bill whose enormity only needs to be stated to be seen and abhorred. One of them is so unspeakably mean and contemptible, that all northern men must feel the insult more keenly than the wrong. It provides that if a commissioner will doom a man to bondage, his fee shall be twice as much as though he restores him to liberty. Now, every body knows that claimants will rarely, if ever, appear before commissioners without a *prima facie* case. If there be no defence, the proceedings will be brief. But a case of discharge presupposes a defence and a trial. A case of discharge, therefore, will probably occupy as much time as half a dozen cases of surrender. Yet for this greater labor, the commissioner is to have but half price. In assailing all we love of liberty, could not the framers and supporters of this measure have forborne to wound us in all we feel of honor!

The cases are to be "heard and determined," as they were under Robespierre, "*in a summary manner.*" Shakspeare enumerates the "law's delay" among the causes of suicide. Under this act, real suicides will doubtless be occasioned by the *law's despatch.** This "summary manner" contains the sum of wrong. Does not every lawyer and every client know that when an action is brought for the unfaithful execution of a contract, in building a house or a ship, or for the balance of an account, or for flowing lands, or for defamation or libel, the defendant needs weeks and often months to make ready for his defence. His witnesses may be in another state, or abroad; it may be necessary to examine ancient titles in registries of deeds or of wills, to make surveys of premises, or investigations into character and conduct. It often happens that when process is first served upon a man, he does not know the grounds of his own defence. They may consist of facts which he has forgotten, or of law of which he is ignorant. Our courts, acting upon this well-known truth, have established a rule that a party, even after he has had fourteen days' notice, shall be entitled to a continuance as a matter of right, unless under special circumstances; and he may always have it on cause shown. I ask any defendant who was ever forced into court to resist a

* Since writing the above, I see that a man in New Jersey was so overcome with fright at the rumor that slave-catchers were in town, that paralysis and death speedily ensued.

claim of any magnitude or difficulty, whether he was ready to do so, on the instant when process was served upon him? Yet this is what the respondent must do under the Fugitive Slave act. On the 26th day of last September, James Hamlet was peacefully pursuing a lawful occupation in Water Street, New York, and earning an honest support for his wife and children. In three hours, hand-cuffed, in irons, and surrounded by armed men, he was on his way to the house of bondage. No time was given him for procuring the aid of counsel. He declared he was free, that his mother was a free woman, and he a free man. But by another provision in the act, it is declared that "in no trial or hearing under this act, shall the testimony of such alleged fugitive be admitted in evidence." In all other cases, within the broad compass of the common or statute law of Great Britain or of this country, a party litigant may give evidence pertaining to the suit. In some cases, he may give evidence on the merits; in all cases, he may make affidavit on interlocutory matters. A man who has been in the state prison, a felon scarred with crime, may still make affidavit, in his own case, under certain circumstances, though he can testify neither for nor against any other person. But an alleged fugitive can make oath to no fact, and under no circumstances, for delay or other cause. It would conflict with that "summary manner" in which it is deemed expedient to dispose of human liberty.

Look at this provision under the light of a few facts. In the case of *Mahoney* vs. *Ashton*, (4 Harris & McHenry's Maryland Reports,) the petitioner for freedom claimed that a maternal ancestor, *four generations back*, who had been brought over by Lord Baltimore, in the early days of the colony, was free; and, by an extraordinary chain of evidence, he traced his descent from that free source. It was a claim which any court in Massachusetts would have sustained without hesitation.

Now how much evidence of history, of record, of parol, does the bare mention of such a case suggest? Who could have been prepared to try it in three hours; ay, as soon as he could be seized and hurried to a lawyer's office?

Among the alleged fugitives in the "Pearl cases," so called, which I assisted in trying in Washington, in the years 1848 and '49, was the family of Daniel Bell, consisting of his wife and eight or ten children. The mother and children had been freed many years before by deed of manumission, executed by their master in his last sickness, and they had been reputed free ever afterwards. Soon after the grantor's death, the device was started of proving him to be of "unsound mind," and thus reclaiming the family to bondage. But the magistrate who prepared the deed, witnessed its execution, and took the acknowledgment, declared that he stood ready to testify to the *competency* of the grantor, and the validity of the instrument. Years passed away and *he* died. Immediately the heirs claimed the family as slaves; and, after the loss of the deceased magistrate's testimony, proved the grantor of "unsound mind," and so set aside the deed and were adjudged owners of the *chattels*. On the ground of newly-discovered evidence, application for a new trial was made; but the family becoming alarmed lest they should be secretly seized and sent to the south, attempted to make their escape on board the "Pearl," on the night of the 15th of April. Now, suppose that they had succeeded, and that, after arriving in a free state, they had been seized and carried before a commissioner, to be tried in this "summary manner," without even waiting for a crier to open the court, and debarred from making affidavit that, in the city of Washington, there existed evidence of their freedom. I will not waste words to point out the impossibility of their defence, and the certainty of their doom! He that hath ears to hear the cry of the oppressed, let him hear!

A few days before the close of the last session of Congress, I was inquired of by a resident in Washington, as to the condition of a family held as slaves in that city. I found they were free by the laws of the District, but they did not know it.

Sir, throughout the Southern States, there are thousands and thousands of reputed slaves, who, legally, and by the laws of those states, too, in which they are held, are as free as the governor of Massachusetts, or the chief justice; but, in their enforced and brutish ignorance, the victims do not know it; and should they come to a free state, and be there hunted, and seized, and carried before a commissioner, they would be debarred from taking an oath as to facts which would furnish grounds for a continuance so that their right to freedom might be established. But, under such obstructions and embarrassments, liberty could not be extinguished in a sufficiently "summary manner."

According to the constitution of the United States, all *criminals*, from the least to the greatest, are to be informed of the nature and cause of their accusation; to be confronted with the witnesses against them; to have compulsory process for obtaining witnesses in their favor; and to have the assistance of counsel in their defence. Yet here, always in the case of an *innocent* man, oftentimes in the case of a free man, there is to be no previous notice, no process for obtaining witnesses, and no provision for counsel; and while the court is forbidden to allow delay, without good cause shown, the party whose liberty is at stake cannot make out that cause by his oath; but, with the full knowledge in his own breast that he *is* free, he must stand dumb before the minister of the law that puts on his fetters.

I will not dwell at any length upon those portions

of the act which affect marshals and deputy marshals. If any man chooses not to hold office under such a law, he can decline to accept it, or resign it. It is, however, clear proof of wicked legislation, when humane and conscientious men cannot hold the offices it creates. But the fifth section contains a provision which is atrocious. It makes the marshal or his deputy liable for an escape, whether made "with or *without* his assent," — that is, *at all events*. Though the alleged fugitive should disable him, though the enemies of the country should capture him, though the act of God should strike him down, though an armed mob should commit a rescue, — yet he is still liable.

All civilized governments have statutes of limitations. Human welfare requires that claims which have long been voluntarily acquiesced in, should not be revived. Hence our laws bar a right of action, otherwise incontrovertible, after that tacit abandonment of which the mere lapse of time is proof. Personal rights are most generally abandoned by a six years' neglect to enforce them. Even real estate may be held, by twenty years' quiet possession, without other title. Crimes partake of this exemption. With the single exception of murder, all crimes are barred in Massachusetts by a six years' delay to prosecute. But the Fugitive Slave act knows no mercy or compassion of this kind. Unrelentingly it fastens its clutch upon all cases. While life lasts, its fangs strike into the flesh. The alleged slave may have been amongst us for fifty years; he may have earned property, be married, and surrounded by children. It is all the same. The inexorable certificate of a commissioner remands him to bondage and despair.

The act not only remands him to bondage, but, under circumstances to which there will be few exceptions, it orders that he be sent home at the public expense. The constitution says, he shall be "delivered up." There the obligation of that instrument ceases. It is only the law that adds, he shall be *carried back*. You and I, sir, must help pay the costs of sending a fellow-being into bondage; when we are under no more constitutional obligation to do so, than to pay the expenses of a slave dealer who ships his cargoes direct from Africa.

But the bill has become a law, and the practical question now is, how can the country be exculpated from the crime, and the dishonor. For myself, I do not adopt the doctrine of forcible nullification. I trust I shall never join a mob to resist a law, until I am ready for revolution. The only true and enduring remedy is repeal. Those who would forcibly resist the law, lose half their motive and impulse for repeal; for if we abolish it without repealing it, it will be likely to remain upon the statute book an eternal monument of the nation's disgrace. Let effort never cease, until the jury trial be obtained.

But this view of civil duty applies only to the *citizen*. It does not touch the fugitive. One liberty the slave always has, — whenever he deems it expedient, he may re-clothe himself in the rights which God and nature gave him, and which, though they may be ravished from him, can never be destroyed.

Until repeal, however, there is one opening for hope. If, as is said by Mr. Crittenden, in the opinion already cited, "Congress has constituted a tribunal with *exclusive* jurisdiction, to determine summarily, and without appeal;" and if, as he further says, "the judgment of every tribunal of exclusive jurisdiction, where no appeal lies, is of necessity *conclusive upon every other tribunal*, AND THEREFORE THE JUDGMENT OF THE TRIBUNAL CREATED BY THIS ACT IS CONCLUSIVE UPON ALL TRIBUNALS;" then the whole case in all its bearings and relations, its sources and its issues, comes before the commissioner; not even the supreme court of the

United States can interfere with him ; and the first question for him to " hear and determine " is, whether in truth there be any such *law*, whether the whole disgraceful enactment be not unconstitutional and void ; and, therefore, whether his first and only duty be not to dismiss the proceedings, and to " let the captive go free." I am not without hope that such will be the result ; and thus, that many conscientious and law-abiding men will be relieved from the moral anxiety and conflict which now oppresses their minds.

Very truly, your obedient servant,

HORACE MANN.

SPEECH

DELIVERED AT DEDHAM, NOVEMBER 6, 1850, BY SPECIAL REQUEST OF A CONVENTION OF WHIG VOTERS OF THE EIGHTH CONGRESSIONAL DISTRICT.

GENTLEMEN AND FELLOW-CITIZENS ;

Having been specially invited to appear before this meeting, and address it, my friend Mr. Russell has introduced me to you with many kind words ; and he has emphatically announced me as "your old friend." By so doing, gentlemen, he has touched a living chord in my heart ; for, as I look around me, I see many familiar and dear faces, and am reminded that, in this town, I spent some of the happiest years of my life. The sight of every object around me awakens remembrances of home. Right opposite to us is the court house, in whose forum my feeble voice was first raised, and where, I thank God, it was never raised in behalf of the oppressor, nor on the side of any cause which I believed to be wrong. Around this church in which we are assembled are the streets where I used to walk, there is the pew where I used to sit, and all around me are persons whom, for years, I saw daily and knew intimately, and knew them only to respect. I feel assured that I do meet "old friends," — true men, who carry their hearts in their hands, and whose lives are anchored to their convictions of duty.

Gentlemen, it is not without embarrassment that I address you. Yet I might plead a high example for my course, if I were worthy, in any respect, to mention myself in connection with my venerated predecessor, who has made the past history of his country so luminous with his wisdom and purity, and the name of this district which he represented so honored and memorable. Would to God I could carry you to some Pisgah height, and show you, under one view, the past, the present, and the future, as he was wont to do, when, as was his custom, he used to address you on those great topics which employed his energies,— on the principles by which you ought to be guided, and on the dangers to which you were exposed.

We have fallen, gentleman, on momentous times. Great events have occurred, in rapid succession, both in this and in the other hemisphere. There seems to have been a grand upheaving of the elements of society from its deep foundations. We have been so often astonished and amazed, by shock after shock, and convulsion after convulsion, that I fear we are beginning to lose our moral sensibility to political catastrophes, however grand or fatal they may be.

You know there is a spot near the Mississippi River famous for the frequency of its earthquakes. A gentleman who visited there some years ago, told me that soon after entering a hotel, at a place called New Madrid, his attention was suddenly arrested by the rattling of the crockery, the jarring of the household furniture, and the shaking of the chair in which he sat. Starting up in trepidation, he sprang for the door. "O," said his landlord, "don't be alarmed. *It is nothing but an earthquake.*" These phenomena, it seems, had become so common as to have lost their power of exciting alarm. So, I fear, it is in regard to the late commotions in Europe; and especially in regard to some of the marvellous doings of Congress in our own country. From their astounding character, and their rapid succession, I fear we are becoming insensible to their importance, like the inhabitants who dwell at the base of Mount Etna, whom neither the rumbling of the mountain, nor the lava rivers which pour down its side, can awake from their stupor, until, like Pompeii or Herculaneum, they are buried in the ruins.

In the old world, things seem already to be settling back into their former condition, and hopes are darkening into fears. In this country, I still trust that we shall redeem something of the past, and secure the future. Yet the events of the last few months are of a disheartening character, if any thing could ever dishearten a true lover of his country. It has been my fortune and duty to be in the midst of these events. I have watched the tide of battle with sleepless eye; and when Liberty at last was stricken down, my heart bled with hers.

I believe I understand, gentlemen, what you wish me to do on this occasion; and therefore I shall endeavor to lay before you, briefly but impartially, the humble part which I, as your representative, have taken in those events which have filled the hearts of good men with alarm.

I would, however, premise a few words, in order to show how we have come, step by step, to the fearful position we now occupy.

Very early in our history, as a republic established to maintain the rights of man, an extent of territory was acquired equal to all we possessed before; and this addition accrued to the special advantage of those who maintain, as the first great article in their creed, the wrongs of man. The same European wars which enabled Mr. Jefferson's administration to purchase Louisiana with fifteen millions of dollars, — a sum mostly paid by the north, — brought the commercial interests of the north also within the destructive sweep of those contests, and the non-intercourse act and the embargo were the consequence. These came upon New England at a time when commerce was her only resource. They brought as great a calamity upon the New England states as it would now be to the south if their whole cotton crop, or to the west if their whole grain crop, were to fail for a series of years. They palsied our industry; and, without industry, men, any where out of Paradise, will be poor. Upon the back of this calamity came the war of 1812, which we bore as well as we could, and performed our full share in carrying the country through it, though it cut off our very means of living. That war revealed a lamentable condition of things. It revealed the fact that, notwithstanding our political independence, we were, in a commercial sense, most deplorably dependent. It pointed to a new policy. It put the country upon achieving its second independence,— its independence, at least for the necessaries of life, of foreign mechanics, manufacturers, and artisans, as it had already achieved its political independence of foreign kings, aristocracies, and ecclesiastics. It gave birth to the American system, in which Calhoun, Lowndes, Cheves, and Clay,—all from the slave states,—took the lead. I mention the first three names, particularly, because they were from the state of South Carolina. So heartily did they enter into the new policy that they took their seats in Congress clad in homespun. They said they would exemplify their principles by their garments, and wear them outside as well as inside of their bodies. I am sorry their principles lasted but little longer than their clothes,—one suit worn out, and all, both without and within, clean gone. Even Mr. Madison boasted that his coat was woven in an American loom. The south led off in this policy, and New England, whose capital had been wrecked on the ocean, was reluctantly compelled to follow their lead. This was the origin of the protective tariff, the child of South Carolina, though, at a later period, adopted by Massachusetts.

It was not, however, until 1824, that New England, and Massachusetts particularly, gave in her adhesion to the protective policy. Then our people engaged in manufactures. The streams were dammed, and the mighty powers of nature were set to spinning and weaving, to dyeing and printing, under the guidance of that genius which had been kindled and nurtured in our schoolhouses. Those establishments were founded which have produced so marvellous a change in our household condition, surrounding all with so many comforts, and filling our dwellings with so vast a variety of the refinements and luxuries of life. Those of you who have arrived at my age, and are therefore acquainted with the condition of things throughout our country towns thirty years ago, know that the change is almost magical. Though opposed in its inception by the cities and the merchants, yet it has promoted their prosperity not less than that of the people.

In the year 1820, a national question of a great moral character arose. The south, whose policy had before secured a territory as large as that of the original thirteen, sought to extend slavery over its whole surface. Missouri applied to be admitted into the Union as a slave state. The morality and religion of the north thought the time had come to arrest the strides of slavery, and they opposed the application. Earnest resistance was made. The battle was obstinately fought; but at last, the north, or rather enough recreants of the north yielded, and the day was lost. The south bought or bullied a sufficient number of the invertebrate creatures whom we send to Congress, and triumphed over us. This was the first great surrender of principle on the part of the north, and a fatal surrender it was. We, and humanity, and all that is dearest to the heart and thoughts of man, might have achieved the victory but for a few cases of foul treachery to the cause of freedom. O, that the retributions for that treason had been so terrible, that the coward motive of fear, if not the angel impulse of humanity, might have deterred all men in after times from ever daring to repeat it.

The next great struggle was in 1833, when nullification first reared its hideous head. At that epoch, the south, and especially South Carolina, observing that our capital had been too deeply invested in manufactures to be withdrawn, changed their policy, and sought to reap a double harvest, — both of the manufacturing system they had introduced, and of the free trade system they had abandoned. She therefore set about to strangle that offspring of protection to which she had given birth. Even in Virginia, Mr. Madison's coat had become an unconstitutional coat, and the idea of American woollens so wrought upon Mr. John Randolph's gentle affections, that he said he would go a mile out of his way to kick a sheep. The South Carolina resistance was beginning to assume a military form. Then occurred a most admirable opportunity to test the strength of our government, — to learn and know whether the pillars of this Union are made of granite or of pipe-stems. We had a clear case of right. In the chair of state was a man of Roman will, who would have rejoiced in the opportunity to *see that the republic received no detriment.* He contemned the nonsense as much as he despised the fraud, of the cry that the Union was in danger. If it was in any danger, he would have saved it in such a way that it would not need saving again every twelvemonth. But the chance was lost. A compromise was brought forward, by which South Carolina consented to a sort of armed truce, on her part, provided the tariff, though not given up, should be tapered down almost to nothing. Though, on many accounts, I have a high respect for the author of that compromise, yet I regard it as the most unfortunate act ever done, — the most fatal precedent ever set by this government. It taught the south the efficacy of clamoring; it taught them that there are cases where a Bombastes Furioso is as powerful as a Julius Cæsar; and it taught them also, notwithstanding all appearances of solidity and firmness, of what a delicate nervous tissue a money-bag consists.

When that compromise law had had time to reach its legitimate issues, you all know the result. A whirlwind of bankruptcy swept over the land. Its ravages reached even the humblest portions of society. The laborer suffered even more than the capitalist. The latter suffered in his gains, but the former in his bread. All classes perceived the cause; and they rallied, almost as one man, to that tremendous effort to change the policy of the country, which resulted in the election to the presidency of General Harrison. Though, but a few days after his inauguration, the reins of government fell from his lifeless hands, yet the tariff of 1842 was the consequence of his election. This restored the drooping fortunes of New England. Then it was, while we were immersed in our business and our money making, that southern politicians addressed themselves to that great scheme of pro-slavery aggrandizement, — the annexation of Texas. You are all familiar with the details of this transaction, and it is painful to revert to them. The kid was seethed in its mother's milk. Northern Democrats cast the votes which gave Texas to the south, and destroyed our own prosperity. Texas was admitted just in season to repeal, by her votes in the Senate, the tariff of 1842, by that of 1846. This again put in jeopardy all our means embarked in manufactures. Would to Heaven that nothing more dear than pecuniary interests had been sacrificed by that measure.

I do not blame the south for seeking an equilibrium with the north; but they do not seek the true equilibrium. If they would sustain themselves in a competition with us in economical affairs, they must encourage labor and render it honorable. They must, all of them, labor as we do, in one way or another, with the hand or with the head; or, — which is the only true way, — with both together. They must build schoolhouses to develop the minds of their children, and churches to cultivate their morals. If they would only do this, and not attempt to carry every thing by slave-begotten votes, and by adding new states to beget more slave votes, they would soon surpass us; for nature has done vastly more for them, in soil and climate and in all the means of earthly prosperity, than for us. A superiority obtained in this way, we, as lovers of human happiness, should not repine at, but rejoice in.

The next struggle in which they engaged for political aggrandizement, was the Mexican war. It could, indeed, hardly be called a struggle, — the north so readily and ignominiously yielded. They wanted more territory. Texas, already gravid with future slave states, was not sufficient. And though it was yet somewhat uncertain whether Congress would not interdict the extension of slavery over that country, even should they conquer it; still, as they had always triumphed in their contests with us, they assumed the risk, and trusted to their future prowess and skill to monopolize the plunder. The territory was conquered; and then, perhaps, the most important question arose which has ever come before this country since the Declaration of Independence. The most momentous consequences were suspended on the decision of this question. We had, as it were, a creative power put into our hands. We had the shaping of the destinies of half a continent intrusted to our keeping. Our authority once exercised, the act would be irrevocable, and the doom of all that region would be fixed, as by a decree of Omnipotence. When God gives to the world a generation of children, and they are ruined through parental neglect, he gives another generation, that another trial may be made. But if we once admit slavery into those immense regions, comprising all the unsettled residue of this continent, God will give us no new continent on which the error may be retrieved.

Now, on this great question, what has been done? I grieve to say that I fear the battle has been lost. If not lost, nothing can save it but a vigor and an energy on the part of the north, such as they have not lately put forth. So far as legislation is concerned, the whole battle field is in possession of the enemy. Let me read a passage from one of the acts of the last session of Congress, which settles this fact. By the law for creating the territorial government of New Mexico, it is expressly provided, —

> "That when admitted as a state, the said territory, or any portion of the same, shall be received into the Union, WITH OR WITHOUT SLAVERY, as their constitution may prescribe at the time of their admission."

The act providing a territorial government for Utah contains a provision precisely similar. In regard to Texas, we have gratuitously given her a right to form one more slave state than she was authorized to do by the resolution of annexation. By the third article of the second section of that resolution, Texas was authorized to form new states, not exceeding *four*, of which those south of 36° 30′ should be admitted, with or without slavery, as their people should elect, while in the state or *states*, (and there must, therefore, be at least one,) which should be formed north of 36° 30′, there should be no slavery or involuntary servitude except for crime. But by the act of the last session, for establishing the boundary of Texas, though the United States buys up the claim of Texas to all the territory north of 36° 30′, yet it authorizes Texas to form as many slave states out of the residue of her territory, as she could have formed by the resolution of annexation, both of slave and free. This is manifest, by the following provision: —

"Provided, that nothing herein contained shall be construed to impair or qualify any thing contained in the third article of the second section of the joint resolution for annexing Texas to the United States, approved March 1, 1845, *either as regards the number of states that may hereafter be formed out of the State of Texas, or otherwise.*"

Here, then, instead of three states, four are provided for, with full consent that they shall all be slave states. Now, I ask, if this gift of a slave state is a trifle to be thrown in like the value of a small coin in the settlement of an account? In some of the pro-slavery papers of the north, which have professed to publish this act for the information of their readers, I have observed that this clause has been left out! They did not dare to trust their readers during the present political campaign with a knowledge of it.

I know it is said, by here and there an individual, that slavery cannot go into those territories. But it is to be remembered that all the south, almost as one man, dissent from this proposition. They say it can and shall; and is not their opinion, on such a subject, of greater weight than that of any northern man? They threaten to dissolve the Union if slavery be prohibited from going there. Are they such lunatics as to dissolve the Union, because we assume to prohibit what nature has already made impossible? Slave states border on those territories, and should there be any rush of emigration towards them, as, by the discovery of mines or other causes there may be, a cloud of slaves would immediately overspread them. If it be said that the local law of the territories prohibits slavery, I reply, so it did in Texas. Slavery had been abolished throughout Mexico, of which Texas was a province. But though slavery was no longer legal there, peonage was. Hence the southern planters, at least some of them, when about to remove to Texas, indented their own slaves to themselves, as peons, so that they might hold them by the Mexican law of peonage, until they should become strong enough to pass a law for slavery. It will be no more difficult to introduce slavery into New Mexico and Utah than it was into Texas.

I will not now go back to the questions which agitated the country and the Whig party at the time when General Taylor was nominated for the presidency. Whatever I may have thought of him, and of the propriety of nominating him, it is but justice to say that I now believe that he was a true man, and an anti-slavery man. He intended honestly to carry out the will of Congress, and execute the laws of his country, regardless of slaveholding dictation. He would have crushed the first movement for disunion; or rather, a knowledge of what he would do, would have prevented any such movement. With his own lips, in his own house, he told me that in case any state should attempt to nullify an act of Congress, he should immediately order a naval force to blockade its coast; he would allow nothing to pass into, or to come out of, the rebellious state; and in six months, said he, it would give up its resistance without the shedding of blood. It was President Taylor's plan, as you well know, to leave the adjustment of the slavery question to the territories themselves; not that he was not prepared to have it settled by Congress, and a prohibition imposed, but because he saw that while a prohibitory act might be passed by the House, it would certainly be rejected by the Senate. He therefore threw himself forward to what he knew the condition of things must be, after all the ineffectual attempts at legislation on the subject had been made; and he adopted that future condition and result of things as his present plan of action. Should the northern members of the House prove true to their constituencies and their pledges, they would never allow the territories to be organized without the proviso; and the fear of such a prohibition would exclude slavery from the territories, as certainly as the prohibition itself. Slaveholders would not venture to carry slaves into a country, where, at any moment an act of Congress might emancipate them. And if slavery could only be kept out of the territories while they remained territories, it would, of course, be prohibited by the state itself, when the condition of territorial pupilage should be succeeded by that of state independence. A boy trained up to virtuous resolves until the day he is twenty-one, will not adopt all the vices the day after.

The recent act has given Texas more than fifty thousand square miles of free New Mexican territory, and the promise of ten millions of dollars in fourteen years, with interest at five per cent. up to that time; which, at compound interest, makes a prospective grant of twenty millions of dollars. This is done on pretence of discharging debts which she owed at the time of her annexation. But those debts, at the highest estimate, do not exceed seven millions, so that a clear gratuity is left to her of at least three millions in addition to the grant of another slave state. The interest of these three millions will support her government, and keep her supplied with the means of fighting the battles of slavery.

There is something most extraordinary in the claim of Texas to the territory for which she has obtained so extravagant a price. Her title was not by conquest, nor by purchase, but by an act of her own legislature. She claimed the territory merely because she had extended her legislation over it, when she had no more right to legislate for it than for Canada. I have brought with me for your inspection, if any of you desire to see them, a series of maps which illustrate the growth of Texas. By Humboldt's map, of 1804, Texas contained 71,752 square miles. By Tanner's map, of 1826, it contained 108,097 square miles. By Austin's map, of 1839, it had grown to 179,567 square miles. The late claim of its legislature was the enormous quantity of 325,000 square miles, which the act of Congress cuts down only to 237,321! By its own legislative assumptions it grew from 70,000 to 325,000 square miles. By good husbandry, in this part of the country, we are able to make greater crops grow on the same land, but in Texas they make the land itself grow. I think Humboldt himself would have been astonished at any such geological theory of the uprising of the earth as would enlarge an area of 70,000 square miles, in an inland country, into more than 300,000, in less than fifty years.

But, fellow-citizens, slavery is already in the territories, whether prohibited by God and nature, or not! The line of 36° 30′ crosses the territory appropriated to the Indians, which is already full of slaves. Whenever the Indian title is extinguished, slavery will be found there in possession of the soil. Utah has slaves to-day, and I was informed by a gentleman chosen as a delegate from that territory to Congress, that the Mormon religion prescribes nothing on the subject.

I need not now dwell on another act of the last session,—the Fugitive Slave Law,—because, as yet, I believe no voice in Massachusetts has been raised in its defence or palliation. It is an act which might turn all of us here, at this moment, into slave hunters; which might break up this meeting at the present time, should an officer, clothed with the authority of the United States, appear at that door and command us to chase an alleged fugitive, perhaps a native-born freeman, over the graves of our Pilgrim fathers.

Standing here, then, before you, my constituents, to give account of my stewardship, I have to say, that with voice and vote, by expostulation and by remonstrance, by all means in my power, I have, to the full extent of my ability, resisted the passage of all these laws. Why have I done so? Because, in the first place, I felt myself a moral and accountable being; and, as such, I could not do otherwise. I have done so, in the second place, because I was your representative, and believed myself to be acting in conformity with your wishes, with the wishes of the Whig party of Massachusetts, and of my constituents generally. Have I been mistaken? [A volley of noes.]

To ascertain what were the wishes of the Whig party, and of those who put me in nomination, I shall refer you to a series of the resolutions of conventions, and of the declarations of the best accredited authorities of that party, on this subject, for years past. The following are among the resolutions of the Whig convention which assembled in this town, March, 1848, to nominate a successor to the Hon. John Quincy Adams. They were unanimously adopted: —

" *Resolved*, That the members of this convention, met together for the purpose of nominating a candidate to supply the vacancy existing in the eighth congressional district, mourn, in common with the state and the nation, the event which has deprived them of the services of that eminent son of Massachusetts, whose voice was ever raised in the cause of freedom, whose vast and varied powers, more than those of any other statesman of his time, were devoted to the service of his country, shedding light upon her institutions, and leading her on in the path of duty, prosperity, and glory.

" *Resolved*, That the loss of his services in the halls of Congress, at this time, is the more deeply to be deplored, when his great weight of character, his influence, his talents, his wisdom, his zeal, and indomitable energy would have been so benignly felt upon the great questions of freedom and slavery, which are to be discussed and settled for our newly-acquired domain, stretching from the Gulf of Mexico to the Pacific Ocean.

"*Resolved*, That it behooves us to unite upon a candidate to represent this district upon the floor of Congress, whose principles shall be in consonance with those of his predecessor, whose fidelity to the great principles of human freedom shall be unwavering, whose voice and vote shall on all occasions be exercised in extending and securing liberty to the human race."

In September, 1848, the Whig state convention of Massachusetts met at Worcester, when the following resolution, among others, reported by the Hon. Joseph Bell, of Boston, since then president of the Massachusetts Senate, was unanimously adopted: —

"*Resolved*, That being impressed with a profound sense of our responsibility, as the representatives of the Whigs of Massachusetts, that responsibility which attaches to our words, acts, and votes, — we cannot fail, on this occasion, as we have never failed on any other general assemblage of the Whigs of Massachusetts, to record, in the most solemn and deliberate manner, our unqualified opposition to any extension of the institution of slavery into our territory, or any acquisitions of territory, for the purpose of such extension. On this question, the voice of the Whigs of Massachusetts has been unwavering and uniform, and never has that voice spoken with higher eloquence and power than when our distinguished senator in Congress, speaking for himself, and for the whole people of the commonwealth, said, 'I consent to no further extension of the area of slavery in the United States, or to the further increase of slavery representation in the House of Representatives.'"

In September of the same year, another Whig convention assembled at this place, to nominate a candidate for the Thirty-first Congress. My views, as recorded by my votes on all the questions of slavery, and as expressed in my speech, delivered on the 30th of the preceding June, were then before the people. That convention, among other resolutions, passed the following, by acclamation: —

"*Resolved*, That we cordially approve of the course of the Hon. Horace Mann, and that his position in regard to *free* principles, *free* labor, and *free* speech, sustained with such signal ability, was but a satisfactory fulfilment of the expectations that we had when we nominated him to succeed the illustrious Adams. Regarding the past as the best and only honorable pledge of the future, this convention unanimously present his name to the people of this district for reëlection."

At the Whig state convention, held at Springfield, September 29th, 1847, Mr. Webster said he would consent to no extension of slavery. Are not the laws which I have just read a consent? — full consent? He claimed the Wilmot proviso as his "thunder," and said it had been stolen from him. Whether stolen from him, or not, I do not decide. He certainly seems to have lost possession of it; for we now find him thundering on the other side; — yes, from the high Olympus to which the votes of Massachusetts had elevated him, he has hurled his bolts against the dearest interests of his benefactors. But it is said we have registered these acts of pro-slavery legislation, at the dictation of the south, in order to save the Union. When Governor Davis was once asked to surrender the rights of humanity to save the Union, he retorted with the question, "How many times have we got to save the Union?" If we yield to every threat of disunion, we shall have to save the Union whenever any factious and unprincipled member of it shall threaten resistance to the laws. Look at the present threat which has been made by Texas. What resources has she wherewith to oppose the general government? She has no funds except a school fund of $34,000, which her governor, in one of his late messages, declared to be inviolably devoted to education. To be sure, since this cry of rebellion has been raised, he has said that this fund, which could be diverted for no useful purpose, might be appropriated to the treasonable one of resistance. But look at the amount of this fund, — $34,000. Military men tell me it would not support a single regiment of mounted rangers more than a month; and all the more settled parts of Texas are at least one month's marching distance from Santa Fe, which is the nearest point of attack. There was never any thing more ridiculous than the threats of Texas, that she will take armed possession of the eastern side of the Rio Grande, if it be not surrendered to her. She cannot even protect herself against the Indian tribes that roam through the regions lying between her and the people she threatens to subjugate. Will the disaffected states of the south help her by munitions, money, or men? The only states on which she could place any reliance are Mississippi and South Carolina. Could a military force be organized, and then marched nearly a thousand, or nearly fifteen hundred miles, across the country, to uphold the Texan banner on the borders of the Rio Grande? Were expeditions to be sent by sea, could not the mouth of the Mississippi, the harbor of Charleston, and that gateway of the Gulf of Mexico, which lies between the capes of Florida and the West India Islands; ay, the whole Texan coast itself, be blockaded and guarded, so as to make a hostile irruption into New Mexico impossible? Talk about Texan resistance to the government of these United States, my fellow-citizens; it is so ridiculous that nothing can be conceived which is not less ridiculous, and which would, therefore, by the very comparison, relieve the supposition of a portion of its nonsense. This surrendering to the threat of disunion, is like the foolish mother who gave her boy a sugar-plum to stop swearing. Presently he belched out a stream of profanity; and when the mother asked him why he did so, he said, "I want more sugar-plums." General

Taylor embraced the whole subject in a short sentence when he said he was more afraid of Texan bonds than of Texan bayonets. Their bonds have been ten thousand times more powerful than their bayonets in consummating this disastrous compromise.

But it is not only in conventions of the Whig party that sentiments have been expressed wholly incompatible with the great surrenders we have made. Such sentiments have emanated from more authoritative sources. They are the voice of our commonwealth, — the repeated voice, reiterated again and again, through a series of years. Let me select a few from among the many resolves of the Massachusetts legislature, covering the time, and preceding the time, that I have been in Congress. The following was passed in 1847: —

"*Resolved, unanimously*, That the legislature of Massachusetts views the existence of human slavery within the limits of the United States as a great calamity, an immense moral and political evil, which ought to be abolished, as soon as that end can be properly and constitutionally attained, and that its extension should be uniformly opposed by all good and patriotic men throughout the Union."

Again, in 1849, the legislature of Massachusetts

"*Resolved*, That when Congress furnishes governments for the territories of California and New Mexico, it will be its duty to establish therein the fundamental principles of the ordinance of seventeen hundred and eighty-seven, upon the subject of slavery, to the end that the institution may be perpetually excluded therefrom beyond every chance and uncertainty."

And again, during this present year, and not six months ago, the same general court passed the following resolve. I might read from the printed volume of the "Acts and Resolves of 1850;" but I choose to read from *this official circular* which I hold in my hand, which is attested by the secretary of state, and was sent to me at Washington, as to all the other members of Congress from Massachusetts, so that we might be informed of the views of the state government, as well as of our respective constituencies, on this important subject: —

"*Resolved*, That the people of Massachusetts earnestly insist upon the application by Congress of the ordinance of 1787, with all possible sanctions and solemnities of law, to the territorial possessions of the Union in all parts of the continent, and for all coming time.

"*Resolved*, That the people of Massachusetts, in the maintenance of these their well known and *invincible* principles, expect that all their officers and representatives will adhere to them at all times, on all occasions, and under all circumstances."

And yet, in six months, we are called upon to support these laws. Is this "all coming time"? Are these "invincible principles" of the Massachusetts Whig legislature to melt, like wax, when touched by the breath of party? They notified me, under their seal and sign-manual, that they expected "all their officers and representatives to adhere to them, at all times, on all occasions, and under all circumstances." And yet, before six months have elapsed, some of the very men who voted to give me such instructions, or injunctions, or whatever you please to call them, having discarded their own solemn asseverations of principle, now upbraid me because I, too, will not be recreant to them. Is this what you are to expect from men whom you have elected by your votes, and to whom the momentous interests of millions, and the honor of the country, have been confided, that their vows should be like those of perfidious lovers, who swear "eternal fidelity" — during the honey moon? We cannot plead the excuse, in regard to these resolves, which a certain hearer of Whitfield did, for appearing unmoved at one of his pathetic discourses, while all others were melted to tears. When asked why he, too, did not weep, he replied that "he did not belong to that parish." We do belong to this parish. These are the "acts and resolves" of our own state, fresh and unsullied from the mint. We cannot deny their genuineness. If we impute fraud any where, it must be to the motives of those who passed them. Hear, too, what Governor Briggs says on this same subject, in his last inaugural address: —

"Entertaining no doubt of the constitutional power of Congress to exclude slavery from its own territories, and believing that such exclusion is demanded by the highest principles of morality and justice, she never can consent to its extension over one foot of territory where it now is not. If the other free states concur with her in this resolution, the thing will be done, and consequences left to themselves."

Thus have the Whig party in this state, and its executive, pledged themselves not to extend slavery "one foot." How many feet in the six hundred thousand square miles, into which the legislation of the last Congress permits slavery to enter? — which legislation the Whig party is now called upon to indorse, — that is, how many myriad pledges do they require us to break?

Let me now quote from another high Whig authority, — General James Wilson, of New Hamphire. For many years, probably no man has been considered a more authoritative expounder of Whig sentiment. He has been employed by the party, or the organs of the party, to traverse the country for the advocacy of Whig principles, and has been every where listened to with great acceptance. In Congress, he spoke as follows: —

"I hold that Congress is bound to take care of the territories, and so execute the trust as will best promote the interests of those who may hereafter be entitled to the beneficial use.

As a member of this Congress, I feel that I sustain a part of that responsibility, and it is my desire to acquit myself worthily in meeting it. I desire so to acquit myself that my own conscience will not upbraid me, and that when I shall pass away, no reproach shall fall upon me, or my children after me, for my acts here upon this momentous question. I have, sir, an only son, now a little fellow, whom some of this committee may have seen here. Think you that when I am gone, and he shall grow up to manhood, and shall come forward to act his part among the citizens of the country, I will leave it to be cast in his teeth, as a reproach, that his father voted to send slavery into those territories? No! O, no! I look reverently up to the Father of us all, and fervently implore him to spare that child that reproach. May God forbid it!

"I have said that it is characteristic of the slave power to accomplish all of its political purposes in this government. I must now say that the power and influence of slavery over the action of Congress is impaired, if not entirely gone. [What an infinite mistake!] I make this declaration, not because I have any confidence in the politicians of the day. No, sir, I have none whatever. The politicians are just as ready now to betray their constituents as they ever have been. I am sorry to say there is evidence enough of this. My confidence is in the people. They have taken the matter into their own hands; they have brought themselves into order of battle and line, without the word of command from any political leader. Here they stand, with front rank, and rear rank, and rank of file-closers in position, with bayonets at a charge. They have spoken to their representatives in a voice of thunder, and warned them against abandoning their interests. They have bid them do it at their peril. The constituents have challenged their representatives to betray their trusts, and skulk and retreat upon them, *if they dared.*

"And, sir, the constituencies have spoken 'upon honor.' They are determined, and will execute their purposes. There was a time, when, if the slave power had any special work to be done, and wanted a northern man to do it, they hunted him up from New Hampshire. Little, unfortunate New

Hampshire was called upon to furnish the scavenger to do the dirty work. That day, thank God, has gone by, and it will not come again very soon. [Wait a short year, Mr. Wilson, and see who the Hazael will be.]

"The north are not disposed to trespass or interfere with the rights of the south. Where slavery exists within the states, the northern people claim no right to interfere with it by any political action of this government. The people ask no action by Congress on the subject of slavery within the states. But gentleman need not ask me for my vote to extend the institution of slavery one single inch beyond its present boundaries. Did I say an inch, Mr. Chairman? Ay, I would not extend it one sixteen-thousandth part of a hair's breadth. I would not extend it, because it would be doing an irretrievable wrong to my fellow-man; because it would be doing irreparable wrong to those territories for which we are now to legislate; because it would be doing violence to nature and to nature's God; and because it would be a wicked and wanton betrayal of the trust confided to me by the free, intelligent constituency which has done me the honor to send me here.

"It shall not be in the power of any man to shake a menacing finger at me, and look me in the face with a jibe of contempt, and say to me, in the insulting language of a former representative from Virginia, [Mr. Randolph,] 'we have conquered you, and we will conquer you again; we have not conquered you by the black slaves of the south, but by the white slaves of the north.' No, sir, that remark shall never apply to me. Gentlemen need not talk to me, or attempt to frighten me, by threats of dissolution of the Union. Sir, I do not permit myself to talk, or even think of the dissolution of the Union; very few northern men do. We all look upon such a thing as impossible. But, sir, sir, if the alternative should be presented to me of the extension of slavery, or the dissolution of the Union, I would say, rather than extend slavery, let the Union, ay, the Universe itself be dissolved! Never, never will I raise my hand or my voice to give a vote by which it can or may be extended. As God is my judge, I cannot, I will not be moved from the purpose I have now announced."

And yet this same General Wilson did vote for every one of these laws, excepting, perhaps, the last, which passed in the night, — fit darkness for so dark a deed, — and the next morning he was off for California. How can such a man stop this side of Botany Bay? .Now, fellow-citizens, did you want me to disgrace myself, and you, and human nature, too, by such an act of flagrant apostasy? [A crash of noes.] Yet if these measures are adopted and sustained by the Whig party, and if those men who committed these nefarious deeds are justified and upheld by you, then how are you less guilty than General Wilson? *

Let me quote a passage or two from a speech delivered by one of my colleagues in Congress, the Hon. George Ashmun, who has, I believe, usually been considered pretty good Whig authority. In a speech made by him on the 27th of last March, referring to the subjects of slavery in the territories and the recaption of alleged fugitive slaves, he said, —

"But I am bound to say, however, if the south persist in uniting to demand the entrance of slavery into our free territories, I, for one, must conform to what are, at the same time, the views of my constituents and the convictions of my own judgment; and if I am driven to the alternative, I shall not hesitate to vote for the proviso." — *App. to Cong. Globe*, 1*st Sess.* 31*st Congress*, p. 401.

"While I desire to do every thing which may protect the rights of property which are guarantied to citizens of the slave states, I cannot consent to sacrifice the rights of liberty which belong to the citizens of the free states. To secure both these ends, I see no other mode than to have those rights settled before legal tribunals, *by the verdicts of juries and the judgments of courts*. . . . . . When a colored man is seized in Massachusetts upon a claim that he is the property of a citizen of a slave state, and he claims to be a citizen of Massachusetts, and invokes the protection

* Mr. Wilson has since been rewarded by the administration with a lucrative office in California.

of the laws of Massachusetts, is it to be said he may be summarily sent away by the decree of any one magistrate without the privilege of vindicating his title to his citizenship before a jury of the country? Why, sir, it could not be done in the case of a horse escaped from one state to another, and found in the possession of a citizen. It could not be taken by strong hand, — by force. The claimant must resort to process of law. He must sue out his writ of replevin, and the title of the defendant must be tried where he lives. That defendant may be a negro; and surely, if without a trial by jury you may not take that which he claims to be his property, you can hardly claim to seize the man himself, and carry him away, before his title to freedom has been tested by a tribunal, as respectable, at least, and as safe, as that which settles a title to his horse." — *Ib.* p. 399.

And another of my colleagues, [Mr. DUNCAN,] even as late as the 7th of June last, emphatically declared, in the House of Representatives, as follows: —

"If territorial bills are presented for the government of New Mexico and Utah, I shall vote for the exclusion of slavery from those territories."

Let me fortify these citations by another from one of the acknowledged leaders of the Whig party, — the Hon. Rufus Choate: —

"On all the great questions of the day, but just slavery; on executive power, on internal improvement, on the protection of labor, on peace, and the constitution, we mean to remain the same party of Whigs, one and indivisible, from Maine to Louisiana, — one vast incorporation of consentaneous feeling throughout the land; and upon this question alone we always differ from the Whigs of the south; and on that one we propose simply to vote them down." *

I will quote a passage also from a recent letter of the Hon. Zeno Scudder, late a Whig president of the Massachusetts Senate, and now a candidate of the Whig party for Congress, in District No. 10: —

* See, also, *ante*, p. 256.

"I was at the Springfield convention when Mr. Webster said, 'Not another inch of slave territory; *no, not one inch!*' By the aid of his remarks on that occasion, I was confirmed in the views which I had before entertained, and have as yet seen no reason to change them.

"In 1847, I had the honor and pleasure of recording my 'yea' in favor of the resolves 'concerning the existence and extension of slavery within the jurisdiction of the United States,' and 'concerning the Mexican war and the institution of slavery,' which passed the legislature of last year; and had I been a member of that body at its last session, I should have given my support to the resolve 'concerning slavery,' which was then passed.

"When I recorded my 'yea,' and advocated the resolves of 1847, I did not suppose them to be *idle words*, written out to be bandied about and declaimed upon in Massachusetts, and be *laid snugly away*, if ever I should depart the jurisdiction. I supposed them to involve great principles of human freedom, which were to be applied throughout the length and breadth of our country, whenever and wherever the time and place might present legitimate opportunities therefor."

At the Whig state convention held at Springfield in 1847, a resolution was submitted by Dr. Palfrey, "that the Whigs of Massachusetts will support no men for the offices of president and vice-president, but such as are known by their acts, or declared opinions, to be opposed to the extension of slavery;" and Mr. William Dwight, then of Springfield, is reported to have said, "You cannot vote for a candidate not known to be opposed to slavery extension; *it would be guilt.*"

But, fellow-citizens, I might go on citing authorities of this kind until sunset; — nay, until sunlight should come round again, and still leave the greater part of my resources untouched. I will refer you but to one more, — a resolution passed at the late Whig state convention, only a few days ago, which was as follows: —

"*Resolved*, That Massachusetts avows her unalterable determination to maintain all the principles and purposes she has in times past affirmed, and reäffirmed, in relation to the extension of slavery; and the measure of success which has attended her exertions is a new incentive to continue and persevere in all constitutional efforts, till the great and good work shall be accomplished and perfected."

And now, gentlemen, let me ask you whether my action has been in accordance with these sentiments, as expressed by the highest acts of the party and the most solemn resolutions of the state? [An acclamation of yeas.]

Here, fellow-citizens, I come to the test question: Did we, as true Whigs, and as honorable men, make all these declarations in sincerity, meaning to stand by them to the end; or was it done, from time to time, to beguile a portion of our fellow-citizens of their votes, on the vile doctrine that "all is fair in politics"? Were we frank and in earnest, or were we hollow and fraudulent?

I know very well what influences have been brought to bear upon us. I know we are a people intent on thriving, and on worldly prosperity. Every young man amongst us sets out in life determined to better his condition. This, to me, is no cause of regret, but of rejoicing. If the spirit of thrift does not transgress the limits of honor and duty, it is not only right but laudable. The animal wants of man must be supplied before he will develop his intellectual or moral powers. You may find individuals who will be virtuous amid want and privation, — heroes in virtue; — but a virtuous community in rags and hunger, you will never find. We must put society in a condition of physical comfort, before it will rise to mental excellence. I am an ardent advocate, therefore, of all measures tending to increase the wealth of the country; but on this ever-present and everlasting condition, that it is done without a sacrifice of principles. Any enlargement of business, any increase of profits, any augmentation of wealth, gained by a community through a dereliction from principle, is as insecure and as ignominious as the gains of an individual through fraud, embezzlement, or peculation.

For the purpose of rewarding our native labor, therefore, I am for a protective tariff. Perhaps some persons may be here present who dissent from this opinion; but I came here to avow, and not to conceal my sentiments and acts. It has always seemed to me that we must protect our labor against foreign labor, or our laborers at home will fall to the condition of the pauper laborers abroad. In Manchester in England, and Glasgow in Scotland, and many other manufacturing towns in Great Britain, there are thousands of wretched, degraded female operatives, who earn scarcely a shilling a day. After their day's work is done, they visit the dram-shops, roam the streets till midnight, and if not invited away by vicious men, they huddle by scores into filthy lodging-houses, where they sleep, men and women promiscuously, till morning summons them back to their tasks. Now where labor is so scantily paid, fabrics can be produced more cheaply; and if these fabrics can be sent into this country, free of duty, they will undersell ours, until the prices of our labor and the condition of our laborers are reduced to theirs. Nothing is left to protect our industry but the cheaper freight of the materials, and that is too trifling a compensation to be of any account. This is the whole philosophy of the matter, and to me it has always seemed unassailable.

It has been thought and said that if we would yield to the south on the slavery question, they would yield to us on the tariff question. We have surrendered the slavery question. Have we got the tariff? Have we got any thing but disgrace in the eyes of the civilized world? To me, it seems that our chance for a tariff is greatly diminished. For the majority which is necessary to enable us to pass a tariff law, we must depend on our opponents. By our yielding to the south, their party discipline has been immensely strengthened, and it is now more difficult than ever to obtain their votes for any measure conducive to northern interests. Besides, they now say they will retain the tariff question as an open one, in order to keep us on our good behavior. What have those now to say for themselves, who beguiled a portion of our people into the delusion, that they might safely barter human rights for pecuniary advantages, and have left to their dupes both the loss of the advantages, and the disgrace of abandoning their principles!

But an appeal is made to us to ratify this surrender to the slave power, because of our love for the Union. And is our love for the Union always to be converted, or rather perverted, into a pro-slavery motive of action? I join you all most cordially, I join any one, in avowing my regard for the Union, and my resolution to stand by it. But the Union ought to be so used as to extend, and not to abridge human welfare. If, in order to maintain the Union, we must sacrifice all the great objects for which the Union was formed, — the establishment of justice, the promotion of the general welfare, and the securing of the blessings of liberty to ourselves and our posterity, — then the Union no longer represents a beneficent divinity but a foul Dagon, and is worthy to be broken in pieces. A Union which must be secured by such sacrifices as have been lately made in New York, in behalf of the so called "Union Meeting," abolishes the benefits it was designed to secure. Eight thousand signatures were obtained for calling that meeting; but to procure them, whole streets were scoured, and men were threatened with the publication of their names, and the consequent loss of southern custom, if they refused to join in the call. Many were obliged to pay *hush money* to prevent exposure. The New York idea is slavery and free trade. Here, it is slavery and tariff. Both cities cannot get the price of their surrender of principle.

No, fellow-citizens, the more we yield to the demands of the south in order to save the Union, the more we may and must. Their longing eyes are already fixed on Cuba. There is more probability and more danger to-day that Cuba will be annexed to this government within five years, than there was of Texan annexation five years before that event took place. I lately said to a Louisianian, "You will soon be for making a slave state of Cuba." "No," said he, "we mean to make two of that."

Gentlemen, I have already occupied your attention too long. But I am constrained to make a few brief remarks on a subject I would gladly avoid. The occasion of your present meeting is known to all. Two years ago, I was nominated by the Whigs of this district as their candidate for the seat in Congress which I now hold. By the favor of my fellow-citizens of all parties, I received more than eleven thousand out of about thirteen thousand votes cast at that election. I felt assured at that time, that I agreed in all essential articles of political faith with those who gave me their support, otherwise I should not have accepted the office at their hands. I have endeavored faithfully, and according to the best of my ability, to carry out the wishes which they then expressed, and which they well knew that I held. Yet, during the last week, a Whig convention, (so called,) assembled in this place to nominate a candidate for the thirty-second Congress; and, after some close voting, they nominated as my successor, the Hon. Samuel H. Walley,—a gentleman, I am happy to say, towards whom I have always sustained relations of personal kindness. In the language of the day, that convention threw me overboard. Now it is known to my whole circle of private friends, that, as soon as Congress passed these pro-slavery measures to which I have adverted, my determination was formed not to be a candidate for reëlection. I resolved to return to the people, and labor at home instead of at Washington, in the cause of human freedom. But it was soon given out, in certain influential quarters, that I should not be returned to Congress again, and that I should be stigmatized by a rejection. Unsurpassed efforts, as you all know, have been made to carry out this threat; even the Secretary of State of the United States has made it the occasion for a practical contradiction of all he had ever said against bringing the influence of the government to bear upon the freedom of elections; and the proceedings of the last week's convention were the first instalment of the penalty which I am to suffer for defending human rights and unmasking their betrayers. It is said that the convention of last week was a packed convention; that it did not represent the wishes of the people. Decorum forbids *me* to make any such charge, even though it were probably true. In a few days, this point will be settled by the sovereign of us all, at the ballot-box.*

But two or three points, to which I wish to call your attention, are contained in the address put forth by the meeting I have referred to. Let me premise, however, that I take no exception to the fact that my acts and opinions should be made the subject of examination and criticism by any body of men, or by any man. It is better that animadversion should be wrong than that it should not be free. Like Aristides, I would write the vote that should banish me, rather than to fetter or control the voter's will. And now, having laid down these principles in favor of free speech for others, I proceed to exemplify them for myself.

* The people settled the question by electing Mr. Mann by a majority over all other candidates. — *Publishers.*

The first charge preferred against me, in the address, is, that I said, in a letter dated on the 3d of May last, and addressed to a portion of my constituents,* that I "sympathized on different points with different parties, but was exclusively bound to none." Upon this, the address remarks, "If we understand his meaning, it is . . . . . that he cannot be our champion and defend our cause, as our true representative should, whenever and wherever called upon." No, I reply to this, I will not promise beforehand to be any man's "champion," nor to defend any man's "cause," "*whenever and wherever called upon.*" This would be to proffer championship and allegiance to men and measures whether they were right or wrong. If any man offers to vote for me on such conditions, I deny him my assistance and disdain his support. Perhaps I do not know what I was made for; but one thing I certainly never was made for, and that is, to put principles on and off, at the dictation of a party, as a lackey changes his livery at his master's command.

Another remark in the address is, that the compromise measures, so called, excepting the fugitive slave law, were "wise, and that they gave to the free states all they could reasonably ask." What a stultification, my friends, is this, of ourselves, of our party, and of every department of our state government, for the last ten years. What have you been doing, but resolving, contending, and placing your words and deeds upon the historical records of the state and the nation, against the identical measures now declared to be "wise," and all for which the free states "could reasonably ask"? I leave this point with a single remark. The address excepts the fugitive slave law from the measures it commends. Before another year is past, will not that most execrable act in modern legislation be palliated or adopted by those who voted for this address?

* See *ante*, p. 237.

A third objection to my position is, that I regard the question of the extension of slavery into our territories as paramount to those questions of a pecuniary character, on which we desire to obtain the favorable action of the government. Let this objection against me have its full force. I admit it, in all its length and breadth. I do regard the question of human freedom for our wide-extended territories, with all the public and private consequences dependent upon it, both now and in all futurity, as first, foremost, chiefest among all the questions that have been before the government, or are likely to be before it. When temporary and commercial interests are put in competition with the enduring and unspeakably precious interests of freedom for a whole race, of liberty for a whole country, and of obedience to the will of the Creator, my answer is, "Seek ye first the kingdom of God and his righteousness, and all these things shall be added unto you."

In an address delivered by Mr. Choate, in 1848, he declared the slavery question to be of "transcendent importance;" and for this sentiment he was universally applauded. Wherein does "*paramount* importance" so differ from "*transcendent* importance," that the one is to be applauded while the other is condemned?

Let me call your attention to one other remark in the address, and I will leave it. It suggests that my course in Congress on the slavery questions has been unacceptable to the south, and that we ought to send a representative who will conciliate them and obtain their good will. Fellow-citizens, do you suppose that any man can be true to the memory of the Pilgrim fathers, and to the love of liberty they bequeathed us, and at the same time true to the spirit of the Cavaliers, and to the wishes of their slave-owning posterity? Eighteen hundred years ago, it was said that no man can serve two masters; but the cupidity of modern times proposes the solution of a problem which Christ declared to be impossible. My opinion is, that the cause of all our present calamity, and of the enduring dishonor of the late measures, is this very desire to conciliate southern favor, instead of giving a manful defence to northern rights.

Finally, fellow-citizens, it is our fortune to live during a great historic crisis in the affairs of the world. This is the age of the useful arts; of discoveries and inventions, which are filling with wealth the garners and the coffers of men. It is the age of commerce, of profit, of finance. One part of our nature is intensely stimulated. Let us beware of the effect of this stimulus upon that nobler portion of our being, which no splendor of opulence nor profusion of luxuries can ever satisfy; which demands allegiance to God, and justice and humanity towards our fellow-men; and which must have them, or die the second death. We may be poor; but let us deprecate and forefend the most calamitous of all poverties, — a poverty of spirit. We may be subjected to great sacrifices; but let us sacrifice every thing else, nay, life itself, before we sacrifice our principles. I commend to you the language of the good Bishop Watson, who, when tempted to stifle the expression of his convictions through the hope of kingly patronage, replied, that it was "Better to seek a fortuitous sustenance from the drippings of the most barren rock in Switzerland, with freedom for his friend, than to batten as a slave at the most luxurious table of the greatest despot in the world."

SPEECH

Delivered in the House of Representatives of the United States, in Committee of the Whole on the State of the Union, February 28, 1851, on the Fugitive Slave Law.

Mr. Chairman;

Some time ago, I prepared a few comments upon those prominent measures of the last session, which have since arrested the attention of all the lovers of constitutional liberty, and of moral and religious men, throughout the civilized world. I am unwilling to suffer the present session to close without expressing the reflections I have formed; because I deem it but a reasonable desire that my opinions should be placed upon the records of the very Congress to whose measures they refer.

Does any one ask what benefit I anticipate from a discussion of this subject at the present moment? I answer, this benefit at least: that of entering a solemn protest against a grievous wrong, and of placing upon the tablets of my country's history, what I believe to be the views of a vast majority of my constituents, in common with the vast majority of the people of Massachusetts.

Some of those compromise measures are destined to be of great historic importance. They will be drawn into precedent. When, in evil days, further encroachments are meditated against human rights, these old measures will be cited as a sanction for new aggressions; and, in my view, they will always be found broad enough, and bad enough, to cover almost any nameable assault upon human liberty. When bad men want authority for bad deeds, they will only have to go back to the legislation of Congress, in 1850, to find an armory full of the weapons of injustice.

Sir, legislative precedents are formidable things. If created without opposition, and especially if acquiesced in without complaint, they become still more formidable. Now, if there were no other reasons for reviving this subject at the present session of Congress, this alone would be an ample justification, — it forefends the argument from acquiescence.

When several of these measures were passed, and particularly when one of the most obnoxious and criminal of them all was passed, — I mean the Fugitive Slave bill, — this House was not a deliberative body. Deliberation was silenced. Those who knew they could not meet our arguments, choked their utterance. The previous question, which was originally devised to curb the abuse of too much debate, was perverted to stop all debate. The floor was assigned to a known friend of the bill, who after a brief speech in palliation of its enormities, moved the previous question; and thus we were silenced by force, instead of being overcome by argument. For, sir, I aver, without fear of contradiction, that the bill never could have become a law, had its opponents been allowed to debate it, or to propose amendments to it. For the honor of the country, therefore, at the present time, and for the cause of truth hereafter, it is important that the hideous features of that bill, which were then masked, should be now unmasked. The arguments which I then desired and designed to offer against it, I mean to offer now. Those arguments have lost nothing of their weight by this enforced delay, and I have lost nothing of my right to present them.

Mr. Chairman, I feel none the less inclined to discuss this question, because an order has gone forth that it shall not be discussed. Discussion has been denounced as agitation, and then it has been dictatorially proclaimed that "agitation must be put down." Sir, humble as I am, I submit to no such dictation, come from what quarter or from what numbers it may. If such a prohibition is intended to be laid upon me personally, I repel it. If intended to silence me as the representative of the convictions and feelings of my constituents, I repel it all the more vehemently. In this government, it is not tolerable for any man, however high, or for any body of men, however large, to prescribe what subjects may be agitated, and what may not be agitated. Such prescription is at best but a species of lynch law against free speech. It is as hateful as any other form of that execrable code; and I do but express the common sentiment of all generous minds, when I say that for one, I am all the more disposed to use my privilege of speech, when imperious men, and the sycophants of imperious men, attempt to ban or constrain me. In Italy, the pope decides what books may be read; in Austria, the emperor decides what books may be written; but we are more degraded than the subject of pontiff or Cæsar, if we are to be told what topics we may discuss. If the subjects of a despotic government are bound to be jealous even of the poor privileges which they possess, how sensitive, how "tremblingly alive all o'er" ought we to be at these threatened encroachments upon freedom of speech and freedom of thought. I think that those who say so much about recalling us to a sense of our constitutional obligations, would do well to remember, that the very first article of the amendments to the constitution secures the freedom of speech and the freedom of the press. By the common consent of this country, manifested in all forms for more than half a century, the old alien and sedition law has been condemned. Has that law been condemned for fifty years in order to make our shame more conspicuous by its revival under circumstances of intolerable aggravation? Sir, I hold treason against this government to be an enormous crime; but great as it is, I hold treason against free speech and free thought to be a crime incomparably greater.

If it be just and heroic to rebel against all arbitrary invasions of free thought and free expression, then is it not proportionably base and dastardly to utter menaces, or threaten social or political disabilities for the unconstrained exercise of these birthrights of freemen? On the face of it, it must be a bad cause which will not bear discussion. Truth seeks light instead of shunning it. He convicts himself of wrong who refuses to hear the arguments of his opponent. It was well said by Montesquieu, that "the enjoyment of liberty, and even its support and preservation, consists in every man's being allowed *to speak his thoughts and lay open his sentiments.*" Wherefore, then, in a country hitherto reputed to be free, are we told that discussion must be stopped, and agitation must be put down? It seems as if, when a freeman debases his soul by lending himself to the defence of slavery, God punishes him on the spot by demoralizing his own nature with that spirit of tyranny which belongs to slavery. Wherein consists the advantage of a republican government over a despotism, if the freedom of speech and of the press, which can be strangled in the one by arbitrary command, can be stifled in the other by obloquy and denunciation?

It is remarkable, too, that of all the "agitators" in the country, there are none more violent than those who are agitating against agitation. Throughout the north, that portion of the public press which volunteers its influence to extend the domain of slavery, and to maintain it by extra-*constitutional laws, is constantly* provoking the agitation it denounces. What are these so-called Union meetings in northern cities but an extensive apparatus of agitation, — a piece of machinery to manufacture and send abroad the very articles which its managers declare to be contraband? Through public assemblies, through the public press, and by correspondence designed for the public eye, they are shaking the common air to keep it calm; they are agonizing and in convulsions for repose; they are vociferating to maintain silence. In the most clamorous days of anti-slavery, there never was half so much said and written against the institution as is now said and written for it. Sir, is the right of agitation to be monopolized by those who denounce it? Is free speech to be only on one side; and is it one of the offices of free speech to silence the sentiments it dislikes? I think this is the second time in the history of this country, that an attempt has been boldly and unblushingly made to stifle free discussion; and I do not believe the fate of those who are now laboring to accomplish so nefarious a purpose will be historically more enviable than that of their prototypes, who passed the far-famed law against seditious speeches and writings.

Is it not extraordinary, too, that this interdict on discussion should be applied to a subject which touches the highest interests of man, and calls into fervid action all the noblest faculties of his nature; which, more than any thing else, tests the question whether a man *is* man? We may discuss the question of bank or sub-treasury, of tariff or free trade; but the only subject too sacred to be approached, is slavery and its aggrandizements. This is a free country, except when a man wishes to vindicate the claims of freedom. All other parts of the temple may be entered, but slavery is the ark of the covenant, and whoso lays his profane hands thereon must perish.

Sir, how comes it to pass that an institution which

even the enlightened heathen of old pronounced to be iniquitous, and which eighteen added centuries of Christian illumination have proved to be the sum of offences against God and man, should now be protected, not merely by constitutions and laws; but that a general warfare should be waged against all those who would restrain it within its present limits, and keep it from arming itself with new weapons of oppression? How comes it to pass that this should be done, not in the despotisms of Austria and of Russia, but in republican America? Sir, it is not to be done, and cannot be done. Almighty God has so constituted the human soul, that while wrong exists upon the face of the earth, all the noblest impulses of that soul will war against it. The order of nature will war against it. "The stars in their courses" will war against it. Discussion, or agitation, if you so please to call it, is one of the Heaven-appointed means by which truth is to be spread until it covers the face of the earth, as the waters cover the sea. It was by discussion and by agitation, in synagogue and in temple, in distant cities and in different empires, that Christianity was carried from its cradle in Jerusalem to the ends of the earth. Did not the disciples of Jesus Christ go "agitating" from city to city, from Palestine to Greece, and from Greece to Rome, notwithstanding they were imprisoned and scourged, flayed alive, and burnt, and persecuted as incendiaries and fanatics, by scribe, and Pharisee, and high priest? The very accusation brought against the Savior was, "He stirreth up the people, teaching throughout all Jewry, beginning from Galilee to this place." The subject on which anti-slavery men now "agitate" is inferior only in importance to that on which Christ and his disciples "agitated." Nay, the only cause why Christianity has not prospered as it ought during the last eighteen centuries, and why it has not already overspread the whole earth with its blessings, is, that LIBERTY has not been given it as a sphere to work in. It is because SLAVERY has existed among men; and Christianity never will and never can pervade the earth until the barriers of slavery are first overthrown. It was by discussion and agitation that the prevailing religion of this country, — the Protestant religion, — broke through the double phalanx of civil and sacerdotal power, and triumphed throughout the leading nations of Europe, under the indomitable energy of that old hero of Wittemburg, who did not heed nor fear that prince of the slave power, the incarnate devil himself. It was by discussion and agitation that the first glowing sparks of liberty in the bosom of the Adamses, of Hancock, and of Franklin, of Thomas Jefferson and of Patrick Henry, were fanned into a flame that consumed the hosts of the tyrant, — that tyrant who sought to put down this dreadful agitation by means not a whit more reprehensible in his day, than those by which certain leading men are striving to silence it now. Where was there ever written or published a more incendiary and fanatical document than the Declaration of Independence? — a torch to set the world on fire. In the present century, what but discussion and agitation, through all the realms of Great Britain and in this country, could have sufficed to extinguish the slave trade, — that foulest blot upon modern civilization? No, sir; agitation is a part of the sublime order of nature. In thunder, it shakes the stagnant air, which would otherwise breed pestilence. In tempests, it purifies the deep, which would otherwise exhale miasma and death. And in the immortal thoughts of duty, of humanity, and of liberty, it so rouses the hearts of men that they think themselves inspired of God; and not the mercenary clamor of the market-place, nor the outcries of politicians, clutching at the prizes of ambition, can suppress the utterances which true men believe themselves Heaven-commissioned to declare.

The President's message tells us that the compromise measures of the last session are "FINAL." I take the liberty to say of that declaration in the message, with all due respect to the high source from which it comes, that I adopt the sentiment, that those measures are *final*, in one sense only. Their substance and object were, in an extreme degree, pro-slavery and anti-liberty. They marked the passage of this government through another long stage in the gloomy highway of oppression. They furnished another argument for those who despair of human nature; and they supply the misanthrope with a plausible reason for hating mankind. They affixed another stain upon the country, and set in deeper shade the contrast between the theory of our government and its practice. They belied still another time the gospel of love and human brotherhood. Once again they defied the vengeance of God, who is no respecter of persons, and who will bring the sinner to judgment. If such measures are to be "*final*," in this sense only do I accept the proposition, — that they are to be the last of their kind; that here, at this point, the career of this iniquity is to be stayed; that here, the confederated powers of ambition and of wealth, — of those who aspire to office and those who lust for gold, have won their last victory. In this sense only do I accept the President's declaration, that the action of the last Congress on this subject is to be deemed *final*; — that, in all future conflicts, the right shall not be trampled under foot, but the victims of oppression shall triumph. Base as human nature often proves itself to be, it sometimes manifests a divine resilience by which it springs with recuperative energy from its guilty fall.

I draw no augury of despair from the calamity that has befallen us. It teaches whatever there is of virtue and of principle in mankind, the task which has been set them to do, and whose accomplishment God will require at their hands.

It has been said by the Secretary of State, in a late speech, that if this subject be reöpened in Congress, the friends of freedom will be found in a "lean and miserable minority." What cares my conscience, sir, whether I am in a minority or a majority, *if I am right?* Has any great and glorious cause ever been started upon earth, that did not find itself, at the outset, in a minority? Did Clarkson and Wilberforce open their twenty years' contest with a majority? or were not all the office-seekers and mammon-worshippers opposed to them? Did the resistance of the revolutionary patriots to the government of Great Britain start with a majority on its side? Did the Pilgrim fathers resist conformity to ecclesiastical oppression because they were a majority of the people? Did the glorious band of reformers count on majorities, when they defied the racks and the flames of Rome? What would now be our condition if the prophets and heroes of olden days, if the warriors for truth and the martyrs of liberty, all over the earth, had yielded to so base an argument as this, and had followed the multitude to do evil, instead of battling for the truth, though it were solitary and alone? I can conceive of but one effect which such a sentiment must produce upon all noble and truth-loving men. It is to make them labor for the right with a zeal commensurate with the infinite baseness of the appeal by which they are urged to abandon it.

But I come now, Mr. Chairman, to the main topic of my remarks, which is a consideration of the character of the Fugitive Slave law, passed on the 18th day of September last.

The objections most generally urged against this law are of two kinds:

1st. That it is unconstitutional; and

2d. That, even if the framers of the constitution did leave an unguarded opening, through which such a law could be introduced without a breach in the structure of that instrument, still, that it is a cruel law, that it discards all those principles of evidence and forms of proceeding which have been devised by the wisdom of ages for the protection of innocence against power, and that in its whole scope and spirit it is in conflict with our fundamental ideas of human liberty.

It will be seen by this statement, that I here accept the constitution according to its commonly-received interpretation. There is a class of defenders of this law whom I wish to meet on their own ground. I do not, therefore, object here to the constitution as they understand it, but to the law. However much a man may reverence the constitution, though he may make it an idol and worship it, yet I mean to show him that this law is an unholy thing in its presence. I object, then, to the law as a departure from the constitution,—not a departure *towards* despotism merely, but *into* despotism. Admitting, what many deny, that when the constitution speaks of "persons held to service or labor," it means slaves, and admitting that it provides for their reclamation when it says they "shall be delivered up on claim," I still impeach the Fugitive Slave law for high crimes and misdemeanors against the spirit and the letter of that instrument.

On the question of the constitutionality of this law, the legal minds of the country are divided. It may not be easy to distribute opinions correctly, on this point, into their proper classes, and to decide upon their relative preponderance. If we include slave owners and those whose pecuniary interests connect them directly with slavery, and especially if to those we add a strong party who, from political associations and hopes, have surrendered themselves to a pro-slavery policy, probably the number, if not the weight, of opinion, is in favor of the constitutionality of the law. But if we gather the opinions of disinterested and unbiased men; of those who have no money to make or office to hope for through the triumph of the law, then I think the preponderance of opinion is decidedly the other way. I know it has been said by one prominent individual, that he has heard of no man, whose opinion was worth regarding, who denied the constitutionality of the law. Now, as it is a fact universally known, that gentlemen who have occupied and adorned the highest judicial stations in their respective states, together with many of the ablest lawyers in the whole country, have expressed opinions against the constitutionality of this law, I have but one single word of reply to a declaration so arrogant and insolent as this. That reply is, that on a great moral and political, as well as legal question,—a question that connects itself with ethics, as well as with partisan politics, and the success of old parties or the formation of new ones,—*integrity* is as necessary to the formation of a sound opinion as *intelligence.*

I think, however, that one further remark should in candor be made, in regard to the difference of opinions held by honest men on this subject. The constitutionality or unconstitutionality of the Fugitive Slave law is not a question to be determined solely by any single and simple provision of the fundamental law. Numerous clauses in the constitution have a bearing upon it. It connects itself with contemporaneous history. It presents a case where commentators and expounders must appeal to precedents and analogies, and to general principles respecting the nature of government and the object of all law. It is therefore a question of construction and interpretation. And, what is a more important consideration still, it belongs emphatically to that class of cases where men, who have been trained under one class of institutions, and whose minds have been moulded and shaped by the universal prevalence of one set of opinions and one course of practice, may honestly come to one conclusion, while those who have grown up under adverse opinions and an adverse practice, — or rather, into whose minds adverse opinions and adverse practices have grown, until they have become a part of the very substance of those minds, — may honestly come to an opposite conclusion. We know, too, that in addition to the powerful influences of education and training, the general cast and structure of men's minds predispose them to take one side or the other of great political and religious questions. Natural biases operate like a law of gravitation to sway different minds in different directions. When, therefore, a southern gentleman, into whose perceptions and reasonings and moral sentiments, the facts and the creed of slavery have been incorporating themselves ever since he was born, tells me that he believes even such a law as this to be constitutional, I can still concede the fulness of his integrity, however strongly I may dissent from the soundness of his opinion. It is a law that might be held constitutional by a bench of slaveholders, while it would be held unconstitutional by all the inhabitants of a free land. It is a law that might be held valid by the courts of Austria, while it would be held invalid by those of England. It is a law which the judges of Westminster Hall might have held valid in the time of the Stuarts, which they might and probably would have held invalid in the eighteenth century; and, in the nineteenth century, would certainly have reprobated and annulled.

My own opinion is, in view of the great principles of civil liberty out of which the constitution grew, and which it was designed to secure, that this law cannot be fairly and legitimately supported on constitutional grounds. I express this opinion because, after having formed it with careful deliberation, I am now bound to speak from it, and to act from it. I have read every argument, and every article in defence of the law, that I could find, from whatever source emanating. Nay, I have been more anxious to read the arguments made in its favor than the arguments against it; and I think I have seen a sound legal answer to all the former. As for any arrogant or supercilious dictum, either that the law is constitutional or that it is not constitutional, unaccompanied by any reason or any reference, all reflecting men must regard it as sheer insolence, come from what quarter it may.

Even should the supreme court of the United States declare the law to be constitutional, then, though we must acknowledge their decision, as to the point decided, to be the law of the land, until it is set aside, yet, without any disrespect to that tribunal, we may still adhere to our former opinion. We know how that court is constituted. A majority of its members are from slaveholding states. Independent, too, of all other considerations, they will feel a strong desire to maintain a former opinion, which was also given when a majority of its judges were from the south. We may, therefore, place our dissent on grounds which, two years ago, when the "Clayton compromise," so called, was under discussion, were so well stated by a distinguished senator from Ohio, [Mr. Corwin,] — grounds perfectly respectful on our part, and not derogatory to the court. He said, —

"It is a sad commentary upon the perfection of human reason, that, with but few exceptions, gentlemen coming from a slave state . . . . . all eminent lawyers on this floor, from that section of the country, have agreed that you have no right to prohibit the introduction of slavery into Oregon, California, and New Mexico; while, on the other hand, there is not a man, with few exceptions, (and some highly respectable,) in the free states, learned and unlearned, clerical or lay, who has any pretensions to legal knowledge, but believes in his conscience that you have a right to prohibit slavery. . . . . . How is this? Can I have confidence in the supreme court of the United States, when my confidence fails in senators around me here? *Do I expect that the members of that body will be more careful than the senators from Georgia and South Carolina to form their opinions without any regard to selfish considerations?*"

Besides, the supreme court have already, as I will show, decided certain points in such a way that, if they maintain the Fugitive Slave law, they will be obliged to overrule those points; and it is more creditable to them to suppose they will overrule their decision in Prigg's case, than to suppose they will overrule other decisions in other cases.

In the first place, I believe the constitution not only authorizes but requires a trial by jury, in the case of alleged fugitive slaves, when claimed in free states.

The constitution declares, "The right of the people to be secure in their persons," "against unreasonable" "seizures, shall not be violated; and no warrant shall issue but upon probable cause, *supported by oath or affirmation*, and particularly describing" "the persons or things to be seized." — *Amend.*, Art. IV.

It also declares, that, "In suits at common law, where the value in controversy shall exceed twenty dollars, the right of trial by jury shall be preserved." — *Amend.*, Art. VII.

And it also says, "No person shall be deprived of life, liberty, or property, without due process of law." *Amend.*, Art. V. And it is most important to observe that these words, "due process of law," are held by all the authorities *to include the trial by jury*. — 3 *Story's Com.* 661; 2 *Inst.* 50, 51; 2 *Kent's Com.* 10; 1 *Tucker's Black. App.* 304–5.

That there may be no doubt about the meaning and force of these words, I quote the following passage from Chancellor Kent: —

"It may be received as a self-evident proposition, universally understood and acknowledged throughout the country, that no person can be taken or imprisoned, or disseized from his freehold, or liberties, or estate, or exiled, or condemned, or deprived of life, liberty, or property, unless by the law of the land, or the judgment of his peers. The words, 'by the law of the land,' as used by the Magna Charta, in reference to this subject, are understood to mean 'due process of law.' That is, *by indictment or presentment of good and lawful men.*" — 2 *Com.* 13.

Now, in most of the cases which will arise under the Fugitive Slave law, there will be a "seizure" under a warrant; and in *all* the cases, the questions both of property and of liberty will necessarily be involved. In every case, the claimant will aver property in the respondent, and will seek to deprive him of his liberty. The respondent will deny the claim of property, and will seek to retain his liberty.

Now, suppose a man to have lived in Boston or New York for twenty years; to have contracted marriage; to have bought and sold; to have hired himself out to others, and to have hired others to serve him; to have pleaded and been impleaded in the courts; to have voted at elections, and to be, in all respects, as free by the constitutions of Massachusetts and New York as the governors of those states themselves; and suppose further, that this man is suddenly seized and taken before a commissioner, is adjudged the property of another man like himself, with no chance of revising the decision, or of having a new trial, is placed in duress, and then transported by force, and against his will, to a distant state, under a claim that he is a slave, and an adjudication that such claim is true, — suppose all this, I say, and then answer me this simple question, Has, or has not, such a man been "deprived of his liberty"? In other words, does such a man retain his liberty? As he is borne away by force, and against prayers, and tears, and struggles, does he remain free? Can a man be adjudged a slave; held, coerced, beaten as a slave; with all his powers and faculties of body and mind subdued and controlled as a slave's, and yet possess or retain liberty? If such a proceeding does not deprive a man of his freedom, by what means can he be deprived of it? What *more*, or what *other thing* would you do to deprive him of it? Would binding him out to serve for life deprive him of it? This declares that he owes service for life. Would imprisonment deprive him of it? This imprisons him, and makes the man his keeper who is interested to make that imprisonment perpetual in himself, and descendible to his children, and his children's children forever.

Is not perpetual imprisonment of the nature and substance of punishment, — of the severest punishment? The constitution has provided that "cruel and unusual *punishments* shall not be inflicted," even for the perpetration of the worst of crimes; yet here is a case where the most cruel of punishments, or of privations, may be inflicted without even a charge of crime. And the argument is, that this form of punishment may constitutionally be inflicted, because it was so inconceivably atrocious and diabolical that the constitution did not prohibit it, — because the constitution only prohibited "cruel and unusual punishments" *for crimes*, and not for having a dark skin.

Does any one say that a victim of this law has not been "deprived" of his liberty because he may sue for it, and possibly recover it, in the courts of the state to which he is carried? I reply, that it would be just as good an answer to say, that he may possibly recover his liberty by escape, or possibly his master may emancipate him, or possibly a St. Domingo insurrection may break out, or possibly the walls of his prison-house may be shaken down by an earthquake, and he may go forth like Paul and Silas; and *therefore* he is not deprived of his liberty by being enslaved. Neither of these events would have the slightest legal relation to the proceedings which did enslave him. Neither of them would be retroactive, undoing or annulling the past. Enslavement and liberty being incompatible, when he suffers the first, though but for an hour, he is deprived of the last. The moment he should arrive within the limits of a slave state, that moment he would be in the same condition as three million other fellow-bondmen; and it would be just as rational to say that they have never been deprived of liberty as that he has not. When our government made war upon Algiers, ransoming American captives from their horrible bondage and restoring them to their homes, did it annihilate the preëxisting fact that they had been enslaved? Did it enable or authorize the historian to say that they had never been *deprived of their liberty?* Had Algiers been "reännexed" as one of the states of this Union, could she have said, "We have not broken the constitution because these men are free again"? I affirm, then, that when a man in Massachusetts, who by the constitution of Massachusetts is free, is adjudged to be a slave, is transported as a slave, and held as a slave, in a southern state, though it be but for a single day, he is deprived of his liberty. That very thing is done to him which the constitution says shall not be done but by a jury of his peers.

But a question of PROPERTY is involved as well as a question of liberty. "In suits at common law," says the constitution, "where the value in controversy shall exceed twenty dollars, the right of trial by jury shall be preserved."

Now, sir, in regard to this important clause in the fundamental law, I propose to demonstrate the three following propositions: —

First; the claim, made before a competent magistrate, for a "person held to service or labor," is, in view of this constitutional provision, a "suit."

Second; it is a "suit at common law."

Third; it is a suit at common law "where the value in controversy exceeds twenty dollars."

As a law term, the lexicographers define the word "suit" to mean "an action or process for the recovery of a right or claim; legal application to a court for justice; prosecution of right before any tribunal; — as a civil *suit*, a criminal *suit*, a *suit* in chancery."

Blackstone says, "in England, the several *suits*, or remedial instruments of justice, are distinguished into three heads, — actions, personal, real, and mixed."

"Suit" comes from "*secta*," and *secta* from *sequor*; and the phrase "to bring suit," denoted anciently, to bring *secta*, — followers, or witnesses, to prove the plaintiff's demand. The scope of the word is now enlarged, so that it embraces the written forms by which an action is instituted, as well as the proof which sustains it.

We are not, however, confined to the authority of the dictionary. The supreme court, in the case of *Cohens* vs. *Virginia*, 6 Wheat. 407, where this very word "suit," as it occurs in the constitution, was the subject of consideration, defined it as follows: —

"What is a *suit*? We understand it to be the prosecution, or pursuit, of some *claim*, demand, or request. In law language, it is the prosecution of some demand, in a court of justice. 'The remedy for every species of wrong is,' says Judge Blackstone, 'the being put in possession of that right whereof the party injured is deprived.' The instruments whereby this remedy is obtained, are a diversity of *suits* and actions, which are defined by the Mirror to be 'the lawful demand of one's right;' or, as Bracton and Fleta express it, in the words of Justinian, '*jus prosequendi in judicio quod alicui debetur*,' — (the form of prosecuting in trial, or judgment, what is due to any one.) Blackstone then proceeds to describe every species of remedy by suit; and they are all cases where the party suing claims to obtain something to which it has a right.

"To commence a suit, is to demand something by the institution of process in a court of justice ; and to prosecute the suit, is, according to the common acceptation of language, to continue that demand."

Now let me take the different clauses of this definition, and see if every one of them does not necessarily include the demand made by a slave claimant against the alleged slave.

"We understand a suit," say the court, "to be the prosecution or pursuit of some *claim*, demand, or request." Here, then, according to the supreme court, a *suit* is the prosecution of some *claim;* and, according to the very letter of the constitution, the fugitive slave is to be delivered up, on *claim.* The slave, then, can be constitutionally and legally "delivered up" in no other way than "on claim," by "suit."

Again, say the court: "In law language, it [a suit] is the prosecution of some demand in a court of justice." When legal process is instituted for the recovery of a slave, is it not the prosecution of a demand? And will any one be rash enough to say that a man ostensibly free, — free according to all legal presumption, — can be "delivered" over to bondage for life, without the intervention of "a court of justice"?

To proceed with the opinion of the court: "The Mirror defines a suit to be 'the lawful demand of one's right;' or, as Bracton and Fleta express it, in the words of Justinian, it is the form of prosecuting, in trial, or judgment, what is due to any one." Here service is alleged to be due; and the one who is said to owe that service is "prosecuted by trial and judgment," that he may render the service claimed.

"To commence a suit is to demand something by the institution of process in a court of justice ; and to prosecute the suit is, according to the common acceptation of language, to continue that demand." In the appeal to a court for the possession of an alleged fugitive, is not something "demanded"? And what is the warrant that is issued for his arrest but the "institution of process"?

If any one, then, will show that a "claim" for an alleged fugitive, by process of law, to be followed up by proof in support of the claim, and to be consummated by judgment, is not a "suit," he must show that it is not "the prosecution or support of a claim;" he must show that it is not "the prosecution of some demand in a court of justice;" he must show that it is not "the lawful demand of one's right;" nor "the form of prosecuting in trial or judgment;" and finally, he must show that it is not "to demand something by the institution of process in a court of justice," and then "to continue that demand" until judgment is rendered for or against him.

But should the claimant of a fugitive slave show any one of these four things, he would show himself the way out of court.

And this brings me to the *second* proposition, namely, —

The claim for a person "held to service or labor" is, in view of the constitution, a "*suit at common law.*"

In a decision bearing directly on the right to a trial by jury, the supreme court has defined the phrase "suits at common law," in special reference to its meaning in the seventh amendment to the constitution, where the right to such trial, "in suits at common law," is secured. These are their words: —

"It is well known that in civil causes, in courts of equity and admiralty, juries do not intervene; and that courts of equity use the trial by jury only in extraordinary cases, to inform the conscience of the court. When, therefore, we find that the [seventh] amendment requires that the right of trial by jury shall be preserved in suits at common law, the natural conclusion is, that this distinction was present to the minds of the framers of the amendment. By *common law* they meant, what the constitution denominated in the third article, 'law;' not merely suits, which the *common* law recognized among its old and settled proceedings; but suits, in which *legal* rights were to be ascertained and determined, in contradistinction to those in which equitable rights alone were recognized, and equitable remedies were administered, or in which, as in the admiralty, a mixture of public law, and of maritime law and equity, was often found in the same suit. Probably there were few, if any states in the Union, in which some new legal remedies, differing from the old common law forms, were not in use; but in which, however, the trial by jury intervened, and the general regulations, in other respects, were according to the course of the common law. Proceedings in cases of partition, and of foreign and domestic attachment, might be cited, as examples, variously adopted and modified. *In a just sense, the amendment, then, may well be construed to embrace all suits, which are not of equity or admiralty jurisdiction*, WHATEVER MAY BE THE PECULIAR FORM WHICH THEY MAY ASSUME TO SETTLE LEGAL RIGHTS." — *Parsons* vs. *Bedford*, 3 Peters's Rep. 456–57.

Here the court say, that the term "common law," in the seventh amendment, meant what the constitution denominated in the third article, "law." The word "law" which is here referred to, as contained in the third article, occurs in the following sentence: "The judicial power shall extend to all cases, in *law* and equity, arising under this constitution, the laws of the United States," &c. And the court declare that the constitutional right to a jury trial embraces "not merely suits, which the *common* law recognized among its old and settled proceedings, but suits in which *legal* rights were to be ascertained and determined," in contradistinction from equity and admiralty cases.

And in the last sentence of the decision quoted, the court expressly say, that the seventh amendment embraces "*all suits which are not of equity or admiralty jurisdiction*, WHATEVER MAY BE THE PECULIAR FORM

WHICH THEY MAY ASSUME TO SETTLE LEGAL RIGHTS." The court say "ALL." After excepting cases of equity and admiralty jurisdiction, they declare that the phrase, "suits at common law," embraces *all* the rest. They recognize no hybrid class, not included under one or another of these heads.

Now it has been proved above, that a warrant for the arrest of an alleged fugitive, together with the allegations and proofs under it, constitute a "suit." And can any thing be more clear, than that a proceeding which decides the issue, whether a man "owes" or does not "owe;" which decides the issue, whether a man has "escaped," or has not "escaped;" and which, as the legal consequence of these decisions, delivers one man into the custody of another as his slave, or enlarges one man from the custody of another because he is not his slave, is, "whatever peculiar form it may assume," a proceeding "to settle a legal right," — one of the highest and most important legal rights that appertain to a man? It is not, in legal language, a right "of equity or admiralty jurisdiction," but exclusively and purely a *legal right*, and nothing else.

The court declare this to be so, *whatever peculiar form the process may assume.* But what gives peculiar pertinency and stringency to this decision of the court is, that at common law there was an original writ, called the writ *de homine replegiando*, — the writ of personal replevin, or for replevying a man, by which the question of property in a man might be determined. It was a writ which the party could sue out of right; one to be granted on motion, without showing cause, and which the court of chancery could not supersede. In the very language of the supreme court, it was a writ recognized by the common law, and is to be found "among its old and settled proceedings." The form of it is contained in that great arsenal of common law writs, the *Registrum Brevium*.

"A man," says Comyn, "may have a *homine replegiando* for a negro, or for an Indian brought by him into England and detained from him; or it may be brought by an infant against his testamentary guardian; or *by a villein against his lord.*" — (Dig., title Imprisonment, L. 4.)

If this writ could be brought "for a negro," or "for an Indian," by a man who had introduced him into England, and from whom he had been detained; and if, on the other hand, it could be brought by the negro, or by the Indian to gain his freedom, as was clearly the case, then it follows that the question of a right to a man, as well as that of human freedom, was a question familiar to the ancient common law, and for the trial of which a well-known process existed "among its old and settled proceedings." But this ancient writ, *de homine replegiando*, carries with it, as every body knows, the trial by jury, as much as an action of assault and battery, or of assumpsit on a promissory note.

I have always understood, that before the revolution, and before the framing of our constitution, Comyn's Digest, from which the above citation is made, was a work of the highest authority. It must have been well known to all the lawyers in the convention. Could they have intended that the mere fact of claiming a man as a slave, — which claim might be made against a freeman as well as against a slave, — should be sufficient to deprive him of this ancient muniment of the subject's liberty? It seems impossible!

But we are not left to the broad and general assertion, contained in the case of *Parsons* vs. *Bedford*, that the seventh article of amendment embraces "all suits" not of equity or admiralty jurisdiction, whatever the peculiar form which they may assume to settle legal rights. Authority exists still more pointed and direct. In *Baker* vs. *Riddle*, Mr. Justice Baldwin, one of the judges of the supreme court of the United States, held that it was not in the power of Congress to take away the right of trial by jury, as secured by the seventh amendment; neither, —

"1. By an organization of the courts in such a manner as not to secure it to suitors; nor,

"2. By authorizing the courts to exercise, or their assumption of, equity or admiralty jurisdiction over cases at law."

"This amendment," says he, "preserves the right of jury trial against any infringement by any department of the government." — *Baldwin's Rep.* 404.

Now, what are the tribunals created by the Fugitive Slave law but a new "organization of the courts"? or rather, the creation of new courts, "in such a manner as not to secure, [the right of trial by jury,] to suitors?" By it, Congress creates tribunals unknown to the common law, and purports to give them power over common law rights.

Having now proved, from the nature of the claim in controversy, — namely, the claim of one man to the personal services and the liberty of another man, and the counter claim of personal liberty and of self-ownership, — that the right in dispute between the claimant of an alleged fugitive, and the person claimed, is a common law right; and that *any* legal process to determine this right, "whatever form it may assume," is a "suit at common law," it only remains, under this head, to establish my *third* point, namely;

A claim to *any* person, as one "held to service or labor," always and necessarily presumes that "the value in controversy exceeds twenty dollars."

On this point, direct authority may be found in the case of *Lee* vs. *Lee*, 8 Peters's Rep. 44. This was an appealed case, where by law no appeal could be taken unless "the value in controversy" should be "one thousand dollars or upwards." It was objected that the apellants, — the petitioners for freedom, — were not worth a thousand dollars. But the court said, —

"The matter in dispute, in this case, is the freedom of the petitioners. The judgment of the court below is against their claim to freedom; the matter in dispute is, therefore, to the plaintiffs in error, the value of their freedom, *and this is not susceptible of a pecuniary valuation.* Had the judgment been in favor of the petitioners, and the writ of error brought by the party claiming to be the owner, the value of the slaves as *property* would have been the matter in dispute, and affidavits might be admitted to ascertain such value. But affidavits estimating the value of freedom are entirely inadmissible, and no doubt is entertained of the jurisdiction of the court."

Suppose there are two claimants for the same alleged fugitive? If his market value exceeds twenty dollars, both of them have a clear right to the trial by jury. And can it be that a man's right to his own *freedom* cannot be tried by a jury, when, if two men dispute about his *value*, each may claim the jury trial, and cannot be denied?

On the three points, then, 1. What constitutes a common law or "legal right;" 2. What constitutes "a suit at common law," and 3. What constitutes "a value which exceeds twenty dollars," — namely; the personal liberty of any human being, though he be an infant just born, or a drivelling idiot, or he be stretched upon his death bed with only another hour to breathe, — I trust I have made out a case which entitles a party to trial by jury under the constitution of the United States.

I might here rest the argument, feeling that, from authority and from reason, from the old and time-honored principles of the common law, as well as from those interpretations of the constitution which have been given by the supreme court, my conclusions are impregnable. But I proceed to notice some of the points taken on the other side; and if I shall occasionally advert to positions that are obviously too shallow and fallacious for discussion, it is only because I wish to omit nothing which any one may think of importance.

It is alleged that the whole force of the above argument, otherwise conclusive, is annulled, because a slave is no party to the constitution, is not under its protecting shield any more than a horse or an ox, and therefore, any provisions, however strong, securing the jury trial, are inapplicable to him. A slave, it is said, is not one of the "people" by whom and for whom the constitution was formed. He is an outlaw, and an outcast. He has no inherent or inalienable rights *as a man*. What he has, he has *ex gratia*, by the good will of those who own him, body and soul, and who are graciously pleased to forego some of their legal rights from generosity in themselves, and not from justice to him.

Now, as it seems to me, a most obvious principle confutes this argument utterly. By the laws of the free states, we know no such being as a slave. Our courts, in their functions as state courts, do not understand the meaning of the word *slave*. To talk to them in that capacity about a slave or slavery, is talking to them in an unknown tongue. In the eye of the legislators of the free states, and in the eye of the courts of the free states, so far as their domestic polity is concerned, there can be no such creature as a slave. The constitution of every free state in this Union must be first altered, before any such being as a slave, or any such condition as slavery, can be recognized under them, as state authorities.

So the constitution of the United States creates no slaves, and can create none. Nor has it power to establish the condition of slavery any where. And I hold further, that if the government of the United

States, by escheat, by purchase, by execution against a debtor, or in any other way, should become possessed of a slave, that moment he would be free. The government of the United States can neither hold a slave, nor make valid title to a slave by sale. It is a government whose powers consist of the grants that have been made to it; and nowhere, by no competent party, has any such grant ever been made.

The relation of the government of the United States to slavery consists in this, and in this alone: that when this government was created, slavery existed in a portion of the states; and by certain provisions in the constitution, the existence of this slavery was recognized, and certain rights and duties in relation to it were respectively acknowledged and assumed. But the government of the United States has no more power to turn a freemen in a free state into a slave than it has to turn a slave in a slave state into a freeman.

The officers of the state government being sworn to support the constitution of the United States, the governments of the free states are implicated indirectly in the matter of slavery, as the government of the United States is directly, and not otherwise.

Both by the constitution of the United States, then, and by the constitutions of all the free states, every man found within the limits of a free state is *prima facie* FREE. No matter what complexion he may wear, or what language he may speak, he is a free man UNTIL some other civil condition is proved upon him, or until he forfeits his freedom by crime. Every man, therefore, in any one of the free states of this Union, has a right to stand upon this legal presumption, and to claim all the privileges and immunities that grow out of it *until* his presumed freedom is wrested from him by legal proof. It is the most cruel of sophisms to say, that because a man is *claimed* as a slave, he is not under the protection of the constitution, and then *to prescribe a base mode of trial for him, by which he can be proved the thing he is claimed for.* On the subject of freedom or slavery, we of the free states know of but one class of men living among us. That class is free. There is no such class as slaves known to our laws. Nor is there any intermediate class, who may be presumed to be slaves on account of their color, or who may be proved to be slaves by less evidence, or by an inferior kind of evidence, because of color.

No axiom is more universal or indisputable, than that the right to freedom in a free state, and the right to be held and treated by the courts as a freeman, has no relation to complexion. If, then, these rights have no relation to complexion, *all* white men may be arbitrarily presumed to be slaves, and be deprived of the form of trial, secured to them by the constitution, just as well as any colored man can be. The former may just as well be proved to be slaves, on dangerous, or on inferior, or on insufficient evidence, as the latter. No; the liberty to which every man, of whatever color, in a free state, is *prima facie* entitled, invests him with its protection, and this investiture cannot be stripped from him but by the judgment of his peers or the law of the land, — which, as we have before seen, means trial by jury.

Any other interpretation assumes this as a postulate, namely, that there is a higher or surer kind of trial applicable to freemen, and a lower or inferior mode of proceeding applicable to slaves. And the inhuman inference from this assumption is, that any man against whom a ten-dollar commissioner may issue a warrant as a possible slave, shall forthwith be subjected to the slave's mode of trial, and be utterly deprived of the freeman's mode of trial; or, at the best, that he shall be sent away a thousand miles, into another jurisdiction, there only to have the slave's mode of trial. According to this form of proceeding, the first thing which the commissioner says to his victim is, "Being a slave, you must be tried in a summary manner." "But I am not a slave," asseverates the respondent, "and I claim to be tried by my peers under the guaranties of the constitution." "You are no party to the constitution," rejoins the commissioner, "and, therefore, not entitled to its shelter. The constitution was made by the people, and for the people, and you are not of them." Then says the victim, "If I could have the trial due to a freeman, I could prove myself a freeman; but under the form of trial awarded to a slave, I may be adjudged a slave; so that my fate is made to depend not upon my rights, but upon your form of proceeding." "Even if so," retorts the mercenary minister of the law, "it is but an imperfection incident to human institutions. Is not one man's property sometimes taken to pay another man's debts? and is not one man sometimes executed for another man's murder? Why, then, should the courts of justice be arraigned, if a freeman, instead of a slave, is sometimes consigned to bondage?"

Sir, the unmistakable distinction lies here; that if there be any difference between the kind or degree of proof applicable to a freeman and that applicable to a slave, then, in a free state, you must first prove a man to be a slave by freeman's proof. If cast on such proof, then, and not till then, does he become the subject of slave proof. Any thing else under the form of justice is a mockery of justice. No man will say that the "claim" imposes any disability upon the person claimed, or takes away from him any rights. A man who has a presumptive right to his liberty, has a perfect right to all the means to prove it. The "claim" imposes no obligation to deliver up, but the proof under the claim; and this proof in a case of "life, liberty, or property," is to be judged of by a jury.

The real question is, *who* is to be delivered up, a slave or a freeman? If the person arrested is prejudged to be a slave, then there is no need of a trial at all. If he is *prima facie* a freeman, then he is entitled to the most perfect mode of trial.

By the theory, I believe, of all the slave states but one, every person of maternal African descent is presumed to be a slave. As such, his civil condition is fixed, special tribunals are constituted to try him, and he is subjected to rules of evidence unknown to the common law and never applied to freemen. Now it would be but the same kind of legal absurdity and preposterousness, for the presumptive slave in a slave state, to demand the form of trial, the tribunal, and the evidence, which there appertain to a freeman, as it is to subject the presumptive freeman in a free state, to the form of trial, the tribunal, and the evidence, which appertain to a slave.

The iniquity of the law is, that it enables a perjured or fictitious slave owner, on proofs most easily fabricated, to seize any individual in a free state, and to *prejudge* him to be a slave, by the very form of trial which this law authorizes. On the contrary, nothing can be more clear, than that the civil condition or *status* of every man found in a free state is that of a free man. His living under a free constitution, without any thing more, invests him *prima facie* with this character. Until divested of this character, he continues presumptively a free man. While such, he is entitled to every security which the constitution gives to a free man. How then can he be subjected to a trial which reverses the whole law of presumption in favor of freedom, and which presumes that he is a slave to begin with? This is not only anticipating the judgment at the commencement of the proceedings, but it is anticipating the worst judgment that can be passed; and, by anticipating, procuring it; as prophecies often procure their own fulfilment.

I put this case, and I challenge an answer that shall refute or admit my conclusion: If any one man in a free state can be seized and suddenly transported into bondage under this law, *then every other man also can be; and there is not a single person left in any free state who has a right to a trial by jury to save him from slavery.* I am not now speaking of the special danger to each particular individual, but of the principle that embraces us all. Under the most oppressive of tyrannies there are persons who are not in danger. But under such a law as this, who can tell what may happen to men arrested away from home, to unprotected women, and to helpless children? Do you say that a public sentiment and a public watchfulness exist, which would protect the whites, the female, and the child? I reply, that we possess our right to protection under the constitution and laws, and are not to be turned over to public sentiment or public watchfulness in order to enjoy it.

Suppose an analogous law to be passed respecting debtor and creditor. Suppose a law to provide some new mode of proceeding by which the indebtedness of a defendant should be so far presumed as to subject him to an inferior kind of defence, or to transfer his case to another kind of tribunal, as from jurors to arbitrators, to be selected by the plaintiff himself. Who is there, though through all his life he had fulfilled the apostolic injunction to "owe no man any thing," that might not be cast in an action that would strip him of all his fortune?

The law punishes murder by death. Could it know with omniscient certainty, beforehand, *who is a murderer*, it might take from him the trial by jury without offence to the eternal principles of justice. It is because the law cannot know with infallible certainty, beforehand, who is a murderer, that it provides the trial by jury to determine the question. Just so, because human tribunals cannot know with certainty who is a slave and who is free, the constitution gives the trial by jury, before any man in a free state shall be deprived of his freedom. And the argument, that if a man be wrongfully consigned to bondage he may be afterwards restored to freedom, is as audacious and as tyrannical as to say that an innocent man may be hanged and sent into another world as a felon, because sometimes the dead have been restored to life.

It is no answer to this view of the case, to say that all processes, whether civil or criminal, are initiated on the supposition that a pecuniary liability exists, or that a wrong has been done. Every body knows that no presumption of this kind follows the plaintiff, or the government, into court. When there, in the presence of the law, the plaintiff must establish his claim affirmatively. The possible debtor is no longer a debtor. So the government must prove the guilt of the man it has arraigned. The possible criminal is no longer a criminal. In the eye of the law, he is as innocent as the unborn child. When they claim the trial by jury, neither plaintiff nor prosecutor can say, You are not entitled to this form of trial, because you *are* presumptively a debtor, or presumptively an offender. Yet this is precisely, and *in totidem verbis*, what the pro-slavery argument says to the respondent when he is brought before the commissioner and put in peril of his freedom. In both the cases supposed, such a doctrine would take away a man's rights in the most odious manner, by taking away the legitimate and constitutional means of defending them.

For the purpose of determining by suit or by prosecution whether a man is a debtor or is an offender, a suit or a prosecution may be commenced against him, but never for the purpose of raising a presumption that he is either the one or the other, or to deprive him of any evidence to which an unindebted or an innocent man is entitled, or to change the tribunal which is to try the question of indebtedness or of guilt. If attachment on mesne process, if even indictment by the grand inquest for the county, does not deprive a man of his right to a trial by jury, how can so great a natural wrong be constitutionally inflicted by the warrant of a commissioner?

The presumption that a colored man is a free man in the free states, is just as strong as that a man of pure, unmixed, Anglo-Saxon blood is a free man in the slave states; and would they tolerate the doctrine for a moment that any perfectly pure-blooded white person could be transformed into a slave, and as such sent from his own state into another, under this law? Nay more; would any slave claimant at the south be allowed to go *into a slave state*, and seize upon a pretended fugitive whom another man might claim to own, under such a process as is now sufficient, *in a free state*, to authorize the taking and carrying away of the same individual?

But to the argument, that the constitution and the law of 1850 apply only to slaves, and that because slaves are not parties to the constitution they are not under its protection, and so not included in the provision for jury trial, there is another answer perfectly fatal. It is this: the constitution does not enumerate the various classes of criminals who shall be entitled to trial by jury; but with the exception of cases of impeachment, and cases in the military and naval service, it expressly declares as follows: "The trial of all crimes shall be by jury." And also, "In all criminal prosecutions, the accused shall enjoy the right to a speedy and public trial by an impartial jury," &c. The right, therefore, is not made to depend upon the *classes of persons* on trial, but upon the nature of the charge brought against them. The constitution does not say that freemen shall be tried in one way and slaves in another; but its language is, "all crimes," and "all criminal prosecutions;" so that it embraces every person *who is prosecuted*, whether free or slave, citizen or foreigner, Jew or Gentile. If an Englishman or a Frenchman were to be tried here for murder, how would the whole world deride the suggestion that he should not have a jury trial because he is a foreigner, — because he is not one of the "people," and so not a party to the constitution!

So the constitution does not say, in suits between merchant and merchant, or between landlord and tenant, and so forth, "the right of trial by jury shall be preserved;" but it says, "*In suits at common law*, where the value in controversy shall exceed twenty dollars." The right is not determined by the character of the litigants, but by the nature of the action. The constitution does not care who the parties are, — man, woman, bond or free, — it is all the same. As soon as parties appear upon the record, the right to trial by jury attaches. The *suit*, and not the *civil condition* of the litigants who instituted or who defend it, tests and determines the jury question.

In the case of *Lee* vs. *Lee*, before cited, the law allowed an appeal only in case the sum in controversy should amount to one thousand dollars. The appellant was of African descent, and therefore, within that jurisdiction, presumptively a slave; not presumptively a freeman, as every man is in a free state; and, if a slave, then he could own no property; for, by the cruel law of slavery, every master may rob his slave legally of all that he earns, or finds, or otherwise receives. Yet the supreme court sustained the appeal. Why was not so astute an exception as this then taken? — an exception which, if they have a bar in Pandemonium, would have done honor to one of its counsellors. Why was it not said that a slave was no party to the law, and therefore not entitled to its benefits? No reason can be assigned why a slave is not as much under the protection of a constitution made for the "people," as under the protection of a law made for the "people." Yet here, even in the case of a presumptive slave, a right was acknowledged, which some freemen, in free states, deny to presumptive freemen.

I have here been combating the argument, that because the Fugitive Slave law is aimed at slaves, no freeman has any ground of complaint against it, even though he should be converted into a chattel under it. He must console himself under the doom of interminable bondage, with the patriotic and pious reflection that he is only suffering, as an exception, to prove the general excellence of the law; and he must leave this consolation also to his enslaved children. For, in his case, it is said that eternal slavery is only one of those exceptions in the working of the law which proves the rule of its general excellence. This argument I hold to be eminently sophistical and cruelly oppressive. But if any one believes it to be a sound argument, then I hold him to all fair deductions resulting from it, — of which the following is clearly one: —

On the same ground on which Congress passes a law for escaped slaves, let every free state pass a law for resident freemen. The presumption in every free state being, that all men within its borders are free, let every such state give the trial by jury, in all cases in which personal liberty is involved, to every one who shall ask for it, and who has not once had it in a litigation with the same party, on the same subject-matter. According to the argument I have been considering, no slaveholder can complain of such a law; for, by its very terms, it applies only to freemen. The law of Congress applying only to slaves, and the supposed state law applying only to freemen, there is no conflict between them. And if, by accident or mistake, any real slave should take shelter under such a state law, and should escape a life of horrible bondage, it will be only one of those mistakes which may arise under the purest administration of justice. It will answer quite as well as its counterpart case, to stand as one of those exceptions in the working of a rule which prove its general excellence. If the occasional subjection of a freeman instead of a slave, to all the horrors of bondage, constitutes no valid objection to the United States law, then, surely, the occasional enfranchisement of a slave from a bondage that was always unjust and cruel, should constitute no objection to the law of the free state. If this Fugitive Slave law continues for a single year, I hope every free state will pass a law inflicting condign punishment upon every man who directly or indirectly assists in sending any man into southern bondage, unless he can prove before a jury that the man so sent was a slave.

So far, I have considered the question, whether a fair interpretation of the constitution does not secure the jury trial in every free state, to an alleged fugitive, and empower him to demand it as a matter of right.

But this is a strange question to discuss in a republican government. The proper question is, not whether the constitution expressly *demands* the jury trial, but whether it will, by any fair implication, *allow* it. The only point which a republican judge or citizen can, with decency, make on this subject is, Does the constitution forbid, prohibit, deny, such trial? — for, if it does not, then the jury should be granted of course. In a free country, under a free government, where the idea has become traditional, where the doctrine has become a household doctrine, that the trial by jury is the palladium of our civil and religious liberties, is it not amazing that we should find men who seem eager to avoid this form of trial, rather than zealous to grasp it? It is the saddest of spectacles; it argues the most mournful degeneracy, to see the children at this early day, from grovelling notions of ambition and of wealth, abandoning those noble principles of freedom for which their fathers so lately shed their blood. Wherever the constitution allows the trial by jury, in a matter of human liberty, in Heaven's name let us have it. Let Russia and Austria curtail and deny this privilege of freemen; let the tyrant, and the tyrant's minions among ourselves, explore the musty records of darker times, to find precedents against it; let them strive, by their shallow sophistries and plausibilities, to gloss over this ravishing of liberty and life from beings created in the image of God; but let every true republican, whenever, in the disposal of these momentous interests, the constitution will, by fair construction, sanction it, cling to the trial by jury, as to the only plank that will save him, — ay, the only one that will save the human race, — from being again ingulfed in the vortex of despotism. The enemy of the trial by jury, wherever human liberty is concerned, is the enemy of human liberty and of the human race. The friends of a repeal of this law, then, need not discuss the question whether the constitution does expressly confer the right of trial by jury upon the alleged fugitive, for it is enough for them if the constitution does not take it away.

It is worthy of remark, that in both of the bankrupt laws passed by the United States, it was expressly provided, that when the commissioners should declare any person to be a bankrupt, he should have the right to a trial by jury to annul their decision. Thus, when the law proposed, not to appropriate a man's property, but merely to enable his creditors to receive it in payment of their debts, the jury trial was secured to him; but here, where the direct purpose is to strip a man of his liberty, and of his property in himself, the jury trial is denied.

This seems an appropriate place to consider the further irrelevant suggestion, sometimes obtruded, namely, that an alleged fugitive is not deprived of a trial by jury, because he may have it in the state to which he is carried.

Here the pro-slavery advocate admits, at least for argument's sake, that the alleged fugitive has a right, at some time, and some where, to the jury trial. If so, then there are numerous and powerful reasons why this trial should be had in the state in which he is found, rather than in that to which he may be transported. I will advert to a few of these reasons.

1. Slaves are held to be personal property. Trover lies for their value where they have been unlawfully converted. Trespass is the remedy for an injury done to them. According to the laws of all the slave states, they are the subject of larceny. Suits to recover them, or to recover damages for an injury done to them, are personal actions; and in personal actions it is required, by all the precedents and all the analogies of the common law, that the action should be tried in the jurisdiction where the writ is served. By the common law, personal actions are transitory. They are to be brought where the defendant resides; or, at least, where the property which is claimed lies. In the case of an alleged slave, both the defendant and the property are where *he* is found. According to the usages and principles of the common law, therefore, the trial should be there.

2. Before trial and judgment, the parties are like any other parties before the court, or they should be so. The claimant stands upon the merits of his claim; the respondent upon those of his defence. It may be inconvenient for a Texan claimant to prove his right to an alleged fugitive in Massachusetts; but it will be

indefinitely more inconvenient for a citizen of Massachusetts to prove his freedom in Texas. If the trial is in Massachusetts, and the plaintiff prevails, he takes immediate possession of his slave, and is invested at once with all the rights which the rigors of the slave law so abundantly give. But if the trial is in Texas, whither the defendant has been forcibly exiled, and there *he* prevails, who is to reimburse or recompense him for his intermediate bondage; for being dragged from his home; torn from wife, children, and friends; for being plunged, perhaps for years, into the hell of slavery itself, with all the untold agonies of an apprehended slavery for life?

What Judge Story says respecting the right of all persons who are accused of crime to be tried by a "jury of the state and district wherein the crime shall have been committed," applies with full force to a trial for liberty. "The object of this clause," says he, "is to secure the party accused from *being dragged to trial in some distant state*, away from his friends, and witnesses, and neighborhood." "Besides this," he continues, "a trial in a distant state or territory might subject the party to the most oppressive expenses, or perhaps even to the inability of procuring the proper witnesses to establish his innocence." (3 *Com.* 654.) For "innocence" read *liberty*, and the argument in behalf of the alleged criminal becomes applicable to the alleged fugitive. And why should the alleged fugitive be treated less mercifully than the alleged felon? The law is unspeakably rigorous in the case of an alleged fugitive, but softens into mercy over an alleged pirate or murderer.

If the trial, then, is where all the practice and principles of the common law indicate that it should be, no great or irreparable injury is done; no inconvenience even is suffered beyond that which is always suffered in enforcing a claim in a foreign and distant jurisdiction. But if a freemen is carried away, a grievous and intolerable wrong is done; a wound is inflicted which mortal medicaments cannot heal, nor the longest continued punishment of the malefactor ever expiate.

3. By transferring the trial to the place of the claimant's domicile, an effective, and, as it seems to me, a most iniquitous advantage is given him, in regard to evidence, while the respondent is subjected to cruel disabilities. By the laws of all but one or two of the slave states, persons of African descent, whether slave or free, are declared incompetent witnesses against white men. The freeman, then, by being removed as a fugitive into a slave state, may lose his evidence, which, under such circumstances, is the loss of his liberty. This violation, therefore, of the principles of the common law, in regard to the place of trial, is, to him, of the most momentous consequence. It is not true, then, in any just sense, that the trial by jury is still "preserved" to the alleged fugitive, notwithstanding his removal to a slave state. The common law trial, as inclusive of the right to adduce common law evidence, is not "preserved."

4. But not only is the evidence different, but, in some of the slave states, *the law itself is different;* so that one man may carry another by force into a jurisdiction where the law will account him a slave, when, had he been tried where he was found, the law would declare him free, — the facts in both cases being the same.

Take the law of Kentucky, for instance, — and I refer to this state because its slave code is of a milder type than that of most of the Southern States, its dreadful rigors being mitigated by an infusion of more humanity.

By the laws of Kentucky, a master may carry a slave *in transitu*, through a free state, or he may allow his slave to go temporarily into a free state, without a forfeiture of the legal right to hold him. *Graham* vs. *Strader & Gorman*, 5 Ben. Munroe, 173, (1844;) *Davis* vs. *Tingle et al.*, 8 Ben. Munroe, 545, (1848;) *Collins* vs. *America*, 9 Ben. Munroe, 565, (1849;) *Bushe's Reps.* vs. *White*, 3 Munroe, 104; *Rankin* vs. *Lydia*, 2 A. K. Marshall, 468, (1820.)

In Massachusetts certainly, and I suppose in most of the Northern States, all such cases would be decided in favor of the respondent.*

Now, what greater outrage can be inflicted upon a man than to seize, and bind, and carry him into a foreign jurisdiction, where not only is the evidence different, by which his rights may be proved, but where the law also is different, by which his rights are to be adjudicated. In Holland, the killing of a stork once was, if it be not now, punishable with death; because this bird devours the animals that would otherwise bore through and undermine its ocean-barring dikes. In a neighboring country, the killing of a stork may not be merely blameless, but praiseworthy. What an atrocity it would be to seize a man in the latter country, and carry him to Holland to be tried and executed for doing an act which, according to the law of the place where he had a right to be tried, may have been not only innocent, but laudable! I leave you, sir, to make the application.

5. But what must shock every man who possesses any just appreciation of the value of human liberty, or has any just perception of the principles on which it is founded, is, that under the Fugitive Slave law, the plaintiff gets possession and control not only of the chattel or article of property claimed, but of the defendant himself. He gets command, not only of the thing in litigation, but of the body and soul of the litigant. A Boston or New York merchant would con-

* Such also is the law in Louisiana. See *Louis* vs. *Marot*, 9 Louis. Rep. 473; *Smith* vs. *Smith*, 13 Louis. Rep. 441.

sider it a grievous hardship, if a southern adventurer could go there and seize upon all his property, transport it to Mobile, or New Orleans, and compel the owner to follow it and try title to it, in the place of the captor's domicile. Still more grievous would the hardship become, if, under the new jurisdiction, the defendant might be deprived of the evidence which, at home, would be decisive of his rights, or find himself controlled by adverse laws which he never had helped to frame. But what an extreme of barbarous tyranny would it be, if, beyond all these enormities, the southern plaintiff could seize him too, — the defendant himself, — the alleged debtor, — and grasp him in his own iron hand, obtaining supreme control over his body by force, and over his mind by fear; could command his powers of locomotion, so that he could go only where the will of his master would permit; could control his speech and his vision, so that he could consult with no counsel, and could see no friend but such as were in his master's pay; and, to enforce his authority, could imprison him, and starve him, and scourge him, and mutilate him, if he but so much as uttered a whisper that he had a right to have a trial by his country, or opened his lips in prayer to God to break the fetters of his iniquitous bondage!

To tamper with the witnesses of the adverse party, or endeavor to suborn his counsel to violate their duty to their client, is not only an act of the grossest baseness, but would subject the offender to penal retribution. Yet what need would there ever be of corrupting witnesses or suborning counsel, if a party could get bodily possession and absolute control of his antagonist himself?

Does not every one see that, in ninety-nine cases in a hundred, a control over the defendant's person and will would be a control over his case? His rights would be lost in his enforced disability to defend them.

You might as well put out a man's eyes, and then talk of his right in the common sunlight. In Baltimore, or Louisville, a kidnapped freeman might find an opportunity of self-redemption; but such a captive will never be carried to Baltimore or Louisville. He will be sent to some interior region, perhaps fifty miles from any court, or the residence of any counsel, where he may never have an opportunity to speak to a white man unless it be to a taskmaster, who is paid to guard and to silence him.

The authors of the Federalist deemed the principle of excluding an interested party from all power of deciding his own cause to be so important, that they laid down the following doctrine: "No man ought certainly to be a judge in his own cause, or in any cause, in respect to which he has the least interest or bias." (No. 80.) Yet the only chance which the Fugitive Slave law allows to a freeman, when carried into bondage, is that which he may exercise while under the absolute control of his robber master.

But more than this: the law imposes no obligation upon the claimant to carry his victim to the state he is charged to have escaped from. A man charged to have escaped from Texas may be carried to Florida. Nay, he may not be carried to any state in this Union; but may be sent to Cuba or Brazil; beyond hope, and into the outer darkness of despair.

All the arguments which I have ever heard, or seen, on this point, gratuitously *assume*, that the persons reclaimed and transported will have an honest master, be surrounded by kind friends, and have a lawyer at hand whom they can consult with every day, and money in their pockets to fee him. Would such be the case of a kidnapped freeman? Would a wretch, vile enough to rob a man of his liberty, carry him five hundred or a thousand miles, and then go to a shire town during a session of the court, and give his pretended slave a purse of money with which to fee a lawyer for investigating his right to freedom? No! the man who knows, or suspects, that he has seized a freeman, or that his victim even believes himself to be a freeman, and will put the claimant to the trouble and expense of a trial, will plunge that freeman into the abyss of bondage, where no ray of hope may ever reach him, and where his voice will be hushed as in the silence of death.

Another objection to the Fugitive Slave law is, that it confers judicial power upon persons who are not judges. Here we are not left to inference or construction, but can stand on the plain words of the constitution. The third article declares, —

> "The judicial power of the United States shall be vested in one supreme court, and in such inferior courts as the Congress may from time to time ordain and establish. The judges both of the supreme and inferior courts shall hold their offices during good behavior, and shall at stated times receive for their services a compensation which shall not be diminished during their continuance in office." — *Art.* III. § 1.

Here I hold it to be clear beyond dispute, that the "judges" mentioned in the second sentence of the above section are the members of the "supreme court" and "inferior courts" mentioned in the first section, and no other. If so, then there can be no doubt about the tenure of their office, and the mode of their appointment, compensation, and removal.

By sec. 2, of Art. II., the President "shall nominate, and by and with the advice and consent of the Senate shall appoint," "judges of the supreme court, and all other officers of the United States, whose appointments are not herein otherwise provided for, and which shall be established by law."

The appointment of *no* judge of *any* court is "otherwise provided for in the constitution;" and therefore the appointment of *all* the judges in whom "the judicial power of the United States is vested," belongs by the constitution to the President and Senate; and this "judicial power" cannot be delegated to, nor exercised by, any persons not so appointed.

The courts may appoint "inferior officers," such as clerks, criers, or masters in chancery; but these are not "judges;" nor would any one of them singly, nor any number of them associated together, constitute a "court," within the meaning of the first section of the third article. Were such the case, then *they* might have power to appoint "inferior officers," and so on, by sub-delegation, indefinitely.

The constitution also defines what it means by "judicial power." It says, "The judicial power shall extend to all cases in law and equity arising under this constitution, the laws of the United States," &c.

Now, my objection is, that the Fugitive Slave law requires the creation of a large body of officers who are not "judges," but whom it purports to invest with "judicial powers."

They are not "judges," because they are not nominated by the President and confirmed by the Senate, as all "judges" must be.

They are not "judges" again, because, if they were, they must hold their offices "during good behavior." But the commissioners may be unmade on the day they are made. "Judges" can be removed only by conviction, on impeachment. Commissioners may be removed by the court that appointed them. Not the President, nor the Senate, nor both together, can remove a judge, unless by the initiatory and concurrent action of the House of Representatives. An "inferior court" can eject a commissioner without notice.

Even if Congress had declared, by express words, that the commissioners appointed by the circuit and district courts should be taken and held to be "judges," it would not make them so; for Congress cannot delegate any power to judges to appoint judges, nor to courts to make courts. If Congress could not do this by express enactment, how can it do so by implication?

Commissioners are not "judges," also, because no person can be a "judge" who is not entitled, "at stated times, to receive for his services a compensation which shall not be diminished during his continuance in office."

This provision necessitates the conclusion that all "judges" must be entitled to salaries payable periodically. These salaries are in no case to depend upon the *amount* or the *quality* of their labors, — far less, if possible, upon their deciding the cases that are brought before them for the plaintiff or for the defendant. One "judge" may have an enviable reputation for talent and integrity, and thus attract suitors to his court. Another may be as corrupt as Lord Jeffries, and repel all honest litigants from him. But, in either case, he has a right to a compensation which shall not be diminished during his continuance in office. Each year gives him a definite, unchanged sum of money.

But the commissioner is paid by fees, and the amount of his fees depends partly upon the number of cases he decides, and partly also upon the party in whose favor he decides. If he decides that a man is free, he receives five dollars. If he decides that he is a slave, he receives ten. If the commissioner is acceptable to slave hunters, suitors multiply. If obnoxious to them, his docket is bare of a case. He is entitled to his compensation, not "at stated times," but on the determination of each case. His compensation may be diminished, or it may cease altogether, during his continuance in office. Each year does not give him any definite, unchanged sum of money.

The "judge" must be paid by the government, and

is independent of all the parties before his court. The commissioner is never to be paid by the government, but is wholly dependent for his fees upon the claimant whose case he tries. The government guaranties the payment of the "judge," but it can never inquire or know whether the commissioner be paid or not.

By the sixth article of the constitution, all "judicial officers" must make oath or affirmation that they will support the constitution. But there is no law requiring these commissioners to take an oath; and as a matter of practice, in some parts of the country at least, it is known that they take no such oath.

Now, by the act, a portion of the "judicial power" of the United States, the *whole* of which is, by the constitution, vested in one "supreme court," and in "inferior courts," is given to the commissioners. The fourth section says they "shall have concurrent *jurisdiction* with the judges of the circuit and district courts of the United States." If the power of these courts, in the premises, is judicial, then the power of the commissioners, being the same, is judicial.

The attorney-general of the United States, in a written opinion, given by command of the President, declares that this power, so given to the commissioners, is judicial. The following are his words: —

"These officers, [the commissioners,] and each of them, have judicial power, and jurisdiction to hear, examine, and decide the case."

"The certificate to be granted to the owner is to be regarded as the act and judgment of a judicial tribunal having competent jurisdiction."

"Congress has constituted a tribunal with exclusive jurisdiction to determine summarily, and without appeal, who are fugitives from service. The judgment of the tribunal created by this act is conclusive upon all tribunals."

Such is the opinion of the attorney-general of the

United States, given upon the precise point, by order of the President of the United States.

But the point needed no authority to sustain it. It results inevitably from the very nature of the power conferred by the law. The decision of the commissioner is to be *final* and *conclusive*, and the subject-matter of the decision is liberty and property. The case cannot be reheard or reëxamined by any judge, or by any court, of any state, or of the United States. The decision acts *in rem* and *in personam*. It delivers the property to the claimant, and puts the body of the defendant into his custody. From that moment, if the law has any validity, the defendant is the slave of the plaintiff, by force of a "judicial" decision. The plaintiff, thenceforth, may control his actions, his words, his food, his sleep. If he chooses to exercise his authority in such a way, he can order his victim to carry him home on his back, and make him bear the loathsome burden of his person as well as of his will. Now, to say that the power which effects these results is not a judicial power, is to do violence to language, and to commit a fraud upon the inherent nature of ideas. In no case known to the common law, or indeed to any other law, is a plaintiff invested with *full* rights, except after *final* judgment.

If, then, this power is a "judicial power," the constitution peremptorily forbids that it should be vested any where but in a "court," whose "judges" are nominated, confirmed, sworn, hold office, are paid, and are removable, according to its requirements. Look at the constitutional distribution of powers. By the first article, all legislative power "shall be vested in a Congress." By the second article, the "executive power shall be vested in a President." And by the third article, "the judicial power shall be vested" in the courts. And it was just as competent for Congress to invest "commissioners" with supreme "executive" or "legislative" power, as to vest them with "judicial" power.

If, by good fortune, or by miraculous interposition, a captured freeman should afterwards obtain a hearing in a court of the state to which he had been carried, such hearing would, in no sense, be in the nature of a review of the former case, either by appeal, writ of error, mandamus, or certiorari. It would be by the institution of *another* suit, under *another* government. The relation of the parties would be reversed. The respondent who was kidnapped must be plaintiff, the plaintiff kidnapper, or some one claiming under him, must be defendant. Were the various *possessory* writs known to the English common law any the less "suits at common law"? or were the courts that tried them any the less *judicial* tribunals, because a *writ of right* could be afterwards brought, in which the previous judgments could not be pleaded in bar, and would be neither estoppel nor proof of title?

But to avoid the force of this, it has been said, that the proceedings before the commissioner do not constitute a "case," within the meaning of the second section of the third article, which extends the "judicial power" of the United States to all "cases" in law and equity. Instead of being a "case," it is said to be only a summary inquiry, designed to operate as a condition for executive action, in order to accomplish a special and limited object; like the inquiry, who are rightful claimants of money held by the government, under a treaty, and how much belongs to each one. It is also said, that if a construction so literal is to be put upon the words "judicial power," then no master in chancery could act in behalf of the courts in equity cases; no commissioner of bankruptcy could be appointed under a bankrupt law, &c.

In answer to the first position, that the proceedings for the reclamation of fugitive slaves do not constitute "a case," we have the most explicit declaration of the supreme court in more *cases* than one. In Prigg's case, 16 Peters, 616, the court say,—

"It is plain, then, that while a claim is made by the owner, out of possession, for the delivery of a slave, it must be made, if at all, against some other person; and inasmuch as the right is a right of property capable of being recognized, and asserted by proceedings before a court of justice, between parties adverse to each other, it constitutes, in the strictest sense, a controversy between the parties, and a CASE, arising under the constitution of the United States, within the express delegation of JUDICIAL POWER given by that instrument."

"A CASE in law or equity consists of the right of the one party as well as of the other, and may truly be said to arise under the constitution, or a law of the United States, *whenever its correct decision depends* ON THE CONSTRUCTION OF EITHER."—*Cohens* vs. *Virginia*, 6 Wheat. 379, (5 Cond. Rep. 101.)

Indeed, almost every page of the opinion of the court, in *Cohens* vs. *Virginia*, may be referred to, to show that they used the word "case" in a sense that embraces the proceedings for the reclamation of a fugitive slave. If so, then any tribunal, having jurisdiction over such a "case," is vested with a part of the "judicial" power of the United States.

In defining the word "case," as it occurs in this article, Judge Story says,—

"It is clear that the judicial department is authorized to exercise jurisdiction to the full extent of the constitution, laws, and treaties of the United States, *whenever any question respecting them shall assume such a form that the judicial power is capable of acting upon it.* When it has assumed such a form, it then becomes a *case*."—3 *Comm.* 507.

"A case, then, in the sense of this clause of the constitution, arises, when some subject touching the constitution, laws, or treaties of the United States, is submitted to the courts by a party who asserts his rights in the form prescribed by law."—*Ibid.*

And, as if these definitions were not clear enough, the learned judge adds, —

"Cases arising under the *laws* of the United States are such as grow out of the *legislation* of Congress, within the scope of their constitutional authority, *whether they constitute the right, or privilege, or claim, or protection, or defence of the party, in whole or in part, by whom they are asserted.*"— 3 *Comm.* 508.

It seems clear, then, that the proceedings authorized by the Fugitive Slave law cannot be taken out of the meaning of the word "cases," (cases in law and equity,) in the third article.

There is another clause in the third article, which embraces these proceedings with equal clearness and certainty. "The judicial power shall extend to controversies" "between a state and citizens of another state." I suppose it will not be denied that a slave state may itself own slaves. They may escheat to it, be taken in execution for debt, &c. Now, a free citizen of Massachusetts may enter the port of Charleston as a mariner, be seized, imprisoned, and then sold into slavery for non-payment of jail fees. The State of South Carolina may purchase him. He may escape and return to Massachusetts. South Carolina may then claim him under this Fugitive Slave law.

In such a condition of things, a "controversy" will exist between "a state and a citizen of another state." The commissioner can take jurisdiction of that case as well as of any other. And who will be bold enough to say that a trial and judgment by him, delivering up the respondent to bondage, would not be the exercise of "judicial power" in a controversy between "a state and a citizen of another state"?

The argument, that if the commissioner under the Fugitive Slave law exercises "judicial power," then masters in chancery, commissioners of bankruptcy, &c., exercise it, is answered by a word.

Masters in chancery assist the court in preparing questions for decision, but they decide nothing. Every act of theirs may be reheard and reëxamined by the court at the pleasure of either party. They enter up no judgment; they issue no execution. They may express the opinion that the plaintiff or defendant is entitled to recover a certain sum of money, or to hold the chattel in dispute; but neither of them can touch it. They are "*judges*," in no legitimate sense. They exercise no part of the "judicial power." The court may call upon them to state an account between parties, as it calls upon a clerk to make up the record, or a servitor to bring a law book, or asks a friend to cast up the interest on a promissory note. Such are the functions of a master in chancery, whose acts have no legal validity until assented to by the parties or sanctioned by the court.

So with regard to commissioners of bankruptcy. Every act they were ever authorized to perform derived all its legal force from the consent of the parties, or from the verdict of a jury, before whom it had been contested, or from the judgment of the court, — as may be seen at a glance, by reference to the acts creating them.

As to the supposed "judicial power" exercised by commissioners, under a treaty to determine who are rightful claimants, and to how much each one is entitled, it is almost too obvious to remark, that as no citizen can bring "suit" against the government, the "judicial power" does not "extend" to such a case, and the suggestion is puerile.

A word more will close my remarks on this topic. We have seen that a decision of the commissioner adverse to the respondent delivers him over into absolute, unconditional slavery. But the prevalent opinion is, that a decision in the respondent's favor is no bar to a subsequent trial of the same person on a new "claim." It was actually held in Long's case, in New York, where the claimant apprehended that the decision of the first commissioner would be against him, that he might abandon proceedings before that tribunal and resort to another. He did so, and prevailed. That is, the claimant may select, from among an indefinite number of irresponsible magistrates, the one whose ignorance or whose turpitude may promise the best chances of success. But if, from any cause, he should apprehend defeat, then, and before the final judgment is pronounced, he can withdraw his suit and commence anew before another magistrate, and so throw the dice of the law again and again, until, by the very doctrine of chances, he shall ultimately succeed. Such want of equity between the parties stamps this law as infamous, — for inequity is iniquity.

An argument in favor of the surrender of alleged fugitives from service under this law has been derived from the provision for the surrender of fugitives from justice. But the difference between the cases is world-wide. In regard to slaves, the constitution says, — "No person HELD to service," &c.; but in regard to criminals, its language is, "A person CHARGED," &c.

Now, who can avoid perceiving the difference between the legal force of the words "held" and "charged"? The obligor in a bond is "HELD and firmly bound." The grantor conveys an estate "to have and to HOLD" to the grantee and his heirs and assigns forever. So a lessee is to "HOLD" for the term specified. A man is HELD to answer a charge, &c., &c. In all these cases the word "*hold*" implies a perfect obligation or certain liability. But a man is "CHARGED" with an offence when a grand jury has found an indictment against him, or when a competent person has made the requisite oath. It is not enough that a man be *charged* to be *held* to service. He must be *proved* to be *held*, or he remains free; the court must know that he is so *held* before they are authorized to surrender him. And how, under our constitution, can the court know such facts as convert a presumptive freeman into a slave without a trial by jury?

Had the constitution said a fugitive *guilty* of murder, &c., shall be delivered up, could a man be delivered up until *proved* guilty of murder? Yet the word *guilty* is no stronger in reference to a fugitive from justice than is the word *held* in reference to a fugitive from service.

Another distinction between the cases is not less marked than the preceding. When the fugitive from justice is *claimed*, he is claimed by a *state* for having violated its law, and when he is delivered up he is delivered into the custody of the law. Legal process must have been commenced against him in the state from which he fled. He is returned, that the prosecution thus commenced may be completed. He is delivered from an officer of the law in one state to the officer of the law in another state. He is transferred, not to avoid a trial, but to have one. The original indictment or *charge*, the arrest in a foreign state, and the delivery and transportation to the place of trial, are but separate parts of one legal proceeding. The shield of the law is continued over him. All the time and all the way, he has the solemn pledge of the government, that if not found guilty on the prosecution *then pending*, he shall be discharged.

But the alleged slave is claimed not by a state, but by an individual, and he is delivered up, not into the custody of the law, where his right might be adjudicated upon, but into private hands; not into the hands of a neutral or indifferent person even, but into the hands of a party interested to deprive him of all his rights, and who himself claims to be judge, jury, and all the witnesses, in determining what those rights are. If he be not a slave, then he is delivered into the hands of a man-stealer. The shield of the law is not continued over him; nay, the Fugitive Slave act expressly provides that, whatever his rights may be, yet, while *in transitu*, the law shall not recognize them. The certificate given by the commissioner to the claimant is to prevent "all molestation of him by any process issued by the court, judge, magistrate, or other person whomsoever." Under this practical interpretation of our constitution, which, as its own preamble declares, was formed to "establish justice, and secure the blessings of liberty," it takes better care of felons than of freemen.

But there are other provisions of the constitution respecting the trial of *criminals*, which would control this provision respecting the delivery of fugitives from justice, even if there should be any doubts about its true construction. By the constitution as orginally adopted, and by the fifth amendment, all crimes, (except in cases of impeachment, or in the land and naval forces,) are to be tried in the state and district where committed. This makes it impossible to try a fugitive from justice in the state to which he has fled. It is an express prohibition against trying him there. But no such prohibition exists, no analogous provision exists, respecting the trial of "suits at common law," or the trial of "cases" or "controversies," in which a man may be deprived of "life, liberty, or property." These cases, therefore, not being taken out of the general provisions of the constitution for securing the rights of the citizen, are left within it, and hence must be tried by a jury in the place where the claim is made.

My next objection to this law is, that it attempts to suspend the writ of *habeas corpus*.

The constitution says, "The privilege of the writ of *habeas corpus* shall not be suspended, unless when, in cases of rebellion or invasion, the public safety may require it." The Fugitive Slave law declares that the "certificate" given to the claimant, his agent or attorney, "shall prevent all molestation of said person or persons by any process issued by any court, judge, magistrate, or other person whomsoever." Now, as a writ of *habeas corpus* is a "process issued by a court or judge," it follows, that, according to the terms of the Fugitive Slave law, the slave owner is not to be "*molested*" by that process. What, then, will constitute a "molestation" of him under this law? Would the service of a writ of *habeas corpus* upon him, and, in case of his refusal voluntarily to obey it, the seizure of his person, and the carrying of him bodily before the court, perhaps a hundred miles out of his way; — would the moral necessity of employing counsel, and being otherwise subjected to great expense, both of money and time; — would any or all of these impediments and privations amount to what this law denominates "molestation"? If they would, then the slave owner is exempted from them. And if so exempted from them, is not the privilege of the writ of *habeas corpus* "suspended," as to his pretended slave? What else can a "suspension" of it mean?

But take the other alternative. Suppose the writ of *habeas corpus* to be issued, and a return of all the facts by which the supposed slave is held to be made. The very return brings the Fugitive Slave act before the court; and if the act is before the court, then, surely, the question is also before the court, whether it is constitutional or not. For, if unconstitutional, it is no law, and no justification of the restraint. Suppose the court to decide the act to be unconstitutional, and to discharge the prisoner. This surely would be a "molestation" of him, in the strongest sense of the word. To say the least of it, then, the law contains an insolent and audacious provision, forbidding the "courts, judges, magistrates, and all other persons whomsoever," to do what it may be their sworn constitutional duty to do, — that is, to inquire into the constitutionality of the law, and, if found to be unconstitutional, to disregard it.

I am aware of the astute reasoning of the present able attorney-general of the United States. He says, first, that the act does not suspend the writ of *habeas corpus*, because such suspension would be "a plain and palpable violation of the constitution, and no intention to commit such a violation of the constitution ought to be imputed" to Congress; and second, that if the certificate of the commissioner is shown "upon the application of the fugitive for a writ of *habeas corpus*, it prevents the issuing of the writ; if upon the return, it discharges the writ, and restores or maintains the custody."

The first reason might be more briefly stated thus: it don't because it don't; or it don't because it can't.

The second is as little satisfactory as the first. If the facts are shown, it says, upon the fugitive's application for a writ, no writ will issue; if shown upon the return of the writ, it will be abated. Is it not most clear that this assumes the very question in dispute, whether the law on which the certificate is founded be constitutional or not? The statement may be all very true, if the law be constitutional; but suppose the law to be unconstitutional, would not the statement be superlatively absurd? Yet whether the law be constitutional or not, is the very question to be determined.

Let me test the soundness of this logic by a supposed case. There is, at the present time, a set of politicians amongst us, who are so alarmed at agitation that each one of them is a kind of Peter the Hermit, getting up a crusade to prevent it. Now, suppose Congress, "*as a peace measure*," should pass a law authorizing the secretary of state to issue his warrant for the arrest and imprisonment, until the 4th day of March, 1853, or at least until after the next presidential nominations are made, of any person who shall be guilty of agitating *on the wrong side of said peace measure*, and should further declare that any jailer having such warrant from said secretary should be free from "all molestation by any process issued by any court, magistrate, or other person whomsoever." Would it be a sound, judicial, and lawyer-like argument, in such a case, to say that Congress could not, and could not have intended to, violate the constitution, and therefore they had not violated it; and that if the warrant for commitment should appear upon the prisoner's application for a writ of *habeas corpus*, it would prevent its issuing; if, upon its return, it would discharge it?

I think it impossible for any one to show that if the argument be good in the first case, it would not be good in the second; and good, indeed, in any case, however outrageously violating the constitution.

Again: suppose the 18th of September last, when the Fugitive Slave bill was approved, to have been a time "of rebellion or invasion," when the public safety required the suspension of this writ, would not such words as end the sixth section of the act be sufficient in law to suspend it? The attorney-general seems to rely upon the fact that the Fugitive Slave law does not mention the *habeas corpus*. He cannot surely mean to say that the privilege of this writ could not be suspended, unless by name. Even slavery is not mentioned in the constitution *by name*. Suppose Congress, in a time of rebellion or invasion, to say, in regard to any class of cases which it might choose to specify, that if one person shall hold another under executive warrant, such warrant "shall prevent all molestation of said person or persons by any process issued by any court, judge, magistrate, or other person whomsoever;" could any man deny that such words would have ample force to suspend the privilege of this sacred and time-hallowed writ?

No! Heaven, and not the thirty-first Congress, be praised for it! Though this infamous Fugitive law *could not* suspend the *habeas corpus*, yet its words are adequate to do so. They purport to put the professional slave-hunter, as it regards the privilege from arrest, or "molestation," on the footing of a member of Congress; and it would not have gone one iota further, in point of principle, had they made his person inviolable while going to seize his prey, and when returning with it.

If the argument of the attorney-general be sound, then the whole "privilege of the writ of *habeas corpus*," under any corrupt law that any corrupt Congress may pass, will consist in the privilege of applying to a court for the writ, and being refused; or in suing out the writ, and having it quashed.

By the principles of the English law, the privilege of the *habeas corpus* attaches to all, whether bond or free. The words *liber homo*, says Lord Coke, extend to every one of the king's subjects, "be he ecclesiastical or temporal, free or *bond*, man or woman, old or young, or be he outlawed, excommunicated, or any other, without exception." — 2 *Inst.* 55.

I now proceed to lay open for the abhorrence of mankind other deformities of this most odious law. In opposing a law, a distinction is to be made between the courts and the people; between the bench and the ballot-box. The courts can hear but one objection to a law. It may be impolitic, unrighteous, atrocious; but if it be constitutional they must sustain it. But before the tribunal of the people, a law may be impeached for any attribute of cruelty, oppression, or meanness. I denounce the Fugitive Slave law for all these qualities. In its scornful rejection of all those common-law principles of evidence which have been ratified by the wisdom of ages; in the "summary" and piratical haste of its proceedings, and in the indelible blood with which its judgments are recorded, I believe it has not a parallel in the modern code of any civilized people.

Should the courts, hampered by previous decisions, and habituated to the spectacle and the support of a cruel institution, pronounce this law to be constitutional, such a judgment would give new force to every reason why the people should demand its modification or repeal. It is not enough that it should be declared void by the courts as against the fundamental law of the land ; it deserves to be branded by the people as abhorrent to humanity, to civilization, and to the gospel of Jesus Christ.

Look at its provisions in regard to evidence. The proof of three facts dooms the victim : first, that the person named in the warrant owes the claimant service ; second, that he has escaped ; and, third, identity.

Now, according to the law, all these facts may be proved in the absence of the party to be ruined by them. The whole case may be established by evidence taken behind the victim's back, without notice to him, without knowledge, or possibility of knowledge, on his part. A freeman may be suddenly arrested, and dragged into court, and on certain papers being read against him, which he never saw nor heard of before, he may be ordered into the custody of officers, and hurried to a returnless distance from wife, children, and friends, reduced to the direst form of bondage the world ever knew, and at the expense of the very government which he has been taxed to support, and which in turn was bound to protect him. I will prove by a reference to the act itself that these atrocities are among its conspicuous features.

By the sixth section it is made the duty of the "court, judge, or commissioner," "upon satisfactory proof being made by deposition *or affidavit*, in writing," "or by other satisfactory testimony," "and with proof, *also by affidavit*, of the identity of the person whose service or labor is claimed," "to make out and deliver to such claimant a certificate," &c.

And the tenth section of the act declares that the transcript of a record "taken in any state or territory, or in the District of Columbia," and "produced in any other state, territory, or district," and being there "exhibited to any judge, commissioner, or other officer authorized to cause persons escaping from service or labor to be delivered up, shall be held and taken to be full and *conclusive* evidence of the fact of escape, and that the service or labor of the person escaping is due to the party in said record mentioned." "And upon the production of other and further evidence, *if necessary*, either oral or *by affidavit*, of the identity of the person escaping, he or she shall be delivered up to the claimant."

Here, then, is a provision unknown to the common law of England, or to any colony, or people, or tribe that ever claimed the common law of England as their inheritance; unknown even to the star chamber, or high commission court; unknown in the bloodiest reigns of the bloodiest tyrants that ever sat upon the English throne; unknown to those judicial villains whom Lord Campbell calls "*ruffians in ermine*" — incorporated into the code of a republican government. Evidence, which may consign to slavery a man who is ostensibly and presumptively free, — free by the laws of the state where he is, and free every where by the law of God and humanity, — may be prepared in his absence, without any notice to him, and by any means of perjury or subornation of perjury to which guilt may resort, and this evidence is made legally sufficient to doom a fellow-being to relentless bondage. Notwithstanding those remarkable clauses in the constitution which provide that "in all criminal prosecutions the accused shall enjoy the right to a *speedy* and *public* trial," "be informed of the nature and cause of the accusation," "be confronted with the witnesses against him," "have compulsory process for obtaining witnesses in his favor," "and have the assistance of counsel for his defence;" yet Judge Story comments upon them in a spirit of dissatisfaction and sorrow; "for," says he, "unless the whole system [of the common law] is incorporated, *and especially the law of evidence*, a corrupt legislature, or a debased and servile people, may render the whole little more than a solemn pageantry." (3 *Com.* 662.) In speaking of a "corrupt legislature," he seems to describe what this Congress has done in enacting the Fugitive Slave law at its last session; and, in speaking of a "debased and servile people," he speaks of just such a people as the advocates and champions of this law are now striving to make the people of the United States become!

The right of cross examining witnesses is a common-law right, appertaining to all kinds of trials. It is a right without which all trials are but mockery. It is oftentimes a hardship to be confronted with witnesses of whom one knows nothing; but to be debarred from all opportunity of getting, by cross questioning, at the knowledge that is in them; to be debarred from the right of showing that they are incompetent even to folly, or corrupt even to wilful perjury, this is a barbarity unknown to any code in the civilized world, save to the code of the United States of America. It is what even barbarians might be ashamed of. It is offering bounties and premiums on villany, and turning the courts into brokers' offices for perjury. Under such a law, is there a single colored person at the north who can rise to his labor in the morning, or lie down to his repose at night, with any feeling of security that avarice and false swearing may not then be at work for his destruction? Who can wonder, if he is tormented in his nightly dreams by images of the man-stealer, in far off regions, plotting for his ruin? Who can wonder if, in his city residence, he starts as he turns the corner of every street; or, in his rural home, if he shudders at the rustle of every leaf, lest some kidnapper should spring from his ambush to seize him? That sense of personal security which every honest man is entitled to feel, this law abolishes. The virtuous man cannot rely upon his government, nor the pious man upon his God, for earthly protection. For him the Prince of Darkness has obtained the ascendency in the affairs of men, and offers impunity to guilt, while protection is withdrawn from innocence. The life of such a man is a perpetual agony of alarm for himself and for his family. A cloud charged with lightning is forever suspended over his head, and no genius can devise the means to turn aside its bolts.

Sir, before God, I believe that, in the judgment of an impartial posterity, this method of taking evidence, by the cruellest of means and for the wickedest of purposes, will be held as atrocious and as execrable as that horrid method of extracting evidence by torture, which once prevailed, but which now even half-civilized nations have abolished. A brave heart could withhold a false confession, even upon the rack. With the images of wife and children before the eyes, martyrdom for their protection has been sweet. But there is no man whom God ever made who will not tremble, and stand aghast with consternation, with the conscious knowledge in his mind that he, his wife and children, and all that he holds dear upon earth, are at the mercy of every pirate-hearted villain between the Atlantic and the Rio Grande; nay, that the government offers inducement to foreign assassins to come here, where, with less risk, they can make more money by false swearing and judicial kidnapping than they could at home by murder and robbery. Better, a thousand times better, had the constitution allowed the citizen "to be compelled to be a witness against himself," and laid its prohibitions upon the fabrication of testimony against him in his absence.

The tenth section of the act declares that this evidence, thus obtained under a foreign jurisdiction and in the absence of the party, shall be "*conclusive.*" Now, the legal force and meaning of this provision is, that no amount or weight of evidence, no array of the most unimpeachable witnesses, not even the personal knowledge of the commissioner himself, who tries the case, though given under the sanction of an oath, which the law does not require him, as a commissioner, to take, shall be admissible to rebut this "conclusive" testimony. It is not made *prima facie* evidence merely against the respondent; it does not merely shift the burden of proof, so that the presumptive freeman becomes presumptively a slave, and must himself establish the freedom he would possess; but the law magnifies it into a species of proof that is "conclusive,"— that is, unquestionable, irrefragable, omnipotent, — like a miracle of God, not to be disputed. And this greatest of legal force is given to the worst kind of evidence. I say that a law so worthy of abhorrence, so truculent, so fiendish, is not to be found upon the statute book of any other civilized nation on the globe.

Such, too, has been the practical construction given to the law. I see by the papers that, in a late case which occurred at Detroit, the respondent declared himself a free man, and prayed for a continuance, to allow him to send to Cincinnati for his free papers. But the commissioner refused the delay, saying that, under this law, even free papers from the very man that claimed him would be of no avail; for where the law made the evidence *conclusive*, nothing could rebut it. Any counter evidence must always be admitted, on the hypothesis that the evidence already received may be controlled by it. But what an infinite absurdity to suppose that one mass or body of proof can be *conclusive*, over another which is *conclusive*. The law might just as well have made *color* conclusive, not only that the respondent was a slave, but that he ran away from the man who claims him. The law, as it stands, is as much a slave-making as it is a slave-catching law.

It declares that the proceedings shall be "summary;" and it provides a different rate of compensation, according as the decision is for freedom or against it. On what principle is this difference of compensation founded? Every body can see at a glance that when a claimant can prepare his evidence beforehand and in secret, he would be a fool not to make out a *prima facie* case. If the respondent adduces no proof, the case goes by default, and judgment, without delay, is entered against him. But if the claim is contested, then witnesses are to be examined, arguments are to be heard, evidence is to be weighed, legal questions to be investigated, and such a decision made as the commissioner is willing to pronounce before the world. It is only in the last class of cases, the contested class, that the respondent will be discharged. The cases, therefore, that result in freedom will ordinarily occupy sixfold or tenfold more time, besides requiring the exercise of more legal knowledge and ability, than those which terminate fatally to the respondent. Yet for decreeing the freedom of a man, the fee is but half as much as when a sentence of bondage is awarded against him. This surpasses the bribery of Judas by the high priests. They had not diabolical wit enough to present a contrast between right and wrong, as a special stimulus for committing iniquity.

The "summary manner" of trial provided for by this law, when considered in reference to rights so momentous, shocks every Anglo-Saxon mind. One's blood must all be corrupted in his veins, before he can hear of it without indignation. It is the noblest attribute of our race, that we hold civil and religious liberty to be more sacred and more precious than life itself. Yet by what safeguards of constitution, of law, and of forms of practice, is life protected amongst us? There must be a presentment, by at least twelve sworn men, before a man can be held to answer to a charge by which it can be forfeited. Then come the traverse jury, the right of peremptory challenge, the assignment of counsel, the right to see the indictment beforehand, and to know the names of witnesses who are to be called against the accused, and compulsory process to insure the attendance of witnesses in his favor! What noble barriers are these against the oppression of a powerful government, and the malignant passions of powerful men! The probable culprit, — the man laboring under the most violent suspicion, — though caught with the blood-red dagger in his hand over the prostrate body of the victim, is guarded by all that human ingenuity has been able to devise; by all the knowledge that we can command this side of the omniscience, and by all the power this side of the omnipotence of God. Yet in the very community where these rights are reverenced and upheld, a man may be seized without notice, hurried to a tribunal without an hour for preparation, and then be borne away a thousand miles, where all that life has of hope and of enjoyment is taken away, and all that it knows of misery and of terror is realized.

Let me ask any man who ever had a case in court that was worth defending, whether he was prepared to meet it the first hour he had notice of its existence? A respondent's witnesses may be resident in different states, and distances of hundreds of miles may intervene between him and them. His proof may consist of deeds, or wills, or records, which cannot be found or authenticated without delay. His defence may consist of matters of law, which the ablest counsel may require time and the examination of books to investigate. All these obstacles to instantaneous readiness may exist together, and yet the inexorable mandate of the law scorns his appeal for that delay on which his highest interests are suspended, and dooms him to bondage because he cannot achieve impossibilities. Under such a law, not one man in ten who will be arrested, even though he should be free, will be prepared to establish his freedom. A great portion of these outcasts from human justice, I doubt not, are better prepared for the summons of instantaneous death than for this summons of instantaneous trial.

Then the cruel haste in executing judgment! The murderer is allowed a season of respite between the hour of sentence and the hour of death; the debtor may turn out goods to satisfy a creditor's demands; but the alleged fugitive has no reprieve. He has no opportunity to solicit money to redeem himself, or to negotiate for the ransom of body and soul. Swift and sure as an arrow to its mark, he is speeded on his way to the abodes of toil and despair. The witnesses who swore away his liberty may have been perjured, but he cannot stop to convict them. The court may have been corrupt, but he cannot remain to impeach it. However honestly rendered, the judgment may be reversible for error in law, but he cannot stay to set it aside.

Now, every one must see that where there is so little caution before trial, there should be a liberal opportunity for revision after it. But here is infinite exposure to error with no chance for rectification. Overstepping the acts of the common tyrant, there is an infliction of the most heinous wrong, with a premeditated purpose that it shall not be repaired. The great and free republic of North America has transferred the unwritten law of Judge Lynch to its statute book.

However clear the constitutional obligation of Congress to enact a law for the reclamation of fugitive slaves may be supposed by any one to be, there certainly are limitations to this obligation, which all the principles of our government forbid the law-maker to transcend.

In the first place, this constitutional obligation must be strictly construed. The main and primary object of the constitution was to protect natural rights; but the object of the Fugitive Slave clause was to protect a legal right in conflict with natural right. All judges of an honorable name, all courts in all civilized communities, have recognized a broad distinction in the principles of interpreting law. They have held that provisions against life and liberty should be strictly construed, while those in favor of life and liberty should be liberally construed, — the one so construed as to inflict as little of pain and privation as possible; the other, to give as much of freedom and immunity as possible. These have become maxims, or axioms, of legal interpretation; and in their long and unbroken recognition, it is not too strong an expression to say, they impetrate and command a strict construction of that clause in the constitution under which fugitives may be claimed. And the same legal maxims, in regard to all subjects touching life and liberty, bind Congress in legislating under the constitution, as bind the judicial tribunals in administering the law.

Yet the Fugitive Slave law contains provisions which there can be no pretence nor shadow of a pretence that the constitution requires. By the constitution, "No person held to service or labor in one state, escaping into *another*, shall be discharged." Into *another* what? Indisputably, into another *state*. It must mean *state*, and can mean nothing else; for the laws of language admit no other construction. The expression, "No person held in one *state*, escaping into *another* TERRITORY," would be not merely un-grammatical and un-English, but nonsensical. No man of common intelligence ever so construed a sentence. Yet the sixth section of the act provides not only for the case of slaves escaping from one state into another state, but for their escape from a state into a *territory*, and for an escape from a *territory* into a state, and for an escape from one *territory* into another *territory*. Four classes of cases are provided for by the law, while but one of them finds any warrant in the constitution.

Now let any one take a map of the United States, and see over what a vast area the law extends, over which the provision in the constitution does not extend. The region is continental over which the law unconstitutionally extends, and this corresponds with the vast inhumanity of the principle which so extends it.

Mark another particular in which the provisions of the law go beyond the requirements of the constitution. The constitution says the fugitive shall be "delivered up." The law makes provision for transporting him to the claimant's home. Is there any similar provision respecting any other species of property? If a northern merchant recovers a debt from his southern customer, does the government assume the responsibility of seeing that it is paid to the creditor at his own home? If a northern man is robbed, and the stolen goods are found in another state, does the government transport them back and pay freight? Then, why should government interpose in this case to bear costs and risks, unless slavery is so meritorious an institution as to deserve the benefactions as well as the benedictions of freemen?

Then observe how artfully the law is worded, to make the assistance rendered to the claimant go beyond any supposed necessity in the case. "If," it says, "upon affidavit made by the claimant, ...

his agent or attorney, ... that he has reason to apprehend that such fugitive will be rescued by force, ... before he can take him *beyond the limits of the state in which the arrest is made*, it shall be the duty of the officer . . . . . to remove him *to the state whence he fled*." Thus, if danger is apprehended, *within the first ten miles*, the government shall see the slave safely home, at its own expense, *though it be a thousand miles*.

But besides the unheard-of principle of saddling the government with the expense of prosecuting the private claims of its citizens within its own jurisdiction, I should like to know what provision the constitution contains, which, though interpreted by the most latitudinarian constructionist, confers any right upon Congress thus to take the money of one citizen to pay the private expenses of another. There is no clause, or phrase, or word in that instrument which favors the idea that the Northern States should bear the expense, as well as the disgrace, of thus remanding our fellow-men into bondage.

Besides, if the limits of the constitution were to be transcended in order to deliver an alleged fugitive to his master, would not the slightest element of equity, or decency, even, require that when a freeman is condemned to bondage under the law, his expenses, incurred in returning to the place where he was plundered of himself, should be reimbursed to him by the government which had failed in its duty to protect him? If the claimant of James Hamlet could be supplied with a force, at the government's expense, to carry him into slavery, why should not the expense of coming back into a land of freedom be reimbursed by the government to Adam Gibson, after one of its venal and villanous instruments had wrested that freedom from him?

The law also provides for another thing which the

supreme court has expressly declared to be unconstitutional, or beyond the power of Congress to enact. It provides that any *state* court of record, or judge thereof, in vacation, may take and certify evidence which shall be "conclusive" in regard to two of the three points which are made sufficient by the law to prove a man a slave. Thus, the two facts of slavery and of escape may be "conclusively" proved by the certificate of a judge of a *state* court, so that the judge before whom the alleged fugitive is brought shall, in regard to these facts, exercise only a mere ministerial function. Now, he who has power to take and authenticate evidence, which it is predetermined shall be "conclusive" in the case, has power to decide the case. This, in its nature and essence, is a judicial power; yet this power is given by the act to any *state* court of record, and to any judge thereof in vacation. Contrary to this, however, the supreme court has said, "Congress cannot vest any portion of the judicial power of the United States except in courts ordained and established by itself." — *Martin* vs. *Hunter's Lessee*, 1 Wheat. 330. "The whole judicial power of the United States should be, at all times, vested in some courts created under its authority." — *Ib.* 331. "The jurisdiction over such cases, [cases arising under the constitution, laws, and treaties of the United States,] could not exist in the state courts previous to the adoption of the constitution, and it could not afterwards be directly conferred on them; for the constitution expressly requires the judicial power to be vested in courts ordained and established by the United States." — *Ib.* 335.

Yet, though it is expressly declared that Congress cannot vest any part of the judicial power of the United States in a state court, the state courts are empowered by this law to take and certify evidence, which is made "conclusive" in the case.

Look at the subject in another of its aspects. Here are some half million of free colored persons in the free states. *They* are unquestionably free. They possess, as fully as you or I, those prerogatives of freedom without which life ceases to be a blessing. Their freedom is guarantied to them by the constitution of the United States, and by the constitutions and laws of the states respectively in which they dwell. They certainly are a part of the people. In some of the states, as in Massachusetts for instance, the law knows no iota of distinction, in any respect, between a black man and a white man ; between one of European and one of African descent. It is the noble privilege of a Massachusetts man to say, that, as all men are equal before the divine law, so are all men equal within our borders, before the human law.

Now, scattered among this half million, more or less, of free colored people in the free states, there are a few hundreds, or a few thousands if you please, of "fugitives from service or labor," as the constitution cunningly and evasively phrases it ; which, being interpreted, means, as the whole world knows, fugitives from toil, and fetters, and stripes, and agony ; fugitives from ignorance and the thick darkness of the intellect ; fugitives from moral debasement, and from that enforced pollution of body and soul that spares neither wife, nor mother, nor a daughter's innocence ; fugitives from the disruption of family ties, and from the laceration of all human affections ; fugitives, in fine, from a heathenism of superstition and religious blindness into the glorious light of the gospel of Jesus Christ.

Now this free class and this fugitive class belong ethnologically to the same race. They speak the same language, and wear the same distinctive characteristics of feature and of form. All the unspeakable privileges, all the sacred titles and immunities of the one class are enshrined in the same complexion and in the same contour of person that attend the debasement and privation of the other. The vessels of honor and of glory are moulded into the same shape with the vessels of dishonor and of shame.

Now, after this debased class has been created by a wicked system of human laws, and after it is mingled with the free class, another law steps in and decrees that the former shall be remanded to their bondage. An awful decree! second in terribleness only to that which shall divide between the blessed and the accursed before the judgment-seat of God. Within the compass of human action, there never was an occasion that demanded more unerring justice and wisdom, that invoked more foresight and solicitude, that appealed more touchingly to every sentiment and instinct congenial to liberty, with which God has endowed and ennobled the soul of man, so to devise the law, if law there must be, as not to involve the free in the horrible doom of the enslaved. If, in the administration of penal laws, a knowledge of human fallibility has forced the maxim into existence and into practice, that it is better that ninety-nine guilty persons should escape than that one innocent man should suffer, ought not the same benign rule to be adopted in our legislation whenever there is a possibility of exposing the free to the fearful fate of the enslaved? But instead of this jealousy and circumspection, what have we? A law whose first utterance abjures the distinction between freedom and bondage; a law which brings the whole free colored population of the United States within the outer circles of the whirlpool of slavery, that they may be ingulfed in its vortex; a law which empowers every villain in the country, by fabricating false testimony at his own leisure and convenience, to use his own freedom in order to rob other people of theirs! I aver, that before any moral tribunal, where right and wrong are weighed in the balances of the sanctuary, there is not a felony described in the whole statute book that is more felonious than such a law.

It has become an axiom in the administration of justice, — an axiom slowly evolved by the wisdom of ages, but now firmly established and incorporated into the jurisprudence of every civilized community, — that the ethical policy of the law will tolerate no rule of action that opens the door to fraud or crime, but will even vacate solemn contracts between parties otherwise competent, in its jealousy and apprehension of wrong. Hence the law applicable to common carriers, which will not allow a man to exonerate himself from liability even by express notice, lest opportunity should be given for collusion and fraud. Hence, too, the principle of law which forbids an insolvent debtor to pay, or even to contract to pay, a *bona fide* creditor in anticipation of bankruptcy. Now, this principle applies with tenfold force to legislators, — withholding and repelling them from passing any law which may involve the innocent in the fate of the guilty, or the free in the bondage of the enslaved.

But the law violates a still deeper principle than these. I do not recollect the instance of a single northern man or northern press, utterly false to freedom, and venal as so many of them have been, that has expressed entire satisfaction with the law. They palliate it, they strive, by seductive party and pecuniary appeals, to beguile men into its support. They look outside of it for pretexts to hide its inherent baseness; but not one of them, so far as I know, has had the effrontery to justify it on its intrinsic merits. Even those northern men who voted for it have sought refuge from the storm of righteous indignation that burst upon them, by alleging that it was an essential ingredient in a system of measures, and entered, as a necessary element, into a desirable compromise.

When this language is translated, what does it mean? Simply this, and no more. California was admitted, and thereby certain political and commercial advantages were gained. This, in legal language, was the consideration. The Fugitive Slave law was passed, and thereby the rights of freemen, the property of men in themselves, all the household sanctities, all the domestic endearments of half a million of men, were put in peril. This was the equivalent given! A mere barter of the holiest interests for wordly advantages! And these interests were given away by men who did not own them, and therefore had no right to transfer them. The whites, north and south, played a game, and made the black people their stakes. Who authorized the law-makers to derive a benefit to themselves from doing this infinite wrong to others? Who gave them the terrible prerogative of making others suffer for their pleasure. I say it with reverence, but I still say it with emphasis, that we cannot conceive of God himself as having power to inflict vicarious suffering without the free consent of the sufferer! Yet the atrocities of this law are defended by those who made it, on the ground that they and other white men have secured benefits to themselves by sacrificing the liberty, happiness and peace of half a million of their fellow-beings of a different color. Cause and counsellor are alike; for the defence is as profligate as the act it defends.

I say, sir, it is the population of African descent in the free states which is specially put in peril by this law. Occasionally, indeed, persons of unmixed white blood are seized and enslaved under it. These cases, however, are comparatively rare. But suppose the reverse. Suppose circumstances to be such that the whole body of the white population should be as much endangered by it as the colored people now are. Suppose that not only the white voters themselves, but their wives and their children, were as liable to be "*Ingrahamed*," as the blacks; suppose this, I say, and would the existence of the law be tolerated for an hour? Would there not be an uprising of the people, simultaneous and universal against it, and such a yell of execration as never before burst from mortal lips? The name of every man who had voted for it, or who should defend it, would be entered upon that apostate list at whose head stands the name of Judas. Christian and Infidel, Jew and Gentile, would execrate it alike. Why, then, if they would do this to avert such peril from themselves and their families, do they not do it when their sable brethren are in jeopardy? Alas! there is but one answer! From selfish considerations, from the love of wealth, or the love of power, they have discarded that heaven-descended maxim, "Whatever ye would that men should do unto you, do ye the same unto them."

And it is this very class of men who have thus abjured the precepts of Jesus Christ, who have trampled upon the divine doctrines of liberty and love, that now so clamorously summon us to an obedience to law.

In answer to this call, let me say, that true obedience to law is necessarily accompanied and preceded by a reverence for those great principles of justice and humanity without which all law is despotism. How can a man pretend to any honest regard for the principle of obedience to law when he is willing, as in the case of this fugitive act, to transcend our constitutional law, and to invade the divine law? It is but an appeal to the lower rule of action to justify a violation of the higher. Under the pretext of rendering unto Cæsar the things that are Cæsar's it denies to God the things that are God's.

And again, a true reverence for law is a general principle, and not an isolated fact. It applies to all laws collectively, and not to any one law in particular. It bestows its greatest homage upon those laws that embrace and confer the most of human welfare; for, were all the laws of a community, or the great majority of them, unrighteous, then disloyalty to law would be the virtue. Can the class of men who demand our allegiance to the Fugitive Slave law stand this test? We have usury laws, which not only carry the legal force of statutes, but the moral power of the greatest names in legislation and in statesmanship. Are the men in New York, in Philadelphia, and Boston, who are most vehement in support of the Fugitive Slave law, signalized for their regard to the statutes against usury?

Is not money lent in all those cities on the same principle that wreckers send a rope's end to a drowning man, — for as much as they can extort? It is notorious that among the great body of merchants and capitalists in those cities, interest is regulated by the pressure upon the money market, and that no more idea of law mingles with their contracts than in California, where there is no law on the subject.

We have laws restricting the sale of intoxicating liquors, and designed to promote the glorious object of temperance. For which practice have our cities been conspicuous, — for their obedience to these laws or for their violation of them? A few years ago, when a question of the constitutionality of a law of Massachusetts for the restraint of intemperance arose, did not its two distinguished senators appear in the supreme court of the United States, and make the most strenuous exertions to annul the law of their own state, and to open anew the flood-gates for overwhelming their own constituents in misery and ruin, — the selfsame gentlemen who are now so intolerant even of discussion?

Look at the complaints which come to us every day

from the friends of a protective tariff. They tell us that our revenue laws are fraudulently and systematically evaded; and they number the violations of these laws by thousands and tens of thousands. Who are the violators? Not men living in the country; not the farmers and mechanics and laborers, — the substratum of our strength and the origin of our power; — but they are the city merchants, the getters-up of "Union meetings," and the members of "safety and vigilance committees," who are so earnest in inculcating those lessons of obedience by their precepts, which they have done so little to recommend by their example.

The Southern States are loud in their calls upon us to execute the Fugitive Slave law. But what examples have they set us on the subject of obedience to law? I think I may be pardoned for mentioning a few cases, to show how their preaching and practice tally.

In 1831, the legislature of Georgia offered a bribe of *five thousand dollars* to any one who would arrest, and bring to trial and conviction, in Georgia, a citizen of Massachusetts, named William Lloyd Garrison. This law was "approved" by William Lumpkin, governor, on the 26th December, 1831. Mr. Garrison had never stepped foot within the limits of Georgia, and therefore it was not a reward for his trial and conviction, but for his abduction and murder.

At a meeting of slaveholders, held at Sterling, in the same state, September 4, 1835, it was formally recommended to the governor, to offer, by proclamation, the five thousand dollars appropriated by the act of 1831, for the apprehension of either of ten persons, citizens, with one exception, of New York, or Massachusetts, whose names were given; not one of whom, it was not even pretended, had ever been within the limits of Georgia.

The Milledgeville, Georgia, "Federal Union," of

February 1, 1836, contained an offer of $10,000 for kidnapping A. A. Phelps, a clergyman of the city of New York.

The committee of vigilance, (another "committee of vigilance,") of the parish of East Feliciana, offered, in the Louisville Journal, of October 15, 1835, $50,000 to any person who would deliver into their hands Arthur Tappan, a merchant of New York.

At a public meeting of the citizens of Mount Meigs, Alabama, August 13, 1836, the *honorable* Bedford Ginress in the chair, a reward of $50,000 was offered for the apprehension of the same Arthur Tappan, or of Le Roy Sunderland, a Methodist clergyman of New York.

Repeated instances have occurred in which the governors of slave states, — Virginia, Georgia, Kentucky, Alabama, &c., — have made requisitions upon the governors of free states, under the second section of the fourth article of the constitution, for the surrender of free citizens, *as fugitives from justice*, when it was well known that the citizens so demanded were not within the limits of the slave states at the time when the alleged offence was committed, and, in some instances, had never been there in their lives, — high executive perversions of the constitution of the United States, by chief magistrates who had sworn to support it!

For nearly twenty years past the post-office laws of the United States have been systematically violated in slave states, the mail bags rifled, and their contents seized and publicly burned; and, in some instances, these violations have been enjoined, under heavy penalties, by a law of the states. There are several of the slave states on whose statute books these laws, commanding a violation of the post-office, stand to-day.

During Mr. Adams's administration, a man by the name of Tassels, in Georgia, was adjudged to be hanged, under a law of the state, as clearly unconstitutional as was ever passed. A writ of error was sued out from the supreme court of the United States, in order to bring the case before that tribunal for revision. But the state of Georgia anticipated the service of the writ, and made sure of its victim by hanging him extemporaneously.

Within a few weeks past,—the accounts having but just now reached us, — an aged and most respectable individual of the name of Harris, a citizen of New Hampshire, has been tried by a mob in South Carolina, and tarred and feathered, because he happened to have *in his trunk* a sermon which had been sent to him by one of his acquaintances, a clergyman at the north; though he had never showed the sermon to a single individual, nor whispered a word of its contents. Another man, a Dr. Coles, belonging to Boston, who had been lecturing on the subject of physiology, was, within a few days, seized and carried before a magistrate, in the same state, his trunks rifled, the private letters sent to him by his wife and family publicly read, with the most indecent comments, and all without any shadow of reasonable suspicion against him.

The unconstitutional imprisonment of northern seamen in southern ports is an occurrence so frequent, and so universally known, that I need not spend time to enumerate or to describe the cases.

The President of the United States has made proclamation, and proffered the military and naval force of the United States, to aid any southern slave owner in reducing his fugitive slave to a new bondage; but I have not heard that he has made any similar proclamation, or manifested any anxiety for the support of that part of the constitution which says that "the citizens of each state shall be entitled to all the privileges and immunities of citizens in the several states."

Now, with a few exceptions, it is these very classes

of men who violate the laws against extortion and usury; who break down the barriers against the desolations of intemperance; who, almost alone of all our citizens, are implicated in the breach of the revenue laws; who annul the post-office laws of the United States; who offer rewards for free northern citizens, that they may get them in their clutch to lynch and murder them; who demand free citizens as fugitives from justice, in states where they have never been, and who imprison free citizens and sell them into slavery; — it is these classes of men who are now so suddenly smitten with a new sense of the sacredness of law, and of the duty of obedience to law, — not of the laws of God, not even of the laws of man, in general, but of this most abominable of all enactments, the Fugitive Slave law in particular.

I do not cite the above cases from among a thousand similar ones, as any justification or apology for forcible and organized resistance to law by those who even constructively can be said to have given it their consent. But the words of a preacher do not "come mended from his tongue," when his name is a scandal among men for his violation of all the precepts he enjoins.

And now, sir, when I am called upon to support such a law as this, or to desist from opposing it in all constitutional ways, while it lasts, my response is, repeal the law, that I may no longer be called upon to support it. In the name of my constituents, and by the memory of that "old man eloquent," in whose place it is my fortune to stand, I demand its repeal. I demand it, —

Because it is a law which wars against the fundamental principles of human liberty.

Because it is a law which conflicts with the constitution of the country, and with all the judicial interpretations of that constitution, wherever they have been applied to the white race.

Because it is a law which introduces a fatal principle into the code of evidence, and into judicial practice, — a principle, before which no man's liberties and no man's rights of any kind can stand.

Because it is a law which is abhorrent to the moral and religious sentiments of a vast majority of the community that is called upon to enforce it.

Because the life and character of so many of its apologists and supporters are themselves potent arguments against whatever they may advocate.

Because it is a law which, if executed in the free states, divests them of the character of free states, and makes them voluntary participators in the guilt of slaveholding.

Because it is a law which disgraces our country in the eyes of the whole civilized world, and gives plausible occasion to the votaries of despotic power to decry republican institutions.

Because it is a law which forbids us to do unto others as we would have them do to us, and which makes it a crime to feed the hungry, to clothe the naked, and to visit and succor the sick and the imprisoned.

Because it is a law which renders the precepts of the gospel and the teachings of Jesus Christ seditious; and, were the Savior and his band of disciples now upon earth, there is but one of them who would escape its penalties by pretending "to conquer his prejudices." And, finally,

Because the advocates and defenders of this law have been compelled to place its defence upon the express ground that the commandments of men are of higher authority than the ordinances of God.

In Hooker's sublime description of law, when understood in its generic sense, he says, —

"Of law there can be no less acknowledged than that her seat is the bosom of God, her voice the harmony of the world; all things in heaven and earth do her homage, the very least as feeling her care, and the greatest as not exempted from her power; both angels, and men, and creatures, of what condition soever, though each in different sort and manner, yet all with uniform consent, admiring her as the mother of their peace and joy."

Now, sir, with these glorious attributes of "law," I say the Fugitive Slave law of the last session possesses not one quality in common, nor in similitude. To say that the seat of such a law is in the "bosom of God," is the intensest blasphemy. To say that it is "the harmony of the world," is to declare that the world is a sphere of ubiquitous and omnipotent wrong, unchecked by any thought of justice, and devoid of any emotion of love. To say that "all things in heaven do homage" to such a law, is to affirm of the realms of light what is true only of the realms of darkness. The "least" do not "feel its care," but tremble and wail beneath its cruelty; while the "greatest" and the strongest *are* "exempt from its power;" for they made it not for themselves but for others. To no class of "creatures," rational or irrational, human or divine, can it prove to be the "mother of peace and joy;" but wherever it extends, and as long as it exists, it will continue to be an overflowing Marah of bitterness and strife.

As the great name of Hooker has been profanely cited in behalf of this law, I will close by quoting his distinction between those laws of human governments which ought to be obeyed, and those which ought not: —

—— "which laws," says he, "we must obey, *unless there be reason showed which may necessarily enforce that* THE LAW OF REASON OR OF GOD DOTH ENJOIN THE CONTRARY."

SPEECH

ON THE FUGITIVE SLAVE LAW, DELIVERED AT LANCASTER, MASSACHUSETTS, MAY 19, 1851, PENDING THE CANVASS FOR A MEMBER OF CONGRESS FOR THE FOURTH CONGRESSIONAL DISTRICT.

FELLOW-CITIZENS;

We are assembled on a great occasion and for a great purpose. The election of a member of Congress, indeed, is not an extraordinary event; but it is extraordinary that principles of the most vital importance to the honor of Massachusetts, and to the cause of human liberty throughout the world, should be involved in a local election. Such, however, is now the fact.

Gentlemen, the assertion and the recognition of the rights of man have made great progress among the nations of Europe within the recollection of many who are now before me. Notwithstanding the partition of Poland by allied robbers, and the obliteration of that kingdom from the map of Europe; notwithstanding Hungarian subjugation to Austrian despotism, and many other atrocious crimes against humanity, such as nations only can commit; for they are too vast and monstrous to be perpetrated by any individual, — I say, notwithstanding these facts, the great fabric of human liberty has been rising in Europe, while the solid structures of despotism have been disintegrating and making ready for their fall.

But truth compels me to acknowledge that, during the last three quarters of a century, our course, in this country, has been downward. While among the other nations of Christendom the altar-fires of liberty have been kindling and burning with a brighter flame, ours have been waning. At the foundation of our government an institution existed amongst us utterly irreconcilable with the fundamental principles of the government itself. But it was then limited in its extent, and its spirit nowhere existed in great intensity. Even those who cherished it most were ashamed of it; and in those provisions of the constitution which were designed for its temporary protection, a common regard for decency forbade the mention of its name. Fatally to our own peace and honor, that which was then regarded as temporary and local, now threatens to be abiding and universal. From speaking of slavery with hushed breath, its bold abettors now shout forth its praises. From providing for the extermination of the African slave trade, they have converted the slave states into another Africa, this side the tropics; and by the successful robbery of a neighboring republic, they seek to create a new America, so that the slave trade, once abolished and declared piracy, may be revived and legalized. The Middle Passage is to be transferred from the ocean to the land. Maryland, Virginia, Kentucky, &c., are to be the Gold Coast, Benin, and the Galinas; the place of supply, the place of demand, and the highways of commerce between them are to be within our own borders and protected by the American flag; and that horrid traffic which all the leading nations of Christendom united in declaring to be a felony punishable with death, is now to be maintained and defended amongst ourselves, under penalty of death and a dissolution of the Union.

Nor does it suffice that the tide of slavery should rise and overflow the vast and uninhabited regions of the west. It surges up against the free states themselves, and all the dikes and barriers of that constitutional law which we have been enacting for seventy-five years, cannot stay its flood. We thought that Massachusetts was the impregnable citadel of freedom; but unconstitutional and inhuman laws, dictated by slaveholders, are now enforced amongst us, and at our very doors; and our services are commanded for their execution.

Thank God, there is a part of our people who, while they suffer, resist. Only a portion amongst us have reached that lowest depth of degradation, where they surrender, not their limbs only, but their wills, to the hateful service of their masters. Slavery has done its perfect work only when the soul is enslaved. I rejoice to believe that we have not only seven thousand in this our Massachusetts Israel, who have not bowed the knee to Baal, but seven hundred thousand; and recent events foretell not only an increasing number, but a more determined opposition.

Why is it, fellow-citizens, that Massachusetts stands first, or among the first, in 1851, in her hostility to the Fugitive Slave law? I answer, for the very reason that she stood first in her hostility to the encroachments of the British crown in 1776. And in less than seventy-five years from this time, those who oppose and those who defend this inhuman law, will stand, historically, as wide asunder, and will share as high an honor or suffer as deep an ignominy, as is now awarded to the lovers of freedom and the minions of power who lived at the era of the revolution. Let all young men beware not to be seduced by any temptations of immediate profit or mistaken honor, to lift a hand in defence of this law. If they do, then, before they have lived out half their lives, they will be as ready as old Cranmer to thrust the offending member into the flames, and to say with him, " This hand, this wicked hand, has offended."

Gentlemen, we in Massachusetts are a Union-loving, and law-abiding people. Mr. Webster and his " retainers" may spare their breath in exhorting us to abide by the Union. Such a work, in this commonwealth, is a work of supererogation. He knows, and they know, that the number of disunionists in this state can be counted on a man's fingers and toes. Whatever influence they exert must flow from their zeal, their talents, and their private character; for they derive none from numerical force. Were they all to settle in one of our small towns, they would be out-voted by its inhabitants. I regard these ever-repeated appeals made to Massachusetts men and to New England men to stand by the Union, as not merely obtrusive, but as affrontive and insulting. Besides, when a man undertakes the mission of going round the country, preaching honesty, or temperance, or chastity, he provokes the inquiry whether he is more honest, temperate, or continent than those whom he exhorts. If the union of these states now is, or has ever been verging towards a point of danger, it is solely and only because ambitious men and mercenary men at the north have given it that direction by recognizing southern threats and bravadoes as realities, and thus encouraging them. Let the greatest coward see that his threats are acknowledged as verities, and he will adopt the cheap mode of threatening instead of the hazardous one of acting. Could the Chinese have frightened away the British fleet by their battery of wooden cannon, having the middle of the ends painted black for a muzzle, they would have been fools to incur the expense of brass or iron. But John Bull did not care whether the cannon were of wood or of metal, and at his first fire the Celestials scampered. But here, when a few men in a few states pointed their wooden guns at us, Mr. Webster, General Cass, and others, for their own ambitious purposes, cried out that the Union was in danger. I say, then, if the union of these states ever has been in any proximity to danger, it was not from menaces uttered by the south, but from northern indorsement of them. If northern leaders had dishonored instead of indorsing this spurious paper, it never would have got into circulation.

We are not only Union-loving men, but, as I said before, we are law-abiding men. Had this not been so, not all the fleets and armies in the world could have carried Thomas Sims into bondage. So intimately blended is the reverence for law with the very soul of our people, that if you could convince them that a statute has legal force and is binding upon the conscience, I verily believe our juries would give a verdict in favor of Shylock, though the pound of flesh which he claimed were to be carved from their own bosoms. This side of a just cause for revolution, they will yield submission to all laws enacted by the government, with one single exception. The exception I mean, embraces those laws of men which are clearly contrary to the law of God. And I trust the time is not now, and never will be, when the children of the Puritans will obey any commandment of human origin if it conflicts with a divine command, though they have to lie down in lions' dens or walk through furnace fires, as the penalty of disobedience.

But with this sentiment of reverence for law is another sentiment, which is its proper attendant and brother, — I mean a desire and a determination to know what that is which is called *law;* what it is that claims this prerogative of controlling the will and challenging the conscience. It is in this spirit that they have discussed and mean to discuss the Fugitive Slave law, and to bring it, Protestant fashion, to the test of individual judgment and conscience.

I have no need to repeat to you the general provisions of this inhuman enactment. No lover of liberty can read them without having their atrocious character burned into his mind ineffaceably. You know that it assumes to dispose of the highest interests of human liberty, — the liberty of soul as well as the liberty of person; — and you know that it also assumes to dispose of the most precious interests of property, — the property that a man has in himself and in all his capacities of physical enjoyment and suffering as well as his property in his money or his goods; — without a single one of those safeguards and protections which the constitution of the country builds up like a rampart of defence around us all. This enactment, too, is no theoretic affair; it is no dead letter on the statute book. It is a living monster, uncaged and turned loose amongst us, to rob and devour at its will.

Now, I have two objections to this law, which absolve me from all obligations to execute it, or, in any way or manner, to assist in executing it. First, I believe it to be contrary to the law of God, which, God helping me, shall be the rule of my conduct, though I should scatter political treasons as the autumn wind scatters leaves. In his dread description of the judgment day, Jesus Christ makes the distinction between saints and sinners to turn upon the fact, whether they have fed the hungry, clothed the naked, and visited those who were sick and in prison. And who so hungry as those who do not own, and cannot own a morsel of bread? Who so naked as those who do not own, and cannot own a shred of a garment to protect them from cold, or from the lascivious eye? And what confinement was ever so hopeless as southern slavery, what prison was ever so deep as that prison-house which holds three millions of our fellow-beings within its melancholy walls,— them and their posterity forever? He that refuses the common acts of hospitality to these victims, when fleeing from their bondage, denies his Lord and Master. He that refuses them, disobeys every precept of the Savior, and has no more right to call himself a Christian, than has the Fejee islander, when he rises from his cannibal banquet. He is the Levite who passes by on the other side.

And next, I hold this law to be contrary to the constitution of the United States, and therefore of no binding force upon my conscience or my conduct. I do not mean to say by this that I shall make forcible opposition to it. I take the Quaker ground upon this subject; I will not assist to execute it, though I shall suffer it to execute itself on me.

The constitutionality of this law has been extensively discussed. But there is this broad difference between the arguments of those who affirm and those who deny that it is constitutional. Those who deny it, argue the question upon its merits, upon principle, upon those legal relations and analogies that so nobly characterize the English law on the subject of human liberty. But those who affirm the constitutionality of the law, base their argument upon technicalities and upon precedents, and they cannot sustain themselves for a moment on any other ground. They found themselves, in the first place, upon the statutory precedent of 1793, which was an act passed with very little deliberation, as its history shows, and passed, too, when it was expected on all hands that slavery would soon die out. In the next place, they rely upon the judicial precedent of Prigg's case, which was made by a bench of slaveholding judges, and some of the points which the court professed to decide did not arise in the case.

Now the statutory precedent covers only a part of the case; for some of the most hateful features of the law of 1850 are not to be found in the law of 1793; and the supreme court has never passed upon the law of 1850 at all. So two points are clear in the outset, that the champions of the law cannot get along without the precedents, and the precedents, in several most important particulars, fail them altogether.*

This question has lately been discussed in our own vicinity. The liberty of a resident of Massachusetts, — a man every way entitled to a jury trial by our constitution and laws, as much as you or I, — has been sacrificed by a United States commissioner in the city of Boston.† He has decided in favor of the law. You would naturally suppose that, in order to shelter himself from the odium of such a decision, he would put all personal and all collateral resources into requisition to make the case as plausible as ingenuity can make it. It is said, too, that Mr. Webster and Mr. Webster's friends, and the commissioner's friends have contributed of their strength to help the debility of the case. While the cause was pending before him, one of the points involved in it was brought before the supreme court of Massachusetts, and also before the circuit court of the United States. The commissioner adjourned the case over after all the arguments of counsel were in. He thereby gave himself an opportunity for preparation and for consultation. I am

* It is substantially conceded by the supreme court of Massachusetts, in delivering their opinion on the application of Sims for a writ of *habeas corpus*, that the Fugitive Slave law stands upon precedent alone, and is disowned by principle. Chief Justice Shaw says, —

"At the same time it may be proper to say, that if this argument, drawn from the constitution of the United States, were now first applied to the law of 1793, deriving no sanction from contemporaneous construction, judicial precedent, and the acquiescence of the general and state governments, the argument from the limitation of judicial power would be entitled to very grave consideration."

I submit that the precedents, on this subject, both legislative and judicial, are substantially divested of all their force, by the fewness of the cases that have ever arisen under the law, by the general obsoleteness into which it fell, and, more than all, by that uniform indifference and neglect, and I may add inhumanity, with which colored people and the rights of colored people, have been almost universally regarded in the different states of the Union.

† Mr. George T. Curtis.

taking no exception to all this. I am glad it was done. I suppose we now have the breadth and length and strength of what can be alleged in favor of the law. I never feel so confident of my conclusions as when strong men have taken the opposite side, and have failed to sustain it.

Now, to this decision of the commissioner, made under such incitements, and with such opportunities, I propose to invite your attention. The discussion may be dry, but it will not be uninteresting; for it involves matters as important as the liberty of the body and the liberty of the will, and the liberty and life of the human soul.

It may be said that these are legal and constitutional questions, and, therefore, that unprofessional men cannot understand them. But most, if not all the points which I shall bring to your attention, are matters of intuition; questions wholly within the jurisdiction of plain common sense, and such, therefore, as can be decided by you as well as by lawyers or judges. And if I can convince you of the inconclusiveness of some parts of this decision, of the legal Jesuitism of other parts, and of the self-contradiction that pervades the whole, you will not hesitate to set it aside, not as null and void merely, but as discreditable to the profession of the law, and dishonorable to the State of Massachusetts.

The first point which the commissioner discusses is, whether in seizing, by his warrant, a man actually free, in deciding, by his judgment, the exact question, whether that man were a slave, and in sending him, by his certificate, where the lash and the law of slavery apply to his body and his spirit, he were exercising "*judicial power*," as conferred by the constitution of the United States upon such courts as *Congress* should establish. He at first decides that he does *not* exercise such power. This was well; for he knows that he was never appointed, nor commissioned, nor sworn, nor is paid, nor removable from office for mal-conduct, as is prescribed by the constitution in the case of judges. Badly heroic as he was, *in fact*, in exercising jurisdiction over a human being, and delivering him over into hopeless and irremediable bondage, he was not mad enough to arrogate, *in terms*, the prerogative of "*judicial power*."

But what says his superior, the attorney-general of the United States? In an elaborate opinion, given by order of the President of the United States, — an opinion which, as I suppose, passed under the supervision of the whole cabinet, and therefore may be presumed to have the authority of Mr. Webster and the other constitutional advisers of the President, and which certainly had the sanction of the President himself, for he acted upon it, — in this opinion the attorney-general says, —

"These officers, [the commissioners,] and each of them, have *judicial power*, and jurisdiction to hear, examine, and decide the case."

"The certificate to be granted to the owner is to be regarded as the act and *judgment* of a *judicial tribunal*, having competent *jurisdiction*."

"Congress has constituted *a tribunal*, with *exclusive jurisdiction* to determine summarily, and without appeal, who are fugitives from service."

"The *judgment* of the *tribunal*, created by this act, is conclusive upon all *tribunals*."

Now, which is right, the attorney-general, with the President and his cabinet as indorsers, or Mr. Commissioner Curtis? I submit to you that the former were clearly right, so far as this, — that when the constitution declares that "no person shall be deprived of life, liberty, or property, without due process of law," (which imports a trial by jury,) then neither Adam Gibson, nor Thomas Sims, nor any other alleged fugitive can be so deprived, without trial by jury, *and the judgment or sentence of the "judicial power" thereupon.* The following position has never been answered, and I think never can be, namely, that if a resident of Massachusetts can be deprived of his "liberty and property," without a trial by jury and a judgment of a *court,* then he may be deprived of his life also; for "life, liberty, and property" are secured in the same section, in the same sentence, and by the same safeguard.

The attorney-general held that, as the power exercised by the commissioner was a "judicial power," it deprived the party of all benefit from the *habeas corpus.* And there was some plausibility in this, though, I think, no soundness. But our defenders of the law hold that this sending of a man into bondage is not a part of the "judicial power," and yet that it deprives him of all benefit of the *habeas corpus.* That is, they hold that a man may be deprived of his liberty and property, (and of course of his life,) *by a ministerial proceeding*, not having its origin in any court, and not to be prosecuted to final judgment in any court, and yet that all the courts in the land, competent to furnish relief in any other case, can afford none in this. If this be true, if a proceeding, held and acknowledged by the officer who initiates and conducts it to be a ministerial proceeding, not originated by a court, and never to be carried before a court, does thus take away the trial by jury, and the security of having one's liberty and property adjudicated upon by a "court," and renders the writ of *habeas corpus* an empty form, then, indeed, we may bid "farewell, a long farewell" to all our liberties. An unprincipled majority of Congress has only to pass a law that any man may be imprisoned or hanged on an executive warrant, and that the hireling marshal or commissioner shall suffer no "molestation by any process issued by any court, judge, magistrate, or other person whomsoever," and despotic power will be enthroned here as effectually as it ever was in England in the bloody days of the Stuarts. Jeffries was at least a judge, though he acted like a commissioner.

Who could have imagined, eight months ago, that a *ministerial* proceeding could put a citizen beyond remedy or reach of our *courts?*

I now come to a position in the commissioner's argument which is not only transparently fallacious, but is contradicted by himself, in the same opinion, again and again. I shall offer a series of objections to it.

The point was pressed upon him by counsel that he was exercising "judicial power." To maintain this, a passage was quoted from Prigg's case, in which the court say, "A claim made by the owner out of possession for the delivery of a slave . . . . . constitutes, in the strictest sense, a controversy between the parties, and a case arising under the constitution of the United States, within the express delegation of judicial power, given by that instrument." Can any thing be more explicit and conclusive, to prove that the commissioner was then presuming to exercise a part of the "judicial power" conferred by Congress exclusively upon courts? And how does he answer it? In this way, and in this way only. He says the court decide two points:—

First,—That a claim for a fugitive slave is a case arising under the constitution of the United States, and so within the grant of "judicial power" as given by the constitution; and

Second,—"That being such a case, belonging to the judicial power of the Union, it was for Congress to regulate and prescribe the remedy, the form of proceedings, and the mode and extent in which the judicial power of the Union should be called into activity."

He then declares his full admission of *both* these

propositions. And how does he answer the *first* one, which, at a blow, unseats him from his usurped bench? He says, "The counsel for the prisoner have insisted most strenuously on the first of these positions, but have said nothing with regard to the second." And what need had the counsel to say any thing about the second, *the first being admitted?* The supreme court had said, and he acknowledged it, that every case like the one then before him was a "case arising under the constitution of the United States, within the express delegation of judicial power given by that instrument." This was equivalent to saying that it was a case which could not be adjudicated upon by a commissioner, because a commissioner is not a judge, — is no court nor part of a court. The plain statement of the commissioner's language is this: The supreme court declare that I have no jurisdiction in this case; but because the counsel said nothing about another point to be found in the opinion of the court, therefore I will take jurisdiction.

But again; this reply of the commissioner, that the counsel said nothing about the second point, (when he had acknowledged the validity of the first, which was fatal,) is not merely an evasion; it is founded upon a false meaning attributed by him to the second point. He says the court held that it was "for Congress to regulate and prescribe the remedy, the form of proceedings, and the mode and extent in which the judicial power of the Union should be called into activity." Suppose it was for Congress to do this. Might they not transcend their power when doing it? and does not his admission of the first point prove that they have transcended their power? — the very point then in question. The two things cannot stand together. If the trial of the issue, "fugitive slave or not," be, "in the strictest sense," "within the express delegation of judicial power given" by the constitution, then this ministerial commissioner cannot exercise it, and Congress cannot empower him to exercise it. Besides, the decision of the court was made in 1842. The law, whose constitutionality they had then under discussion, was passed in 1850. Did the court in '42 declare, or could they declare, that any law *thereafter* passed by Congress on this subject should be held constitutional? Did their decision act prospectively, and adjudge a law to be constitutional, which was to be passed eight years afterwards? So far from this, the points then under discussion, — namely, the power of a commissioner to adjudge a case more important than life or death, and the obligation of a commissioner to hear *ex parte* evidence, and to be concluded by it when heard, — these questions did not come before the supreme court in '42, and have never been before the supreme court at all. But because that court had said, years before, that it belongs to Congress to prescribe the mode of recovering fugitive slaves, *therefore*, says the commissioner, if Congress should vest this power in commissioners, (and in slave traders or pirates just as well,) it would be valid. And because the counsel did not answer this point, the commissioner decides an admitted point, conclusive in their favor, against them.

But this is not all. After declaring, in the first part of the opinion, his full conviction that the delivery of an alleged fugitive comes within "the express delegation of judicial power," he uses, farther on, the following language: "It would seem," says he, "that it only remains to inquire whether the act of 1850 authorizes or requires any thing more than a summary ministerial proceeding in aid of the right secured by the constitution, namely, the right of removal." And he holds that it does not. The act which, in the first part of the opinion, was acknowledged to belong, "in the strictest sense," to the "judicial power," has now ceased to be "*any thing more* than a summary ministerial proceeding."

And again he says, "I have endeavored, in the foregoing discussion, to show that this is a summary ministerial proceeding," &c. "If this be so, *and I can entertain no doubt that it is*," &c. This sudden transmigration from a judge to an executioner, from one who acknowledged that the delivery of an alleged fugitive is an act of "judicial power," to one who holds that it is NOT "*any thing more* than a summary ministerial proceeding," may suit a disciple of Pythagoras, or the priests of the Hindoo religion, but it ill becomes an expounder of American jurisprudence.

I proceed to another point in the commissioner's decision, namely, the nature and authority of "judicial power;" and when I have discussed it, I shall submit to your good sense whether I do him any injustice in saying that it is most perspicuously fallacious and lucidly absurd.

"In all governments formed upon the English model," says he, "there is a certain class of inquiries, [powers?] judicial in their nature, but which are confided to officers not constituting a part of the judiciary, strictly so called." (I do not like this substitution of the word "inquiries" for "powers." If any thing under heaven should be called a *power*, the prerogative of sending a human being, presumptively free, into bondage, is surely one.) He then instances certain officers in Great Britain, who, though not judges, perform, as he says, certain judicial functions. A brief remark will suffice for this. Great Britain, having no written constitution, the current of its legislative enactments and its judicial decisions makes its constitution. If, then, it has been the prevailing practice of that government to confer any given description of powers upon any given class of officers, then that is what the British constitution allows and approves.

But we have a written constitution, and therefore are not to tolerate a law, (as in the case of this Fugitive Slave law,) which is repugnant to its fundamental provisions. By this constitution, all legislative powers therein granted are vested in Congress; executive power in a President, and judicial power in the courts. The constitution of Massachusetts is equally explicit. It says, "In the government of this commonwealth the legislative department shall never exercise the executive and judicial powers, or either of them; the executive shall never exercise the legislative and judicial powers, or either of them; the judicial shall never exercise the legislative and executive powers, or either of them; to the end it may be a government of laws, and not of men."

In both these constitutions, the three functions of government, namely, to legislate, to adjudicate, and to execute, are expressly recognized; and the *whole* of their distinctive powers are lodged in separate departments. No mention is made of any hybrid or mongrel class, half judicial and half executive, or half ministerial and half judicial, or compounded of aliquot parts of each. Such an officer, under either constitution, would be a monster; he would hold the same relation to their legitimate functionaries that Caliban does to the human race; and, if created for executing the Fugitive Slave law, that half devil and half beast would be the fitting prototype.

The commissioner professes to have found a class of cases, both under our state and national constitutions, where powers, "judicial in their nature, and special in their purpose, may be confided to the determination of officers who are not judges." On this point he has expended himself. Here lay the pressure and travail of his case. Seeing that, in deciding the great issue before him, "slave or free," he was exercising judicial power, and in ordering an armed force to convoy the victim to his house of bondage he was exercising ministerial or executive power, (thus blending the functions which both constitutions have separated,) the commissioner felt that he must find some analogy or some precedent to cover up this obvious violation of all principle, or his argument was in ruins. It is in ruins; for he has found no such precedent, and cannot find any.

The instances he cites from Massachusetts are,— 1. Sheriffs, who may preside over juries when assessing damages for laying out highways, and may decide such questions of law as arise on the trial; 2. Auditors, who may examine vouchers and state accounts between parties, and make report thereof to the court; 3. Commissioners of insolvency, appointed to distribute insolvent estates; and, 4. County commissioners, who lay out highways.

Now, nothing can be clearer than that, in no one of these cases does the officer named exercise "judicial power." Indisputably, universally, and necessarily, by force of the phrase itself, the term "judicial power" embraces the idea of a *power* whose decision can be enforced *in invitum;* that is, against an unwilling, contesting, resisting party. The sublime power of a court becomes nothingness, and is ridiculous, if its decrees cannot be executed to the very death of the party against whom they are made. For this purpose, they are backed by all the civil power of the state; and should this prove insufficient, they are backed by all the military power of the state; and, even beyond this, by the whole military and naval power of the United States. Without this, judges are but puppets, or no better than "men in buckram." "Judicial power" does not consist in a sheriff's presiding over a jury, nor in an auditor's casting up accounts, nor in a commissioner's ciphering out the dividends of an insolvent's estate, nor in county commissioners' laying out roads; but it consists in entering up a judgment which has the armories at Springfield and Harper's Ferry, which has the standing army and militia of the United States, which has fifty line-of-battle ships, which has the treasury of the nation, to back it, and to visit with death one man, a thousand men, or a hundred thousand men, if need be, who shall confront it with resistance.

Look, fellow-citizens, at this wretched sophistry. The sheriff must make return of the verdict of the jury to the court of common pleas, — *which is a* COURT, — and if either party suggests good grounds of dissatisfaction, the whole proceeding is a nullity, and the investigation must be made again; and again and again, and ten times again, until every act and letter of it become unexceptionable. The auditor must make his report to the court that appointed him, and if the court see cause, they set aside both it and him. The acts of the commissioners of insolvency derive all their validity from the consent of the parties, or from the judgment of a court, which substitutes the force of law for consent. And no act of the county commissioners, in taking a man's land, is worth the paper it is written on, until the verdict of the jury is returned to the *court* of common pleas, and there formally accepted and recorded. Nay, every intelligent farmer in the country knows the fact, that though the commissioners have laid out a new road, or ordered an old one to be shut up, still, if a party, feeling himself aggrieved, demands a jury, the former cannot be worked, nor the latter closed, until the *court* of common pleas shall have passed upon the proceeding and ratified it.*

* I object to Mr. Curtis's calling the county commissioners "*the court* of county commissioners." They are nowhere so called in the act creating them, or in the act defining their duties. On the contrary, they are expressly contradistinguished from the "court of common pleas," which is a court. This may have been an inadvertence, but it shows how he mistook the nature of their powers.

If, however, in all the above cases, the parties in interest *consent* to the acts of sheriff, auditor, or commissioner, then those acts become binding, by virtue of such consent. The party consenting is afterwards estopped from questioning them. But they derive no authority from any "judicial power" vested in the officers performing them. We have a case more exactly in point, and better illustrating the principle, in the fourth section of the ninety-seventh chapter of our Revised Statutes, where it is provided, that "in actions upon promissory notes and other contracts, where the amount due appears to be undisputed, the debt or damages may be assessed and ascertained by the clerk, either under a general order of the court, or by a special reference of the case to him; and the judgment, in either case, shall be entered in the same form as if it had been awarded by the court, on an assessment or computation made by themselves." Yet who will pretend that this act of the clerk, which is performed only where there is no dispute between the parties, emanates from any "judicial power" in that officer?

The instances cited under the United States constitution have, if possible, still less plausibility. The commissioners appointed by the courts can initiate certain proceedings, by holding parties to trial, &c., but this function is no more *judicial* than that of the grand jury in finding an indictment. It is a preliminary to a judicial act, but not such an act. The commissioners are not even required to be sworn, and, in many instances, it is known they are not sworn.

So of the case of which so much is attempted to be made, — that of the commissioner of patents. Any party feeling himself aggrieved by any of his decisions can appeal directly to the courts of the United States for redress.

Compare all this with analogous instances in the legislative department of government. The legislatures of most of the states have created commissions to revise their codes of statute law. Massachusetts has had several such. Our revised statutes are a monument of the labor of one of these commissions. But were they legislators? *Was their proposed code of any validity until enacted by the Senate and House of Representatives?* Just as much as the acts of sheriff, auditor, or commissioners of the different kinds, were acts of judicial power, and no more. Are the selectmen of our towns legislators, because they decide, in the first instance, who are elected as members of our House of Representatives? Are our governor and council legislators, in both the state and national governments, because, on an examination of votes transmitted to them by the selectmen, they issue certificates of election to our state senators and to the members of Congress elect? Do they exercise any part of that power which makes "each house the judge of the elections, returns, and qualification of its own members"? Just as much, I reply, as sheriff, auditor, commissioner, or clerk, does of "judicial power." They perform acts preliminary or antecedent to legislation, but no legislative act; just as the above-named classes of officers perform acts preliminary or antecedent to judicial decisions, but never, in any case, the authoritative and compulsory judicial act itself.

The strength, or rather, the weakness, of the commissioner's argument, on this point, consists in the obtrusive, projecting, self-shouting fallacy of using the exact, technical, constitutional phrase, "judicial power," as synonymous with the popular expression, "*a judicious act*," or "*the exercise of judgment.*" Officers of all kinds exercise "judicial power," in this broad and popular sense of the phrase; that is, they perform acts requiring good judgment. Umpires, arbitrators, and referees perform acts precisely like those of judges, but they cannot put the whole physical strength of the government in motion to enforce them. So sheriffs decide upon the identity of the party named in their precepts; postmasters, to whom they shall deliver letters, and what postage they shall demand; custom-house officers, upon the nature and value of dutiable goods; assessors, in levying taxes; parents and teachers, on matters of discipline, &c., &c. In a popular sense, they may all be said to exercise judicial power; but no particle of that power which, by the fundamental law of our government, is vested in the "courts." Their acts are all examinable by the courts. They cannot set the arm of the government in motion to execute their judgments. Indeed, the whole argument of the commissioner on this point is but a play upon words. It is only a trick of verbal legerdemain. The premises he starts with are unknown to the constitution, and the conclusion he comes to is abhorrent to humanity.

Does not every body see that, in order to make the cases parallel, in order to obtain any legitimate ground of comparison between them, Sims should have had the same power of appealing from the commissioner's decision, to a court, which power of appeal belongs *of right* to a party who feels aggrieved by the act of sheriff, auditor, or commissioner; and that the certificate should bind him only by his voluntary assent?

But there is another point in the commissioner's opinion which is worthy to be companion to this. I proceed to consider it.

He repeats, and keeps repeating, that his decision, dooming Sims to all the horrors of bondage, and putting him under the control of a man who claims title to his body and his soul, to be carried into a jurisdiction where such titles are acknowledged, is not "FINAL." It is not *final*, he says, because if Sims be free, he may extort that freedom from the laws of Georgia which has been denied to him by the laws of

Massachusetts; that is, if the judgment which the commissioner is giving against a free man, in a free state, is a false judgment, he may go to a slave state to obtain redress, — which is ten thousand times worse than if a jury, in a capital case, should say, We may find this prisoner guilty; for if he be wrongfully hanged, God will make him amends.

Besides the inhumanity of this position, it contains a fallacy which is twin-brother to the one just considered. The judicial word, "*final*," has a legal, technical, and certain meaning. In the courts, and in the law books, it means the last judgment in a judicial proceeding. It means that judgment from which a party cannot appeal, though he may ever so much desire it; or it means that judgment, after which, however dissatisfied the party may be, he cannot have his cause retried or reheard by a court, ***but is compelled to submit.***

"Final judgments," says Blackstone, "are such as at once put an end to the action." This is a precise description of the judgment rendered by the commissioner against Sims. That victim resisted by prayers and tears, by the subduing eloquence of his counsel, and by their irresistible logic, which the commissioner has never yet begun to answer. But the self-constituted judge was inexorable. Though he knew that, according to the terms of the Fugitive Law, there was no escape from his decision; though he knew that his certificate was to protect the man-hunter from all "molestation by any process issued by any court, judge, magistrate, or other person whomsoever," yet, like Pilate, he washes his hands and says, "I am innocent of this man's blood, see ye to it;" for my decision is not "final." And why? Because, in another jurisdiction, in another suit, where the plaintiff is to be defendant, and the defendant plaintiff, or perhaps against another party; in a place, too, where all the common-law presumptions in favor of freedom are reversed; where the law is different, and the rules of evidence are different; and where the respondent himself is reduced to the condition of a chattel and a brute, a decision, at some indefinite future period, may be had that the man, whom the commissioner now declares to be a slave, is free, and has always been so. Because of this future and contingent event, because of this almost impossible possibility, the commissioner's decision is not *final*. I deny this. The decision is *final*, because, as Blackstone says, it "at once puts an end to the action." But let us test the question, not only by its legal definition, but by its actual effects. It decides that Sims is a slave. It decides that he owes service to James Potter. It decides that Potter and his heirs and assigns forever are the lawful owners of Sims and the heirs of his bondage forever; and when Sims and his posterity shall be scourged, torn, flayed, mutilated, starved, the only consolation which the commissioner has for him and them is, Shall the clay say to the *Potter* that fashioneth it, What makest thou? It not only decides that Sims is a slave, and that he shall be sent to Georgia, but it sends *familiars*, like those which once disgraced even the purlieus of the Inquisition, to see that the devilish deed is done.

The whole argument of the commissioner, that this act of his is not *final*, is founded on a quibble, — on the use of the legal word "final," as though it were synonymous with the popular word *eternal* or *perpetual*. The slavery of Sims may not be *eternal* or *perpetual;* because, by some miracle of God, or otherwise, he may escape. But in a technical and juridical sense the decision of the commissioner is *final;* and he might as well doom a man to be hurled from the Tarpeian rock, and say that the act is not final, because he only commits the victim to the laws of gravitation, as he has committed Sims to the laws of Georgia.

If by any possibility this doctrine, that the decision is not *final*, could be for a moment sustained, then I will submit a case with which to compare it.

The constitution says, "No state shall pass any law impairing the obligation of contracts." Here we have a constitutional basis, — the same as for the reclamation of fugitive slaves. Some states have passed laws impairing the obligation of contracts, as the stop-laws of Kentucky, and so forth. Suppose a Massachusetts creditor to claim to have a Kentucky debtor, whose contract has been so impaired. Could Congress, in order to give efficacy to this constitutional provision, authorize this pretended creditor to go to Kentucky, seize enough of the alleged debtor's property to satisfy the alleged debt, and carry it home, or have it ordered home by a magistrate, under some "summary" process, which, on its face, excludes the trial by jury; and thereby debar the supposed defendant of all right under that provision of the constitution which gives a jury trial when the value in controversy exceeds twenty dollars? And could the Kentucky magistrate, in the supposed case, deny the jury trial on the ground that the proceeding before him was not "final," because the defendant might follow the plaintiff to Massachusetts, and there institute an action of replevin, trespass, or trover, to try, before a jury of the country, the right of the former plaintiff to the property he had seized?

The commissioner says much in different places, with the apparent hope of showing that the proceeding before him was only for what he calls a "limited and special purpose," namely, "*removal*."

I confess myself unable to understand why the certificate of the commissioner is any more restricted to a limited and special purpose than any judicial act, sentence, or execution, of any court whatever. The commissioner declares a *prima facie* freeman to be a slave.

He declares that James Potter owns Thomas Sims, and the posterity in his loins forever; or that Thomas Sims and his posterity forever, owe service to James Potter and his heirs and assigns forever. Does this "*forever*" limit the meaning of the certificate, as to time? If so, then a *general* or *unlimited* award or execution, against Sims, as contradistinguished from this *limited* and *special* one, must extend and run into the next world. When our courts decide that one man owes another man money, they award execution against his property, with certain humane exemptions as to clothes, furniture, provisions, school books, Bible, &c. But when this commissioner decided that Sims owed Potter service, he awarded a certificate against the adjudged debtor, which made no exemption whatever; but included property, clothes, books, skin, flesh, heart, brain, soul, and all that was in him, or of him, with all appurtenances and appendages, present emblements, and future increase. Yet, according to the commissioner, the first judgment is a common or general one; the last "special and limited." Under our old laws, (and under the laws of some states yet,) courts could sentence offenders to the barbarous punishment of flogging. But they were and are bound to specify the number of lashes. This is general. The commissioner delivers over a slave to be flogged by his master, *ad libitum*, and *in perpetuum*, to be flogged in his own person, and to be flogged in the persons of his children, and their posterity, *in secula seculorum*. The defined flogging of thirty-nine, or such other number of lashes as can be computed, the commissioner calls general or indefinite. But the incomputable number of lashes; the vast, unknown, algebraic quantity; the infinite series; that which Newton with all his mathematics could not compass, nor Rosse with his telescope see the end of, — that is "special and limited." The taking of a limited amount of a man's property, carefully set down in dollars and cents, both in the text and in the margin of the execution, the commissioner calls a general purpose. But the robbing of a man, not only of all he has earned, but of all his capabilities of earning as long as he breathes, with full authority to do the same thing to his posterity to the latest generation, this is "special and limited." To sentence a man to be hanged by the neck till he be dead, though with privilege of priest, prayer book, and Bible, — this, too, is general and proper; though in Massachusetts it can be done only by a majority of the judges of the supreme court. But to send a man to be worked to death in five years on a sugar plantation, where his being taught to read the gospel of Jesus Christ is a felony, — this is "special and limited," and so may be done by any hireling commissioner who will do what Judas did for one third part of his silver pieces.

Fellow-citizens, I submit to any man, clerical, legal, or lay, who is capable of appreciating moral distinctions, whether this whole doctrine, about delivering a man up as a slave, and putting him bodily into the hands of the claimant, and thrusting him into slave jurisdiction, under the pretext that it is done only for *the special and limited purpose of removal*, be not atrocious. It is more like a forgery than an argument. Assumed learning and logic never practised a greater imposition upon themselves, nor attempted a greater one upon others, than when they fabricated this notion, that adjudging a man to be a slave, stripping him of his *liberam legem*, that is, of all his rights and immunities as a citizen, and delivering him into actual bondage, is "for a special and limited purpose of removal," — only to give him a voyage, or a pleasure excursion of a few hundred miles, — *out*, — *but not back*. When the successor of St. Peter, claiming to hold the keys of heaven, and to have death and hell for his ministers, excommunicated whole sects and peoples, and delivered them over to the great soul-hunter, and sent his *familiars* with them to see that the "claimant" suffered no "molestation" while conveying them to the bottomless pit, *he* might as well have said that he did it only for a "special and limited purpose." It was not damnation, it was only "removal." And do you suppose the devil, could he have got possession of those outcast souls, would have cared any more under what pretence the great pontiff commissioner made the delivery, than does the southern slaveholder, when he gets possession of a man of whom he can make a slave?

This fallacy about the "special and limited purpose of removal" did not originate with Mr. Commissioner Curtis. I exculpate him from that guilt. He only adopted it and gave it a "bad eminence" by making it, in part, the basis of his decision. But henceforth let the people brand it. Let them classify it and denounce it, and detest it, as belonging to that impious and blasphemous kind of arguments by which our first parents were beguiled, when Satan told them that, though they sinned against God, they should not die; or by which Mr. Webster cajoled and cozened so many honest men, when he assured them, that though they should violate the moral law, by opening all the territories to slavery, yet some physical law of geography or the weather would avert the penalties.

In the absence of all decent materials for an argument, the commissioner resorts to that ten times exploded position, that there is an analogy between fugitives from justice and fugitives from service. Where could he find a bandage of prejudice thick enough to blind him to the distinction, that the condition of delivering up the former is that he be *charged* with crime, while the condition of delivering up the latter is that he be *held* to labor, and that he *owes* service? How can it be said that a man *owes* service, until the *fact* of the *indebtedness* be proved? Such reasonable suspicion of guilt as justifies a grand jury in finding a bill of indictment is sufficient in the one case, but such positive proof as would require the court to enter up judgment and award execution is absolutely necessary in the other. The government demanding a fugitive from justice seeks possession of him for a trial, *before a court and jury*, of the question of *criminality;* but the claimant of an alleged fugitive from service seeks possession of him to avoid a trial, *before a court and jury*, of the question of *freedom.* The constitution requires that every person accused of crime shall be tried in the state and district where the crime shall be charged to have been committed; but it makes no such provision in regard to the alleged fugitive from service; and this injunction in the one case, and omission in the other, create the irresistible inference, that there is a difference between them, and that the alleged fugitive from service, according to all the analogies of the common law, is to be tried where he is found.

But there is one distinction which is broad enough and luminous enough to make a blind man see it. An alleged fugitive from justice is not adjudged to be a criminal previous to delivery, nor is he made a criminal, in the eye of the law, by the act of delivery. But the alleged fugitive from service is adjudged a slave, and made a slave by the certificate of the commissioner. The state receiving a fugitive from justice does not proceed forthwith to punish him. But the receiver of an alleged fugitive from service *owns* him, and may proceed to control him, and beat him, and rob him, and starve him, on the very instant that the commissioner puts the certificate into his hands. If any one cannot see this distinction, no act of the moral oculist can give him sight.

The papers inform us that when Sims was landed

in Savannah, he was taken to jail and received the "*usual reprimand*," which, as every body knows, is a flayed and blood-streaming back. By whose certificate was the nine-thonged cat laid on? Had he been a murderer or a pirate, would excoriation have been the first act of welcome on his arrival? No! Murderers and pirates would have had a jury. The law is beneficent to them; it saves its terrors for the slave. A man who will not *see* such a distinction as this, would excite no pity should he be made to *feel* it.

In treating this topic, the commissioner makes one assertion that seems insane. He says that, to authorize the delivery of a fugitive from justice, in order to his removal, "*it must be proved that he has committed a crime.*" Such a declaration was never made before, and I do not believe it will be ever made again. You could not find a lawyer south of Mason and Dixon's line who would venture to say this. Every body knows that the supposed criminal needs only *to be charged* with crime. It is the alleged slave who must be proved to *be held* to service before he can be constitutionally surrendered. But as though this was not absurd enough, the commissioner goes on to say, that though the alleged fugitive from justice must be proved, in the place where he is taken, "to have committed a crime," yet, after his removal, he must be proved again to have committed it. How can a man be proved, in any legal way, to have committed a crime, without being confronted with the witnesses against him? Why, after having been so proved, is he put upon trial again?

As to all the commissioner says in denial of the right of trial by jury, I shall make but one or two remarks. I have argued that question elsewhere; and, until I see some answer to that argument, I have no occasion for repetition or corroboration of it. After using the word "*person*" some twenty times, to signify the President of the United States, electors, senators, representatives, United States officers, Indians, Africans, &c., the constitution declares that "no *person* shall be deprived of life, liberty, or property, without due process of law;" — this "due process of law" meaning trial by jury. This is one fact. Adam Gibson, Henry Long, Thomas Sims, and many others, some of them now acknowledged on all hands to have been free, have been sent into slavery without this trial. This is another fact. Now put these two facts together. No man shall be deprived of liberty or property, except by the jury trial. These men have been deprived of liberty and property without the jury trial. These are the two ends. Now fill up the space between them with what you please, and call it argument, law, gospel, or what you will, every body must see that it is nothing, and can be nothing but Mephistophiles' jugglery. I dismiss this point with a single proposition: In Massachusetts, we know no legal distinction founded on color. Through all the gradations, from the person who has the preternatural whiteness of an Albino to one whom you can see in the darkest midnight, because he is so solid black, — all, *all*, under our constitution and laws, are alike freemen, or alike slaves. Notwithstanding the commissioner's decision makes us all slaves, yet I maintain that, in the eye of the law, we are all free. How then can any one of us freemen be robbed of liberty and property, and turned into a slave, but by freeman's proof, — that is, trial by jury? I acknowledge that after we have been proved to be slaves by freeman's proof, then all the unutterable consequences of slavery follow, of course; just as when a man has been proved to be a murderer, the consequences of murder follow. But UNTIL, mark this, UNTIL a man has been proved to be a slave by freeman's proof, he remains legally free. And a magistrate who takes jurisdiction of a proceeding by which a man may be deprived of liberty or property, without freeman's proof, prejudges his victim, when he allows the first witness to be called, or the first paper to be read; and he might just as well do it, in a case of "life," as in a case of "liberty and property."

The next position of the commissioner which I shall notice relates to the right of Congress to make use of state courts to execute United States laws.

Now we have the express authority of the supreme court of the United States for saying that "Congress cannot vest any portion of the judicial power of the United States, except in courts ordained and established by itself." — *Martin* vs. *Hunter's Lessee*, 1 Wheaton, 330. "The whole judicial power of the United States should be, at all times, vested in some courts created under its authority." — *Ib.* 331. "The jurisdiction over such cases, [cases arising under the constitution, laws, and treaties of the United States,] could not exist in the state courts previous to the adoption of the constitution, and it could not afterwards be directly conferred on them; for the constitution expressly requires the judicial power to be vested in courts ordained and established by the United States." — *Ib.* 335. But the commissioner refers to a passage in Prigg's case, in which it is said that "while a difference of opinion exists . . . . . whether state magistrates are bound to act under it, [a law of Congress,] none is entertained by the court, that state magistrates may, if they choose, exercise the authority, unless prohibited by state legislation."

Waiving all exceptions to this doctrine, the utmost that can be made of it is this: that state magistrates may execute a law of Congress, unless forbidden by a law of their state; but when so forbidden, they cannot; and Congress can neither compel them to do so, nor annul a prohibitory law of the state, by giving validity to the act of the magistrate, performed in violation of the state law. Now mark the *non sequitur* of the commissioner's logic. See how his premises belong to one subject, and his conclusion to another. Because a *Massachusetts* magistrate may execute a law of Congress, unless the Massachusetts legislature forbid him, but if so forbidden he can no longer do it, therefore, when the Massachusetts legislature has so forbidden him, Congress may send the magistrates of Georgia, or of any other state, into Massachusetts, to do what our own state had forbidden our own magistrates to do. I say "*send the magistrates of Georgia here;*" because Congress may just as well, and even better for us, authorize the magistrates of any state in the Union to come here, set up courts, and pass sentences which shall convey our citizens into bondage, as to stay at home and make records, which, when brought here, shall have the same effect. This, then, is the law-logic of the commissioner: Because a Massachusetts magistrate may aid in reclaiming an alleged fugitive on Massachusetts ground, unless forbidden by his state, yet, if so forbidden, then the legislatures of fifteen slave states may send their magistrates, or the acts of their magistrates here, to do the same thing. The state might prevent its own magistrates from aiding in this nefarious work, but this would be of no avail, for any one, or all, of fifteen sets of slave state magistrates may come and do the forbidden act.

Pierpont Edwards once said of a clergyman, that if his text had a contagious disease, the sermon would not catch it; and a blind man, being asked to describe his conception of color, compared it to a clap of thunder. But all their ideas were coherent and homogeneous compared with those premises and conclusions of the commissioner, by which the State Rights' doctrine is expounded to mean, the right of one *state* to send its magistrates into another state, to do what the latter has *lawfully* prohibited its own magistrates from doing. South Carolina never claimed so much as this.

Under the first head, where it had been urged by counsel, that a freeman might have no opportunity to prove his freedom in the state from which he was alleged to have fled, because the claimant was under no obligation to carry him to that state, but might send him to the Cuban or Brazilian market, the commissioner shuts his eyes to these very probable consequences, and refuses to consider them ; but under the fifth head, where an argument in favor of the slaveholder could be derived from consequences, he not only argues elaborately from them, but bases his judgment upon them.

There are two remarks thrown out in the course of the commissioner's opinion so shocking to every feeling of humanity, that any one, in commenting upon them, may well be excused for passing from the language of argument to that of emotion.

If there be any one right known to the common law more important and sacred than all others, it is the right of confronting and cross-examining the witnesses who are brought to testify against us. Without this right, there is no fraud that cannot be practised upon the most honest man, and no guilt that cannot be proved against the most innocent one. Doubtless this right of cross-examination is sometimes abused ; but there are few spectacles more exciting or more gratifying than to see the demons of falsehood driven out, one after another, from a perjured villain, until the truth, at last, is wrenched from his heart, notwithstanding the double boltings and barrings with which he had locked it there. The fear of this cross-examination "casting its shadows before," has prevented thousands and tens of thousands from swearing falsely. Next to honesty, this fear is the greatest protection to property, liberty, and life.

Now the testimony which doomed Sims to slavery, and which may doom any of us with our wives and children to slavery, when men grow, not more wicked, but only a little more bold in their wickedness than they are now, was wholly *ex parte* testimony; taken, not merely behind the victim's back, but a thousand miles behind his back; of which he had no knowledge, and, unless he were omniscient, like God, could have no knowledge. And when the counsel of Sims urged upon the commissioner the enormity of this outrage against all principle, what was his reply? It was this, and it makes a man's blood run cold to read it: Sims's absence from Georgia, "so that he could not be served with notice, if he was entitled to it, was in his own wrong, and he cannot now complain that he had no opportunity to cross-examine the witnesses."

I appeal to all history to prove, that no judge who ever sat upon a bench where the common law was recognized and administered, however corrupt he may have been, ever advanced a more atrocious doctrine. Why, gentlemen, if a debtor absconds for the very purpose of defrauding his creditors, he must have notice before he can be proceeded against for the recovery of a debt. If he flees from the state, lurks and hides himself, he must have the best notice the court can contrive to give him. If the plaintiff recovers and takes out execution, he must file a bond conditioned to make restoration; and years afterwards, if the defendant shall come back and show cause, he shall be entitled to a review to annul the whole proceedings against him. Ay, when a criminal, a robber, a murderer, an incendiary, is brought to trial, even he must be "confronted with the witnesses against him, have compulsory process for obtaining witnesses in his favor, and the assistance of counsel in his defence." And yet the commissioner *makes proof out of nothing*, that

Sims escaped from slavery, and then, because of this nothing-made proof, he inculpates him with being absent "in his own wrong."

The other point referred to arose from certain testimony, (if it can be called testimony,) that the mother of Sims begged the witness, "whether her son was in a free state or in a slave state, for God's sake, to bring him back again." "This," says the commissioner, "certainly disarms the case of any unpleasant features"! Why, even the kine of the barn-yard, when the butcher cuts the throat of her young, will weep and low, and bellow, for days and days, and say, as well as in her inarticulate moanings she can say, "For God's sake, let it be brought back again;" though the only consequence of its return would be to have its throat cut by the butcher again. And are we to expect that the brutalized, chattelized "cattle" of the south will have less of that natural yearning and longing of the soul, at the loss of their offspring, than the animals of the farmer's yard? Can we suppose that God has not planted the instinct of a mother's love too deep to be destroyed but by the destruction of the being herself in whom it was planted? No! debase the mother as you will, by ignorance, vice, superstition, lust, concubinage, incest, and this wealth of affection will still glow at the bottom of her heart, "rich as the oozy bottom of the deep in sunken wrack and sumless treasures." And because this mother's love had not been all extinguished, the commissioner says that his sending a human being into the abyss of bondage, on evidence that an intelligent barbarian would reject, "certainly disarms the case of any unpleasant features." But I shall not expostulate with the commissioner. A man must have a heart before he can feel, as he must have eyes before he can see.

"O, who can paint a sunbeam to the blind,
Or make him feel a shadow with his mind?"

Fellow-citizens, I might occupy your attention much longer upon this unprecedented opinion of the commissioner; but there are two or three other topics to which I wish to call your attention, and I therefore forbear. In saying what I have said, I disclaim all personal ill will or discourtesy towards that magistrate. Even should I appear not to have succeeded in suppressing my own feelings, I certainly cannot wound his more than he has wounded mine, and those I believe of nine tenths of all who have ever read his opinion; — not by a thousand fold as much as he has wounded the law, whose servant he is, or the fair fame of Massachusetts, of which he is a citizen; not so much as his decision will wound the hearts of an intelligent posterity, who shall look back upon it as a partisan and an ignoble act, not to be remembered without a sigh.

If the legal relations of slavery did not sustain the moral ones, as the root sustains the branches and nourishes the fruit, those moral relations would seem to demand all our attention. I know but comparatively little, and no man living at the north can know but comparatively little, of the various and ever-repeated wickednesses of this institution. It has been my lot, however, to live for about half the time, during the last four years, in the midst of a milder form of slavery. And besides this, I was once engaged for about six weeks in the trial of causes growing directly out of slavery; and that experience gave me some insight into its dreadful mysteries. For a moment, the wind blew the smoke and flame aside, and I looked into its hell. I saw, then, as I had never seen before, what a vital and inextinguishable interest every human being has in this subject; — not the slaves alone, but the free men; not voters only, but all who can be affected by votes; not men only, but especially women.

For this reason, I am glad to see so many ladies in

this audience. It becomes them to be here. If any mortal should cultivate an abhorrence of slavery, the female sex should do it. Whatever any one may hold to be the social relation between free women and slave women, yet before God and Christ, and all the holy angels, they belong to the same sisterhood of the human race. They are your sisters. And what is the condition of these your sisters, in regard to every thing that a virtuous and noble woman holds most sacred and dear?

Ladies, there are now in this land of pretended freedom and pretended gospel a million and a half of women who have no practical knowledge of what a woman's higher life should be, or what a woman's most precious rights are. Since the Declaration of Independence, the number of slaves in this country has increased from less than five hundred thousand to more than three millions; and before the close of this century, their descendants will increase to more than thrice three millions. And yet, neither as to the living nor as to the dead, has there ever been a lawful marriage among them all. There has never been a man slave who could say, "This is my wife, heart of my heart, and life of my life, and no mortal power shall pluck her from my side." There has never been a woman slave who could say, "This is my lawful, wedded husband, whom I promise to love and cherish, and to whom I vow inviolable constancy." "For this cause," says Christ, "shall a man leave father and mother, and shall cleave to his wife, and they twain shall be one flesh." But the "twain" of slaves are never one. And even when any sham ceremony is observed, to distinguish this holy relation of husband and wife from the cohabitations of beasts, and he who officiates comes to those other words of Christ, "What, therefore, God has joined together, let not man put asunder," he stops; for he knows, and they all know, that a few dollars, at any time, will bring oereavement upon both, — a double bereavement, he a widower and she a widow, both still surviving. Their life, at best, is but a life of concubinage; — not even that concubinage, which, though not founded upon a lawful contract, has still something like conjugal fidelity in it, and therefore a semblance of virtue; but a various and vagrant concubinage, traversing the circle of overseer, master, master's guests, and master's sons. The fate of the children born to the slave mother you all know. Those objects upon which all maternal affections meet and glow as in a focus, are torn from her bosom, like lambs from the flock when the shambles are empty.

And as to those females who are young, sprightly, and handsome: —

Charge me not with indelicacy in touching upon this theme. *Honi soit qui mal y pense.* I speak not to fastidious ears, but to the pure in heart, to whom all things are pure. I speak of eternal verities, before whose massive force the heart trembles and bows itself, as reeds before the tempest. It is the grossest and most shameless of all indelicacies to patronize and multiply vice, through pusillanimity in exposing it, —

As to those females, I say, who are young, sprightly, and handsome, whom God has damned with beauty of form and beauty of face, because they only attract the gloating eye of passion, who can describe the loathsomeness of their life? They are ripened for the New Orleans, or for some other market, whence southern harems are supplied; as, under the Mahometan religion, white Caucasian beauties are sent to the slave marts of the darker-skinned Turk.

In that company of seventy-six persons who attempted, in 1848, to escape from the District of Columbia in the schooner Pearl, and whose officers I assisted in defending, there were several young and healthy girls who had those peculiar attractions of form, of fea ture, and of complexion, which southern connoisseurs in sensualism so highly prize. Elizabeth Russell was one of them. She fell immediately into the slave-traders' fangs, and was doomed for the New Orleans market. The hearts of those who saw her and fore-saw her fate were touched with pity. They offered eighteen hundred dollars to redeem her, and some there were who offered to give, who would not have had much left after the gift. But the fiend of a slave trader was inexorable. He knew how he could trans-mute her charms into gold through the fires of sin. He demanded twenty-one hundred dollars, (though for menial services she would not have been worth more than four or five,) and would take nothing less. She was despatched to New Orleans, but when about half way there, God had mercy upon her and smote her with death. Perhaps, foreseeing her fate, she practised what, under such circumstances, we might call the virtue of suicide. There were two girls named Ed-mundson in the same company. When about to be sent to the same market, an older sister went to the shambles to plead with the wretch who owned them, for the love of God, to spare his victims. He bantered her, telling her what fine dresses and fine furniture they would have. "Yes," said she, "that may do well in this life, but what will become of them in the next?" They, too, were sent to New Orleans, but they were afterwards redeemed at an enormous ransom, and brought back. There was one girl, who, after her recapture in the Pearl, was sold six times in seven weeks, in Maryland and Virginia, for her beauty's sake. But she proved heroically and sublimely intractable. Like Rebecca, the Jewess, she would have flung her-self from the loftiest battlement, rather than yield her person to a villain. Notwithstanding her masters' pre-tence that they had bought her with their money, and owned her soul, yet she had wealth, which, though all the earth were "one entire and perfect chrysolite," it could not buy. It was not difficult, therefore, to purchase her, and she was redeemed and came to New York; and I have been informed in the most authentic manner from the lady of the very respectable family of which she became an inmate, that, on an examination of her person, after the healing-time of the journey had passed, her body was found scarred and waled with whip marks, which the villains inflicted upon her because she would not come to their bed.

Now, suppose a sister or daughter of yours, of this heroic soul and spotless purity, should find herself on the way to New Orleans; — suppose, by almost superhuman power and adroitness, she should escape, and should thread her solitary and darksome path, for hundreds of miles, towards the north star; should lie down in caverns, with poisonous reptiles by day, and pursue her lonely journey by night, finding the beasts of the forests to be less terrible than man; should swim rivers, and keep off famine by roots and insects, until at last, thanks be to God, she sets her mangled and bleeding feet upon the soil of freedom. Perhaps some echo of the fame of the Pilgrim mothers has reached her ears. She has heard of Boston and its noble women of old, and she hies hither as to a city of refuge, — as to a sanctuary where virtue has an altar, and where she can lay down her hunted and weary body, and be at rest. Fallacious hope! The lecher pursues his prey, and he is here. He goes to some Glossin lawyer who sues out a warrant; and to some Jack Ketch who serves it. The victim is seized at midnight, under some lying charge, and she is carried before a commissioner, whose conduct, were he a *quasi* judge, as he pretends to be, would be enough to make every hair of the judicial ermine forever detestable. Here a process is gone through which she does not understand,

and some papers are read of which she never heard, and then a judgment is pronounced that her "labor" is "due" to her pursuer, (and such labor!) that she "owes service" to him, (and such service!) and then the commissioner delivers her into his arms, and pockets a fee which common pimps would be ashamed to work for.

And, my friends, the keenest pang in the grief of all this is, that there is no fiction or romance about it. A commissioner who could bring himself down to send a *man* to a Georgia cotton-field under this law, the first time trying, could send a virtuous and spotless woman into enforced harlotry the second time; and the prince of darkness only knows what he could not set him to do afterwards. The clergymen who could defend the enslavers of Sims because he "owed" the "service" of one sex, could defend the enslavers of a woman because she "owed" the "service" of the other sex; — the clergymen of the rich parishes I mean; — for it happens, with the constancy of a law of nature, that it is only the clergymen of the rich parishes who do this. Do they not know how to serve and reverence their Lord and Master, — that is, their Landlord and Paymaster!

But, fellow-citizens, as our feelings are stimulated to the keenest sensibility, in looking at the infinite of wrong which slavery commits; as we see the millions and millions of human beings dimly emerging into view, and crowding down the vista of futurity to blast our eyes with the vision of their woe, a potent voice rings in our ears, exclaiming, "*Conquer your prejudices*," "CONQUER YOUR PREJUDICES." And this execrable counsel is uttered in reference to the infinite crime and disgrace of sending into slavery, without a trial, those who are free under our laws, — the men to stripes and death, and the women to the body's shame and the soul's perdition. Fouler, baser, more ungodly counsel was never uttered, since it was said to our first parents in the garden of Eden, "On the day thou eatest thereof thou shalt not surely die."

And what is it that this long-honored eulogist of liberty, but now its great apostate, blasphemes with the name of "*prejudice*"? If there be one sentiment more deeply rooted in the public heart of Massachusetts than any other, more intertwined and grown together with all the fibres of its being, it is the sentiment of liberty. We have drunk it in with our mothers' milk; we have imbibed it from all the lessons of the school-room and the teachings of the sanctuary; we have inspired it with the atmosphere we breathe, and our organs have been attuned to it from our birth, by the anthems of the mountain's wind and the ocean's roar. It was from the love of liberty that our earlier fathers plucked themselves up by the roots from that natal soil into which they had been fastening for centuries. For this they wandered abroad upon the ocean, deeming its ingulfing surges to be more tolerable than a tyrant's power. For this they transplanted themselves to this land, at that time more distant and more formidable to them than any part of the habitable globe could now be to us. For this they performed the double task of enduring all privations and dangers, and at the same time of laying the foundations of all our free and glorious institutions; and as the sires were stricken down by toil and death, the sons took up the work and bore it on, generation after generation.

For this noble sentiment of liberty our later fathers encountered the perils and deaths of a seven years' war, and amid poverty and destitution, amid hunger and cold and nakedness, without any of the protections and defences of battle which the wealth of their foe could command, they bared their noble breasts to the shock of the mailed legions of the British crown. And when the struggle was ended and the triumph won, they achieved labors of peace not less magnanimous and wonderful than their labors of war.

They were the pattern men of the world; — not aggressive, not submissive; not hostile, not servile; doing right, demanding right; they were the men who would never wield the oppressor's rod, and would go mad at the touch of his heel.

Now, there is not one of all those glorious deeds, from the embarkation at Delfthaven to the signing of the peace of 1783, or the inauguration of the federal government in 1789, which was not begotten by the love of liberty, or would have been performed without its creative energy. And yet, the arch-apostate, standing in the city of Boston, the home of old Samuel Adams and John Hancock, within a stone's throw of the spot where Benjamin Franklin was born, in sight of Bunker Hill, and with Lexington and Concord, as it were, just hiding themselves behind the hills for shame, calls all this a "prejudice," and commands us to cast it from us as an unclean thing. Was it not enough to make the stones in the streets, and every block in that eternal shaft which marks the spot where Warren fell, cry out "with most miraculous organ" to rebuke him?

We have another, and it is a kindred "prejudice." We have a "prejudice" of sixty years' standing in favor of the principle of the ordinance of 1787. That ordinance has been cherished in our memories, it has been taught to our children, and we have displayed it before the world both as the pledge and the promise of our devotion to liberty. Five states, now numbering five millions of men, were the battalions whom that ordinance wheeled from the ranks of Belial to the Lord's side. Hundreds of times have the Whig party and the Democratic party resolved that the principle of that ordinance should be maintained inviolate. Mr. Webster claimed the application of it to the new territories, as his thunder, and swaggered as he rattled it. Now he calls the great achievement of Thomas Jefferson and Nathan Dane a "*prejudice,*" and dishonors their graves by his scoffs. He abandons the vast regions of Utah and New Mexico to the slaveholder; he gives more than fifty thousand square miles of free territory to Texas; he gives ten millions of dollars in money, (more than, with all our devotion and self-sacrifice, we have been able to appropriate to public education in Massachusetts for the last ten years;) and worse than this, he gives permission that she may carve out of her territory a slave state *additional* to what had been unconstitutionally contracted for when she came into the Union.

And for what does he flout us, by stigmatizing all these sacred convictions and sentiments and instincts as "*prejudices*"? Only to feed the famine of his ambition. He began to see, what every body else has so long seen, that his vices were bringing upon him the retribution of premature old age and decrepitude; and that, unless he could enter the White House the next term, he must wait, at least until the great Julian period should bring the world round again. He parleyed with southern tempters, and fell.

Nor did he outrage our feelings only. He sacrificed our pecuniary interests, our very means of subsistence. Massachusetts would be prospering under an improved system of protection for our domestic industry to-day, but for Mr. Webster's apostasy, which stripped us of all our power and of all our unity, and inflamed the spirit of southern aggrandizement to demand every thing and yield nothing. Could the issue be now formed, and the case tried, whether Daniel Webster's course in 1850 did not deprive the working-men of the country of a tariff for the protection of their labor, not an intelligent and impartial jury could be found that would not bring him in guilty. This result every unbiased man at Washington saw, last summer; while he was cajoling the men of the north with the delusion that, if they would surrender liberty, they should have their reward in a tariff. I speak of this with confidence, because there are hundreds of my constituents and acquaintances who will bear me witness that, in personal interviews, and by correspondence, they were warned, that if they followed Mr. Webster in his recreancy to principles, he would leave them without relief in the matter of property.

Fellow-citizens, I will trespass upon your attention but for a moment longer. I wish to advance one idea for the consideration of all sober, moral, and religious men; and when this idea is duly considered, I trust to its working a revolution in public sentiment. In selecting men to be our political leaders, we have sometimes committed the gravest moral error. We have assumed the falsity of a distinction between a man's public and his private life. We have supposed that the same individual might be a bad man and a good citizen; might be a patriot and an inebriate, a faithful officer and a debauchee, at the same time; might serve his country during "office hours," and the powers of darkness the rest of the twenty-four. But I say, as of old, no man can serve God and mammon.

We have been too prone to judge of men by their professions and by their connections. We seem to have forgotten that the tree is to be known by its fruit, and a man by his life. If we are to take the Pharisee's rule, and determine a man's piety by his creed, and by the number and length of his prayers, then piety will be the cheapest thing in the market, and as worthless as it is cheap.

In choosing teachers to be the guides and exemplars of our children, we demand high moral worth; and we would as soon thrust our youth into the centre of pestilence, as amid the contagion of vicious and profligate men.

In selecting our religious guides, we feel almost justified in being captiously and morbidly critical; we hardly admit that we can be strict to a fault; and the man who fails to carry personal purity and exemplariness into the pastoral life, is driven from it with indignation and contempt.

I admit too, rejoicingly, that, in Massachusetts, this preventive and praiseworthy discipline has been more extensively applied to political men than in any other state in the Union. Our highest state offices have been filled for years, saving very rare exceptions, with men of distinguished probity and a spotless life. And why, in this department, should we *ever* grant dispensations and absolutions; or, like the old popes, sell indulgences to sin?

Now, let this doctrine be applied; for I hold it to be no unwarrantable invasion of private character to apply these principles to public men. When public men openly and notoriously practise vice, they make the vice public, and bring it within public jurisdiction. If it is public for example, it is public for criticism; and, under such circumstances, the moral and religious guides of the community are as solemnly bound "truly to find, and due presentment make," of these offences, as the grand jury is in the case of crimes against the laws of the land. I say, therefore, let us apply this doctrine.

How long have all good citizens in Massachusetts labored in the glorious cause of temperance! They have devoted time, expended talent, lavished money, incurred obloquy; but, as their reward, they have plucked the guilty from perdition; rescued the young, just losing their balance over the precipice of ruin; saved the widow and the fatherless from unutterable woe, and driven demons of discord from domestic

Edens. Now why, after all our toils and sacrifices to uphold and carry forward the cause of temperance, and to make its name as honorable as it is blessed; why should we demolish all our work by elevating a man to a high political station, or by upholding him when in it, who, in the face of the nation and of the world, will become so drunken that he cannot articulate his mother tongue? Is this an example you desire to set before the ingenuous and aspiring youth of the land; ay, before your own children?

We have had men in the presidential chair not without faults and blemishes of character; but hitherto we may proudly say, that we never have had one there who drowned his reason in his cups. God grant that we never may. Think of this magnificent ship of state freighted with twenty-three millions of souls, and laden to the scuppers with the wealth of the world's hopes, with a pilot at the helm — *drunk!*

We are an industrious and a frugal people. The aptitude is born with us. A true Massachusetts boy seems to take to ingenious labor and to labor-saving contrivances from his birth, — like a duck almost impatient to be hatched, that it may get into the water. We prize and honor the home-bred virtues of diligence and thrift; for they bestow upon us all our comforts, the means of educating our children, and leave us a magnificent surplus for godlike charities to be scattered over the world.

Dr. Franklin has stamped a family likeness upon us all. His economical wisdom is domesticated among us. Take a sound and pure specimen of a Massachusetts farmer or mechanic, and analyze him, and you will find that, of his whole composition, from six to ten ounces in the pound is made up of Dr. Franklin. Now, why should we root out this luxuriant, fruit-bearing virtue? Why welcome and court and feed the prodigalities and sensualities of the old world, to corrupt the pristine virtues of the new? Can he be a republican after the severe simplicity and grandeur of the old Roman type; can he be an exemplary citizen, who must have his thirty, forty, or even fifty thousand dollars a year, to squander upon what I must not call, "to ears polite," his vices and passions, but, more genteelly, "his tastes and feelings," while millions of honest laborers thank God if by incessant toil they can earn their daily bread for their families, and the bread of knowledge for their children? Can they be good citizens, or, at least, are they not grievously deluded, who will give such purses to such a man for being the advocate and agent of their special interests, while there are hundreds of suffering men and women, and more suffering children, at their own doors? Do you want your children to grow up inflamed by such examples of excess and wantonness? I know that all this is defended on the ground that something must be done for a great man's family. *Ay, that family!* The progeny and costliness of the vices, what Californias shall be able to support? I know, too, that it is also said we must have great talents in the public councils, at whatever price. Well, if this be your philosophy, don't do the work by halves, but import Lucifer at once!

Now, fellow-citizens, you know that all the men who are guilty of these great derelictions from civil and social duty are the men who uphold the Fugitive Slave law.

I might touch upon more holy relations in life; upon virtues without which there is no home and no domestic sanctuary; without which there may be children, but the sacred institution of the family is gone. But I forbear. I only desire to awaken your attention to the great duty of extending the domain of conscience over politics; of holding public men answerable for those vices which it is a great misnomer to call private when they are committed in the face of the world. "The pulpit is false to its trust" if it does not follow and rebuke them, under whatever robes of official dignity they may hold their revels.

Three great stages of development belong to the world. First, there was the period of physical development, when the tallest man was crowned king, when the strongest muscles enacted the laws, when brute force was "His Royal Majesty," and claimed and received the homage of mankind. That age has passed; and how contemptible does all its greatness now appear! Then came the age when the mind towered above the body, when a nation's power no longer consisted in the millions of its men, but in the treasuries of its knowledge; when the intellect took up the vastest concentrations of animal strength, which seemed omnipotent before, lifted them off their fulcrum, and they became like a feather, in the breath of its power. That age is the present. The moral age is yet to be ushered in. In this age, the intellectual forces shall still retain all their dominion and supremacy over the physical world, but the moral shall preside over the intellectual, and move them as God moves the stars, bringing them out of chaos, and wheeling them in circuits of unimaginable grandeur, and for purposes of beneficence yet inconceivable. In that day, the lawgivers of the land shall be no longer "compromisers" between duty and mammon, and the judges shall judge in righteousness. In that day, the merchant, for the lucre of trade, shall not pay tribute in human beings, and send his flesh-tax across the free waters. In that day, the gospel of human brotherhood, of doing as we would be done by, and of loving our neighbors as ourselves, shall no longer be doled out to us by priests of the broad phylactery sort, in homœopathic doses, reduced to the five hundredth dilution. But in that glorious day, the men who sit in the Areopagus of the nation, clothed with the ermine of the law, shall be, as the heathen of old figured the emblem of Justice, blind in the outward eye; and all they know of color shall be to give no color to the law. In that day the successors of St. Paul shall preach what he preached, when standing "in the midst of Mars Hill," — a God of equity, of righteousness, of justice, of benevolence; the God who made "of one blood all nations of men," who, alas! to so many in our day is "the UNKNOWN GOD."

In that day, when a whole people are aroused to ponder, with unwonted intensity, upon the great principles for which Sidney and Vane bled; for which Hampden smote the tyrant of his day; for which the heroes of the revolution pledged fortune, life, and sacred honor; no voice shall strive to seduce them from their sacred work by its Belial cry, "CONQUER YOUR PREJUDICES!"

Fellow-citizens, if you wish to coöperate in bringing on this glorious era, your first step is to vote for that noble man who ransomed his own slaves, — JOHN G. PALFREY.

SPEECH

DELIVERED, ON TAKING THE CHAIR, AS PRESIDENT OF THE GREAT MASS CONVENTION, CALLED, WITHOUT DISTINCTION OF PARTY, IN OPPOSITION TO THE FUGITIVE SLAVE LAW, AND HELD AT THE TREMONT TEMPLE IN BOSTON, APRIL 8, 1851.*

GENTLEMEN OF THE CONVENTION;

I thank you cordially for the honor of being called to this place; though I could have wished that your choice had fallen upon some one of the many more meritorious men whom I see all around me.

Gentlemen, I have come here to-day to add my feeble voice to the thunder tones of execration against the Fugitive Slave law, with which every free state in this Union, and every free community upon the earth, are now echoing and reëchoing.

I do not propose to occupy your attention long. Where so many things are to be said, and so many persons, far better qualified than I am, are present to say them, I shall consult at once your advantage and my duty, by being brief.

We have come together with especial reference to the Fugitive Slave law; but that execrable statute connects itself so directly with almost every other prominent measure of the government, and with the

* This meeting was held pending the trial, before Mr. Commissioner Curtis, of Thomas Sims, an alleged fugitive slave from Georgia. During the trial, the Boston court house was surrounded by a large police force, and was enclosed in chains, beneath which the judges of the supreme court of Massachusetts bowed as they entered and retired.

leading acts of our public men, during the past year, that it opens the whole subject of human liberty, and our duty, as freemen, in regard to human rights. Especially does it behoove us to inquire, by what means, by whose instrumentality, the country has been instigated to this treason against the rights of men, and when we may expect their machinations will be brought to an end.

Some of our official dignitaries are giving us law lectures on the subject of high treason against the government. I hope they will not object, if we reciprocate the favor, by giving them a lecture on the higher treason against God and humanity, of which they are guilty.

Gentlemen, it is with unspeakable humiliation and regret that I look back and see where Massachusetts stood twelve or thirteen months ago, and where so many of her citizens stand now. Up to that ever-accursed day, the 7th of March, 1850, there was not a Massachusetts man, in the councils of the state or nation; — nay, so far as I know, there was not a single Massachusetts man any where, of any standing or respectability, who did not assert and proclaim his hostility to the extension of slavery; his purpose to maintain at all times the principle of the ordinance of 1787; and his "resolute and fixed determination," (to use Mr. Webster's language,) "to make no further concessions to slavery and the slave power." The public men of the state, the press of the state, the legislature of the state, avowed these sentiments; and the political conventions of the state rang with these declarations from side to side.

But on that ever-memorable day a senator of the United States, from Massachusetts, saw fit to trample under foot every thing that he had ever said in behalf of human freedom and against human bondage. He saw fit to curl his lip and to intonate his voice in scorn of the principle of the ordinance of 1787, and to dishonor the memory of Nathan Dane, whom, a few years before, on the same spot, he had eulogized. He saw fit to contemn what he knew to be the honest sentiments of Massachusetts. He went far, far out of his way, to fortify and extend the institution of slavery. He offered to add new states to its power, and to take two hundred millions of dollars from the treasury of the United States, to be expended for its extra-constitutional security and defence.

I shall not dwell upon the perfidious nature of that deed, nor upon the obvious motive that prompted it. I will rather advert to the measures which have since been taken to corrupt the public sentiment of Massachusetts, and of the whole north, and to bring over the people, some to a palliation and others to a full indorsement of it.

As soon as the stunning effect of that treacherous blow upon all the moral and religious sensibilities of the state, and upon its traditional and inwrought love of liberty, had begun to subside, a systematic effort was commenced to debauch the patriotism and humanity of the people, by an appeal to their cupidity. Our manufacturing and commercial interests were suffering. A majority of the slave states were the antagonists of these interests. Political ambition and mercantile cupidity associated these two facts together, and the flagitious idea was engendered that by surrendering our liberty we might have a tariff. The poison of this idea was first openly and directly infused into the public mind by Mr. Webster, in his speech at the Revere House, April 29th, 1850, when he said, "Neither you nor I shall see the legislation of the country proceed in the old harmonious way until the discussions in Congress and out of Congress upon the subject to which you have alluded, [slavery,] shall be in some way suppressed. Take this truth home with you, and take it as truth. Until something can be done to allay the feeling now separating different men and different sections, there can be NO USEFUL AND SATISFACTORY legislation in the two houses of Congress."

Of this declaration there can be but one interpretation. It was perfectly understood by those to whom it was addressed. It says, without enigma or riddle, surrender the territories to the incursions of the slave states, pacify the slave power, give up blood-bought rights for this life, and Savior-bought hopes for another, and you can have your pay in a cent a yard on calico, and a cent a pound on iron. And, as a means of accomplishing this object, it says the discussion of the slavery question must be "*suppressed.*"

From that time until the close of the last session of Congress, in every form in which so intrinsically wicked an idea could be set forth without shocking not only all principle, but all decency, this idea was inculcated upon the public mind of the north, especially upon the cities. In unofficial speeches and letters, Mr. Webster urged this seduction more and more pointedly and earnestly, until, on the 17th of July, 1850, in the last speech which he ever made in Congress, he appealed to the senators of the north, and to the people of the north, in language as explicit as he could make it, to adopt the compromise measures, to take even the abhorred Fugitive Slave bill itself, for the sake of the money to be made out of them. Throughout that speech he held out the apple of temptation before their eyes, he jingled the thirty pieces of silver in their ears, to seduce them into the surrender of liberty for pelf.

I appeal to the common knowledge of the citizens of Boston, if, during the last summer, it was not an expression as familiar to their lips as the salutations of the day, that they had Mr. Webster's authority for saying, that if they would surrender the great questions involved in the compromise, they could have a tariff.

Now, on this state of facts, I have two observations to make, —

1st. That a proposition to barter or to jeopard the liberty of our fellow-beings for any amount of money, however great, was intrinsically inhuman and wicked.

2d. That every new concession we made to the south on the subject of slavery, for the sake of getting protection for our manufactures and other industrial interests, only impaired and postponed our chance of getting that protection.

For the correctness of the first of these propositions, I appeal to every man who has a conscience, or even any elementary ideas of right or wrong, which are not smothered by his interests or his passions. And for the second, I appeal to the case of Texas which defeated the tariff of '42, and to the fact that, though we did consent to all the detestable provisions of the compromise, — slave territories, slave states, ten millions of dollars for Texas, Fugitive Slave bill, and all, — yet we get no tariff, and have now no rational prospect of one.

That the surrender of all our glorious patrimony of free principles should help to make some northern man President, I can readily understand. That is intelligible. Before the 7th of March speech, it was announced, from high southern sources, that they would take the northern man for the next presidential term who would do the most for slavery; and since that time, the same declaration has been reiterated. [See, among others, Mr. Toombs's speech before the Georgia Union meeting.] But I state it as a fact within my own personal knowledge, that there was not an intelligent man in Congress who was not implicated, on the one side, in the manufacture of goods, or, on the other, in the manufacture of presidents, who did not then foresee and predict that every forward step we took towards the compromise was a step backwards from protection. And we now have this stubborn fact to show for the soundness of that opinion, — the event has ratified it. They have not obtained the tariff they were promised, though they have given for it the price of blood.

Now I wish to ask the manufacturers and commercial men of the north, whether, if they had seen, — as it was seen by every unbiased man at the seat of government, — that upholding the compromise would put down protection, they would have consented to the compromise? And a further question which I wish to put to all Massachusetts and all New England is, if, during the last year, we had had the tariff of 1842 in full operation, and if the current of prosperity had filled the deepest channels that enterprise and industry had cut for it, whether then Massachusetts citizens would have unsaid and retracted all the noble things they have been saying in favor of liberty for the last ten years; whether then the Massachusetts press, or so large a portion of it, would be found openly advocating doctrines which they have always heretofore professed to hold in utter detestation and abhorrence? No man will pretend it. If we had had the tariff of '42 last year, the compromise measures never could have passed, and it would have been impossible for any presidential aspirant, or all of them together, to have subdued the northern mind to their acceptance.

The commercial and manufacturing interests of the north, then, have been deceived, grossly deceived and imposed upon. When their real interests were all on the side of freedom, they have been made to believe that it would promote those interests to unsay all they had ever said, and undo all they had ever done adverse to slavery. Their chance for a tariff lay in standing to their principles like men, and not in abandoning them like cowards. President-making has been the agency, and Cotton has been the instrument, of this deception. It has been said that the Press is the fourth estate in the realm; but I say Cotton is the fourth estate, for Cotton subdues the Press. The eyes and ears and nose and mouth of a portion of our people have been so filled with cotton, that they have come to consider cotton not only as their daily bread, but their bread of life.

Gentlemen, whatever convictions or doubts there may be on the subject of Animal Magnetism, I am a firm believer in Cotton Magnetism. The southern planter seems to possess some wizard art, unknown to the demonology of former times, by which he impregnates his bales of cotton with a spirit of inhumanity, with a contempt for all the dearest, tenderest, holiest ties that bind man to man and heart to heart; he fills them with this spirit as an electrician fills a Leyden jar, and then he sends them here; and if the man who comes within the circle of their influence is not himself filled with the strong, counteracting, disinfecting magnetism of duty and truth, of love to God and love to man, he is overcome and subdued by the infernal spell; he is brought into "communication" with the southern sorcerer, and into subjection to his will; and then he seems bereft of reason and conscience, he belies his Pilgrim parentage, talks gibberish about the dissolution of the Union, kneels, lies down, eats dirt, and says to his southern master, as Balaam's beast said to him, "*Am I not thine ass upon which thou hast ridden ever since I was thine?*"

Still worse is it, when this cotton, so diabolically impregnated, gets beneath the rich velvet seats and embossed cushions of the pulpit; — unless, indeed, a double measure of the spirit of the Lord shall descend upon the preacher and exorcise both him and it, of the evil spirit it contains. When the soul of the clergyman is struck with this cotton magnetism, he grows delirious over his Bible, ignores the new dispensation, seeks out all the pro-slavery parts of the old, discards Jesus Christ as his example, and the precepts of Jesus Christ as the law of his ministrations, and proves himself a pagan, discoursing paganism in a Christian pulpit.

God grant that this kind of cotton may never stuff the cushions of our judges! I fear we are not wholly out of danger of so unspeakable a calamity. Give us the old English woolsack for them, within whose magic presence the chains of the slave drop from his limbs, and he is gloriously transfigured into a man.

Compare the newspapers of our cities now with what they were only one short twelvemonth ago, and see what demoralization cotton can work when it gets into editorial chairs.

As for those slave-catching commissioners who assume to exercise the functions of judges, to abolish human liberty, and to find property in the bodies and souls of men, but are no more a judge than an image "made after supper of a cheese-paring" is a man, — as for them, I say, they seem to have this virus the natural way; and if all moral diagnosis does not fail, it would be found, on an anatomical dissection of their hearts, that their right and left auricle and their right and left ventricle were only four cotton bolls.

But I believe that the reign of Cotton is to be short-lived. Improvements in the arts give confident promise that some new textile substance will soon be discovered which will supersede this slave-made and slave-making material. Even should this hope fail, every body sees what an unnatural attitude of power and strength the cotton-producing states now occupy. Extending over only a small area of territory, which you can cover on the map with your hand, they raise a staple which clothes, more or less, a great part of the world; while there are Brazil, Egypt, India, and regions of unknown vastness in Africa, to all of which, or nearly all of which, the plant is indigenous. Either then by the progress of the arts, or by an extension of cultivation, the majesty of Cotton will soon be dethroned; and then, *then*, how will these men appear, historically, who are now willing to trample upon human rights, and to send men, women, and children into all the horrors of southern bondage for the temporary profits which cotton can bestow?

I rejoice that this reference to the demoralizing power of interest gives me an opportunity to bestow well-deserved honor and praise upon a class of men who have nobly withstood its temptations. Not every man engaged in manufactures or in commerce has yielded to the seductions of this tempter. There are many noble exceptions. I have in my mind one of my own constituents largely interested in manufactures, who told me last summer that half his spindles were lying idle, and property that should have yielded income was incurring cost; "but," said he, "do you see them *all* stop, and the mills decay and go down stream, before you vote for that compromise." Another of my constituents told me he was largely interested in three ships, then at sea; but declared he would see them all sink to its bottom before he would disgrace the country by passing the Fugitive Slave bill. These are but specimens of that noble spirit which was expressed with such Spartan terseness and vigor by Bowen & McNamee, of New York, when the foul panders to southern slavery threatened them with a loss of custom. Said they, "Our goods, and not our principles, are in the market."

O, how these declarations contrast with what a manufacturer in a neighboring county is reported to have said, — that if he could work his mills any cheaper with slave labor than with free, he would employ slaves! And what, also, as I am credibly informed, another has said, — "The south want slaves to raise cotton to sell; we want slaves to raise cotton to manufacture; therefore, we must unite with the south to uphold slavery." Now, I believe these things to have been *said;* but it is of no consequence whether they were said or not; we know they have been *acted.* Every man who upholds this Fugitive Slave law *acts* them, whatever his language may be.

The compromise was forced through Congress partly by government interference, and partly by the delusive hope of a tariff. An appeal is now made, in behalf of the Fugitive Slave law, to the same mercenary motives. It is said, if opposition be made to this law, however legal or constitutional such opposition may be, we shall lose southern custom. Base and infamous appeal! Such men are made of the stuff of the tories of the revolution. Even if this appeal were true, it would be one that no honorable man could hear without indignation. But it is not true. The south must have their goods from somewhere, and our industrious artisans will make them, whoever the go-betweens may be. Will the south go bare-headed and barefooted and unkilted, because they cannot have a law to catch freemen and slaves promiscuously? But it is said the south will abandon their slothful habits, become industrious, and manufacture for themselves. I wish they would. It would be most fortunate for us. They would then have the means of buying more from the north, and paying us better for what they do buy. Instead of spending only the money which their slaves earn, they would then have money to spend earned by the whites, and would become better customers for those ever new forms of commodities which our industry and inventive skill, while we keep our schoolhouses in operation, will always be able to supply.

Now, fellow-citizens, I have gone into these considerations for the purpose of ascertaining and of measuring the extent and the efficacy of the motives brought by our opponents to bear against us. You see they are mercenary, almost exclusively so. As for that bugbear of a dissolution of the Union, I say, without fear of contradiction, that no practical man has ever believed in it for a day. United States stocks at a hundred and sixteen, on the eve of a dissolution of the Union! The whole South Carolina, and Mississippi, and Texas delegations in Congress contending for every local advantage, for the establishment of new United States courts, for the increase of salaries, for appointments at home and abroad, as though the Union had been just insured for a thousand years! Show me one intelligent man in the whole country who has sold his stocks or his farm, or changed his residence, or altered his course of life in any respect, through fear that the Union was about to be dissolved. I think some persons may have left South Carolina, to get rid of the clamor about dissolving it. Why, what would the English national debt be worth under any well-founded apprehension that the British monarchy was crumbling to pieces? There would not be a pound of government securities that could not be bought for a penny. Confidence in the stability of our Union has not only pervaded this country, but other countries. The great bankers abroad who deal in our stocks have never changed their terms one mill in a million of dollars, through any such idle fear. They are the men whose barometers presage political storms. With such facts before us, to say that the Union has been in danger is as absurd as to say that a whirlwind is raging when the leaf of the aspen is pendulous, and cannot be seen to move. If the south wishes to dissolve the Union, let them do it, and at the end of thirty years there will be no slave in all their borders.

The slaves will have made a new Jamaica or a new St. Domingo of it, as the masters shall behave themselves. No, this is nothing but a clumsy trick of the politicians; and if any one of them could be nominated for the presidency, we should hear nothing more from him about any deluge which threatens to submerge the Union. They profess peculiar love for the Union. Their clamorous notes bring to mind what Dr. Franklin remarked of self-righteous people. He said they always reminded him of scarcity of provisions; — those who had enough said nothing about it; it was the destitute who made all the clamor.

I say, then, the only remaining motive with which our adversaries can work is the loss of southern trade. This interests but few of our people. The farmers are not interested in it. The mechanics and artisans are not. The operatives in our mills are not. All our substantial, industrious classes are above this temptation, and would spurn it if they were not above it. The Fugitive Slave law champions, then, can make no more converts among them. Let us, then, continue to oppose this law in all constitutional modes. Let us explain its religious and moral bearings to the Christian. Let us tell the patriot of the disgrace it brings upon our country. Let us show to the working-man that those who are ready to make slaves of his fellow-beings for lucre will be equally ready to make a slave of him whenever interest shall supply the temptation.

Fellow-citizens, it has been asked why we are assembled here to-day, and not in the Hall consecrated to liberty. It is because the doors of that hall have been closed to Liberty knocking for admission. But there is a melancholy propriety in this. When the court house is in chains, Faneuil Hall may well be dumb. Those chains which girt the courts of justice are but typical of the chains which tyrannous men are striving to put upon our lips. This is not the first temple that has been unrighteously invaded and taken possession of by money changers and those who sold doves, — doves! *doves!!* No, not doves, — but men, women, and children. But I trust the time is not far distant when a better spirit shall enter their doors, and shall scourge out their invaders with cords, smaller or larger, as the exigencies of the case may require.

SPEECH

DELIVERED AT WORCESTER, SEPTEMBER 16, 1851, ON TAKING THE CHAIR AS PRESIDENT OF THE FREE SOIL STATE CONVENTION.

GENTLEMEN OF THE CONVENTION;

Accept my thanks. It would be an honor at any time to stand in this position before a body of men so large in their number and so influential by their respectability. But, gentlemen, at this hour of trial, at this time of peril to great principles, when the lights upon earth seem to be going out around us, and we must look for guidance to the lights above, — at this hour, I say, of trial and of peril, it is an especial honor to be called to a post of duty. The position of the friends of freedom at the present time reminds me of a beautiful sentiment expressed by one of the noblest of the old Roman philosophers, who said that those who were called to fill stations of danger and self-sacrifice should thank God for the honor of being deemed worthy of such a trust.*

Gentlemen, it was not until this morning, and since sunrise, that I was waited upon by a delegation from your state committee, requesting my presence on this occasion. They knew, and you all know, how strongly my heart throbs, even at the mention of the great principles for which you contend. They knew, as you all know, how happy I should be if I could do any thing to deepen or to diffuse a feeling of devotion to human freedom.

* Seneca. [The passage is quoted in the Dedication, pp. ix., x.]

But, gentlemen, there were certain circumstances connected with my position which seemed to make it necessary for me to say to your delegation, that, if I should appear here to-day, it should be with an entire privilege to speak out my mind fully on any political subject, and to say in what relation I stand to the present condition of public affairs, both state and national.

I say, then, gentlemen, that I stand where I have always stood, holding the principles of human freedom first and foremost in my regards, and, after these, our pecuniary, or merely worldly interests; holding, according to the order in which they are mentioned in the constitution of the United States, "life and liberty" to be before "property." I stand where I stood in 1848, when I was first elected to Congress; and where my recorded votes and speeches show me to have stood through all the struggles of 1849 and '50. I stand on the same principles yet. If other men have seen fit to go off to the right hand or to the left, I remain where I was. And if any individual of any party,—Whig, Democrat, or by whatever other appellation he may be known,—shall ever return from his wanderings to the good old homestead of Massachusetts principles,—Free Soil, Free Speech, and Free Men,—there, in that immortal birthplace of human liberty, he will find me, early in the morning and late at night, hard at work, to maintain the honor of the Pilgrims and the principles of our revolutionary sires.

Gentlemen, the perusal of the address, and resolutions put forth by the Whig State Convention at Springfield, last week, brought me here. It seems to me that no true lover of human freedom can read that address and those resolutions intelligently, and understand their full scope and bearing, without being struck down by conviction, as suddenly as was St. Paul,—though the light and the voice come from an opposite quarter. Whatever the design of those papers may have been, their whole argument and office are to wheel the Whig party into line, to fight the battles of slavery.

Under these circumstances, I do not ask with a certain distinguished individual, on the prospective breaking up of parties, "Where am I to *go?*" I believe I do but echo the sentiments of thousands of as good and true Whigs as can be found in this commonwealth, (and there are none better any where,) when I say that, let others go where they will, here, *here*, on the old Whig platform of opposition to the extension of slavery, either into New Mexico *or into New England;* of freedom for the District of Columbia; and in favor of the old guaranties of *habeas corpus* and trial by jury, — *here I remain.*

Gentlemen, the Free Soil party, as the name imports, is the party of freedom. The cardinal principle of their *creed* is, that "all men are created free and equal," and that they have an inalienable right to "life, liberty, property, and the pursuit of happiness." Their *faith* consists in the assurance that, in the good providence of God, the day will yet come when the blessedness of their creed will be realized among men; and by their *works* they seek to hasten the advent of that glorious day.

A party of Freedom has existed in all ages of the world, but a mightier party of oppression has been arrayed against it. And though the lovers of human liberty have consisted of the greatest and best men who have ever lived, yet they have been overborne by violence, crushed and trampled upon by power, buried in dungeons, gibbeted on scaffolds, burnt at the stake! God, like the householder who sent servants to his vineyard from a far country, has, from age to age, sent great and mighty souls into the world to redeem it from oppression; but the oppressor has seized and mutilated and martyred them, with every form of ignominy towards the messengers themselves, and of impiety towards the Lord who sent them. The possessors of power and wealth seek to perpetuate these advantages in their families, their clan, or their caste; and over almost all the earth they have established dynasties for governments, landed or moneyed feudalisms for lords, and entails for individual families.

That we may see how fearful a thing this spirit of oppression is, not only for its cruelties, but for the tenacity of its malignant life, let it be remembered that the world had existed almost six thousand years before the principles of human liberty, civil and ecclesiastical, were clearly and fully set forth even on paper. This was first done by Mr. Jefferson, in 1776, in the Declaration of American Independence; and every body knows how intensely the same partisans who are now summoning their forces against the party of Freedom have hated him for his glorious efforts in favor of the freedom of man; how they pursued him with maledictions to his grave, and still break through the sanctity of the tomb to blacken his memory.

The immortal principles of the Declaration of Independence were partially embodied in the constitution of the United States. But, as the preëxisting metaphysics and mythology of the heathen nations mingled with the pure spirit of Christianity, and corrupted it, so the preëxisting laws and usages of oppression deformed to some extent the doctrines of the Declaration of Independence, and stamped some hideous features upon the otherwise fair face of the federal constitution. But such a preponderance of good did that instrument contain, that it was adopted by all the states. It was adopted, however, with the universal understanding that the healing influence of time would purge away the virus of the disease; and with no apprehension of the now undeniable fact, that the disease would be allowed to spread, like a gangrene, over the healthy parts. Had our fathers foreseen that the pro-slavery clauses in the constitution would prove a curse to whole classes and races of men entitled to protection under it, that they would be a shame to its administrators, and an opprobrium, throughout the civilized world, to the name of Republic, — it would be impious towards their memories to say they would ever have ratified it. But instead of the sounder parts diffusing healthful influences, and gradually eradicating the disease, the diseased parts have shot their infection through all the veins and organs of the body politic, until, from the heart to the extremities, there is not now to be found an uncontaminated spot.

Or to leave metaphor for literal speech: The constitution of the United States gave the most comprehensive and fundamental guaranties in favor of freedom, with here and there only an exception in behalf of slavery. It allowed "persons" who were held to service or labor and who should escape into other states to be retaken, but it also secured the trial by jury to every "person" who should claim it on any question of life or liberty, and on all questions of property even down to the paltry sum of twenty dollars. Yet there is not now, in the United States, a single spot, from ocean to ocean, where a free man is free from danger of being kidnapped and carried into horrible bondage for himself and his posterity forever; or, — what is as keenly torturing to every mind penetrated by the spirit and amenable to the precepts of the gospel, — of being called upon, under penalty of fines and fetters, to surrender his soul to this accursed work.

Now, as a true disciple of Christ ought to feel if he saw the imbruting dogmas and Moloch rites of heathenism returning to invade Christendom and to extinguish the lights of the gospel, so should every lover of liberty feel when he sees the fell spirit of slavery regaining its lost empire over the institutions of freedom.

The analogy between the present condition of this country and that of Europe is too striking not to attract attention. In 1848, there was a great uprising of the friends of liberty in both hemispheres. Thousands and tens of thousands sought to redress the wrongs of humanity, — by the cartridge box there, and by the ballot box here. The phalanx of tyranny and of mammon was unprepared for so sudden an onset, and for a moment their ranks were broken by the violence of the shock. But despotism and wealth have almost inconceivable advantages in a contest with the honest and toiling millions. In Europe, they have the military force, — a soulless machine, always ready to be turned against the people who are made to maintain it. They have also the whole ecclesiastical power, which leans upon the government for support, and fights with spiritual weapons for the masters whose plunder it shares.

In this country, owing to our different institutions, the means of quelling the spirit of liberty have been different. The administration have an immense amount of patronage at their disposal. They give contracts to the amount of millions, and select the contractors. Directly, or indirectly, they appoint some thirty thousand office-holders; and, by a lamentable reduplication of the powers of evil, they control twice or four times that number who are aspirants for office. Their influence bought over the slave power, by surrendering all our new territories to the invasion of slavery, and by giving fifty thousand square miles of free New Mexican territory to be turned into Texan slave territory, thus adding to the already enormous size of that slave-begotten state. Ten millions of dollars of almost worthless Texan stock were raised to par value by the signature of Millard Fillmore. During the whole pendency of the compromise measures, agents and brokers, reputed to be interested in this stock, hovered about the purlieus of the national Capitol. The stock was transferred from hand to hand, without record and without daylight, so that, besides the accomplices, Heaven and Satan only know into whose possession it came. And, as though the means of patronage and seducement on so magnificent a scale were not sufficient, a private purse, almost up to the figure of fifty thousand dollars, was presented to the "foremost man of all this world" in his apostasy to the principles of human liberty. These, fellow-citizens, were among the agencies and seductions which caused the discomfiture of the friends of freedom in the national contest of 1850. The tyrants of Europe had no vacant lands, or Texas stocks, wherewith to put down humanity, and so they used gunpowder and bayonets. Our slave power and its northern allies, being debarred by the principles of our government from bullets and bayonets, accomplished their work by the Judas articles of scrip and "dotation." To carry out these purposes, the generals Haynau and Radetsky were found there; the senators, Webster and Cass, here.

The origin and the present necessity of the Free Soil party may be briefly stated. Some years previous to the annexation of Texas, an apprehension existed that that great breach of the constitution and outrage upon northern principles and feelings were meditated. Mr. John Quincy Adams sounded the alarm; but men were so engrossed by their business, and by their paltry local and temporary political strifes, that even his voice, potent and prophetic as it was, passed by unheeded. Some respect, however, was due, at least from policy if not from principle, to the many humble but earnest opponents of so flagrant a wrong. Before the consummation of that iniquity, the Massachusetts legislature passed strong resolutions against it. The question was taken by yeas and nays, and all the

Whigs and almost all the Democrats in the general court recorded their names on the side of the constitution and liberty. But the slave power then had possession of all the departments of the national government, and under the auspices of a slaveholding President, a breach was made in the walls of the constitution wide enough to let in a foreign government, with all its burden of slavery on its back. Yet, notwithstanding this perfidy to all the principles of a true democracy, such was the external pressure brought to bear upon the members of the Democratic party, that but few of them abandoned its ranks. They "*acquiesced*," as the modern phrase is, when any thing specially iniquitous is to be sanctioned. They were told, as the Whigs are now told in regard to the compromise and the Fugitive Slave law, that the act was *done and irrevocable*. The merchants were told, as the Whig merchants now are, that the crime of extending slavery would at least be attended by increased profits of trade. The manufacturers were told, as the Whig manufacturers now are, that if the number of slaves were increased at the south, it must create an increased demand for whips and negro cloths. And the mere blind political partisans were told, as the same class of Whigs are now, that if God designed to stop the heaven-defying enormity of spreading slavery over this continent, he must do it in some way consistent with the integrity of the Democratic party. Precisely the arguments which were then used to seduce and corrupt the Democratic party into "*acquiescence*" are used by leading Whigs and Whig presses now for the same unhallowed purpose. They are alike, except that in the one case there was the crime of originality, and in the other, the meanness of plagiarism.

But from the fatal day of the annexation of Texas, thousands and thousands of honest and intelligent Democrats, though still remaining true to what they believed to be the principles of the party, became alienated from its leaders. From that day, the claims of the party lay lightly, but the sins of the party heavily, upon their souls; and some there were who, like Daniel of old, went into their chambers three times every day, and, throwing open the windows which looked towards the Jerusalem of liberty, prayed aloud to the true God, although within hearing of the wild beasts which had been prepared to devour them.

The Whig party at the north, and particularly in Massachusetts, flourished under the reäction of the Texas fraud. Some of its leaders, it is true, shouted a welcome to Texas, though yet afar off; and, even while she stood outside of the Union, they threw their arms around her blood-besmeared form, hideous as Milton's picture of Sin, with all her hell-hound progeny of future slave states howling in her womb, and gave her a fraternal embrace; and when the time came, they were also ready to vote men and money, — human blood and human souls, — for the robber atrocities of the Mexican war, which a majority of the House of Representatives in Congress, on motion of Mr. Ashmun, of Massachusetts, declared to be "unnecessarily and unconstitutionally commenced." My friends, in your observations of men, you will find there are some moral nonentities, — political availabilities though they may be, — who can listen most sanctimoniously to the Saint Stephens, when they prophesy, and then hold the clothes of the Lynchers who stone them to death.

During all this period, however, the managers and the presses of the Whig party discoursed and printed very edifying anti-slavery homilies. As the harvest months came on, an anti-slavery zeal became an epidemic among them; and sporadic cases happened at other times, depending upon the days and places appointed by the governor and council for special elections. Every body remembers how the Boston *Atlas* used to stir up the pure minds of the Democratic party by way of remembrance, by publishing, — periodically, as they say, and sometimes oftener, — the names of those Democratic senators or representatives in our general court who had voted for freedom and against Texas, in order to show their flagrant inconsistency in still adhering to a party that had been false to liberty. That paper has done some good service to our cause, especially in holding up for a long time the Fugitive Slave act to reprobation, while the other Whig presses in the city were daily striving to hide its atrocities from public view, and to defend what they could not hide. I trust the reluctant and struggling editors of that paper are not to be overcome by the mammon of slavery, whatever disguises it may assume or compulsion it may use. I trust the slave power will never be able to use towards them the language which hell's portress addressed to Satan: —

> "At first they called me *Sin*, and for a sign
> Portentous held me; but, familiar grown,
> I pleased, and with attractive graces won
> *The most averse; thee chiefly.*"

Those prosperous days of the Massachusetts Whigs continued until 1848. They thrived in basket and in store, until, like Jeshurun, they waxed fat, and, at least in the fourth and fifth congressional districts, they performed some very hard kicking. Then came the nomination of General Taylor. General Taylor was a Louisiana slaveholder. He had been the hero of the Florida war, — as great an outrage against a race as ever Rome or Russia committed. He had been a prominent, and, as many believed, a willing instrument in spilling the innocent blood of a sister republic. Even should the executive divest him of military command, or he should grow too old for service, it was universally known that there was a full black battalion on his own plantation which he would always command. The south demanded his nomination absolutely. They would hear no terms, and would offer no terms. In the northern canvass it was strongly asserted that he had written a letter, saying in so many words that he would not veto the Wilmot proviso; but that letter was so warily kept in a certain unmentionable part of a Whig merchant's wardrobe, that neither Mesmerizers nor spiritual rappers could read it aloud to the people.

Hence all omens foreboded evil. Those which we looked for on the earth augured ill to our earthly interests; and those which we looked for above were in the wrong quarter of the heavens. The character of many of General Taylor's friends brought distrust upon himself. He owed his election far more to the repulsion which good men felt towards his opponent, [General Cass,] than to any attraction they had towards him.

It was an occasion that tried the sagacity and the discretion of honest men, and I have always felt great charity both for his advocates and his opponents;—each being able to make out so plausible a case. The course which the Connecticut clergyman took on that occasion always commended itself to me. He voted the Taylor electoral ticket, but indorsed a prayer on the back of his ballot, saying that he was painfully uncertain as to the course of duty, and imploring that his vote might be sanctified for the good of the country.

But I am happy to avail myself of this, and of all opportunities, to do justice to the name of General Taylor. He turned out a very different man from what his friends or his foes supposed him to be. I believe he desired freedom for all the territories; and, could he have been permitted to carry out his own plans, he would have secured not only the freedom of the territories, but would also have consummated all the great national measures of the party that brought him into power. Mr. Clay threw the first stumbling-block in his way, by his compromise scheme. This, alone, might have been surmounted. But Mr. Webster's apostasy, on the seventh of March, turned the tide of battle. It broke up General Taylor's phalanx, both north and south. It roused the drooping and just yielding spirits of the slave power to frantic exertion. An enemy on the field General Taylor was always ready to meet; but he was not prepared for treachery in his own camp. Still, he maintained his ground resolutely, until struck down by the power that conquers the conquerors. There are many who believe it was Mr. Webster's perfidy, with the nameless labors and anxieties that came in its train, which caused General Taylor's death. It remains to be seen whether the political Macbeth shall succeed to the Banquo he spirited away, though all the "weird" brethren of the slave mart and of the "Union and Safety Committees" still tempt him onward by their incantations.

But it was under the circumstances of General Taylor's nomination, and not of his death, that a portion of the Free Soilers parted company with the Whigs; as another portion did with the Democrats, because of General Cass's avowed subserviency to the south,—and the conduct of all men is to be judged by the circumstances contemporary with their acts, and not subsequent to them.

If, however, there are those who judge of motives by results, this certainly can be said in vindication of the Free Soil party, that the now acting President of the United States, who came in on General Taylor's ticket, and is now completing his presidential term, has done more for slavery than the Free Soil party ever predicted or feared would or could be done by the candidates whom they opposed. Even now, when the third year of the presidential term is but half spent, the Whig administration, aided by many leaders in the Whig party, is carrying out, with a relentless hand, and a more relentless heart, worse pro-slavery measures than the Free Soil party ever charged upon them during the canvass, or ever believed or conceived they could commit.

Such was the position of affairs in Massachusetts in 1848, when, almost for the first time within the memory of man, the Whigs failed, at the polls, to elect electors of President and Vice President.

Let us dwell for a moment on that crisis. It was during the canvass of 1848 that the Whigs became so amorous towards the rank and file of the Free Soil party. No knight-errant ever protested more fidelity, or vowed to do more valorous deeds in his mistress' cause. Than some of them, no dove ever cooed with a sweeter gurgle. Than others, no stag ever offended with a ranker breath. They wooed them by daylight, by moonlight, and by torchlight. They swore belief not only in all the Free Soil scriptures, but in the traditions of its rabbins. The Ordinance of '87 they loved; the Wilmot proviso they loved better; and would the coy damsel of Free Soilism but consent to the affiance, the abolition of slavery in the District of Columbia should gladden the espousals. Every Whig rally, from ward and school district meetings to monster mass meetings, resounded with Mr. Webster's *slogan*, or war-cry, "No more slave states! No more slave representation in the Congress of the United States!" The Boston Daily *Advertiser*, the *Courier*, and the *Journal*, which are now south of South Carolina, in the impiety of the grounds on which they defend the wrongs and the aggressions of slavery, and shout on slave hunts over Pilgrim burial grounds, — all gave back the cry, with three times three, "No more slave states! No more slave representation in the Congress of the United States!" At all their conventions, the Whigs "resolved and re-resolved," and — but I hope we may not be compelled to finish the line. You were told there was no more need of a Free Soil party in Massachusetts than of two suns in the heavens. The Whigs were the true Free Soilers; they held Free Soilism as a hereditament, or as an heir-loom long possessed by the ancient family of the Whigs. Even Mr. Webster, who had very much withdrawn from public gaze after the Philadelphia convention, and who, like Achilles, sat "sulking in his tent" and musing over the lost Briseis of a nomination, was at las' tempted, by a succession of brilliant retaining fees, tc come forth and reason with these recusant and contumacious Free Soilers face to face. And what did he say? Addressing himself distinctively to Free Soilers, he said, "If, my friends, the term 'Free Soil' party, or 'Free Soil' men, is meant to designate one who has been fixed, unalterable, to-day, yesterday, and for some time past, in opposition to slavery extension, then I may claim to be, and may hold myself, as good a Free Soil man as any member of that Buffalo convention. I pray to know where is their soil freer than that on which I have stood? I pray to know what words they can use, or can dictate to me, freer than those which have dwelt upon my lips. I pray to know with what feelings they can inspire my breast *more resolute and firm in resisting slavery* EXTENSION OR ENCROACHMENT than have inhabited my bosom since the first time I opened my mouth in public life."

These, gentlemen, were his words, spoken at Marshfield, on the first day of September, 1848. If he were here to-day to address you, could he speak any *words* more grateful to your ears? If only truth and a heart were in that language, could he speak any thing better?

It was by such false pretences as these that thousands, and I doubt not tens of thousands, of men wholly penetrated and imbued with Free Soil principles, were kept in the Whig ranks. I was one of them. I had faith in men; and I have it still, — with important exceptions however. The needle points to the pole; but if you bring a huge black mass of pig iron and place by its side, it trembles, yet deviates, like a man struggling to be virtuous before overwhelming temptations. Remove the disturbing force, and it returns to its fidelity. So, when the next presidential election is over, I believe the great body of the rank and file of the Whig party in Massachusetts will return to their duty; for I venture to say, that if the Whigs of Massachusetts, in November, 1848, could have foreseen the present position of their party, and the demoralization which its leaders have been able to work in it, not one third of them, no, not one quarter of them, could have been induced to vote the ticket that elected Mr. Fillmore, brought in the present cabinet, and brought on the present disastrous policy.

But, gentlemen, I am occupying too much of your time. I will add but a few more words. I said the address and resolutions of the Whig State Convention, held at Springfield, last week, brought me here. I have read them with profound sorrow. It was the first Whig convention that ever met in Massachusetts that did not at least put forth some noble doctrines in favor of freedom, whether they meant to stand by them or not. Yes, even the convention of 1850, — only one year ago, — passed the following: —

"*Resolved*, That Massachusetts avows her unalterable determination to maintain all the principles and purposes she has in times past affirmed and reäffirmed, in relation to the extension of slavery."

And yet the late convention, the first one that has met since the resolution which I have just read was adopted, has endorsed the present administration, which has done more to corrupt and deaden public sentiment at the north, as to the wrongs of slavery to the enslaved, and its injury to the free, and to aggrandize the pro-slavery south, and foster and encourage, ay, and *reward* its aggressions; — has done more, I say, than any other administration that ever existed under this government. History will bear me out in this statement. Yet, at this crisis in human affairs, the one idea, the master purpose of the address and resolutions of that convention, seems to have been, to disparage and depreciate the great, eternal principles of freedom, and to bring odium and contempt upon the only party now organized for their support.

Gentlemen, the Whig leaders, in this respect, and in regard to this most important and paramount attribute of the Whig party, have lurched and lurched round, until they have got into the very trough of the pro-slavery sea. Its members, I admit, are free to follow them to their ruin, if they will; but free, too, I thank God, to go on in their old course, steering for the haven of honor and liberty. I give the great majority even of the Whig leaders the credit of having yielded to this pressure reluctantly, and under what they deemed a sort of political duress; for, gentlemen, a new and most alarming fact in the history of the Whig party of this country has been developed within the last two years. It is this: formerly, and universally, the Whig administration was supposed to be chosen to carry out the views of the Whig party; but the present administration, having abandoned the grounds on which it obtained power, and having, for its own purposes, taken new grounds, now demands of the Whig party to carry out, — not the old policy of the Whigs, but the new policy of the administration.

Fellow-citizens, could Mr. Fillmore by any possibility have been elected, in 1848; could he have got so many as ten thousand votes among all the Whigs of the Northern States, had his present attitude on the subject of slavery been foreseen?

Was there ever an hour when Mr. Webster could have obtained one tenth part, — one fiftieth part, — of the votes of the Massachusetts legislature for the office of senator, had the curtain of the future been lifted up, and his present position been revealed? You know there never was. But, during the year 1850, without any initial change, or symptom of a change, on the part of northern Whigs, the administration, prompted by its own purposes, or yielding from its own weakness, faced square about; and ever since that time it has been striving, by all the lures of patronage and the terrors of denunciation, to force the Whigs of the north on to a kind of political turn-table, like those railroad turn-tables you see at a car-house, so that the whole party, too, should be faced square about, made to retrace their course, by going backward among the same people who had seen them go forward, shouting down all they had shouted up, and forswearing all the glorious doctrines of liberty to which the whole world had heard them swear. Gentlemen, if, in this stress of circumstances, any body asks me, "Where shall I go?" my reply is, Don't get on to that political turn-table which the administration has prepared for the Whig party, and not the Whig party for the administration; for it will carry your country to ruin, and yourself to dishonor.

During the canvass last autumn for a member of Congress for the eighth district, when, as you all know, there were such "godlike" exertions made against my election, I was asked, as a test question, by numbers of most respectable members of the Whig party, what I thought of the Free Soil party, and their proposed coalition at that time. I replied to them in the following words, and my answer is now on record in the hands of my constituents: "I say, as I have often said, that, if the Whigs will live up to their professions a hundred times made, I see no reason or warrant for separate organizations or coalitions. But if the great body of the Whigs mean to belie all their professions, and to persecute and punish all who remain faithful to the lessons which the Whig party itself has been teaching so strenuously for so many years, then what true Whig can blame any man for attempting to carry out what the Whigs themselves have promised to do, but have abandoned?"

But the Massachusetts Whig State Convention at that time passed the most pointed and emphatic resolution, affirming anew what they avowed themselves to have affirmed and reäffirmed so often before, on the subject of slavery. I reposed trust in their honesty; I believed in their veracity; and, as a consequence of my faith, I voted the entire Whig state ticket. Having read their last address and resolutions, I must now say, that if they desire any more votes of mine, they must revive my faith by some new evidence of their good works.

Let me advert to a few of the more salient points in that address. It labors to sustain a charge of coalition against the Free Soil party. Well, before I either approve or condemn a "coalition," I must know by whom, and for what purpose, it was formed. A coalition, I suppose, like other acts, must be right or wrong according to the motive that prompts it.

But it is said the Free Soil party formed an alliance with those who, on some important points, had no sympathy with it. And where is this said? Why, in a land where our revolutionary fathers, fighting for freedom and for a republic, formed an alliance or coalition with monarchical and despotic France, and with monarchical and despotic Spain. What were the points of resemblance or unison between the American

Confederation on the one side, and France or Spain on the other? In government, in policy, in manners, in education, in religion, nothing could have been more different. In what did they agree? In hostility to Great Britain alone; but not in a single one of the reasons for that hostility, nor in but one of the objects to be accomplished by it, — the humiliation of a haughty and overbearing power.

At the same time, Great Britain formed coalitions with the North American savages, to extinguish the rising dawn of freedom. And in this they have been too faithfully imitated by the old hunkers of both parties; — *imitated*, I say, not only in the object and spirit of the coalition, but in the weapons with which the warfare is waged. Yes, fellow-citizens; for there is an attempt, and that attempt is to be followed up, to overwhelm the Free Soil party by obloquy and denunciation. There is to be a cry of "bargain and corruption" to put down the Free Soil party, just as the administration of Mr. John Quincy Adams was put down by the same cry. Who now believes any thing about the charge of "bargain and corruption" against Mr. Adams, — except that it was a villanous charge? I believe the same charge against the Free Soil party will have come, twenty years hence, to the same result, — that of conferring honor upon its object, and infamy upon its authors.

But it is said the Free Soil party have seized the offices and emoluments of the state. I was absent last January at the time of the organization of the state government; but I have heard that those who were distinctively called Free Soilers received only the office of secretary of state, and president of the senate, and two or three out of the nine councillors; — all of them nearly or quite without patronage. I suppose all their emoluments combined would not equal what is received by the Boston postmaster, or the collector of the Boston port. Vast "ways and means" these for the corruption of the people! The whole of them would not suffice a cabinet officer for a *bonne bouche* or a tidbit.

And now I suggest a further point. Was there a single Free Soiler who received an office last winter, on what is called the *division of the spoils*, which the people, when they voted for him at the polls, did not desire and mean that he should receive?

Now, I need not say that when men conspire or coalesce for a selfish purpose, whether that purpose be office, or emolument, or the profits of trade, or the increase of dividends, and especially if they sacrifice great principles of public utility, or morality, or religion, for the selfish end, I condemn the deed with my whole heart. So when representatives, or agents of any kind, are elected or appointed for special purposes, and by votes or influences without which they could not have obtained their posts, and then, for their own ambitious or mercenary objects, *they* coalesce to defeat the will of their constituents, any severity of language, in holding up their conduct to reprobation, may be used with my full consent. Precisely of this nature was the coalition between Mr. Webster and General Cass, to carry through the compromise measures and the Fugitive Slave bill. Both were agents, both betrayed and violated the will of their principals. Could Mr. Eliot, of Boston, have been elected to Congress, had he avowed his intention to vote for the Fugitive Slave bill? Every body knows he could not. Yet he coalesced with the secessionists, Messrs. Clingman and Venable, of North Carolina, and with the whole South Carolina disunion delegation, in voting for the Fugitive Slave bill. For Massachusetts, it was said that the passage of that bill would raise the price of manufacturing stocks; as, for North Carolina, it would increase the profits of negro-breeding. Here, then, are cases of coalition between persons mutually hostile on other points; and all the northern members engaged in it, not to carry out, but to defeat, the will of their constituents.

But the coalition entered into by the Free Soil party in this state, last year, was a coalition planned, formed, sanctioned, and executed, as far as they could execute it, by the people themselves, acting in their original, sovereign capacity, at their primary meetings, and at the ballot box. It was not originated by representatives against the wishes of their constituents; but the representatives carried out what the people who chose them willed. What conclusively proves this to be so is, that the people who elected these representatives were satisfied with what they did; and, since the work has been done, have shown their approval of it in every practicable way.

There may be wrong motives prompting to the most useful and beneficent acts, as good motives sometimes lead to the most pernicious conduct; but I am speaking of these acts of alleged coalition which were instituted by the people themselves, discussed in their hearing at all the primary meetings and all the conventions, and afterwards ratified by their votes; and I say, to compare such a coalition with that which took place between Whigs and Democrats in the Senate of the United States, and between unionists and disunionists, slave-breeders and manufacturers, in the House, to carry through the compromise bills and the Fugitive Slave bill, seems to me illogical, preposterous, and absurd. But it is said that the bargain in the one case was open and public; and that its terms were reduced to writing, like a bond or covenant between individuals. Is it any the worse for that? Had you not as lief have an open bargain that you can see, as secret ones, like the Texas stock bargains, that you cannot see? I suppose that coalitions can be *implied* and *understood*, as well as contracts. Why, have you not seen such an implied coalition carried out in Faneuil Hall within a year, when the Hon. Benjamin F. Hallett led on his cohorts, and the Hon. Rufus Choate advanced his forces to join them; when Mr. Benjamin R. Curtis joined hands with Mr. David Henshaw, who was present by letter, if not in person, — honorable men all, — and formed one of the most loving and harmonious coalitions out of as heterogeneous and repulsive elements as ever chaos jumbled together, — a coalition not to lift the bleeding form of liberty up, but to crush it down.

The coalition entered into by the Free Soilers certainly did one thing which would atone for many errors. They elected Mr. Charles Sumner to the Senate of the United States. And I cannot believe there is a man to be found in any party so shameless and depraved as to charge Mr. Sumner with any dishonorable coalescing, or with being tainted, in a hair of his head or in a filament of his garments, with "bargain and corruption." Mr. Sumner was not elected on any principle of availability, but on the principle of "*Detur digniori*," — "Let it be given to the most worthy." His lofty pedestal is too firm to be shaken by any such accusation. His character is not to be affected by any office which he shall hold, but only by what *he does*, whether in office or out of it.

While defending, in this way, the principle of coalitions, when formed by the people themselves, no one, of course, could be understood as pledging himself to vote for all their measures. This would be the old and wicked partisan principle of standing by our party, right or wrong. I am also free to say that there is, in my opinion, a *prima facie* objection against coalitions; but I cannot doubt the existence of cases where they are not only justifiable, but laudable. I lay down this great principle: I think the Free Soil party should act at any time, on any point, with any party through whom they can help the cause of freedom.

The Whig address remarks as follows: "We are now able to say, after the experience of nearly a twelvemonth, that it, [the administration,] has fully earned the confidence which we awarded to it in advance. *The great interests of the country have been faithfully cared for!*" I ask, What great interests of the country have been faithfully cared for? What interest of the Whig party, assuming to be the country, has been faithfully cared for? Have we got a tariff? Mr. Webster dissipated all chance of that for the present, and I fear for years to come, when he taught the south to threaten and prevail. Have we any river and harbor appropriations? Alas! northern capital and northern lives still go to the bottom on our western waters. Is the financial policy of the country changed? Let the condition of the money market for the last few months, and also its prospective condition, grinding the middle classes of tradesmen and manufacturers as between the upper and nether millstone, answer this question. A reform in all these particulars would doubtless have been affected but for Mr. Webster's apostasy; but where are these reforms now? If they exist at all, they exist in some indefinite future. What interest of the country, then, has been faithfully cared for or secured? Not one! Not one! The most prominent member of the administration has been engaged in carrying out the policy of the south,—in visiting southern cities to pander to the slave power, and northern cities to stifle the spirit of freedom. Two armed expeditions have been fitted out in our own ports against the territory of a government with which we are at peace, resulting in the loss of hundreds of lives, while the President and his first secretary have been spending their time gayly at watering-places. When some of our citizens, a few years ago, afforded some assistance to the "Liberals" of Canada, in favor of a movement which Canadians themselves had already set on foot, the government promptly and energetically interfered. But Canada and Cuba are wider apart *politically* than they are *geographically*. Slavery makes the difference between them.

The only valorous exploit of this administration was the issuing of a proclamation, when one southern slave, from among three millions, escaped from the house of bondage, and found that protection under the British ensign which was denied to him by the American flag, and that right to a trial by jury under a monarchy which was denied to him by a republic. Or, if any other act should be added to the preceding, it was the President's letter to Dr. Collins, of Georgia, offering the use of the army and navy of the United States to catch one poor white woman, Ellen Crafts, and her husband, and return them to bondage.

In another passage of the Whig address all disguise is cast off, and it is openly declared, that the giving of an extra slave state to Texas, with territory enough for half a dozen more as large as Massachusetts, and ten millions of dollars in addition to that, and the statutory permission that slavery may go into New Mexico and Utah, and even that abhorred enactment, the Fugitive Slave law, are only "factitious and imaginary" grounds of complaint. The Free Soil party is condemned because it takes any notice of such "factitious and imaginary" causes. A three-penny tax on tea was a real grievance,—one fit to be resisted unto blood, to be historically recorded, and to which we are not ashamed to refer when descanting upon the honor of our fathers. But such largesses to slavery as kings could not afford to give, and the robbery of an entire race of all its rights,—yes, and with authority, too, to make us help commit the robbery,—

these are "factitious and imaginary" causes of dissatisfaction. Men of Massachusetts! moral and religious men! lovers of freedom and of your country, were you prepared for this?

But the address goes still further. It goes into an elaborate palliation of the Fugitive Slave law itself. It first attempts to shift the question by asking the Free Soilers what they would do with regard to the constitutional provision respecting escaped slaves. The views of the Free Soil party on this point, and their purpose of fidelity to the constitution, have been set forth a hundred times. In further answer, therefore, to this question, I trust it is only necessary to remark, that the Free Soil party *will do what they say*, and not pass ten long years in asserting, and protesting, and resolving, and calling Earth and Heaven to witness their devotion to Freedom, and then disavow all they had ever avowed, and forswear their oaths.

Let me read to you the disparaging and contemptuous remark of the address on that great palladium of human liberty, the trial by jury. "Is nothing meant," it gravely asks, "but the substitution of the verdict of a jury for the decision of a judge." Nothing but —*what?* "The verdict of a jury for the decision of a judge," that is, of a commissioner! And are the persons who prepared that address so nearly stone blind as not to recognize the infinite difference between the verdict of a jury and the decisions of such commissioners as Messrs. Ingraham, Smith, and Nelson? Ingraham, of Philadelphia, sent a man into bondage whom the alleged claimant refused to receive as soon as he saw him, knowing that all his family, and all his slaves, and all his neighbors would see that he had no right to him. Smith, of Buffalo, gave a certificate to carry Daniel into slavery, when not a single item, or particle, or tittle of legal and admissible evidence was before him as proof, as was afterwards shown by Judge Conkling, of the United States court. Nelson, of New York, forced the facts in Bolding's case to bring them within the law which he himself had laid down, as much as ever a fraudulent book-keeper forced balances to cover an embezzlement. Sims, instead of having common-law notice and time to send for evidence, was seized at night on a false and trumped-up charge of stealing. Daniel was knocked down by the claimant's agent with a club, tumbled and tortured upon a hot stove, his scalp torn open, and then compelled to go to trial, while, as described by an eye witness, "he sat dozing, unable to talk with his counsel, with the blood slowly oozing out of his mouth and nostrils." Hamlet, Long, and Bolding were sprung upon as remorselessly as a tiger springs upon a lamb, and carried to trial without being allowed to go to their respective homes to bid farewell to their families. An alleged slave has lately been taken from Pennsylvania who was seized in the night, tried in the night, and carried away on the same night, without any opportunity for preparation, for counsel, or for defence. The kidnapper, Alberti, now lies in a Pennsylvania prison for carrying away a mother and her child; but the mother and the child are now groaning under the lash of a southern task-master. Had this villain, Alberti, and his accomplices been detected while the victims were still in their hands, I suppose he would have carried them before Mr. Commissioner Ingraham, and had the wrong *legally* rectified, — the blackness of the crime *judicially* washed white. These are but specimens of what the Fugitive Slave law has already done, before the public mind has become familiarized with its brutalities, and while there is yet some sensibility to the claims of justice and mercy left among us. And yet the writer of this address and the committee that offered it, ask us whether all we mean is the substitution of the verdict of a jury for the decision of a commissioner. I answer, that this difference which they so be-little and disparage will often be all the difference between freedom and bondage, between life and death, between honor and infamy, between happiness and perdition.

And now, fellow-citizens, if, in addition to having our northern freemen kidnapped in southern ports, and imprisoned and sold into bondage; if, in addition to fighting for foreign territory to be added to the domain of slavery; if, in addition to being taxed, in sums of millions and tens of millions, to fortify the slave power; — if, in addition to all this, we are to be deprived and defrauded of that noble and venerable institution, the trial by jury, — an institution sanctified by the blood of martyrs, hallowed by the prayers of sainted patriots, held sacred by all good men, and taught to their children like the living oracles of God; — if this attempt is to be made, as the late Whig address foreshadows, — then I say, a more flagrant case of apostasy is nowhere to be found on the records of any history, sacred or profane, since Satan broke into paradise and *Websterized* our first parents.

I shall advert to but one more point in the address. It speaks of the "pitiable humbug of ballot envelopes." Now, gentlemen, I may be all wrong on this subject. My instincts, reason, judgment, conscience, may all mislead; but from the first time, now years ago, when I heard this subject broached, my instincts, reason, judgment, conscience, have all been in its favor. Why, fellow-citizens, the ballot is worse than useless, if it be not FREE! Better be debarred from the privilege of voting at all, than to be mocked with the form, while cheated of the substance. A southern slave stands higher, politically, than a northern laborer, if the latter must vote as his employer dictates. It may be very well for an opulent man, one of vast fortune, who is dependent on nobody, and so cares for nobody, who goes quarterly and takes his thousands of dollars for rents or dividends; it may be very well for him to laugh at the secret ballot, and call it a "humbug;" but let us look at the other end of the scale. Let us look in the thousands of day-laborers, of workmen on corporation grounds, of dependent clerks, of subordinates at custom-houses and other public offices, and so forth, who have no capital but their industry, no resources but their daily earnings, who have an aged mother or dependent sisters to support, or a family of children to be fed, clothed, and educated; who may be turned out even of the humble tenements where they live, as winter is coming on; who may be refused promotion or advancement in their work and in their wages; and in regard to some of whom the wolf of hunger sits growling at the door; let us look at these, I say, and then answer the question, whether they ought not to be protected in voting according to their judgment and conscience. The liberty of voting includes all other liberties. The man of independent circumstances has this liberty; and no man's circumstances, not even the poorest and the humblest, should be so dependent as to take it away.

I do not desire this secret ballot law for myself. I like to lay my ballot in the box, face upwards, looking heavenward; looking the Paul Prys who hover round, full in the eye; but I am willing and glad to put that ballot in an envelope, in order to protect my poor neighbor, the bread of whose mouth, the shelter of whose family, and the education of whose children, may depend upon the vote he gives. Ay, I go further. I should think that any high-minded man, any man having proper sensibilities respecting his relations to his social inferiors, would rejoice in such a law as this; because it would take away all ground of accusation or imputation that he would do so unrighteous and dastardly a deed as to invade a dependant's right of voting as it might seem to him good.

Gentlemen, it is said, in one of the Springfield resolutions, that the last legislature cost the state an extra fifty thousand dollars. Whether it did or not is not of any very vast importance; though I confess I have a great respect for Poor Richard's economy, and would save all that I could. But does not the very mention of this sum of fifty thousand remind one of another sum, almost precisely the same, which was spent last year on one of Mr. Sumner's predecessors in the senatorial office? And if it cost fifty thousand dollars for a ticket to pass Mr. Webster out of the Senate, it was surely worth as much for a ticket to pass Mr. Sumner in.

Gentlemen, I close by remarking that it is in view of these great questions of human freedom, — in view of the solemn responsibility in which we stand to our country and to posterity, that we have assembled here to-day. May this meeting prove to be a concentration of rays of scattered light and wisdom, meeting and burning in a focus, and then sending back illumination and cheering to all the parts of our beloved commonwealth. If, in my humble way, I can do any thing to promote so glorious an object, my services are at your disposal.

www.ingramcontent.com/pod-product-compliance
Lightning Source LLC
LaVergne TN
LVHW021230110826
845150LV00002B/287

* 9 7 8 1 4 2 5 5 6 2 7 8 6 *